William Galbraith Miller

Lectures on the Philosophy of Law

designed mainly as an introduction to the study of international law

William Galbraith Miller

Lectures on the Philosophy of Law
designed mainly as an introduction to the study of international law

ISBN/EAN: 9783337078799

Printed in Europe, USA, Canada, Australia, Japan

Cover: Foto ©Suzi / pixelio.de

More available books at **www.hansebooks.com**

LECTURES

ON

THE PHILOSOPHY OF LAW,

DESIGNED MAINLY AS

AN INTRODUCTION TO THE STUDY OF INTERNATIONAL LAW,

BY

WILLIAM GALBRAITH MILLER, M.A., LL.B.,

LECTURER ON PUBLIC LAW (INCLUDING JURISPRUDENCE AND INTERNATIONAL LAW)
IN THE UNIVERSITY OF GLASGOW.

LONDON:
CHARLES GRIFFIN AND COMPANY,
EXETER STREET, STRAND.
1884.

(All Rights Reserved.)

Ὅταν γὰρ ἔθνη τὰ μὴ νόμον ἔχοντα φύσει τὰ τοῦ νόμου ποιῇ, οὗτοι νόμον μὴ ἔχοντες, ἑαυτοῖς εἰσι νόμος· οἵτινες ἐνδείκνυνται τὸ ἔργον τοῦ νόμου γραπτὸν ἐν ταῖς καρδίαις αὐτῶν.—St. Paul.

Das Geschäft der Philosophie besteht nur darin, dasjenige, was rücksichtlich des Denkens den Menschen von Alters her gegolten, ausdrücklich zum Bewusstseyn zu bringen.—Hegel.

TO JAMES LORIMER, LL.D.,
*Professor of Public Law and The Law of Nature
and Nations in the University of Edinburgh.*

Dear Professor Lorimer,

In dedicating to you this small contribution to the discussion of your favourite science, I take the opportunity, not only of recording my sense of gratitude for the many favours and much encouragement I have received from you ever since I was a student in your class, but also of expressing my conviction, that, although I have ventured to differ from you on some points, no one will receive this work with greater gratification than yourself, since the goal for which we strive is identical.

I remain

Yours sincerely and affectionately,

WM. GALBRAITH MILLER.

PREFACE.

To those who are acquainted with the state of Scientific Jurisprudence in this country a new book on that subject from the metaphysical point of view needs no apology: but it is desirable to explain the aim and scope of the following attempt to deal with the subject.

This volume is practically an expansion of an essay on "Evolution in Law," which I read to the Glasgow Legal and Speculative Society about seven years ago; and it forms the course of lectures on Jurisprudence, which, with some alterations, I have delivered during the last six sessions as introductory to the course of Public Law in this University.

By the ordinance of the University Commissioners this course extends to forty lectures, and it might have been consistent with the letter of the ordinance to deliver lectures only on the doctrines of Public, and perhaps also of Private International Law. But it would have been a bold innovation, of which I did not feel inclined to accept the responsibility, in the university of Francis Hutcheson and Adam Smith, to separate the *Jus Naturæ* from the *Jus Gentium*. And not only so, but such a course would have been quite inconsistent with the traditions of Scottish legal learning, which from the time of Lord Stair—himself a Glasgow professor—and certainly from the time of Lord Kames, has always associated Law with History and Metaphysic. Besides, at the time I commenced to lecture, it seemed to be a tenet of the orthodox English school of Jurisprudence that International Law was not law, and the most satisfactory mode of answering such a contention was to examine the nature of law in general. Although, therefore, the subject of Jurisprudence was dealt with by the professor of Ethics in the Faculty of Arts, I felt it to be my duty, on receiving my appointment as lecturer on Public Law, to deliver such a short course of lectures on Jurisprudence as would at once supplement and illustrate the lectures given in the Ethic class, and serve as an introduction to the study of International Law on a scientific basis. This explains the necessary shortness of the course, and why many important topics are either passed over in silence, or only alluded to casually.

By publishing this volume I expect to be able to overtake some of those subjects in future sessions; and, if I have leisure, to expand into greater detail than I have been able hitherto to do, the lectures on the History of International Law, sketched in appendix D.

Among the friends who have kindly assisted me in preparing my lectures for the press, I must name particularly Mr. W. R. Herkless, M.A., who has read the last two. His friendly criticism of the twelfth lecture has enabled me, I trust, to make my argument more complete and somewhat clearer to the general reader.

Students who may not have a previous acquaintance with philosophy may postpone the reading of Lecture I. till they have read Lecture XI.

GLASGOW, *February*, 1884.

ADDENDA ET CORRIGENDA.

Page 5, line 2 of note,[1] for "Ferguson" read "Hutcheson."
,, 39, ,, 16, insert semicolon after "spectator."
,, 54, ,, 18, after "Session" add "at the present moment."
,, 56, ,, 17, after "courts" insert a comma.
,, 66, ,, 9 from bottom, after "powers" insert "of the Court of Session," and delete these words in lines 7 and 8.
,, 135, ,, 15 from top, read "There is a modification of the nature of the servient. For example, as a general rule," &c.
,, 157, ,, 2, read "except within certain limits, arrangements" &c.
,, 168, ,, 3, after "abolished" add "under certain limitations."
,, 181, ,, 10 from bottom, for "preventative" read "preventive."
,, 197, ,, 7 from top, for "idea" read "ideas."
,, 210, ,, 5, insert "who" before "is."
,, 214, ,, 3 from bottom, after "restitution" insert comma.
,, 224, bottom line, *dele* "for example."
,, 232, line 3 from top, for "to" read "of."
,, 237, ,, 11, for "or" read "and."

TABLE OF CONTENTS.

INTRODUCTION.

	PAGE
The Art, Science, and Philosophy of Law—Utility of Philosophy,	1

LECTURE I.
LAW AND METAPHYSIC.

The Problems Presented—The Theological School—Utilitarianism—Hobbes—The "Greatest Happiness" Principle—Montesquieu—Professor Lorimer and the *de facto* Principle—Evolution and Mr. Spencer—Subjective and Objective Law—Legal Judgments synthetic,   9

LECTURE II.
LEGAL FORMS.

Ancient Forms—Forms prior to Rights—Legalised Violence—Lynch Law—Warrants for Execution—Judges of Fact and Law—Judge-made Law—Equity and Legal Fictions—Relation of Judicial, Legislative, and Executive Bodies—Modern Judicial Legislation—Functions of Legislative Bodies—The House of Lords—Grand Committees—Professional Lawyers—Revolt against them—Retrospect of the Movement,   46

LECTURE III.

LEGAL FORMS—*continued.*

Corresponding Forms in Constitutional and International Law—Legal Aspect of Rebellion—Modern Development of Legislation—Legal Aspect of Intervention in International Law—*Causes Célèbres*—Treaties—Summary, ... 75

LECTURE IV.

OBLIGATION.

Obligations prior to Rights of Action, &c.—Implied Obligations—Wrong reveals Right—Crime and Civil Injury—Reparation and Punishment—Capital Punishment—Punishment of Children—Negative Wrongs—Negligence—Police Offences—Insanity—Legal and Medical Views—Corporate Responsibility—International Responsibility—War—Neutrality—Obligations arising from Contract—Development of Duties in Modern Society, ... 89

LECTURE V.

MATERIAL RIGHTS—PERSON AND PROPERTY.

These Rights implied in Contract and Delict—Idea of Property in Body—Nature of "Thing"—Idea of Property in Things—Origin of Property—Labour—Marking Object—Analysis of Idea—Literary and Artistic Property—Compulsory Purchase of Land—Formal Aspect of Property—Lawyers and Economists—*Condominium*—Tenants, Lessees, Mortgagees, &c.—Servitudes—Possession—Prescriptions—Duties of Proprietors—The Land Question—Communism—Land Nationalisation—The Modern Credit System, . 120

LECTURE VI.

THE FAMILY.

Rights spring from Relations of Individuals—Groups of Men—The Family—Marriage, Foundation of Family—Relation Ethical—Development of Relation—Forbidden Degrees—Divorce—Rights of Husband and Father in Relation to Wife and Children—Guardianship—Breaking up of Family by Action of State and of Contract, . 150

LECTURE VII.

THE STATE.

Expansion of Family into State—The Social Contract—Functions of State—Police—Poor Laws—Public Works—Education—Forms of States—Franchise—Rights of Majorities—Progress of Democracy—The Idea of Party—Relations of State to Burghs, the Church, and other Bodies, ... 176

LECTURE VIII.

CONTRACT.

Contract determines Rights within State—Definition of Contract—Condition of early Society—Development of Roman Contracts—Relation to Property—Analysis of modern Contract—Interference of Law—Error—Fraud—Force—Freedom of Contract—Trades' Unions—*Laissez-faire*—Importance of Contract in modern State—Insurance—Classification of Contracts—Extinction of Contracts—Prescription—Bankruptcy, . . . 204

LECTURE IX.

THE COMMUNITY OF STATES.

Development of Person and Expansion of State—Progressive Integration of States—The State in International Law

—Property of Monarch in his State—Independence Intervention—Modern Multiplication of Treaties—Free Trade—Private International Law—Naturalisation—Individualism—Piracy—War—Neutrality—Friendships and Alliances—Humanity an Organic Whole, . 229

LECTURE X.

SUCCESSION.

Rights with reference to *Time*—Hereditary Trades and Offices—Theories of Succession which found it on Right of Property—Intestate Succession—The Family and Succession—Modern Law—Distribution by State—Rights of State—*Ipso Jure* Investiture—Ancient and Modern Conceptions of a Will—A Will an Act of Legislation—Entail and Primogeniture—Arguments for and against Entail—Mortmain—Organic Relations of Individuals and Nations in Succession, . . 250

LECTURE XI.

PERSON.

Late Development of Idea—Individual not Member of Family or of State, but of Humanity—Not a Citizen merely, but a Man—Fallacy of the Psychological and Analytical Methods—Development of Personality in Children—Infancy—Minority—Women—Recognition by Law—Rights over One's own Body—Imbeciles—Monsters—Corporations—Rights of Paupers—Animals—Vivisection—Freedom of Will—The Individual and Humanity, . . . 277

LECTURE XII.

RETROSPECT OF THE DEVELOPMENT OF LAW THROUGH THE CATEGORIES.

Correspondence of Legal Institutions with Categories of Formal Logic—Tendency to rise above them—Kant's

List of Categories—Illustration of Development through Categories of Quantity, Quality, Relation and Modality—Progress from Quality to Modality on Side of State, and from Quantity to Relation on Side of Individual—Ideas of Individual and Humanity give Rise to Sciences of Natural Law and Law of Nature and Nations- Latter raises Antinomies—Nature of these — Examination of Kant's four Antinomies—Their Origin—Popular Solutions—Solutions in Practical Life, . . . 303

LECTURE XIII.

LAW, MORALITY, AND RELIGION.

Differentiation in Human Life and Activity—Legal, Ethical, and Religious Views of Actions—Analogies of these Ideas—Uniform Customs—Positive Institutions and Ideals—The three Ideas ultimately identical—Transition from the one to the other—Their mutual Relations in the State—The Individual, the Universe, and God, . . 339

APPENDIX.

A.—Note on the use and meaning of the terms "Law," "Positive Law," "Natural Law," . . . 373
B.—Note on the history of secondary responsibility for servants in Scotland, ... 384
C.—Note on the history of *ipso jure* investiture in Scotland, 393
D.—Note on the relation of Law and History, . . 396
E.—Bibliography, ... 408

INDEX, . . . 425

LECTURES

ON THE

PHILOSOPHY OF LAW.

INTRODUCTION.

ART—SCIENCE—PHILOSOPHY.

As practical arts invariably precede science, law first appears as "Positive Law." This does not necessarily involve the existence of a legislative body or a king, or even a judicial tribunal, for we find rudimentary traces of law before these exist in any form. But when law has become separated from other social phenomena, and where, as in active communities, there is much intercourse between individuals, its growth is rapid and its bulk often overwhelming. This was one of the causes of codification in the time of Justinian, and this is also the cause of the agitation for codification in our own day. The objects of a code in such circumstances are practical. They are, first, the instruction of the student of law, and, secondly, the necessities of the practising lawyer or judge. Setting aside compilations in the form of dictionaries, we have various codes, digests, and treatises, arranged on some definite principle. Thus, treatises on the law of property, husband and wife, contract, succession, evidence, procedure, or bankruptcy, though nominally treating a single subject, may be so expanded as to cover a large area of the law. Such treatises are invaluable as supplying a theoretical knowledge of law, which is supplementary to the skill acquired by practice. A treatise on law, or a code, occupies, in this view, precisely the same position as a treatise on whist or cricket.[1] Now, the ideas which form the basis of a code may be philosophic, and, in truth, the only satisfactory arrangement of legal rules will be one where the philosophical ideas underlying them are kept clearly in view. But the scientific arrangement of a great body of laws for practical purposes must not be taken for the sum and substance of the philosophy of law. There is with most English writers a distinct tendency to do so. They confound science with technical education—subjects which are related but are not identical. Beyond physics and chemistry we have metaphysics; beyond anatomy and physiology we have biology; beyond biology, the ultimate problem of life. Beyond practical jurisprudence we have the Philosophy of Law. The scientific stage indicates that the idea of Right is explicit—that mankind has become conscious of

[1] Mr. Justice Markby (*Elements of Law*, Introduction) points out that, until shortly before his time, English lawyers learned law only as a practical art, in the same way as an apprentice learns a trade—*i.e.*, by rule of thumb. In Scotland, before the institution of university chairs for the teaching of conveyancing, a knowledge of that subject was acquired in the same manner.—See Inaugural Lecture by Prof. Dicey, *Can English Law be Taught in the Universities?* Macmillan, 1883.

Right, as an idea distinct from other ethical and intellectual phenomena. But science merely arranges and groups legal phenomena, and stops there; its practical end is served, and it has no need of going further, either to inquire into the history of the doctrines laid down, or to discover whether there is any ultimate reason for them. In point of fact, however, science and philosophy shade into one another, and no hard and fast line can be drawn between them. And so, as in the physical sciences, discussions on legal topics frequently assume a philosophical aspect. The systematic development of positive law in treatises may be taken to represent the "Natural History" stage of the science in which the legal phenomena are catalogued and arranged. But the human mind refuses to stop arbitrarily at this point and ask no more questions. If we could conceive law in an ideal state of perfection, and reduced to a perfect code, so that litigation would be a practical impossibility, and legislation absolutely unnecessary, a series of questions would still present themselves, and press for a solution. What is Law, as distinguished from a particular law? Is it a decision of every conceivable case that can occur? Or is it a general rule that embraces a large number of individual cases? Whence does it derive its authority? Is it the authority of the parliament or king who has enacted it, or its own inherent reasonableness? Whence is our knowledge of law derived? Is it a revelation from God? Is it a mere generalisation from the facts of external nature ? Is it an arbitrary invention of man himself? By what faculty do we declare one act to be right and another wrong ? Are legal judgments merely a portion of our moral ones ? These questions, and such as these, belong to the philosophy of law.

It is absolutely essential that any department of human knowledge should in some form pass through the stage of science before it comes to that of philosophy.[1] This may account for the backward state of the philosophy of law in England at the present day. Thus so recent and so popular a book as Professor Holland's *Elements of Jurisprudence* is only an attempt to systematise the positive law of England.[2] No one could take exception to such a task, but the mistake made by Professor Holland is in expecting to find any assistance in German works on *Naturrecht*. It is like trying to learn geometry from Kant's *Kritik of Pure Reason*, or Hegel's *Logic*. The philosophy of law in England at the present day appears to be in the same position as ethics in ancient Greece.

---

[1] See Hegel's *Logic* (Wallace's translation), p. 12 ; and Prolegomena, p. xxxiv.; Caird's *Hegel* (Blackwood), p. 166, and foll. A bigoted Comtist will, of course, see that the period prior to Hobbes is the religious epoch of English law; the period from Hobbes to Bentham, the philosophical ; and from Bentham to the present day, the scientific. As I have not space to discuss this, I would only observe that philosophy has not said its last word in England, but it will not make further progress until English law has become more scientific.

[2] It is instructive to compare the reviews of this work and of Professor Lorimer's *Institutes of Law*, contained in Pollock's *Essays in Jurisprudence and Ethics*, and in the *Revue de Droit International*, xiii., p. 647.

Every one who writes on jurisprudence has practical ends in view.¹ The art and the science of law are hopelessly confounded. On the other hand, the object of the scientific inquirer is knowledge for its own sake.² It is not improbable that the knowledge, when obtained, will have an important bearing on the corresponding practical art; but this to the scientific inquirer is a pure accident. We do not study the philosophy of religion to make us pious, or ethics to make us moral, or æsthetics to make us poetic.³ And so the primary object of the philosophy of law is not to make us either better citizens, or better lawyers or statesmen. To quote the words of Mr. Wallace:⁴ "Practical statesmen and theoretical reformers may do their best to correct the inequalities of the world. But the very terms in which Bacon scornfully depreciated one great result of philosophy are to be accepted in their literal truth. Like a virgin consecrated to God, she bears no fruit. . . . Philo-

---

[1] Zeller's *Pre-Socratic Philosophy*, by S. F. Alleyne, vol. i., p. 5. Even Ferguson defines moral philosophy as the "*art* of regulating the whole of life." See Sidgwick's *Methods of Ethics*, Book I., chap. i., Introduction, particularly section 2; Green's *Prolegomena to Ethics*, Introduction, pp. 4 and 9; Bradley's *Ethical Studies*, p. 175; Spencer's *Data of Ethics*, Preface, p. 4, and chap. xvi.

[2] On the general subject of the relation of art and science, reference may be made to Whewell's *Novum Organon Renovatum*, Bk. i., chap. 8; Mill's *Logic*, vol. i., p. 2, and vol. ii., pp. 448 and 546; and the authorities quoted in the above note.

[3] Caird's *Philosophy of Religion*, p. 45; Bradley's *Ethical Studies*, p. 175.

[4] *Logic of Hegel*, Prolegomena, p. xxiii.

sophy has to comprehend the world, not try to make it better. If it were the purpose of philosophy to reform and improve the existing state of things, it comes a little too late for such a task." And to the same effect he quotes Hegel,[1] where he says, "As the thought of the world, philosophy makes its first appearance at a time when the actual fact has consummated its process of formation, and is now fully matured. This is the doctrine set forth by the notion of philosophy; but it is also the teaching of history. It is only when the actual world has reached its full fruition that the ideal rises to confront the reality, and builds up, in the shape of an intellectual realm, that same world grasped in its substantial being. When philosophy paints its grey in grey, some one shape of life has meanwhile grown old; and grey in grey, though it brings it into knowledge, cannot make it young again. The owl of Minerva does not start upon its flight until the evening twilight has begun to fall." These statements may seem to be exaggerated, but I have quoted them as a protest against the exaggerated ideas which prevail in some quarters as to the immediate practical utility of the philosophy of law, or rather against the spirit in which it is sometimes studied—a spirit which may lead to the most bitter disappointment. When a naturalist traces the life and growth of some microscopical animal, or an astronomer tries to resolve a nebula, he has no practical end immediately in view. His aim

[1] *Philosophie des Rechts* (Gans' Ed.), p. 20.

is knowledge for its own sake. So the legal philosopher must not expect to reform the world by theories. He may make discoveries which will revolutionise society, but he will stumble across them by accident when they are least expected. His sole immediate aim must be knowledge for its own sake. He may have to be content with explaining some catastrophe after it has taken place; but even this humble function is not without its uses. The philosopher here gathers human experience into a focus, and brings it to consciousness, and thus enables a step of further progress to be made, for the theories of one generation may be the commonplaces of the next. But the practical utility of such studies is conclusively shown by the disastrous effects of false theories, which men have sometimes tried to put into practice. Such experiments, on a gigantic scale, are very instructive, but the question may be put—Can the knowledge not be obtained without so much human suffering? Can a political question not be solved without a riot or a battle? Can nothing but a famine or a rebellion suggest a reform? What is Free Trade, if it can be established by one starving rabble and abolished by another? Such questions are asked every day, and must be answered.

It has been said by a high authority that lawyers have no more concern with such questions than any other class of men. This is true in the sense that clergymen have no exclusive interest in theology; and medical men should not monopolise the study of natural science.

But, just as has occurred in those cases, our pursuits and our studies directly raise ethical and sociological problems, of which we see the inner working more closely than other men. It is fashionable in certain circles to denounce theology; and there are determined theorists who would exclude pure science from the medical curriculum. But in law there appears to be no danger of an agitation in this direction, because philosophy is not an obligatory part of legal education, and, in spite of theoretical objections, lawyers will persist in this study, even from motives of mere curiosity. And I would submit that no place or time is more suitable for the calm and profitable discussion of such questions than the end of an university course in the Faculty of Law. We are here removed from the temptation to make philosophy, like some ancient oracle, give a reply to please the inquirer —a reply which will subserve some passing want, and give an apparently philosophical foundation to the grossest selfishness. Liberal or Conservative philosophies are as absurd as Catholic or Protestant histories. We must approach our subject as free from prejudice as an anatomist or a botanist. The only danger is that we may lose ourselves in abstract theories; but if we remember that the subject of our study is Humanity, as it actually lives and moves, and that the book of nature is open to us, as to other inquirers, it will only be the result of our own blindness or folly if we fail to reap a rich reward.

LECTURE I.

LAW AND METAPHYSIC.

A POSITIVE law, in its widest sense, may be defined as the expression of the idea of right involved in the relation of two or more human beings. What is this idea of right? An answer to this question will involve an answer to all the questions to which I have referred as belonging to the philosophy of law.

It will have been noticed that there are three aspects of the problem presented, which may be distinguished as the psychological, the logical, and the metaphysical. The psychological question is, By what faculty do we become acquainted with the idea of right? This is the common form of the question in modern ethical speculation,[1] and writers who discuss law from the ethical standpoint have adopted the same line of treatment. For a full discussion of the subject from this point of view, I would refer to Trendelenburg's *Naturrecht*,[2] and Professor Lorimer's *Institutes of Law*.[3] The logical question is, What is the nature of the process of reasoning

---

[1] Grant's *Aristotle*, vol. i., p. 378.
[2] P. 9.
[3] Second Ed., p. 184. Compare Bradley's *Ethical Studies*, pp. 63, 194, and Green's *Ethics*, pp. 327, 351, and *passim*.

involved in legislation or a judicial decision? And lastly, the metaphysical question is, What is the nature of the idea of right in itself? I shall refer to the logical question incidentally while discussing shortly the metaphysical.

A series of problems precisely similar to those just indicated is raised by our investigations into the physical universe. What is the nature of our knowledge of the external universe? How is external knowledge possible? In ethics we have the question as to the nature of our ideas of moral right and wrong; in æsthetics we have the question as to the existence of an absolute standard of taste; and in theology, the question as to the existence of God and His relation to the world. In each of those branches of science, if any particular answer is given to the question proposed, it will be found that a corresponding answer can be given to the questions in the others.

Without enumerating all the answers which have been given to those questions, as that would involve a complete history of the philosophy of law, I would direct your attention to one or two leading ones.

And first, it is sometimes said that the idea of law is created by God, and revealed by Him to man—in other words, that law is an arbitrary addition by God to a *de facto* relation. In ancient systems this was always a sufficient answer. The Hebrews in the wilderness came to Moses "to inquire of God."[1] The laws of

[1] Exodus xviii. 15.

Moses were written by God on tables of stone. Both judicial decisions and legislative enactments were thus directly given by God. So with the Greeks, the θέμιστες—judicial decisions—were inspired, and their ancient law-givers were on terms of familiar intercourse with the gods.[1] In modern times this view has been adopted by a school of jurists, of whom Stahl is the most prominent on the Protestant side. He regards law as a demand made by God on humanity as a whole, while morality is a similar demand made on the individual man.[2] The ancients assumed this theory in regard to *positive* law, the moderns push it a step further back, to *natural* law, and leave the details of legislation and jurisdiction to mere human judgment. There are two modes in which we may regard this revelation. It may either be at certain definite epochs in the history of mankind, or it may be a continual operation of God on the minds of men. Every legal judgment would thus be a revelation. This latter view corresponds to the Cartesian theory of the universe; but such a pantheistic conception explains away our notion of right. Its apparent necessity to us is an hallucination. Whichever view of this revelation is adopted, it is obvious that the mere fact of God creating law gives no information as to why particular principles are just or unjust. If law is an arbitrary creation of God, then He might have made every principle

---

[1] Jowett's *Plato* (Laws), vol. v., p. 193.
[2] *Rechtsphilosophie*, vol. ii., pp. 191, 217.

of justice the very reverse of what it is at present. And if His own nature made it impossible for Him to do so, then the question is still unsolved, for we have here something apparently independent of God. But are legal principles revealed to man any more than mechanical, or architectural, or artistic principles? I do not suppose it will be maintained that the Romans had any special revelation; and if this is so, it remains for us to explain how the greatest legal people the world has yet seen—for our English neighbours have not yet produced a code—developed their system of law. The history of Roman law is quite inconsistent with the idea of a revelation. Even Christianity did not revolutionise that system, for it had already advanced a great portion of the way to meet the new religion.

It is useless to attempt a compromise with the theological school, as Professor Lorimer tries to do,[1] by saying that the assertion by a jurist that God is the source of law, is just the same as if a botanist said, at the outset of his system, that God created the world. When theologians appeal to the sciences, they generally make the nature of the Creator of the universe a deduction from the nature of the created objects. It is certainly strange that jurists, when the argument from design has been discarded by theologians, should reverse the process, and infer the nature of the object created from the assumption that they are the direct creation

[1] *Institutes of Law*, 2nd Ed., p. 21.

of a just and holy Creator. The reasoning is a circle, because we infer the character of God from the notions of right and justice which we ourselves possess.

So far for the theological school. I pass now to a school which we may consider as placed at the opposite pole—the English Utilitarian School, represented by Hobbes and his successors. Austin is the first name that will occur to most; but, as all his philosophy is borrowed from Hobbes,[1] it is better to go direct to the fountain-head. Hobbes' answer to our question is that law (including the state which recognises and enforces it) is an arbitrary addition to human relations, generally by man, and in some cases by God. His position may be gathered from the following passage in the *Leviathan*: —"By art is created that great Leviathan called a commonwealth, or state, in Latin *Civitas*, which is but an artificial man, though of greater stature and strength than the natural, for whose protection and defence it was intended, and in which the *sovereignty* is an artificial *soul*, as giving life and motion to the whole body: the *magistrates* and other *officers* of judicature and execution, artificial *joints; reward* and *punishment*, by which, fastened to the seat of the sovereignty, every joint and member is moved to perform his duty, are the *nerves*, that do the same in the body natural; the *wealth* and *riches* of all the particular members are the *strength; salus populi, the people's safety*, its

[1] Maine's *History of Institutions*, p. 354.

business; counsellors, by whom all things needful for it to know are suggested into it, are the *memory; equity* and *laws*, an artificial *reason* and *will; concord, health; sedition, sickness;* and *civil war, death.* Lastly, the *pacts and covenants* by which the parts of this body politic were at first made, set together, and united, resemble that *fiat*, or the *Let us make man*, pronounced by God in the creation."[1] And again, he defines law thus:—" Civil law is to every subject those rules which the commonwealth hath commanded him by word, writing, or other sufficient sign of the will, to make use of for the distinction of right and wrong—that is to say, of what is contrary and what is not contrary to the rule."[2] And in the same way he explains custom by the tacit consent of the monarch; and, even as to interpretation, he maintains it is only competent to the monarch. The objections to this theory, which is completely contradicted by the facts of history, are the same as I have urged against the views of the theological school. It had been anticipated by Cicero when he says,[3] that if law is constituted merely by the enactments of peoples, decrees of princes, or sentences of judges, then it might be legal to rob, commit adultery, and forge, if these acts happened to be approved by the votes or ordinances of the multitude. The law is here external

[1] Introduction (Molesworth's Ed., vol. iii.), p. ix.
[2] *Leviathan* (Molesworth's Ed.), p. 251.
[3] *De Legibus*, i., 43.

to the subject of it. He could not discover it himself. If he could, it is not a command, and it ceases to be law. Two men have no more relation to each other than two figures in a waxwork, unless a ruler steps in and commands one of them to do, or abstain from doing, something to the other, or unless the two men make a compact which, however, as we shall see hereafter, really implies and presupposes law for its recognition. The subject can never adopt the law and make it a part of himself. His sole motive is to escape from a penalty. He does not try to obey the command so much as to escape the punishment. Just and unjust, right and wrong, here mean simply commanded or forbidden. This whole system is an outrage on common sense. The commands of the Irish Land League are as true laws as the statutes of the Imperial Parliament. In a word, if law is merely an arbitrary command, then, as Cicero points out, theft, murder, and other crimes may become law, as they did with the Irish Land League. Such a view is pure scepticism, or only one step removed from it. And if we concede to Austin the honour claimed for him by Professor Amos, of being the true founder of the science of law,[1] it will be in the same way as we give Hume the credit of awakening the critical philosophy.

To obviate this objection that the command may be perfectly arbitrary, Hobbes and his successors have

[1] *Science of Law*, p. 4.

adopted the theory of utility. This theory raises difficulties somewhat similar to those to which it gives rise in pure ethics. It is closely connected with the assumption—which is gradually becoming discredited through the influence of Sir Henry Maine's works—that all law is due to legislation. It is true that legislative changes have always some practical end in view—are, in fact, intended to be useful for some purpose. But law existed ages before legislation, and early legislators, as we shall see hereafter, disclaimed any intention of *making* law as much as modern judges are in the habit of doing. The theory, so far as it goes, applies only to a few late laws, consciously evolved and expressed, just as in the history of language utility may explain a few words or phrases deliberately added to a language, but is quite inadequate to explain the origin of speech or of thought, of which it is the expression. Again, this theory assumes that law is *merely* mechanical in its working; but it is more. It is the conscious expression by at least a portion of the community of their ideas of justice. But, even on the mechanical view (which is true to a certain extent), utility explains nothing. Coal gas is useful, and is used; but utility does not explain the chemical phenomenon of combustion. As I have already remarked, utility is late of appearing in the history of law. It is only when men have come to criticise cumbersome and antiquated forms on theoretical principles that this idea is called to their aid. Thus the Roman law was an ancient institution when Cicero turned against it the shafts of his ridicule; and it was long after his day that the reforms pointed out by him were actually carried out. The difficulty of accepting utility as an explanation of the phenomenon of law, is that it has no definite content. The most opposite principles may still appear equally useful, according to the object in view. Thus the reforms advocated by Bentham were plausibly opposed on the very same ground of utility. It has been attempted to overcome this difficulty by saying that the end of law is the "greatest happiness of the greatest number." Law is thus a collection of rules to promote the happiness or pleasure—which is used as a convertible term by those who maintain this view—of as large a number of persons as possible. Now, if any one, not a philosopher, were asked if this were so, he would unhesitatingly pronounce it nonsense. It is another phase of the attempt to reduce benevolence to selfishness, and the appetites of hunger and thirst to the mere pleasure of eating and drinking. But the case seems if possible clearer than that of eating and drinking, which Mr. Green thinks is now beyond controversy.[1] And so we may ask, Does Parliament legislate to promote pleasure? Surely that is never its direct object. And if so, the maxim applies, "*In jure causa proxima non remota spectatur.*" To remedy an injustice will certainly cause pleasure,

[1] See Green's *Ethics*, p. 167, and Butler's *Sermons*, No. xi.

both to the legislator and the persons wronged, but it is a confusion of thought to imagine that this is the object aimed at. This form of the utilitarian theory is closely connected with the fallacy that a *sanction* is necessary to make a true law. Men are supposed to obey the law in order to avoid the pain of punishment, or to obtain the pleasure of reward. And if it is asked why men should make laws and invent rewards and punishments, it will probably be answered, To avoid *natural* punishments, which are the result of the violation of *natural* laws. If certain acts became common, society—nay, life—would be impossible, and in order to avoid such consequences, artificial punishments are created. But what is the connection of *natural* laws and *natural* punishments? Is it ethical, or merely physical? Again, this principle of happiness or pleasure does not explain the rude instinct of revenge. It cannot explain the statement, "*Fiat justitia, ruat cælum,*" which impels men to vindicate their supposed rights, when a cool calculation of the consequences to themselves and the world would dissuade them from so doing.

While hedonists speak of pleasure and pain quantitatively, they make no attempt to lay down a unit of measurement. Their difficulty is well stated by Shakespeare: " I were little happy if I could say how much."[1] They assume tacitly that if a certain quantity of pleasure is given up or thrown away, like a bushel of wheat, a

[1] *Much Ado about Nothing*, Act ii., Scene 1.

larger quantity, twenty or thirty bushels, will be reaped. By whom? If by the individual who has given up the pleasure, it is understandable; but why should he give up his pleasure if others are to reap the result? And if these others compel the surrender, where is the limit to be drawn? Can they sacrifice the individual entirely? No; it will be generally admitted that only a partial restraint is put on the conduct of the individual. Here, again, we have a merely *mechanical* balancing of the powers and capacities of individuals, without consideration of their *organic* relations. Is it conceivable that an individual should derive pleasure from suffering pain imposed on him for the benefit of others? Could others have pleasure when they know that it is causing pain even to one individual? Is a humane emperor entitled to deprive a hundred thousand poor people of great pleasure, involving perhaps real pain in disappointment, by saving the life of one Jew, who would have been " butchered to make a holiday?" Can we weigh the pleasure of the one man, or at most two, against that of the thousands? Perhaps, too, the gladiator was sick of life, and death would have been a pleasure to him.

But this difficulty is increased, if we take posterity into consideration. If money is required for a war, why should we pay it if we can leave the debt to our descendants? If a debt has been left to us, why should we pay it? Can it be suggested that the act of last session for liquidating a portion of the National Debt in the beginning of next century, was passed on the consideration that, if thirty millions of people paid sixpence a year just now, and saved fourpence a year to forty millions a generation hence, there would be a balance of pleasure on the transaction? If pleasure was actually taken into consideration, which I do not admit, it was undoubtedly that of the minister who devised the scheme, of the members who voted for it, and of the present inhabitants of the country who enjoy the satisfaction of paying their debt, and not that of posterity, who may reap the benefit, but can hardly feel so much pleasure as they would if they had endured the burden. The only pleasure which can be taken into account is that of the generations which successively pay the debt. If the debt is cleared off at the end of five or ten centuries, it will only be a few students of history who in calm moments will be able to realise, at the best in a vague way, what their ancestors have done for them. In point of fact, it is an utter impossibility for a legislator to estimate, even in the vaguest degree, the effect of his laws on *the pleasure* of untold myriads of beings who may succeed him.[1] But, further, no legislator tries, or can try, to deal with the pleasure of more than a small number of the inhabitants of the earth. We have, to a great extent, got rid of monopolies and class legislation; but most people appear to draw the line at

[1] See Sidgwick's *Ethics*, p. 383.

their own nation, and seek the happiness of as many as possible within a limited territory. Thus, instead of being "universalistic," it appears that in law at least hedonism for the present is "egoistic," the nation taking the place of the individual.

The confusion of thought, which is at the bottom of hedonistic theories of law, is more apparent there than in other branches of ethics. There is a pleasure which accompanies the normal exercise of functions, such as eating and drinking, and even of mere existence. Any disturbance of these functions causes pain, and suggests the removal of the disturbing cause. Writers, who are accustomed to algebraic calculations, find no difficulty in assuming that a *plus* pain is a *minus* pleasure, and without further proof translate every feeling into one of pleasure. But, instead of saying that laws are intended to cause the greatest pleasure to the greatest number, it would be more correct to say that they are designed to cause the least pain to the fewest number. Positive laws, like medicines and other human contrivances, are intended to alleviate a certain description of pain. If great wrongs are perpetrated on individuals or classes of the community, or on nations, it may be necessary for judicial or legislative bodies to interfere for their redress, and without doubt pleasure will result from their interference to all concerned; but the philosophy of law must not explain only the few cases where judicial or legislative interference is necessary, but it must explain also the multitude of cases in which such interference is uncalled for. Any derangement of the social organism causes pain, and is a grievance which demands a remedy. The lawyer, like the physician, devises a remedy to restore normal, healthy action. The pain shows that something is wrong, and he devotes himself to the removal of the *cause* of the disease. Law is thus entirely utilitarian in so far as it deals with material interests. It aims, in its practical aspect, at the maintenance of the individual man in life, and strives to keep him in possession of the material conditions necessary for life. Pleasure accompanies the result of interference, but it is a pleasure mixed with pain. The pleasure would have been much greater, in the estimation of most men, if there had never been any necessity for interference. The utilitarian forgets that for one dispute, which we term a legal one, there are myriads and myriads of transactions between men in which no dispute arises. These are all subject to and regulated by law; or, rather, we should say, men are perpetually in contact with each other in the organic unity of society, and law is involved in all their relations. The error of supposing that law is only involved in cases of contention between men, is as great as if we supposed that nobody but a dyspeptic had a stomach or a liver, or that electricity existed only in thunder clouds and electric batteries. In the faculty of medicine and in engineering we have a clear line drawn between the scientific and the practical courses of study; but in the faculty of law we have been apt to forget that there are studies corresponding to anatomy, physiology, and pathology, in which the subject of research is the body politic. We cannot understand or explain the irregular action without some knowledge of the normal functions of society. As I have already remarked, law as a practical art, like medicine or surgery, is utilitarian, in so far as it strives to remedy grievances by removing their physical cause.[1] But neither the pleasure which accompanies existence in society, nor the pain which results from a disturbance of normal relations, explains the idea of right which underlies all the relations which are involved in man's existence.

I now turn to Montesquieu, whose system may be regarded as an answer to that of Hobbes. The opening paragraph of the *Spirit of Laws* is often quoted. "Laws, in the widest signification, are the necessary relations which spring from the nature of things; and in this sense all beings have their laws. Deity has His laws; the material world has its laws; intelligences superior to man have their laws; the brutes have their laws; man has his laws." If the word "law" is used throughout here in a secondary sense, as meaning

---

[1] Is not this what Mr. Sidgwick's partial adoption of the utilitarian theory amounts to? If ethics is an art of conduct, it must be utilitarian; but the science discusses questions beyond this, as to the end involved in utility. Compare Green's criticism of Sidgwick (*Prolegomena to Ethics*, p. 406).

generalised statement of phenomena, the statements are quite true, except with regard to God, who cannot be described as a phenomenon; and Austin's criticism that laws proper and laws metaphorical are confounded is beside the point. But, assuming that he refers to human laws as true positive laws in the ordinary sense, it is evident that Montesquieu's view is quite the opposite of that of Hobbes. Law, according to him, is in the relations of men. It is not added to them either by a Divine command or revelation, or by the command of a ruler. Laws are the necessary relations which spring from the nature of men. This view has recently been revived, and put in a more explicit form by Professor Lorimer as an answer to Austin. He lays down the following propositions[1]:—"(1.) The laws of nature are logical, and as such necessary inferences, which it belongs to the scientific jurist to make from the facts which consciousness or internal observation, and experience or external observation, reveal to him as the necessary conditions of human life. (2.) The laws of the nation, public and private, and the laws of nations, public and private, are similar inferences which it belongs to the legislator or practical jurist to make (*a.*) from the laws of nature, which he accepts as facts; and (*b.*) from the local and temporal facts or circumstances of the nation, or of the nations, which it is his business to ascertain. (3.) Judicial sentences or judgments—*i.e.*, the laws of the

[1] *Institutes of Law*, 2nd Ed., p. 250; 1st Ed., p. 194.

individual case—are inferences equally necessary which it belongs to the judge to make (*a.*) from the laws of the nation, or of the nations, which he accepts as facts in themselves, and consequently as decisive of the law of nature; and (*b.*) from the facts—*i.e.*, the characteristics and circumstances of the individual—which it is his duty to ascertain." As I shall show hereafter, this order of development is the reverse of the historical one. But, passing over this, it will be at once apparent that this is merely an application to law of the metaphysics of Locke, who denies the existence of an innate law in the sense of a complete code possessed by all men at birth, but admits the existence of a law of nature which we may learn by the use of our faculties. "There is," he says, "a great deal of difference between an innate law and a law of nature, between something imprinted on our minds in this very original and something that we, being ignorant of, may attain to the knowledge of by the use and due application of our natural faculties."[1] Ideas, according to him, are derived solely from sensation and reflection. The notions of father and son, husband and wife, purchaser and seller, are merely deductions from single ideas obtained in those two modes.[2] But sensation—or external observation—and consciousness, if mere internal observation or reflection, are merely empirical. There is nothing

---

[1] *Essay on Human Understanding*, I., 3, 13.
[2] *Ib.*, II., 28, 18. As to what Locke means by "sensation" and "reflection," see Green's *Hume*, vol. i., Introduction, p. 9.

necessary in them. If our experience is exactly opposite on different occasions, what becomes of law? Is it lawful to expose children in China, and unlawful to do so in Europe and America? Is it ever lawful to put persons to death who are afflicted with incurable and intolerable disease? Are lying, cheating, and murder unlawful in the case of individuals, and lawful in the affairs of states? In a word, if law is merely an inference from sensation, there is no such thing as right and wrong. The *de facto* principle on which Professor Lorimer insists so strongly thus breaks down; it is utterly unsatisfactory as a criterion. And if he answers, as he does in another connection, that in taking the facts of nature we must look to the highest races of mankind, the most highly-developed members of these races, and the higher nature of those individuals, he begs the whole question.[1] If I can tell what are the highest races, the most highly-developed individuals, and their higher nature, then there is no need of appealing to facts for information. It is I who interpret the facts. I put a meaning into them, and pronounce a judgment on them, and pronounce some relations to be right and others

[1] *Institutes*, 2nd Ed., p. 67. Comp. Caird's *Philosophy of Religion*, p. 60. Prof. Lorimer appears to be approaching a sounder doctrine at pp. 331, 334 (2nd Ed.) It may be observed that it is the same question which has been raised and discussed by Mr. Ruskin in his artistic works. He disapproves of the Dutch and Flemish painters who count the straws in a stack and the bricks in a house, as well as of the French ones, who manufacture impossible trees and concoct "classical" landscapes.—See *Modern Painters*, passim.

wrong. If any thought is *necessary*, it must be *à priori*. We can never discover the necessary in the contingent matter of sensation and observation, whether internal or external. All that we can say is, that such a relation exists in point of fact. Fathers support their children until they are able to support themselves. This is a fact which we might find in ten million cases, and in the ten million and first we might find a father who did not support his child. Our induction does not then hold. From observation, we can only find that something *is*, not that it *ought to be*. But, even if our experience were absolutely uniform, we could conceive an exception to it. We might then say that the law—in the sense of a physical phenomenon—was for the father to support his child, but then we cannot go further and say he *ought* to do so. We cannot proceed from law in the physical to law in the jural sense—from mere "is" to "ought."[1] But, again, from the logical point of view, we may admit that laws are inferences from the facts of nature, if we do not use the word "laws" in the jural sense. If by laws we mean the generalised phenomena of man's nature, and the phenomena of his legal relations, then the statement is true. In this sense we have the laws of man's nature, physical, intellectual, and moral, as the laws of physiology or the laws of thought. We thus may have even laws of law. In the succeeding Lectures we shall see examples of these. Thus it is a law, in the

[1] Sidgwick's *Methods of Ethics*, p. 361.

physical sense, of law, in the jural sense, that law always begins with judgments, and that legislation is uniformly the last mode adopted for the amendment of law. These are true physical laws—inductions from a series of isolated facts—and if our experience were reversed, the laws deduced would be the opposite. But laws in the jural sense are not merely inductions from the common conduct of mankind. They are not mere general rules put into an imperative form. There may be customs universally observed in certain communities which we would denounce as wrong—murder, infanticide, robbery, drunkenness. And, again, there may be true law in an individual case which never happened before, and might not happen again. The theory—sometimes called a fiction—whereby our courts assume that the common law applies to every case presented to them, if there is not a law specifically dealing with it, is a practical application of the fact to which I refer. There can be no induction from a single fact, and thus the judges, assuming they administer the law of nature in such cases, must find their law elsewhere than in the customs of the community.[1] There is, however, another logical aspect of the matter. Professor Lorimer is in the habit of representing the process of legislation or judgment as a merely formal logical one.[2] This shows, I think, that in

[1] See, on this subject generally, Bradley's *Principles of Logic*, Book II.; Mill's *Logic*, 10th Ed., vol. i., Book II., chap. iii.
[2] *Institutes of Law*, 2nd Ed., p. 9.

the preceding observations I have not misapprehended his meaning. In a formal syllogism, the conclusion gives nothing which is not already contained in the premises. Thus, if the work of a legislator is merely syllogistic, if he merely discovers certain external or internal phenomena called "natural laws," and certain other facts to which these apply, then the positive law is nothing. It is merely a repetition of the natural law in the particular case. As we shall see hereafter, a statute is only an indefinite number of hypothetical judgments, and so a decision founded on a statute does not contain anything which is not already implied in the statute. And this leads me to observe a fact which cannot be too early and too strongly insisted on, that *whenever a natural law is expressed in words it becomes a positive law.* There is not and cannot be such a thing as a natural law apart from concrete positive laws. There cannot be beauty apart from beautiful objects. A man cannot be religious without believing something—without having a *positive* religion.[1] What are sometimes called natural laws in the jural sense—*e.g.*, the obligation to maintain infant children[2]—are only higher generalisations of positive laws, and are as true positive laws as the statutes of the realm. This is pointed out by Professor Lorimer

---

[1] Caird, *Philosophy of Religion*, p. 318.
[2] See, for example, Erskine, *Institute of the Law of Scotland*, I., i., 17. The whole title is worthy of perusal, as illustrating the traditional confusion.

himself in regard to morality.[1] If, therefore, the phrase "natural law" is used in jurisprudence—and I think it ought to be avoided—it should only be in the sense of a generalised statement of a series of facts, keeping in view, however, that the generalisation involves thought,[2] or it may be used, as it is by Hegel and Trendelenburg, as equivalent to the "science of law."

Before leaving Professor Lorimer, I may observe that his relation to Austin is not unlike that of Reid and Hamilton to Berkeley and Hume. Berkeley denied the existence of an external (transcendental) world beyond consciousness; Hume denied the existence of causation. The Scottish school answered them by an appeal to common sense. Austin denied the transcendental existence of law, and reduced natural law to a command of God or our nature, and positive law to a command of a government. Professor Lorimer's answer is practically Reid's. Examine any human relation, and you will find law is necessarily involved in it, even if the Government should tyrannically decree the reverse. They both appeal to instinct. We have an instinctive belief in an external world, and in the idea of cause. We have an involuntary instinctive power of inferring rights from the facts of existence. But an instinct is merely an inferior reason. It is blind, and any light it possesses is drawn from a

---

[1] *Institutes of Law*, p. 359 (2nd Ed.)
[2] See Mill's *Logic*, Book VI., chap. v., and following chapters.

higher power, which shows itself in this particular direction. What, then, is the reason of which this instinct is an example? The question is shifted, but not answered.[1]

The solutions to which I have hitherto referred have looked at law as a result, and tried to explain it as it actually exists, ignoring very much its historical development, or referring to history merely to prove that there has been no change in particular laws or ideas. This omission has been met by the evolutionist school, of which Mr Herbert Spencer is so prominent a representative. His answer to the question, "What is the idea of right?" is, that law is a phase of the evolution of conduct. If the common sense school says "law is an existence," the evolutionist school says "law is the result of a process." It is a little difficult to give an adequate account in a few sentences of a doctrine which its author takes eight large octavo volumes to explain. But I may state generally that Mr. Spencer defines a right action to be one in which there is a surplus of pleasure somewhere; a wrong one, where there is a surplus of pain. If there is no pain from an act, either immediately or remotely, then the act is "absolutely" right.[2] Some acts affect only the agent immediately, others affect other men immediately or remotely. Of the latter some are *just* and others are *unjust*, according as they do not interfere or do interfere "unduly" with the pursuit of

[1] Stirling's *Kant*, p. 23. [2] *Data of Ethics*, pp. 27, 261.

ends by others.[1] He holds, further, that our present customary conduct has been evolved by the action of individuals and nations on each other, in conjunction with their physical surroundings. They adopt the course of conduct which is most agreeable and pleasant in the particular cases that arise. If repeated, the acts tend to become instinctive habits.[2] These are transmitted to subsequent generations, and confirmed by imitation, as well as by the feeling of fitness which arises, as often as the act is repeated. Painful acts, or acts which interfere with vital functions, and therefore wrong, gradually disappear, either by being abandoned or by destroying the agents. What is commonly called morality (including, of course, law) is only this conduct "formulated"—put into a scientific form, so that it may serve as a basis for an art of conduct.[3] This art will generally be represented by positive law. This view is open to the objections which I have urged against the view of Montesquieu and Professor Lorimer, and also to others, of which I shall indicate one or two:—And, first, we cannot assume that the progress of the thought is identical with that of its physical embodiment. A word may connote ideas which have been completely forgotten, and so the derivation may give no clue to the idea now conveyed by it. Poetic feeling may

---

[1] *Data of Ethics*, p. 282.   [2] *Ibid.*, p. 275.
[3] *Ibid.*, p. 271. See Spencer's *Social Statics*, "Definition of Morality."

be in advance of technical skill, so that works of art may convey but an imperfect idea of the artist's conception. A spiritual religion may retain much of fetichism in its embodiment. And so laws and customs are not necessarily identical with the moral ideas of a people. The thought and its embodiment act on each other, but it is the former which gives meaning to the latter. The thought regulates and determines the growth of the embodiment, but as they cannot be identified in the ultimate result, it is impossible to identify them while the idea is becoming revealed to consciousness, and is only partially known through its external material form. And if it is suggested that the idea and its embodiment develop independently, and that we know nothing of their connection, we must answer that we do not know what is meant by the idea or the embodiment apart from each other. An idea which changed with its embodiment could not be the same. The idea must remain one and the same while the embodiment changes, or the whole object and its relations become unintelligible.

But, secondly, in Mr. Spencer's theory the notion of ethics is either entirely excluded or is presupposed. Take, for example, the two instances he gives of acts absolutely right.[1] "Consider," he says, "the relation of a healthy mother to a healthy infant. Between the two there exists a mutual dependence, which is a source

[1] *Data of Ethics*, p. 261. The same may be seen in his use of the word "unduly" in his definition of "just" conduct, p. 282.

of pleasure to both. In yielding its natural food to the child the mother receives gratification, and to the child there comes the satisfaction of appetite—a satisfaction which accompanies furtherance of life, growth, and increasing enjoyment. Let the relation be suspended, and on both sides there is suffering. The mother experiences both bodily pain and mental pain, and the painful sensation borne by the child brings as its results physical mischief and some damage to the emotional nature. Thus the act is one that is to both exclusively pleasurable, while abstention entails pain on both; and it is consequently of the kind we here call absolutely right." It will be noticed at the outset that reference is here made to a specific act, and not to a course of conduct. We may elaborate the circumstances in Mr. Spencer's favour by assuming that the quantity of food required by the infant is precisely the quantity the mother can give, and that the moment it feels the impulse to seek it she is impelled to give it. And suppose, finally, that the child is withdrawn, the instant that the supply is exhausted, when it is satisfied. There are then only two hypotheses possible. Either she is conscious of the relation or she is not, for we may surely set the infant aside in considering the *ethical* aspect of the relation. If she is unconscious of the relation, and it is merely physical or governed by instinct, there is admittedly nothing ethical in it. And if by any chance the child did not get the sustenance required, and died in consequence, no law would hold her guilty of murder. But if she is conscious[1] of the relation, and has the power of controlling it, and in consequence of that knowledge and that power withdraws the child *at the proper instant*, then without doubt the act is *right*—not, indeed, absolutely, as Mr. Spencer says, but in relation to the specific circumstances. By hypothesis she consciously and deliberately withdraws the child before there is the slightest indication of pain on either side to suggest that she should do so. This involves some ethical principle in her conduct. It may be an idea that the act is for the benefit of herself and her child, and its descendants to a remote posterity. But here, then, is a most important factor in her conduct which must be explained. She cannot have acquired it by painful experience in her own person, perhaps not even from painful experience of several preceding generations, for by hypothesis she is *perfectly* healthy. If it is developed in course of hereditary transmission, and so instinctive, then it is not ethical. But this is excluded by the hypothesis, for she consciously adopts and obeys the rule. Before acting, she did what Mr. Spencer now does after the act—contemplated her conduct as a whole, and passed judgment on it. And so her act was ethical, because both in motive and in results it was perfect. When, therefore, the word "healthy" was used by Mr. Spencer, it meant *morally*, as well as physically, healthy. If the act is un-

[1] See Green's *Ethics*, p. 106, as to ambiguity of this word.

conscious or instinctive, it is hard to see how it is absolutely right for *her*. It is Mr. Spencer himself who can survey the act in its development, and in the results on the whole universe of beings present and future, and pronounce it "absolutely right." The other example given by Mr. Spencer illustrates more forcibly this unfortunate use of the word "absolute." It is that of a father of whom he draws a very fanciful picture as he participates in the amusements, and superintends the education of his boy; "giving and receiving gratification from moment to moment while furthering ultimate welfare." Mr. Spencer does not tell us, but we must suppose that the father has no other pursuit, or study, or trade which will engross his attention. He is not a philanthropist or a statesman, or even a church elder. He has a competent income. Perhaps, too, he is a widower. And so we may proceed, until we strip him of his ethical surroundings, and eliminate every duty which might clash with his one pursuit of training the boy, and the problem disappears. Or, again, as I observed before, the father may be conscious of his various relations, and deliberately and consciously pursue his course of conduct (and Mr. Spencer seems to have made a slip when he hints that the father may have a *theory* of education), and so it will be right. Or, once more, it is only the spectator who can say that the acts, being "pleasurable alike in their immediate and remote effects," are "actions absolutely right."

I may observe in connection with this, that in our search for a science of absolute ethics it is clear that we cannot fall back on mathematical abstractions. If we could conceive beings so constituted that an *infinite* number could exist in one point of space, or *infinitely* rigid, or *infinitely* compressible (using these words in their ordinary mathematical sense), then law disappears. A collision between two atoms would not be assault or murder. Property would be impossible and unnecessary, and so with other legal relations. Or, again, if, as Mr. Spencer seems to prefer, we attempt to construct an abstract ethical science corresponding to physiology in medicine, we must assume, as he points out, a condition of perfect health.[1] That is to say, we must assume perfect morality—no vices—no passions—no conflict of egoism and altruism. A moment's consideration will show that we may know as much of the functions of society in this abstract form as we know of human physiology. This knowledge has frequently been formulated in a poetic rather than a scientific form—in pictures of ideal societies. And even of social "pathology" our knowledge is, alas, only too great. It is not in the physiology or pathology of society that our greatest difficulties arise. The problems which present difficulties to the student of ethics are (1.) the philosophical one *prior* to this physiology and pathology, and (2.) the practical one *posterior* to them, of what is to

[1] *Data of Ethics*, p. 276 and foll.

be done to restore normal action, and cure the social diseases disclosed. Mr. Spencer will probably advise us not to trouble our heads about the former, as it is insoluble; and if his principles are logically carried out, we shall leave the diseases of society to mend themselves, provided we can secure ourselves from injury.

Again, thirdly, to put the objection to this theory in yet another form, I would observe that Mr. Spencer ignores the self-conscious stage of law—legislation. In tracing the development of a plant or animal, the man of science follows the unity throughout the process. The plant or animal is not conscious of the process, and does not deliberately interfere with it or attempt to modify it. But with man it is different. Here we find individuals successfully struggling with adverse circumstances, and moulding their own character by searching for or creating ideal societies. And, further, we find one part of mankind striving to mould the character of the rest, not only of their contemporaries, but also of posterity, by making laws and creating educational and other institutions. But even if the only effect of this effort is to hasten a development which is certain to take place, if only sufficient time is allowed, it is an additional phenomenon which must be explained or taken into consideration in examining the process. So strongly has the presence of this element been felt that it has led, in epochs of great political and legal activity, to the denial of the objective reality of the law, and the elaboration of such theories as Rousseau's "Social Contract," and the theories of Hobbes and Austin above referred to. It is this element of self-consciousness in the individual, in the nation, and ultimately in the world, which remains one and single throughout the multiform development of the embodiment. And it is this same element which is presupposed in pronouncing the action of the mother or father, in the examples above referred to, to be "absolutely right." To Mr. Spencer self-consciousness is only a phenomenon, bounded on both sides by instinct, for law and ethics have developed from instinctive acts, and when they reach perfection they will again be instinctive,[1] and if conscious, then only in the sense that the individual will have no more to do with his own acts than a spectator, he will feel his motives, and see the acts, and admire and approve, but his relation to them will be accidental.

Perhaps the most extraordinary aspect of Mr. Spencer's ethical views is that he expects his theory to have a beneficial effect on conduct.[2] Now, if a man were convinced of the theory of development, as described by Mr. Spencer, and were placed in circumstances where a conflict arose between present pleasure, and very remote problematical pleasure to himself and others, he would not hesitate to prefer the former. The perfection of the individual in such a case can be no end even to himself.

[1] *Data of Ethics*, p. 275.　　[2] See Pollock's *Essays*, p. 353.

Exalted virtue and self-denial, not to speak of martyrdom, are all mistakes. A slowly evolving conservatism, which denied the existence of change, would arrive at the same result after, perhaps, a few more years, and time is nothing to an evolutionist. In this view legislation is mere ingenious trifling. If we leave things to themselves they will all come right in the long-run. It may take a few years longer, but, in the meantime, the philanthropic legislator will save himself a world of trouble.

I would now observe that every expression of a relation of right is a *synthetic* judgment. In the rudest conception of a crime we add something—we think something into the mere physical phenomenal relation presented to us. It is only to self-conscious beings (persons), and in relation to them, that right can arise. A bull gores a man. It may be an accident, and we, therefore, do not conceive any notion of right. But if the owner of the animal has allowed it to wander along the highway, the notion of law which was already involved in that of owner is extended by that of fault, and a relation of right is created between two persons. We do not hang lunatics, because the relation towards his victim of a lunatic, who has killed a man, is not a legal one. It is purely physical. And so through the whole series of legal relations; they consist of a physical phenomenal relation, and a thought added by one or both of the parties, and also by the state, and expressed, if necessary, by a judge or arbiter. The individuals concerned implicitly or explicitly subsume the relation under a universal conception. A judge or professional lawyer always make the subsumption explicit. To a certain extent, and when society becomes properly organised, this universal is supplied through the state, but afterwards a higher conception is found, when an appeal is made to humanity through the idea of equity.

Is it true, then, that all law is declaratory? It is, if by this statement is meant that there is an objective reality corresponding to the subjective notion. To use the words of Hegel, " What reflection elicits is a product of our thought. Solon, for instance, drew from his own judgment the laws he gave to the Athenians. This is half of the truth, but we must not on that account forget that the universal (in Solon's case the laws) is the very reverse of merely subjective, or fail to note that it is the essential, true, and objective being of things."[1] When, therefore, Austin maintains that there can be no true law which is not sanctioned and enacted by the universal in the form of the state, and when Professor Lorimer maintains the contrary thesis, that there is an objective necessity in human relations, that Parliament with all its omnipotence cannot do certain things, and *must* do certain others, they are merely maintaining separately the opposite sides of one relation. We cannot separate the objective law, which, as Montesquieu puts it, " springs from the nature of things," from the subjective

[1] Wallace's *Logic of Hegel*, p. 36. Compare prolegomena, p. lx.

law which enacts it, and recognises it as right. The external relation, apart from the thought, is nothing. It is a puzzle to which we have no key—a writing, the language or even the alphabet of which we do not know. The subjective notion, apart from its material content, is void. The *de facto* relation, apart from thought, is meaningless —nay, is inconceivable. We may illustrate this from the ordinary process of perception. In looking at a tree I have a number of sensations, and I group these together into a unity by means of the subjective notion of a "tree." We often find that an external object may alter to us, according as we subsume it under one category or another. For example, clouds on the horizon may be taken for a range of hills, or *vice versa*. A rough block of wood, in certain circumstances, may be mistaken for a polished marble pillar. As Dr. Stirling says,[1] "Any individual object is to us a compound of matter from the senses, and of form from the mind. That house, that tree, this table, this pen, outward, external, as they are, are not wholly so, but have forms projected into them from within my own self, even in the very act of my perceiving them, which forms, however, present themselves to me as much externally as the products proper of sense itself, and constitute thus, notwithstanding their origin within, veritable outward realities." Now the process in a legal judgment is the same as in perception. We add something to our

[1] *Kant*, p. 24.

sensations in order to make them perceptions; but the two moments cannot exist separately. And so with the legal judgment, the mere co-existence of beings and things does not make law *apart* from thought. Pure formal thought unrealised in persons or things is not law.[1]

Again, as knowledge progresses by a gradually extending synthesis, so does law.[2] In both cases synthesis is implied in the simpler acts, while analysis is a later process, and implies a previous synthesis. We see this very clearly in astronomy. The Copernican theory was one step. Kepler's laws were another, and Newton made these laws one by the theory of gravitation. In each step thought added an idea to the physical facts of observation. So in law. It is not the mere physical act, but the act *plus* the judgment passed on it by a self-conscious being which makes the legal relation. The judgment of the spectator or judge, or the person aggrieved (if he can rise above the mere physical annoyance), is synthetic. As law progresses, the judge becomes scientific, and classifies legal acts. Instead of dealing with isolated cases on equitable principles, he groups specific acts, and when one is presented to him he refers it to its class. We see this process gradually perfected in the Roman law, and it is this that constitutes Austin's merit as an English lawyer, that he

[1] See Green's *Ethics*, book i.
[2] See Caird's *Kant*, p. 203.

attempted to arrange the multitude of laws under scientific categories. But we cannot stop abruptly here, even if we would. The impulse which makes law scientific makes it metaphysical. We cannot stop until we arrive at absolute unity. I would only remark, further, that even the progress of legislation, or the complete codification of the law, would not make the judicial function merely analytic. The duty of referring a case to one of two or more conflicting provisions in the code, or perhaps the deciding whether a deviation from its rules is material or not, all involve synthesis. This is, of course, obvious in cases not provided for, where the judge has to find the major premises for himself. In such cases it is only by a fiction that his function can be called analytic. And, lastly, in cases of disputed fact, where evidence is circumstantial, it is the inference from the facts which makes his decision. It is a greater or less link from his own mind which he supplies, in order to reduce the chaos of facts to a single point for decision, and here again the judicial function is synthetic.

What, then, is the nature of the addition made to facts, in order to constitute a legal relation? If it is an error in psychology to add special senses and faculties to the human mind when required, it is as great an error in metaphysics to add to the forms of thought. The "idea of right" is a convenient expression for the *à priori* element abstracted from any legal relation; but it must be observed that it cannot exist apart from the facts, and the facts are meaningless without it. It may be suggested that all law may be reduced to personality—the consciousness of self in relation to other persons; but even in the notion of self we have the idea of right, so that law and right are prior even to the notion of "person." Law is thus not only *à priori* or *à posteriori*, but both at once. It is not merely a pre-established harmony between two unrelated things—the claim made by one individual, and the right accorded by other individuals—or between physical external phenomena, and the notions of justice implanted in men. The two elements—the subjective thought, and the objective phenomenon—cannot be separated without the annihilation of both. This will be amply illustrated in the following lectures, in which I shall indicate the *forms* in which the idea of right has been embodied, and trace to some extent their development.

LECTURE II.

LEGAL FORMS.

EARLY law is at once municipal and international, civil and criminal, strict law as well as equity. And, lastly, the form of expression or application is at the same time legislation, judicial decision, and execution. In other words, the process of differentiation, which has advanced so far in our own day, has not yet commenced. As in the lower orders of animal life one organ may fulfil several functions, so in a remote and semi-barbarous age one legal institution embraces relations which in modern practice are quite distinct. And even in our own day, in our modern law we can observe the various branches shading into each other. In some cases the ancient forms are still living and operative; in others we have merely fossilised remains embodied in the modern law. In pursuing our inquiry we might avail ourselves either of the comparative or of the historical method. We might regard legal phenomena in succession or as they actually exist at any particular epoch of the world's history. These methods would certainly lead us to the same result—namely, that the phenomena which we designate positive laws, in their development, as well as at every stage of that development, however diverse they may appear, are simply realisations of one principle—the idea of right.

Ancient law was both municipal and international. The legal unit was the family—the state in miniature. Many examples of this are given by Maine, as in the institutions of adoption and marriage.[1] The only modern parallel to the ancient adoption is the modern process of naturalisation. The formalities are equally solemn, and the result is precisely similar. The individual severs his connection with one unit, and enters into the same relation with another. He is treated as an alien by the former, and as a native by the latter. In the ancient Roman law the forisfamiliated son was a stranger, while an adopted son was regarded as standing in a close relationship to the paterfamilias. We observe the same principle in the criminal law of murder. The kinsmen of the murdered man were his avengers. In some cases the crime involved the destruction of the whole family of the culprit. In the old Anglo-Saxon law, the kinsmen received a share of the fine imposed for murder, and they had to contribute a proportion of the fine imposed on one of their brethren who committed that crime,[2] just as in our own day, when an individual is unable to obtain redress for a wrong done by a foreigner, his state will demand it from the foreign state, and may

---

[1] *Ancient Law* (4th Ed.), pp. 130 and 154.
[2] Stubbs' *Constitutional History*, vol. i., p. 82. See Kames' *Historical Law Tracts*, vol. i., p. 15; Grotius, *De jure prædæ*, cap. viii.

even declare war to enforce it. The rule which makes all the individuals of one state, which is at war with another, enemies of all the individuals in that other state, was thus once completely recognised between families in municipal law. It has long disappeared there, and it is gradually becoming obsolete in international law; one of the last traces of the rule being the right of capture of private property at sea.

Again, ancient law is both civil and criminal. In examining ancient codes we are struck by the fact that criminal law bulks very largely in them; and, further, that many acts which we call crimes are there treated as merely civil injuries. We shall see hereafter the difficulty of distinguishing a crime from a civil injury,[1] but it is sufficient here to observe that they are entirely confounded in early law. In Roman law, the whole law of theft belonged to the private law; and, as Maine points out, the old Roman penal law is not truly a law of crimes, but a law of torts or civil injuries. The same remark applies to the Anglo-Saxon law of murder. We may thus conceive a period in the history of law, when it would consist entirely of flagrant wrongs, which we would now characterise as crimes, but treated simply as private wrongs.

Further, it is obvious from the nature of things that in the earliest stages of law the distinction of law and equity must have been unknown. Early law was a

[1] Lecture iv., *infra*.

decision applicable to the circumstances of each special case as it arose, and so far it was equity.

And, lastly, the form of expression of early law is at once legislation, judicial decision, and execution. Legal formalism or "ritualism" has been a favourite subject of sarcasm from the earliest times. But regular forms of action are the first attempt to make law scientific. The Twelve Tables begin with the law of procedure, and even the Digest of Justinian does not give a description of men's rights, but sets forth the actions they have if they are invaded. So the laws of Æthelbirht[1] begin by describing the *punishments* for various crimes. They assume that every one knows what murder and theft are, and definition is unnecessary. The later Anglo-Saxon codes refer more to procedure at trial,[2] but it is only now, at the end of ten centuries, that we are endeavouring to find definitions of crimes. The attentive reader of Mr. Justice Stephen's interesting *History of the Criminal Law in England*, which, it will be observed, commences with the history of procedure, will notice that, speaking roughly, the reform of the criminal law has proceeded in the same order as procedure itself. *Punishments* were first mitigated through the exertions of Howard and other philanthropists. In order to discriminate guilt and consequent punish-

---

[1] Thorpe's *Ancient Laws of England* (Record Publications), vol. i., p. 3.
[2] See Stephen's *History of Criminal Law*, vol. i., p. 245.

ment a fair trial is necessary. Hence, we have the amendment of laws of procedure and evidence, simplification of indictments, and so forth. And, lastly, we have attempts to *define* culpable homicide and other crimes. The last thing that occurs to us is to deal with the individual *before* he has committed a crime. In early law form is, therefore, all in all,[1] and forms are the first stage in the development of right.

The earliest legal forms of which we have an account clearly indicate that mankind had just emerged from a stage when each family, if not every man, was legislator, judge, and executioner. The earliest law was undoubtedly lynch law. The murderer caught red-handed, or the thief taken "with the fang," did not expect, and did not get, any very protracted trial.[2] The analogy of international and inter-family law will enable us to understand this. The fact that there can be no power superior to individual states has led some to deny the existence of international law, because the last resource is always war where a state which is aggrieved must be legislator, judge, and executioner. This is, to some

[1] This is true of English municipal law down to a very recent date, and hence the danger of indiscriminate citation of English cases in Scottish courts. In many cases the judges do not deal with the point in dispute, but merely decide whether the appropriate remedy is sought.

[2] Innes' *Scottish Legal Antiquities*, p. 210; Maine's *Ancient Law*, p. 379.

extent, the position of public international law at the present day; but there is a tendency to rise above it by states which go to war founding on ancient treaties or issuing manifestoes as to the justice of the war, or, in some cases, getting a "mandate" from Europe.

But this was not confined to criminal cases. Lord Kames says, "It appears to have been of old, both in England and Scotland, a lawful practice to force payment of debt by taking at short-hand from the debtor a pledge, which was detained by the creditor till the debtor repledged the same by paying the debt or finding security for the payment." This practice was prohibited in England by the Statute 15 Henry III., cap. 1, and now it survives only in the law of distress.[1] In Scotland it was dealt with by several statutes, and it now survives only in the modified form of sequestration for rent and poinding of the ground for feu-duties, to which I shall refer presently. This form of positive law is clearly most applicable to obvious wrongs, and so would prevail extensively where law was prominently criminal; and, as we should expect, it is universally recognised in criminal law at the present day. A person assaulted may defend himself by violence; a husband may even kill an adulterer, if he is taken in the act.[2]

---

[1] Kames' *Law Tracts*, vol. i., p. 226; Maine's *History of Institutions*, chap. ix., p. 263, &c.

[2] French *Code Pénal*, § 324; Macdonald's *Criminal Law of Scotland*, p. 152 (1st Ed.)

But in such legal forms, and in the society in which they would prevail, the idea of right is only implicit. It is an unconscious instinct of the race which finds expression in the acts of individuals, and the idea of right is only made explicit when a legislative act of indemnity is passed, or when a court or a jury declare that the act, which in other circumstances might be a crime, is justifiable.

Up to this point it is hard sometimes to draw the line between legality and illegality; but we rise beyond the caprice of the individual, and come to a much higher stage, when we find an intervention by the state in the person of a king or chief magistrate. Maine points out that certain early forms of procedure had reference to the conduct of private persons in a quarrel which was stopped by the intervention of a magistrate. This is true both of the *actio sacramenti* and the English wager of battle, in which we see law step forward in a religious form to settle the dispute.[1] At first the question would no doubt be solved by the magistrate interfering, his interest being rather to put an end to violence than to do justice between the parties. When the power of the magistrate becomes established, weaker persons who feel aggrieved appeal to him for assistance. In the first instance, this application is for the purpose of obtaining a warrant for execution—for the *enforcement*

---

[1] Puchta, *Cursus der Inst.*, vol. i., §§ 40, 161; Innes' *Scottish Legal Antiquities*, p. 210.

of a right.[1] The complainer or pursuer, if we keep up the rude metaphor which suggests the preceding age of barbarous violence, has no doubt of his right. His appeal to the judge is, "avenge me of mine adversary." The adversary does not, and cannot, dispute the claim, and a preliminary examination is therefore superfluous. We may take the Roman action of *pignoris capio*, which Gaius admits to have existed prior to the date of the Twelve Tables, as a type of the legal procedure which prevailed during the first three centuries of Roman history. It was practically a form of execution, and would apply where there was no dispute as to facts or law. We have traces of this idea in our modern procedure. In Scotland we are familiar with arrestment on the dependence of an action. An action is raised for a sum of money, and before the defender can say a word in defence, or perhaps even hear of the action, the pursuer may obtain a warrant which enables him to tie up all the bank accounts of the defender, as well as all debts owing to him, and so put them, for a time at least, effectually beyond his control. In like manner, in the process known as poinding of the ground and the action of maills and duties, warrant is obtained at once on an *ex parte* statement, and carried into effect by attaching the debtor's movables or his rents before it

---

[1] See Pollock's *Essays*, p. 208, and Bigelow's *History of Procedure in England*, p. 153. Maine, *History of Institutions*, p. 271.

is possible to have a decision as to the merits of the dispute between the parties. So with bonds containing a clause consenting to summary execution, and under special statutes, with bills of exchange, summary warrants are issued, and the defender must *suspend* the diligence thereon, and show cause why it ought *not* to proceed, besides finding security for payment of the debt and expenses. In all these cases Scotch law proceeds on a principle diametrically opposed to the maxim, *melior est conditio defendentis*. It will be admitted, I believe, that in practice no inconvenience is felt even by the extraordinary remedy of arrestment on the dependence, because these *lower forms* of procedure for the enforcement of right are adapted to the circumstances with which they deal. But we have clear evidence that such forms were once the usual and proper ones in all cases, in the form of summons employed in the Court of Session, and in the Sheriff Courts down to 1876. There the whole narrative, although put in the mouth of the sovereign or the sheriff, as the case may be, points to the fact that the defender is in the wrong and the pursuer is simply enforcing a right. In appearance a Court of Session summons is a decree, with an addition, calling the defender into court that the matter may be inquired into. The substitution of a petition for a summons, and the alteration of the names pursuer and defender to plaintiff and respondent, indicate an advance to a higher stage.

It used to be more common than it is now to sneer at judge-made law. We shall see presently how far such sneers are historically justified. But the fact seems clear that for some indefinite period prior to the existence of legislation or even judge-made law, a form of positive law existed which we may call policeman-made law. The state is here appealed to, but it is in its executive and not in its judicial capacity.[1] The only form in which this power is now generally exercised is in the royal prerogative of pardoning criminals who have been convicted, unless we should treat as a revival of this primitive form of law the provisions of the Peace Preservation (Ireland) Act of 1881, as to imprisoning suspects. There can be no better evidence of the sad state of barbarism, which characterises so many of the inhabitants of Ireland, than the fact that the legislature in the year 1881 was compelled to abandon the forms of judicial procedure common to all civilised countries, and to allow the Secretary of State for Ireland—the Executive Government—to take a man, try, and punish him, in what otherwise would be an arbitrary manner. The official disclaiming of an intention to punish, and the unusual liberty which was allowed to the culprits, do not alter the fact that this was a revival of a rude and primitive form of justice, and that it was quite in

[1] Kames gives some excellent examples of this in his tract "on the history of brieves."

harmony with the state of society to which it applied.

If the right of the claimant was not self-evident, or if the respondent had a claim *primâ facie* as good, or if the intervening magistrate did not feel competent to settle it, a preliminary investigation would be necessary to determine the question of right. The whole function of the magistrate would be the stopping of the quarrel and the appointment of a judge. *Judex esto.* The judge may be merely a private arbiter. The Roman *judex* was little more, but he determined the *rights* of the parties, and the state, in the person of the prætor, merely enforced the judgment. The Roman jurists thus define litiscontestation as a judicial contract. Like any other contract, it was enforced by the state. Law was then treated as a question of fact is dealt with in our courts as being a matter for the jury and not for the judge. The Roman magistrate would remit it to a lawyer as we now make remits to architects, engineers, and accountants. The law administered in this process is essentially judge-made law. In many cases all that is wanted is the common sense of a third party, whose judgment is not biased by his interest in the question at issue. But a judicial system implies more than an impartial examination of conflicting claims. It is the first step towards a scientific treatment of jurisprudence. The discovery has been made that the idea of right involved in any particular case is not merely an accident, but it is the very essence of the relation between the parties—that the idea of right involved in the particular case is involved in every similar relation, although no actual dispute should arise. "Common sense" is soon found to be inadequate to the task of discovering right. It requires skill and experience. We can trace the process clearly in the history of Roman law. In the early days of the Republic the prætors were changed annually, and, prior to their appointment, they had no special training which could be called legal, and so they could not determine difficult law cases. But even in later times they were in the habit of occasionally deciding cases where perhaps the remedy was obvious without the intervention of a *judex*. But as occurred at a later epoch in the case of advocates, who even in the days of Cicero were not lawyers, it would become more and more common for magistrates to be versed in the law, and this tendency would be confirmed by the necessity of publishing an edict. Under the formulary system the magistrate generally dealt with the law and the *judex* with the facts; but when Diocletian, in the year 294, A.D., abolished the *judicia ordinaria*, the judges were put on a footing more resembling that of our modern Scottish judges. The modern custom of appointing trained and experienced lawyers to the judicial office is thus coincident with the modern development of the law which they administer. An extension of the same principle is seen in the creation of Tribunals of Commerce, and such tribunals as those of the Railway Commissioners, the Wreck Commissioner, and the Irish Land Court. In these cases the judges are specially skilled in the class of *facts* with which they have to deal, as well as in the law. As the magistrate started by treating law as merely fact, the tendency now is to recognise that all facts involve law.[1]

We may realise more clearly the function of the ancient judge from some remarks as to the function of the modern judge passed by Lord Justice Brett in deciding a very recent case.[2] This judge said:— "To my mind merchants are not bound to make their contracts according to any rule of law, but the court of law, from the language which has been used, and from the known course of business among merchants with regard to the subject matter of such contracts, must determine what is the interpretation to be put on such contracts amongst reasonable merchants, and when they have ascertained what that is, the court ought to apply it to the particular contract in question in the way in which reasonable business men, in the ordinary course of business, would apply it." Although this is not very scientifically expressed, it is nevertheless true. All

---

[1] This explains why, in our practice, commissions to take evidence are granted only in exceptional cases, and the strong feeling against jury trials in Scotland.

[2] *Honck* v. *Muller*, L.R. 7 Q.B.D. 103.

judicial law is necessarily *ex post facto*, and yet it is not unjust. Mr. Justice Brett has only put in another form the old truth that you do not require a knowledge of physiology to enable you to eat, or an acquaintance with statics or dynamics before you can walk. The law is implicit in the relation. The court makes it explicit. It is true law, although no similar case should occur again. It is law in that particular case—the law of the case.[1] The decision is not a haphazard arbitrary determination of a particular dispute ; it is the exposition of the idea of right involved in the particular relation of two self-conscious beings. Now, what is here laid down by Mr. Justice Brett as applicable to modern mercantile law is applicable to *all* ancient law. It is now an admitted historical fact that the great bulk of our laws have been laid down by judges acting in a judicial capacity. The maritime codes of the middle ages were nearly all collections of judicial decisions. This was especially the case with the most famous of them, the *Consolat del Mar*. These facts are now universally recognised, and so judge-made law is now condemned on another ground than that it is not the function of a judge to legislate. Austin's objection to this mode of enacting laws is, that it is not sufficiently bold and thorough owing to the conservative instincts of lawyers.[2] But this ancient

---

[1] The word "law" is used in this sense by Earl Cairns, L.C., in *Phosphate Co.* v. *Molleson*, 6 *Rettie* (H.L.) 114 ; L.R. 4 App. Cas., 810.

[2] *Province of Jurisprudence determined*, vol. i., p. 224.

form of legislation in particular cases still survives in another form. "It is a question for a jury" merely means that there is no particular rule of law to decide the case in hand, and that men of common sense must decide it by taking all the complicated details into account.

It has been remarked and fully illustrated by Maine that the *amendment* of the law is effected by means of legal fictions and equity—that is, judicially—long before actual conscious legislation comes into play.[1] The three modes of amending the law correspond in historical order to the three modes of creating it—execution, judicial decision, legislation. In a single sentence I may explain that a legal fiction is an assumption which is false in fact, and which is made by a judge in order to enable him either to bring a case under a particular rule of law, or to exclude any case from such a rule. For example, when imprisonment for civil debt was illegal in Scotland, except in the case of royal debtors, the device was hit upon of procuring a royal order to a debtor to pay his debt. If he failed to do so he was "put to the horn"—denounced as a rebel at the market cross, and thereupon imprisonment became legal because he was a king's debtor and a rebel.[2] It was by a similar process that

[1] *Ancient Law*, p. 25. Among the Jews the appointment of the seventy judges was prior to the Mosaic legislation (*Exodus* xviii. 13). See Robertson Smith, *The Old Testament in the Jewish Church*, p. 334.

[2] Kames' *Law Tracts*, No. 11.

the Court of Queen's Bench in England attained its present extensive jurisdiction.[1] Again, in the Scotch feudal law, when subinfeudation was prohibited, our conveyancers devised the plan of making artificial feu-duties in the form of ground annuals. They observed the letter of the prohibition, but defied its spirit. The remedy of legal fictions was peculiarly applicable to the amendment of old strict forms of law, which were nearly related to summary execution. They clearly indicate that a rough body of rules already exists, but they show that the execution of the law is still of paramount importance, for all that the magistrate is asked to do is to decide whether or not a particular case falls within a particular rule. A legal fiction is merely a quibble, but it is quite possible that the statements made would not appear so glaringly false as they do to us. I have noticed in practice a far greater tendency to quibble among laymen than among professional lawyers—and the same has been observed as to children. The more ignorant people are, the more prone are they to exercise their faculties in that way,[2] and so in a barbarous age such fictions would be accepted without perhaps any

---

[1] Maine's *Ancient Law*, p. 26.

[2] See the scene between Titmouse and Huckaback in *Ten Thousand a-Year*, bk. i., ch. viii. The Employers' Liability Act, 1880, affords an example of a fiction being deliberately enacted by Parliament without its falseness being observed. Instead of providing that the contract of hiring shall, in certain cases, imply a contract of insurance, it attributes constructive negligence to the employer.

question. In some systems—as, for example, in India—we notice a tendency to follow absurd analogies, and this may assist us in understanding the corresponding tendency to draw absurd distinctions. In fictions we see the power of drawing distinctions in embryo, but they are soon found insufficient to adapt legal forms to the growing necessities of social intercourse. Equity is the next stage, but it is only a higher and more general description of fiction. It would involve a higher power of drawing distinctions. All that the judge has to do is to show that the particular point submitted for decision is a *new* one, and forthwith he is empowered to invent a new rule. If he is unable to draw a distinction then he must boldly appeal to a higher source of law, for it would be absurd to decide new cases justly, and old and frequently recurring ones unjustly.

It is interesting to note the relation of the office of judge to that of executioner on the one hand, and that of legislator on the other. The close relation of the office of judge to that of executioner is illustrated by the names of various judicial functionaries. Thus the Roman prætor was formerly the chief executive officer in the state. In the early days of Venetian history the doge combined judicial and executive functions.[1] With ourselves the sheriff has lost nearly all his executive functions, the chief exception being executions for murder, and even these he is permitted to carry out by

---

[1] Hazlitt's *Venetian Republic*, iv., p. 256 and foll.

deputy. The Scotch sheriff formerly executed royal writs,[1] but now he has become almost entirely a judicial officer, while the English officer of the same name has lost his judicial functions, and retains only his executive ones. The Scotch sheriff, besides, has limited legislative functions in making general rules for the regulation of business in his court.

There can be no doubt that the judicial prerogative, as well as the executive, formerly belonged to the king in this country. Now the power of execution alone remains with him. The student of the constitutional history of England is familiar with the struggles between the judges and parliament. Which is supreme? The king who gives the judge his commission, or the judge who determines the nature and extent of the royal prerogative; the parliament which *makes* laws and which can practically remove a judge, or the judge who interprets the acts of parliament. Again and again we find the crown and parliament deferring to the opinion of the courts of law, though these are subject to the control of parliament and the executive government. In all those cases the opinion of an upright and skilled man is adopted and approved by the national conscience. The judges stand to the other governing powers in the same relation as their spiritual, medical, artistic, and scientific advisers. Parliament is omnipotent, but it cannot paint a fresco, or amputate a limb, or decide a law case.

[1] M'Glashan's *Sheriff Court Practice* (Barclay's Ed.), § 32.

The king can do no wrong, but he is most likely to accomplish this feat by restricting his acts as much as possible. In the United States of America the law courts are in some cases superior to the legislative bodies; as, for example, when they decide whether a certain law is constitutional or not.[1] As the judicial function becomes more perfect it becomes more clearly legislative. Instead of deciding a particular individual quarrel between two litigants, a modern judge, whose judgment will be carefully recorded and appealed to as a precedent in all similar cases, is making a rule of universal application. He knows that this judgment will bind him and perhaps his successors, and his anxiety is as great to make a sound precedent as to do justice between the parties. The City Bank cases in the Court of Session illustrate this position very well. Each decision ruled a group of cases, and was to all intents and purposes legislative. To refer again to the Irish Land Act of 1881, Parliament shrank from defining a "fair rent," but left that duty to the judges, because the circumstances of individual cases were so diverse that it was found impossible, or thought dangerous, to lay down a general rule, especially as it would ultimately come to be interpreted by the judges. The well-known case of *Lickbarrow* v. *Mason*[2] is a good specimen of the process of judicial legislation. The varying judgments

---

[1] Kent's *Commentaries* (10th Ed.), vol. i., p. 503.
[2] Smith's *Leading Cases* (7th Ed.), vol. i., p. 756.

of the various courts, from the King's Bench to the House of Lords, indicate a struggle between the old idea of strict conservative law and the new ideas of commercial freedom, which refused to be trammelled by strict form. Disguise the matter as we may, when the House of Lords decided *Lickbarrow* v. *Mason*, it became a "leading case," and men spoke of the law as being settled by it. It recognised for the first time the right of merchants to transfer by simple indorsation goods represented by a bill of lading, just as the Act 19 and 20 Vict., c. 25, recognised their right to cross cheques. In both cases the practice had grown up from convenience. The law merely recognised, formulated, and expressed the practice which it found ready to its hand. A perusal of Justice Buller's opinion delivered to the House of Lords[1]—and as he was in the minority of the consulted judges, his opinion was presumably not good law before his day—will convince any one that he was not merely trying to discover a rule already existent, but that he decided the question on theoretical grounds, and showed that the previously understood law could be explained away. It was the House of Lords which adopted his opinion, and so made it law. Though really acting in a judicial capacity, the House of Lords feels less trammelled in such cases by precedent than other courts, while it feels conscious that it is creating a precedent of the very greatest weight

[1] Smith's *Leading Cases* (7th Ed.), vol. i., p. 792.

for all the other courts of the country, and one the force of which is inferior only to statute.

The judicial function has often developed into express legislation, a legislative act being merely a decision of an indefinite number of hypothetical cases. Prætorian edicts exemplify this very well. At first a decision was given in each case as it arose, but afterwards it became the custom for the prætors to issue a list of the decisions which they would give in certain cases. Each prætor, on his accession to office for the year, issued such an edict. This was purely and simply an act of legislation, and its essential character was not changed when Hadrian promulgated the *edictum perpetuum*. On many subjects those who administer the law are the best legislators. It is for this reason the subject of judicial procedure is generally dealt with by the Court of Session in a legislative capacity. This function of the Scotch court has been adopted in England for the High Court of Justice, and it has been extended in Scotland in certain cases to sheriffs.[1] But the powers formerly were much more extensive, for we find several of the Court of Session acts of sederunt dealing with points in municipal law. Thus the Act 1621, cap. 18, as to bankruptcy was preceded by an act of sederunt. Erskine says that parliament generally ratified such

[1] Act of Sederunt, 10th July, 1839; 39 & 40 Vict., c. 70. By the Act 44 & 45 Vict., c. 44, sec. 2, the Lord Chancellor is directed to take the assistance of a solicitor in preparing tables of fees.

acts,[1] and he tries to explain away the true character of the legislative proceeding by saying that they probably declared what was the existing law of Scotland. The same remark might be made about any of our acts of parliament, for it has been said that all law is merely declaratory.

When we turn to proper legislative bodies we find that the strict separation between legislation and judicial action is a recent development, and that no clear line of demarcation can be drawn between them even at the present day. Among the Romans, as Maine points out, the private transaction of adoption was a legislative act. The earliest criminal prosecutions partook of the nature of bills of pains and penalties.[2] So among the Anglo-Saxons the witenagemot was both a legislative assembly and a court of justice.[3] The double functions of the House of Lords at the present day are a very obvious example of this. The trial of Queen Caroline is a well-known example of a purely judicial proceeding in a legislative form. But every private act of parliament is an example of the same thing. The committees of the Lords or Commons decide on the rights of rival claimants or promotors. There is no essential difference between a divorce obtained by act of parliament and one decreed by the judge in a divorce court. The grounds on which it is obtained are the same in both cases. The effect

---

[1] *Institute*, I., i., 40; Bell's *Commentaries* (M'Laren's Ed.), ii., 171.
[2] *Ancient Law*, p. 373.   [3] Stubb's *Const. Hist.*, vol. i., p. 132.

when obtained is identical. It would be interesting to discover who first enunciated the principle that a judge cannot *make* law. It might be that some unjust judge gave a decision at variance with custom, and so led people to see that as private individuals must not take law into their own hands, so too must judges be prohibited from so doing. Justice cannot be left to the arbitrary caprice of a judge any more than of a suitor. Hence the interference of legislative bodies with municipal law.

The distinction between a legislative act proper and a judicial act is this, that in the former a decision is given in a hypothetical case, generally with the intention of creating a future rule, whereas in a judicial decision there must be an actual case presented to the court, and, at least in early times, the creation of a rule is secondary and accidental. The legislature decides an indefinite number of cases, the judge only one, while the reporter generalises the particular case, or leaves that to be done by a future judge in deciding a future case. The act of legislation and the act of judgment are ultimately and essentially the same, but the true unit is the judicial decision however it may be given. An enactment is nothing till it is clothed with a case. Till that takes place there is no law. No relation of right has yet arisen. The law is only hypothetical.

But within the last year or two legislation has taken a further development. We have seen that Parliament, with all its omnipotence, has long since abandoned the right of interpretation of the law. It would appear that it will soon abandon legislation. High authorities have shewn that it is utterly impossible to expect Parliament to prepare a code. Acts dealing with technical subjects are generally passed in the form in which they leave the draughtsman's hands. This has been particularly the case with the English Criminal Law Consolidation Acts. Amendment in such cases often means mutilation. The referring of certain bills to Grand Committees, the members of which have some technical knowledge of the subject of legislation, is therefore a step of great importance towards perfecting the form of the law, and it is to be hoped that the experiment will be honestly carried out, before a judgment is passed on the proposal. What then will be the function of Parliament? The voting of supplies and a general superintendence of the conduct of the Executive is amply sufficient to occupy the most of its time. And the answering of questions is not such waste of time as some people seem to think, if the questions are put by men who realize the responsibility of their position. As to legislation we can only expect the whole house to deal with broad questions of general principle, such as arise on the second or third reading of a bill, and to deal with details only when the subject is one of universal interest and overwhelming importance.

Under the head of legislation we must include acts of sederunt of the Court of Session, and rules and regulations by judges already referred to, proclamations under particular acts by local authorities, regulations by the Privy Council for the Post Office, for traffic in cattle, navigation, and many other matters; provisional orders by the Board of Trade, treaties entered into with foreign powers by the Executive Government, and such like. These are all a true source of positive law, and, as far as the subjects of the state are concerned, they are acts of legislation. Thus treaties, such as those of extradition and copyright, are simultaneous acts of legislation by two states for their respective subjects.

But in modern times the most common application of the law is by the private individuals who practise as counsel and agents, solicitors, attorneys, and notaries public. The arbiter who decides a dispute is undoubtedly acting as a judge; so also is the lawyer who advises a client as to whether he has a good cause. And even when a case comes to be argued in court, is it not more correct to regard the counsel or agents employed as judges or arbiters who have honestly differed in opinion, than as clever rogues who hire their ingenuity and eloquence for so many guineas a day? Again, the function of a notary who takes the protest of the holder of a bill, or of the master of a ship, is purely judicial. This is also the case in the execution of notarial instruments in Scotland as to the transfer of rights in property in land.[1]

[1] Austin has pointed out the effect of the profession on the law.— *Lectures on Jurisprudence*, vol. ii., p. 667.

In like manner, the whole operation of preparing contracts, agreements, settlements, conveyances, and such deeds, is purely *legislative*. The conveyancer who prepares a contract of copartnery, or articles of association of a company, is framing a code for a greater or smaller group of persons. A marriage settlement or a will is equivalent to a private act of parliament regulating the succession of a particular person or persons. As we shall see hereafter, such deeds bear to the general law of intestate succession the same relation as special articles of association do to those provided by the Companies Act of 1862. All such deeds *make* the law for the persons involved.

But the movement for freedom does not stop here. The exigencies of commerce refuse to be trammelled by the formalities of the civil law. Contracts *in re mercatoriâ* are privileged in their forms. They are made by merchants in their own words, or in any manner they please. And now it is said, why not dispense with the quirks and quibbles of lawyers? why not transfer land like goods or stocks? The revolt here is against professional lawyers, and within certain limits no fault can be found with the movement. Small pecuniary disputes between intelligent men can often be settled without legal assistance; and in ordinary agreements, if a person expresses himself clearly, there is no reason why he should use particular words if others are as clear.[1]

[1] *E.g.*, Use of the word "Dispone" abolished by the Scotch Conveyancing Act of 1874.

To all appearance each step in the process here indicated is a complete negation of the preceding one. Thus, any one "who takes law into his own hands," as the phrase goes, is a wrongdoer, and will be punished criminally. The intervention of a judge prohibits, except in very rare cases, the private enforcement of right. In like manner, legislation supersedes jurisdiction. The legislative body prohibits the judge from *making* law. Again and again we find judges laying it down that they merely administer the law, and cannot alter it. In this view a judge who avowedly alters the law is guilty of malversation of justice, and it is only by a legal fiction that he can exercise his ancient functions. Then, again, it is laid down that parliament cannot *make* laws, it merely *declares* them. And it will be observed that almost all legislation of the present day is for the purpose of freeing men from the trammels of antiquated laws, and allowing them to determine their rights by self-legislation,—contracts and private deeds. If you ask politicians what pressing questions are awaiting a decision by Parliament, you will be told it is the disestablishment of some institution, or the abolition of some old law. Thus, within the last few years, we have had the abolition of the usury laws; the abolition of the navigation laws; the abolition of the corn laws; the abolition of church rates; the abolition of the law of deathbed; the abolition of the landlord's hypothec; the abolition of cumbrous forms in conveyancing and in the making of wills; the disestablishment of trade guilds, of close burghs, of the Irish Church, of exclusive privileges of legal bodies. The air is still filled with rumours of disestablishment, and the abolition of entail primogeniture. This movement, which in some aspects is called free trade, merely signifies that individual men are allowed *to make the law for themselves.* In this view the Irish legislation of the present parliament has apparently reversed the natural order of the growth of legal forms. But this must be explained on the ground that the persons legislated for are so weak and helpless that they cannot realise their true freedom, or maintain it against others who are so strong and so unjust as to encroach on their rights. One of the first results of a consciousness of freedom will be a demand for the repeal of statutes which restrain this power of self-legislation—a demand for freedom of contract — a species of home-rule of which Irish agitators have apparently no conception. Modern legislation where positive, is only supplementary to the private creation of law. Thus the Succession Acts give a general form of will. The Married Women's Property Acts contain a rather unfair marriage settlement, and so with the other acts referred to. And, finally, in the revolt against professional lawyers, it appears as if law would disappear and human relations come back to arbitrary force.

We have thus come back to where we started. It is

again the private individual who determines and enforces his rights, but with the difference that his particular right has absorbed and transmuted all the previous stages. It has now become filled with a fuller and richer content. His right is now recognised and enforced by the state through its judicial and executive bodies. The state cannot refuse him permission to enter into legal relations. The legislature merely interferes in default of the exercise of his powers by the individual. The judicial office interprets and explains his rights, and the executive enforces them. Instead of an arbitrary determination of an individual, enforced by his own individual power, it is the rational determination of the state, adopted and enforced by its power. If in the first might alone was right, in the last might and right are identified.

LECTURE III.

LEGAL FORMS—*continued.*

Hitherto our attention has been confined to the consideration of municipal law; we must turn now to the other great departments of constitutional and international law, which take their rise from the development of the notion of a state, or from men dealing with each other in organised groups. It will be observed that constitutional law is the first branch of law which becomes disclosed by legislation. As in India, one conquest after another may sweep over a district without affecting the primitive legal customs of the people,[1] so in Rome, and at a later period in England, the private law was being slowly developed, while the greatest changes were taking place in the constitution by express enactment. The Twelve Tables, though so antiquated, are dated three centuries from the foundation of the city, and after the establishment of the Republic. In England, a large proportion of early statutes are constitutional or administrative, the extensive employment of legislation in private law as presently developed being very late indeed. For this reason it may be thought that I should have commenced with

[1] See p. 91, *Note.*

constitutional law; but in view of Austin's position, that constitutional and international law are not law proper,[1] it is more satisfactory to show the substantial identity of the forms in those branches and in municipal law. In constitutional law we find the three forms to which I have already referred, with this difference that, whereas in municipal law the judicial enactment of law is the common type, in constitutional law it is the most rare. In early times we find governments set up and overturned—one king deposed and another put into his place, without any idea of a theoretical constitution. In this way the constitutions of nearly all ancient states were gradually moulded. The English constitution is an example of an intermediate class. Point after point, relating to the rights and powers of the monarch and the relations of the two houses of parliament, has been settled by a struggle between the parties concerned. Sometimes the judges have been appealed to as expositors of the law; sometimes the two parties made a compromise; often one yielded; but whatever the process, the result has been the expression of something which is essentially a positive law. Much of the law which relates to this subject has grown up from custom. For example, the rights of burghs to send members to parliament; the powers of the cabinet, the number of members of which it should consist; the

[1] See Amos' *Science of Jurisprudence*, p. 409, where this position is refuted as to international law.

powers and duties of privy councillors; these and such matters may be taken as corresponding to the municipal law which is made simply by being put into force.

The most difficult class of cases which fall under this form of law is that of rebellions. One recent writer says of revolution that "its essence is illegality, and its justification is its success."[1] The same view is expressed more at length by Dr. Abdy in regard to the English revolution of 1688. To a passage in which Chancellor Kent quotes Vattel with approbation, in bringing forward the interference of William of Orange as an example of justifiable interference, he says:—"But however deep may be our debt of gratitude to those by whose help and means the revolution of 1688 was happily accomplished, and however close may be the connection between that event and the assurance of our present liberties, we must not shut our eyes to the fact that the conduct of William, if judged by principles of international law, was above and beyond its spirit to be avoided as a precedent, and certainly not to be assigned as a good and substantial example of a rule neither founded on reason nor warranted by precedents."[2] If a revolution took place once a month in any state, it might be possible to find "precedents." But even then it would be difficult for a state to have such method in its madness as

[1] *Letters of Historicus*, p. 41.
[2] Abdy's Edition of Kent's *Commentaries* (2nd Ed.), p. 82.

to reduce revolution to a science, and embody its rules in a code.[1] It is impossible, when you are stopped by a highwayman on a lonely heath, to proceed to the metropolis and get an act of parliament to deal with him, or even to call in the assistance of a magistrate in the nearest town. The best precedents you can follow advise you to shoot him if you can, and the law does not declare that to be illegal.[2] Fortunately, revolutions do not occur often, and the circumstances must be dealt with as they arise. The original text of Chancellor Kent, which Dr. Abdy has spoiled with the above quoted interpolation, puts the matter in its true light, when he says, "The right of interposition in this class of cases" (and the same remark applies to rebellion) "must depend upon special circumstances, cannot be precisely limited, and is of the utmost delicacy in its application. It must be submitted to the guidance of eminent discretion, and controlled by principles of justice and sound policy." When tyranny and oppression become unbearable, justice and right can only be vindicated by force. It makes no difference that the act of rebellion cannot be judged by a jury, as in the case of a common assault by a private individual. The rebellious subject must be content to be judged by foreign nations, or perhaps by a remote posterity. For this reason the true patriot does not hesitate to risk

[1] Amos' *Science of Politics*, chap. xi.
[2] Lady Bloomfield's *Reminiscences*, vol. i., p. 2.

his own life, for he knows that the striking example of his death will be strong evidence of the sincerity of his opinions. The patriotism which commits murder with the certainty of impunity is of a very suspicious description. The feeling to which Dr. Abdy has given expression is the one to which I already alluded in speaking of municipal law—viz., that the individual aggrieved must not take law into his own hands. But as we have seen, this rule does not apply when delay would be dangerous. In such cases a judgment can afterwards be passed on the act. The mistake into which Dr. Abdy has fallen is one that seems peculiar to lawyers. From the very earliest times down to our own day, we find that forms of procedure have overruled substantive rights.[1] And though we do not go so far as the Romans in adhering strictly to the forms of the *actiones legis*, we still show a tendency to be hampered by them. Dr. Abdy would sacrifice substantive right to form in constitutional law.

Very little of our constitutional law is due to judicial decision. In most cases, where judicial action is necessary, the legislative body acts in a judicial

---

[1] See Holmes' *The Common Law*, where many examples of this are given. See also decision in *Watt Bros.* v. *Foyn*, 1st Nov., 1879, 7 *Rettie*, 126, where it was held that a suspension was incompetent after an appeal had been allowed *per incuriam* to drop. The modern tendency is shown in the powers of amendment of records given to judges, and in the extensive powers of the appellate courts. See Court of Session Act, 1868, and Sheriff Court Act, 1874.

capacity, as in the case of the Earl of Strafford. The consideration that an act of legislation and one of judgment are ultimately identical would have resolved the difficulties in this case which Hallam discusses with such judicial impartiality.[1] The objection to that proceeding arises from the fallacy which is commonly accepted in England, and from which even Sir Henry Maine cannot shake himself free, that law is properly a result of legislation, and that, however atrocious a crime may be, if it is perfectly new in its conception, it must go unpunished until it is prohibited by act of parliament.[2] This is a doctrine on which Paine, in his *Rights of Man*, insists with great force, and it was recently revived by the Conservatives in the House of Commons in discussing the rebellion of Arabi Pasha. Other examples of the judicial application of law will be found in the Wilkes cases, the Hansard case, and the Bradlaugh case, which is still pending. The tragedy of Marino Faliero shows that constitutional law has sanctions even without enactment, and while we may regard the trial of Charles I. of England as a miscarriage of justice, we see from the execution of Louis XVI. of France and Marie Antoinette that judicial crimes are not confined to municipal law.

[1] *Constitutional History*, chap. ix.
[2] See what is perhaps an example of this in Taylor's *Manual of Medical Jurisprudence* (8th Ed.), p. 47, where he states that some doubt once existed whether administering poison *externally* was murder. In Scotland there would never have been any doubt on the point.

The mere fact of a trial being given in those famous cases shows the feeling that it is demanded by a regard for outward decorum.

But at the present day we observe distinctly the third stage of constitutional law—the legislative. The manufacture of constitutions is a favourite pursuit of the statesmen of the nineteenth century. In new states, as in our American, Australian, and African colonies, and in states which try to make a fresh start, we have all the powers and duties of all the constituent members of the government laid down in a code. This is so in France and Belgium. In Germany the constitution has generally been laid down in a treaty between the small states. In this country, again, we have had, during the present century, two Reform Acts, the Catholic Emancipation, the Jewish Disabilities, the Naturalisation Act, and others.

Turning now to international law, we observe that the customs which in early times regulated the intercourse of nations in peace and war took their rise in isolated acts, which made the law for the occasion. And even in modern times, the necessities of war continually modify rights. The purely theoretical difficulties which have been raised as to the doctrine of intervention may be resolved by keeping in view that the right in every case must be decided according to circumstances, and, if necessary, carried out by force. Historicus has, therefore, erred most grievously when he says: "The emancipation of Greece, effected by Europe[1] was a high act of policy above and beyond the domain of law. As an act of policy it may have been, and probably was, justifiable, but it was not the less a hostile act, which, if she had dared, Turkey might properly have resented by war."[2] The error here corresponds exactly to that referred to a little ago in the case of rebellion. If we understand that the act was *just*, for Historicus does not say it was a politic crime, it *cannot* be beyond law. If the three powers—Britain, France, and Russia had been private individuals, they would have been reprimanded for not interfering. In Scotland, one who looks on at a rape, which he might do something to prevent, is punishable as an accessory.[3] The difficulty seems to be caused partly by the act being on a large scale, and partly by its being of rare occurrence. Historicus might as well say that Shakspeare's "Hamlet" is a high effort of genius above and beyond the domain of art! A similar remark might be made as to works of art like Wiertz's colossal pictures, Wagner's lyric dramas, or great engineering works like the Suez Canal, the tunnels through the Alps, the Menai tubular bridge, and so forth. The statement above quoted is as amazing as if an astronomer had declared that the motions of the moon and of comets were above and beyond the domain

---

[1] In 1830.   [2] *Letters*, p. 6.
[3] *H.M. Advocate* v. *Kerr*, December 26, 1871; 2 Couper's *Justiciary Reports*, 334. See Ruskin, *The Crown of Wild Olive*, p. 128.

of dynamics, or that the laws of falling bodies applied only to small stones, and not to large bodies like the earth or moon! I have said that the difficulty raised is purely theoretical, for mankind have not hesitated at intervention when a clamant case presented itself. Intervention to redress an obvious wrong, or to help the weak against the strong, is a human instinct.[1] But even in a case of intervention between belligerents, the notion of right may be explicit if the act is conscious and deliberate. Thus, if Parliament directs the Government to interfere, we have a resolution which is at bottom judicial.

But, perhaps, the best illustration of the judicial stage in international law is afforded by the *causes célèbres*, which have arisen between various states, particularly between the date of the Peace of Westphalia and the Congress of Vienna (1648–1815). In these there was an appeal to abstract law; and whether the dispute was decided by the parties themselves, by mediation, or by arbitration, the result has been a judicial decision and generally a precedent for future conduct. The frequent congresses which have taken place in recent times, either for the purpose of arbitrating between contending parties, or for the purpose of giving one power "a mandate" to carry out the wishes of the other European powers, are an approach to judicial forms. Here, again, the idea is that a state which takes law into its own hands is a wrong-doer.

[1] Amos' *Science of Politics*, p. 353.

But the period since 1815 has been emphatically one of legislation, and that legislation has taken the form of treaties. Two small volumes contain all the commercial treaties of Great Britain for about two centuries prior to 1815. Those of the period succeeding that date—little more than half a century—occupy twelve volumes in Mr. Hertslet's collection, each twice or thrice the size of the first two. Instead of international affairs being left to custom or the sense of justice of individual states, codes are from time to time prepared dealing in detail with particular subjects. In this way we have extradition treaties, postal treaties, monetary unions, conventions for the regulation of the navigation of particular rivers or for the prevention of collisions at sea, regulations as to diplomatic etiquette, as to weapons of war, as to the treatment of the killed and wounded in battle. In international law legislation and private contract coincide. In form many treaties are contracts, but in substance they are simultaneous acts of legislation by several states.

The three divisions of municipal law, constitutional or state law, and inter-state or international law (or, perhaps more correctly, co-national or co-state law), exhaust positive law. The first (municipal law) determines, declares, and enforces the rights claimed by the individual as a person. But the same individuals, who enjoy rights as persons, recognise and enforce them as citizens. The same individuals who are subject to the state form the state. Constitutional or state law determines the relation of the individual citizen to the state. The individual molecules of which each state is composed commingle and form relations with those of other states. These relations must form the subject of joint action by the states to which they belong, and hence I suggested co-national or co-state law as a better name than international law. Much of what is called international law is truly municipal law, common to several states, in many cases enacted by a treaty or a simultaneous act of legislation. This is more evident, if all the states which are parties to the treaty require to get it ratified by the legislature, as in the United States of America. Take, for example, the recent treaty and subsequent legislative acts dealing with outrages on the fishermen on the North Sea. Here, then, the *jus gentium* and the *jus inter gentes*, which it was thought modern science had distinguished, are identified by modern practice.[1] It is quite an error to rank *private* international law as another branch of positive law. The obligation on any state to consider the problem, and to recognise the laws of a foreign state, falls under public international law. The solution of the problem belongs to municipal law, and has been so treated by Savigny. International law is, in this view, an expansion of constitutional law, since it takes means for declaring and enforcing the rights

---

[1] An *international* exhibition is one common to all states. This is the common use of the word outside of law.

of our subjects residing in a foreign state, and in other cases for enforcing the rights of foreigners against their own state. By international law an individual becomes a citizen of the world. Historically constitutional and international law frequently coincide. In the sixteenth century the constitutional law of the states occupying the Netherlands was a kind of international law. In the successive constitutional changes of the German Empire, prior to 1871, we see an example of the same phenomenon. In the middle ages the relations of Venice, Genoa, and Milan fell under the law of nations. At the present day they belong to constitutional and municipal law.[1] In the United States of America, if we substitute plenipotentiaries for the present members of congress, we have international instead of constitutional law. In both of these branches the ultimate appeal is to war, and in form they are therefore ultimately the same. I must return to this subject in a future lecture, but perhaps enough has been said here to show that municipal law and state law (with its two branches of constitutional and international law) exhaust the sphere of positive law.

We may now sum up the result at which we have arrived. The recognised forms of positive law in its three great divisions are :—

---

[1] At a still earlier period the islands, which afterwards made Venice, were independent states. Hazlitt's *History of the Venetian Republic*, vol. iv., p. 251. So with Switzerland down to 1848.

I. THE LEGAL USE OF VIOLENCE OR FORCE, the idea of right being only implicit, as in the case of self-defence against assault; the putting down of a rebellion, as in the civil war in America; or in repelling a sudden invasion by a foreign state. The firing on a mob during a riot, and the burning of a prize at sea before it has been condemned, may also be taken as examples under this head.

II. JUDICIAL DECREES MERELY FOR SUMMARY EXECUTION.—The common mode of recovering rates illustrates this. The procedure against persons suspected of crimes under the Irish Peace Preservation Act of 1881 may serve as an example from constitutional law; while the old system of "reprisals," which still holds its place in our text books of international law, is a good example in that branch of law.

III. JUDICIAL DECREES AFTER INVESTIGATION.—This is the common form in municipal law; in constitutional and international law it appears, when a war is declared against rebels or a foreign state, as the case may be, after due deliberation.

IV. LEGISLATIVE ACTS.—Under legislation are also included proclamations by the Executive Government, the Privy Council, the magistrates of burghs, by-laws of railway companies, &c. The declaration of Paris, 1856, and the Geneva and St. Petersburg Conventions are good examples in international law.

V. THE DEEDS OF PRIVATE INDIVIDUALS, including

charters of companies, articles of association of companies, trust deeds for churches, or creditors, or a family, leases, by-laws of clubs, &c. In constitutional and international law there is nothing corresponding exactly to this head, except, perhaps, treaties on any particular point between two or a few states. But we see the same influence at work in the greatly extended facilities for naturalisation in foreign states, which are a growth of the last twenty years, and also in the recent rapid growth of private international law, where the right is now practically recognised of any individual to choose the law to which he wishes any particular transaction to become subject—a right which was formerly denied in Scotland.[1]

VI. And finally, along with an almost unlimited elasticity of form we find a tendency to disregard form in order to attain substantial justice. It may be, as in America, by allowing the supreme court to judge of the validity of legislative acts, or by allowing deeds, however solemn, to be set aside for fraud or in consequence of error. Or, again, it may show itself in the gradual transference of debates, from parliament to the press and public meetings, where legislative changes are not discussed by representatives of the nation, but the nation thinks aloud for itself.

[1] Act 1425, cap. 48.

LECTURE IV.

OBLIGATION.

RIGHTS, as we have now seen, are declared and enforced by legislators, judges, and rulers. But the question may be asked, Are the rights then created for the first time? Is there no "prior consideration" to the judicial decision, as in the question, which is solemnly discussed in the Scotch books, whether cohabitation with habit and repute constitute marriage, or whether it requires a sentence of *declarator* to complete it? A further investigation shows that the judge merely declares rights, and when he declares one man to have a right he expressly or implicitly declares another to be bound; but he cannot attribute rights to a person unless he has them already, and he cannot declare a person to be "bound" unless he is so already. What then is the nature of the rights enforced by a judge? This brings the scientific lawyer to "substantive" as opposed to "adjective" law.[1] He must now classify rights themselves, and one of the earliest divisions is that of rights arising from delict, and rights arising from contract—the former arising from the negation of a wrong, and the latter being the result of the affirmative self-determination of a free man.

[1] Holland's *Jurisprudence* (1st ed.), p. 61.

If we may conceive such a state, the earliest form of obligation would arise in a state of primitive innocence, where obligations would be performed without their being specifically felt to be burdens or bonds. This is still the great source of obligations in the family and the state, and it is only in recent times that these have been formulated by legislative enactments into obligations to pay rates for the poor, for education, for roads, gas, water, and other common purposes of large bodies of men. These obligations are often spoken of, not very happily, as "implied contracts." We shall see this more fully when discussing the subject of the family and the state. It is these "implied obligations" which become now and then crystallised into "police offences." It will be more convenient to deal with these after discussing the idea of crime. But it is wrong which first reveals rights, as disease calls our attention to organs which are generally unconscious in their operation.

I have already observed the prominent place assigned to legal procedure in the Twelve Tables. The next most prominent subject in that code is the law of delict—wrong.[1] This is a striking characteristic of ancient codes from the Ten Commandments downwards. Thus, the laws of Æthelbirht and nearly all the laws of Alfred are penal.[2] These codes, which are an important

---
[1] Ortolan's *History*, by Pritchard and Nasmith, p. 139.
[2] Thorpe's *Ancient Laws of England*, pp. 3, 44.

step in the scientific development of law, prove that men had then become conscious of criminal law, while the ordinary municipal law was floating about still undetermined. The comparatively simple relations of men in other respects were regulated entirely by custom, or by an appeal to the king, or bishop, or council of the tribe. Criminal law and punishment are so obviously concerns of the state, that express enactments come to be made in regard to them as in ordinary matters of government and taxation. And so, as I have pointed out before, in India, successive rulers may hold sway for centuries without noticing or affecting in any way the private relations of their subjects, or the development of the municipal law which governs them.[1]

It is in and through wrongs that rights are revealed, and Hegel therefore calls wrong "the evidence of right." Right reveals itself first as the negation of its negation. It is through wrong that we become as gods, "knowing good and evil." As we shall see more fully hereafter, in each of the notions of person, property, and contract, the family and the state, we may distinguish four elements—(1.) a physical fact; (2.) a conscious claim by the individual concerned, either for himself or as a member of an organic group; (3.) an organic state or other group of persons physically existing;[2] and (4.) a

[1] Lyall's *Asiatic Studies*, p. 178. Maine's *History of Institutions*, p. 380.

[2] The word "state" is used throughout in this connection as a convenient expression for the *universal*. It is the common *Vor-*

recognition by the state or group, of that fact and claim as a right. So, conversely, a wrong involves (1.) an interference with the physical fact, as assault, physical violence, slander, abstraction of, or injury to, a thing, or a forcible interruption of a voluntary relation, or in relation to the family, adultery, or in relation to the state, treason, or piracy, an attack on civilisation itself; (2.) consciousness of the act; (3.) implicitly, if not explicitly, a denial of the existence of the state or organised group; and (4.) a denial of the right recognised by the state. In crime all those moments are present, and so, as a general rule, a crime involves a civil injury, and affords ground for a claim of reparation; but damage, as a general rule, must be substantial. In criminal law, however, we may punish mere *intent* when exhibited in overt acts; and in cases where character is involved, and in some others, nominal damages may be given to carry expenses by way of penalty. In civil injury, the first and third moments may be admitted, and only the second and fourth denied; but in crime the individual sets himself up in the place of the state, and boldly declares that it is wrong. He deliberately puts his particular will for the universal. He affirms to be right what the universal reason calls wrong.

stellung of the universal. But it should be remembered that in this sense *two* persons may form a state, because there is more in the group than the qualities and powers of the two individuals added together. See Lectures vi. and vii.

Crime and civil injury merge into one another. Maine has illustrated this historically in the gradual development of modern crimes by the transference of acts to that category, which in early times were only treated as torts. But the connection may be illustrated in modern every-day practice. Two persons claim as their property a piece of ground. The one, who is not the true owner, is in possession. This is a physical act in violation of the right of the other. Both admit the general right of the *true* owner to possess, and the only dispute is as to the wrongful claim by the present possessor. As soon as it is shown to be wrong, the wrong-doer cedes possession voluntarily; he adopts the universal will voluntarily, and makes it his own. His will was never anything else than the universal will. This is shown by the fact that the state presumed his possession to be lawful, and protected it until it was shown to be wrong. But suppose the wrongful possessor refuses to leave in obedience to a decree of a competent court. Force must be used to carry out the universal will, and thus the wrongness of his particular will is brought home to the individual. This person would not technically in our law be a thief, though he was so in the Roman law, and his act may be morally criminal. It may be thought, however, that the enforcing of the judgment of the court is a sufficient penalty. In Scotch law a person who wrongfully holds subjects may be found liable in "violent profits" or penal rent. This makes the act really, though not technically, criminal. Again, the dispute may be as to whether the state recognises one view or another—a pure point of law as it is called. Then, as soon as the universal will is ascertained by the highest court, the individual ought to submit. If he resists, force again adjusts the contradiction. It may be said, then, that every person who refuses to pay a just debt, or to fulfil the decree of a competent court, is to that extent criminal. This is partially recognised in practice, for he is treated as a criminal, as in the recent cases of Mr. Green and Mr. Tooth, the famous ritualists. And the Debtors (Scotland) Act of 1880, which abolished imprisonment for civil debt, still allows it for twelve months in cases where the decree or obligation is *ad factum præstandum*, and some others. In the evidence given before the recent commission on the abolition of imprisonment for debt, frequent reference was made to the criminal aspect of a refusal to pay alimentary debts, and it has been pointed out that in the Scotch act, by some inexcusable oversight, the provisions of the English act[1] have been omitted, which enable a judge to imprison certain debtors who have been guilty of misconduct, or who have means to pay and refuse to do so.

But when we come to crime proper, we see that the act of the criminal could only be declared right, if it were possible for the universal to be negated—if it were

[1] 32 and 33 Vict., cap. 62, sec. 4 and 5.

possible for the state to reverse its previous judgment on such conduct, and declare wrong to be right. The state only represents the universal to the criminal, in the same way as a father or a guardian to a child. The law to which it appeals is not an arbitrary creation of its own. As our Scotch indictments put it, "by the laws of this and *every other* well-governed realm," the particular act described is a crime. Every one of our libels and indictments thus sets itself above even the state and passes a judgment on other states, as well as on the criminal who is in the dock.

Each crime, as we have seen, involves a civil injury, and hence a claim for reparation is always competent against the wrong-doer. In English law this seems to be sometimes refused, apparently on the ground that the delinquent has nothing with which to make reparation, or perhaps it is a mere survival of the primitive idea that punishment and civil reparation are identical. In the Roman law this claim was allowed in the particular action, and the assertion of the universal was only implicit or appeared in exemplary damages. When the wrong-doer is poor and cannot make reparation, or the person wronged is poor or weak and cannot sue, or is disinclined to do so from timidity or any other cause, the state, as representing the universal, is still wronged. If the universal will were not reasserted, society would fall to pieces. Hence the interference of the state with punishment. In most European

States this is administered at the instance of the state in its corporate capacity; but in England any member of the state may represent it as prosecutor. If it is borne in mind that the function of a public prosecutor is really in the first instance judicial, the distinction will not appear to be of much importance. Certainly, a Scotch Lord Advocate appears in our eyes to be much more judicial than a French judge.[1] Punishment is an express reassertion of the universal will. It is more or less emphatic, according as the assertion of the particular will has been strong or not. With the criminal his act might only be a transitory aberration, or it might be a long pondered, slowly developed, and determinate effort. The punishment will thus vary from an admonition— a solemn warning—to blowing the culprit from the cannon's mouth, as was done with the Indian mutineers.[2] The physical infliction is therefore an accident. Two theories are current in this country on the subject of punishment. The first is, that punishment is a deterrent; the second, that it is a means of reforming the culprit. These views are both rejected by Hegel, who holds what has been called a bloody doctrine—that punishment is an end in itself. Trendelenburg criticises this, and points

---

[1] Compare the trial of Madeleine Smith at Edinburgh in July, 1857, reported by Mr Irvine, with the trial of the Monk Léotade, reported in Stephen's *History of the Criminal Law*, vol. iii., p. 466.

[2] There was perhaps too much of mere revenge in our treatment of the natives of India during the mutiny. See Kaye's *History of the Sepoy War*, vol. ii., pp. 268, 274, 399, 482.

out that punishment here is mere dialectic with the criminal. It applies his own logic to himself, but it still leaves unanswered the question, whether we are justified in applying force to him as he has done in committing the crime, or whether we are bound to do so. Now, I think the punishment is primarily for the benefit of the state, and secondarily for the reform of the criminal. His act must be condemned. But we must remember that "a reproof entereth more into a wise man than a hundred stripes into a fool." It would be absurd to give the identical physical amount of punishment in each case, and a discretion is and must be given to judges in this matter. It was only ignorance which could complain of the sentences awarded to the City Bank directors. To men in their position, the verdict of a jury was a heavy punishment. Anything more than the punishment awarded them would have been mere revenge. In other words, we cannot estimate punishment merely by quantity. But, in dealing with a fool, we must set up the universal in a more distinct form than his own conscience can do. Here a mere declaration will not suffice. We must make the judgment awful in proportion to his crime; or, rather, in proportion to the amount of disapprobation which the national conscience feels for the crime. A community can hardly express an idea in words, and hence an external physical act is the most natural vehicle for its thoughts. As punishment in this view is an expression of the national conscience, all mere particular revenge is excluded, and hence torture or cruel punishments are not allowable. The state cannot allow the crime to pass without punishment, because that would imply a degradation of the national conscience and ultimate ruin to the state itself, but it is bound to punish with the least possible waste of energy, and punishments should not therefore be more severe or protracted than is absolutely necessary. In this way the criminal is benefitted. As a member of the community he has heard the judgment passed on his act, and it has been brought home to him in his own body. It is only the poverty of the delinquents which has made punishment so important compared with reparation. To a rich man heavy damages will be sufficient punishment, and hence ancient codes are filled with pecuniary penalties. Poor criminals were more summarily dealt with. This explains, I think, why in modern practice so many cases of fraud come only before the civil courts.

Now, capital punishment excludes the idea of reformation of the criminal so as to enable him again to take his place as a useful member of society. How, then, can it be justified? Hegel's answer that it is an infinitely negative judgment corresponding to the wrong is unsatisfactory. It is not dignified for the state to answer the fool "according to his folly"—to answer his force with the mere dialectic of force. If it is true, as I have indicated, that the idea of physical force in punishment is accidental, then death is not the *necessary* punishment for murder, as Hegel would make it. The branding of Cain was a punishment greater than he could bear, and it must always be a question of circumstances whether death is the most appropriate punishment that can be devised. Imprisonment for life is not a very humane substitute. It has been remarked that a large proportion of persons imprisoned for life go mad,[1] but this may be due to the fact that they have been predisposed to insanity, and their crime may only have been a premonitory symptom. It is therefore a most proper provision of our law which allows criminals undergoing such a sentence to go free, after a certain period of good behaviour. They are subject to police supervision, and so are not altogether free from restraint. But, if death is the best and most emphatic method of carrying home to a community the nature of a crime, or if it is the only mode in which it can express its horror and detestation of crime, then capital punishment is proper. It was thus that the British Government conveyed to the natives of India their ideas as to the crimes which the mutineers had committed. The punishment awarded intimated to the people that an eternal punishment only could expiate their deeds, and the peculiar horror which the mode of death would inspire would naturally lead

---

[1] Reports on the laws of foreign countries respecting homicidal crime (Miscellaneous, No. 3, 1881), pp. 62, 63. See Maudsley, *Responsibility in Mental Disease*, pp. 25-33.

them to think on the nature of their crimes. A similar course of reasoning has led Mr. Justice Stephen to advocate an extension of capital punishment to other crimes than murder. While there is a chance of reformation, criminals ought to be pardoned or punished lightly, and young persons should be sent to reformatories or such institutions, but there is no reason why we should preserve the life of a hardened professional thief or resetter. While we are complaining of overpopulation and many honest poor are starving, it is cruel to tax them in order to keep such characters clothed, fed, and lodged in comfortable and healthy prisons. A crab has no compunction in cutting off a limb which has become useless, and why should we hesitate so to deal with social limbs which are dead and harmful? It can hardly be maintained that criminals are necessary for the social life, and if the sacredness of human life is pleaded, some attempt should be made to save it before the disease has run its course. If our prisoners' aid societies could contrive to remove young persons to the colonies, or even to other localities, where they would be free from their old associates, and where the ostracism of jail-birds would not be so likely to bar the way to a return to paths of honesty, it would be a decided advance on our present treatment of these unfortunate beings.

Public executions have been abolished with us, for they were believed to defeat their purpose by throwing a halo of glory round the culprit. They were apt to transform detestation of the murderer into sympathy; and even to the criminal himself they robbed the penalty of much of its solemnity.

We may now without difficulty apply the idea of punishment to children. It is absurd to send a child to prison before sending it to a reformatory. There is nothing sacred in a prison's walls. The universal will may be here restored by a slow process of education in a reformatory school. Thus, whether the magistrate admonishes the child, or warns its parents, or sends it to prison, or sends it to a reformatory, he does the same thing. He vindicates and re-establishes the universal against the caprice or the particular will of the child in so far as it has any will. The training given to it is simply a course to lead it to subject its particular will to the universal. This is what a good father should do when he refuses to spare the rod. The idea of punishment in the case of children is thus identical with that recognised in adults, and so Trendelenburg applies the notion of punishment in a school—the school being the community and the schoolmaster representing the universal.

As the national conscience grows more sensitive, severe punishments become less necessary. Thus imprisonment for debt, flogging in the army, the pillory, are all abolished. Hence, also, the present agitation for the abolition of capital punishment. It would certainly be advisable to remove the present uncertainty as to whether the penalty will be exacted or not. But the penalty must be retained for those who are outside of the community, and do not participate in the national consciousness. We must return to this in discussing the relation of law and morality. To sum up: Punishment may be looked at—(1.) From the point of view of the wrong-doer; (2.) from that of the person injured; and (3.) from that of the state. For the first it is reformatory, for the second it will take the form of reparation, and for the third it will be for self-satisfaction, and indirectly as a warning to others,[1] and therefore for the state itself ultimately reformatory. The order of ideas is the following: Punishment takes its rise in the value attached to the person of the individual wronged. Any wrong to a person is infinite, and hence the severity of early punishments. When law interferes it restrains and regulates this severity. Punishment is thus legalised revenge, the notion of *punishment* implying the universal. If punishment takes the form of a physical infliction, it is a physical infliction *plus* the idea that the state inflicts it. It is soon observed in punishments we are dealing with persons. The personality of the wrong-doer comes into view to such an extent that we have now more sympathy with the murderer than with the murdered man. Our punishments become reformatory. And, lastly, some propose to abolish punishment altogether.[2]

[1] Plato, Gorgias. Trendelenburg, *Naturrecht*, 136 and foll.

[2] On the whole subject of crime and punishment reference may be made to Hegel's *Naturrecht*, secs. 90-103 ; Kant's *Metaphysic of Ethics, Works* (Hartenstein's ed.), vol. vii., p. 149 ; Trendelenburg,

So far we have been considering positive acts where the particular will was deliberately set up in the place of the universal—not mere indifference, but an absolute worship of another god in place of the true God. We must now consider negative wrongs. Take the following cases:—

1. A person looking after his friend's business gratuitously and neglecting it;

2. A clerk or salaried manager neglecting his master's or employer's business, and (*a*) no loss ensuing, or (*b*) loss ensuing;

3. A fraud committed by either of them in the form of permitting peculation by others; or, again,

4. A pointsman falling asleep, and allowing a train to pass at a wrong time, but no damage resulting;

5. The same case, where an accident occurs and some person is injured;

6. The same case, where an accident occurs and some one is killed;

7. Where a pointsman, who has an enmity towards an engine-driver, allows his engine to go full speed into another in order to cause his death;

8. A coach-driver driving recklessly through the street, and injuring no person;

9. Doing same, and injuring some one;

l.c.; Ahrens' *Droit Naturel*, vol. i., p. 225 and foll., vol. ii., p. 438 and foll.; Amos' *Science of Law*, chap. x.; Holland's *Jurisprudence*, p. 254; Bentham's *Morals and Legislation*, chap. xiii. and foll.; and *The Proceedings of the Social Science Congress*, 1883.

10. Doing same, and killing some one ;

11. Doing same, and wilfully running over one.

No. 1. is a pure case of proper mandate, which is gratuitous. The friend gives a gift of his services, and the extent of the gift is what is given. The other cannot complain of the neglect, because it is precisely what he has done himself.

No. 2 is different. The clerk or manager has already freely submitted himself to the will of his employer by entering his service. The transaction belongs to the sphere of contract, and therefore the force used by the master is simply for the purpose of obtaining what the servant should have given voluntarily. It supplies the place of the servant's act, and supplements his will.

The 3rd case is a pure crime—is really a positive wrong, and a contradiction between the individual and the universal will. The same remark applies to cases 7 and 11.

The 4th and the 8th cases are not crimes in Scotland at common law, because the person offending does not set his will up as right in antagonism to the universal will. But, from the terms of his contract the railway servant may be punishable, and the reckless driver may be punishable, by police regulations, as we shall see immediately, in order to prevent accidents.

If, however, a person is injured or killed (cases 5, 6, 9, and 10), the act is assault or culpable homicide, or it may be libelled as culpable neglect of duty, according to circumstances. It thus appears that the criminality of the offence really depends on whether any person is injured. The reason of this anomaly is that the act is not properly a crime. The culprit does not set up his will as right against the universal will. He is punished on the theory of prevention, or perhaps it is a survival of mere revenge. In cases of drunkenness, however, the getting drunk is a positive act, and if an accident results punishment may be justified; but it is hard to see the use of punishment for mere errors of judgment.

From these examples we may gather—(1.) That if a negative wrong is a crime, it can really be resolved into a positive act of will; (2.) that a negative wrong may constitute a claim for civil damages when there is a *titulus* in the person claiming them, *e.g.*, in the shape of a contract (compare cases 1, 2, and 3); and (3.) that negative wrongs, not crimes proper, may be made punishable by positive law, either as crimes or in the shape of police offences. Unreflective instinct looks to results without considering the mental state of the actor. It presumes depravity from the nature of the act itself. When law interferes it merely gives articulate expression to the feelings prompted by this instinct. But the modern tendency is to a more thorough analysis of the act, and a corresponding mitigation of punishment in cases where criminal intent is evidently absent.

It is a similar difficulty which has caused the confusion in cases of reparation for negligence, as to the burden of proof. In some cases there is an absolute presumption of negligence, or the owner of the thing insures the outside public against damage by its use. This is the case with people who make reservoirs or keep wild animals. If the reservoir bursts, or the animal injures anyone, the owner is liable, in any circumstances. In other cases, the happening of the accident merely raises a presumption of negligence, which the owner must redargue, and in a third class fault must be proved.[1] In the case of servants, these presumptions shade into one another, and, however the rules of law may be expressed now, it will be found that they are all resolvable into a mode of proving negligence. In earlier cases the master is found liable, that it may be a warning to others in the choice of servants. By degrees the presumption of negligence against the master has become absolute.

We have come already on the notion of a police offence. In our police courts petty crimes are generally dealt with, but such is not the proper idea of a police offence.[2] Those are true crimes, and show the same depravity. A police offence is an act which, if perfected and carried out to its result, would or might end in a crime or legally punishable offence; *e.g.*, negligent use of firearms or property is not generally punishable unless actual injury ensues, but, as

[1] Pollock's *Essays*, pp. 119-122. Compare *Fletcher* v. *Rylands* L.R., 1 Ex., 265; L.R. 3 H.L. 330, and *M'Gregor* v. *Ross and Marshall*, 2nd March, 1883, 10 Rettie 725.

[2] Stephen's *History of the Criminal Law*, vol. iii., p. 263. Ahrens' *Droit Naturel*, vol. ii., p. 435, and foll.

prevention is better than cure, we punish these acts in an inchoate state by a small penalty. Many enactments in our police statutes are more matter of general consent than anything else—general regulations, where all that is wanted to secure uniformity of conduct is a general rule. But the offences specified in the following clauses of the General Police Act (25 and 26 Vic., cap. 101) stand on a different footing:—

"Every person who discharges any firearm, or throws or discharges any stone or other missile, or makes any bonfire, or throws or sets fire to any firework.

. . . .

"Every person who fixes or places any flowerpot or box, or other heavy article, in any upper window, without sufficiently guarding the same against being blown down.

. . . .

"Every person who leaves open any vault or cellar, or the entrance from any street to any cellar or room under ground, without a sufficient fence or hand-rail; or leaves defective the door, window, or other covering of any vault or cellar; or who does not sufficiently fence any area, pit, or sewer left open, and who leaves such open area, pit, or sewer, without a sufficient light after sunset, to warn and prevent persons from falling thereinto."

The persons who do such things are not fit for civilised society. They act as if their own selfish individual will was supreme. They take no cognisance of the existence of their neighbours. And why should the law wait till some one is injured before it interferes? No doubt, if some one were to break his neck or his leg in consequence of the negligence of some careless person, the fact would be very good proof of the negligence. But, as a mere matter of proof, we may do for the culprit what he should have done for himself—viz., look a little beforehand and prevent any injury. In a police statute, therefore, the community tries to supplement the weakness of will in the individual. Professor Amos complains of the multiplication of these offences in our modern law.[1] No doubt they interfere with the individual freedom, in so far as they make the universal an external law instead of placing it in his reason. But no good citizen rules his conduct solely by reference to the Police Act, and in many cases the universal embodied in a policeman accomplishes its object simply by directing the attention of the offender to his offence. One who persists in a police offence, after his attention is called to it, is really criminal, and punishment is therefore appropriate. Such offences form truly a part of the criminal law.[2] Reparation is impossible as, *ex hypothesi*, no actual damage is done.

With the exception of children we have been considering only the case of persons *sui juris*—persons to whom their own will was a law. We of course exclude from our consideration persons who are fatuous, maniacs, idiots, imbeciles, and such like, who are only one degree removed from the lower animals. If they are unconscious of, or only partially conscious of, their acts,

---

[1] *Science of Law*, p. 257.

[2] Mr. Justice Stephen seems to deny this (*History*, iii., p. 266). If so, his error is the converse of Dr. Abdy's. See pp. 77 & 82 *supra*. We must bear in mind that the dust on the highway is subject to the same law of gravitation as the largest planet.

the state cannot treat them as criminals. The law of their conduct must be impressed upon them from without, and so true punishment is out of the question. The difficulties arise as to partial insanity. In the French Code the provision is very general, that " there can be no crime nor offence if the accused was in a state of madness at the time of the act." So the New York statutes provide that " no act done by a person in a state of insanity can be punished as an offence." So again the German Penal Code says—" An act is not punishable when the person at the time of doing it was in a state of unconsciousness or disease of mind by which a free determination of the will was excluded." In this country the law was settled in the case of M'Naughten in 1848. In that case the House of Lords consulted the judges, who returned their opinion on the point.[1] The law, as laid down there is that, if the person knows right from wrong, or, if he knew he was acting contrary to law, he is liable to punishment. In those cases, where the person does not know the law or the difference between right and wrong, it is clear that punishment is inapplicable. The treatment must be purely medical. But the intermediate cases are more difficult, *e.g.*, a person knows that murder is forbidden by law and morally wrong, but he has an impulse which it is said he cannot resist. Again, he knows murder is wrong and forbidden, but he thinks he has

---

[1] Guy's *Medical Jurisprudence*, (4th ed.), p. 214; Stephen's *History*, chap. xix. See Macdonald's *Criminal Law* (1st ed.), p. 14.

a special mission to assassinate a special individual. If it can be established that such cases exist, then it would seem to follow that punishment is useless with regard to them. The universal could not be brought any closer to the individual. Their particular wills cannot be brought into accordance with the universal, for in both cases their wills are not under their control. At the moment of committing the particular act they have no will. In this view it is hard to see how, even on the theory of prevention, punishment is of any use. A murderer may have committed the crime for the purpose of being hanged. The execution of the punishment has no penal meaning to him. Besides, the mere execution has no meaning to the state unless it is a *person* who suffers. It is not generally said in so many words that a homicidal maniac is to be destroyed like a dangerous animal, for we shoot a mad dog but do not punish it, but there is evidently a feeling in this direction. If the reason for punishing such persons were put into words, it would generally be said that it was done for the purpose of deterring others from committing like crimes. But surely confinement in an asylum as a lunatic is a greater punishment than hanging. Even if it is not so fully realised, it will to all sane persons be an awful deterrent. Dr. Maudsley in his work on *Responsibility in Mental Disease*,[1] maintains that the English doctrine is utterly unsound, and that it ought always to be left to the jury

---

[1] Preface to third edition, and p. 110.

to say whether the accused knew the quality of his act and whether he could refrain. This appears to be the American practice. It must be confessed that there is an unreasoning aversion on the part of lawyers to accept the conclusions of medical men on this subject. The vicious system under which medical witnesses are hired to support a side has cast great discredit upon "mad doctors." But there is no reason why we should shut our eyes to settled facts; and if it is a fact that a person may know right and wrong, and yet have an irresistible impulse to do the wrong, then the law ought to recognise it.[1]

It must be observed that this question is only one branch of a larger one which affects the whole theory of wrongs (torts). Is merely *formal* consciousness of an act sufficient to constitute liability for all its consequences? Or, must there be *actual* malice or intent? The rude instinct of revenge would punish beasts or things as well as men, and it is a step in advance to require even formal consciousness. But the question between the lawyers and doctors is, Must we stop here? Is this the only advance to be made on untutored instinct? As might be expected, the formal view is the one supported by the lawyers, as in the case of insanity. If the man *knew* what he was doing, that is sufficient. But in describing the acts reference is generally made to

---

[1] This is Sir James Fitzstephen's view—*History of Criminal Law*, vol. ii., p. 171. The whole discussion is worthy of perusal.

moral obliquity, as if all the consequences were intended.[1]

It is perhaps unnecessary to add that the sphere of the state in wrongs is seen, not only in the interference of courts to vindicate right and re-establish the universal, but in the definition of what constitutes particular crimes. Thus, some states tolerate duelling, or permit homicide in many circumstances, or with certain classes of persons, as slaves.

The state, we have seen, interferes to set up the universal in the case of crime, and to indemnify also the individual wronged, as well as set up the universal in the case of a civil injury. But if the state fails to recognise, or recognising, fails to enforce the universal, what then? The state becomes accessory to the wrong, and instead of a concrete embodiment of the universal, it becomes a mere particular. This leads us to consider corporate responsibility. Punishment may then be directed against the corporate unit, which affords shelter to the culprit or fails to punish him. We see a familiar example of this in the responsibility of communities for riots committed within their jurisdiction. This is a very ancient relic of Anglo-Saxon times. It has been recently applied in the last Irish Coercion

---

[1] See Holmes, *The Common Law*, Lectures ii., iii., and iv. We see the same difficulty in the question, "Can a young child be guilty of contributory negligence?" See case of *M'Gregor*, quoted above, page 106, note[1]; and article from *Southern Law Review*, quoted in *Journal of Jurisprudence*, 1880, p. 199.

Act. Particular localities are to make good the damage done by individuals within the district. For their own sake, it is hoped that the law-abiding subjects in those districts will do all in their power to prevent outrage, or at least to punish the perpetrators. The instinct of self-preservation will make them, like the sailors in the story of Jonah, discover the culprit, and bring him to justice. In French law we find an example of the same, borrowed from the Roman idea of the family. By that law a father or mother is responsible for the delict of a pupil child. This will act as an external incentive to make them train their children properly. We do not admit this principle in the case of children, but we do so in the case of servants. The head of the *family* is responsible as well as the servant, though the liability of the latter is seldom enforced.[1] We may find examples of the same principle in our history when "letters of fire and sword" were issued against certain Scottish clans for the crimes of individuals.[2] Another example may be seen in the enactment which makes every person who is present at a riot, after the riot act is read, though it may be from pure curiosity, guilty as an accessory; and, again, in the disfranchisement of constituencies, in which numerous cases of bribery have occurred at an election.

The legal aspect of modern warfare falls under this

---

[1] Holmes, *The Common Law*, p. 228.
[2] Sir Walter Scott, Introductions to *Rob Roy*, and *A Legend of Montrose*.

rule. Whenever a state becomes so degraded that it refuses to do what is just and right, force may become necessary to reassert the universal. Nothing short of war may suffice. Even civil war may be justified in such a case. If a government is violating every rule of law and morality, and supporting itself by force, force *must* be used to oppose it. A true universal must be established in its place, and might and right will then be identified again.

War between two *civilised* states is therefore an absurdity. There is a decided tendency towards its development into duelling between the armies and navies of the two governments. A modern battle does not therefore settle much, and it is not impossible to conceive a commission of military experts deciding the result of the fight without bloodshed and perhaps even without wasting the powder and shot. We employ professional policemen to enforce civil rights, and professional soldiers for international ones, but it looks a little like breach of contract to set them to fight "affairs of honour." If therefore one civilised state declares war against another, it must be because it considers that other to have relapsed into crime or insanity.

The change which has taken place in the "laws of war," a phrase which troubles many people, illustrates the point. These are not intended to put the combatants on the same level like duellists or pugilists. In a riot good citizens must side with the police or stay away.

And so, in a modern war, neutrality does not mean keeping both sides impartially supplied with munitions of war. Neutrals must make up their minds on which side right is, and give assistance to that side, or at least deny assistance in every form to both sides, and *particularly to the one in the wrong*, which it may be suggested is practically the *losing* side. So the significance of the Alabama award and the previous negotiations was that Great Britain sympathised with, and assisted to some extent, rebels against the Government of the United States, and she admitted liability and paid the penalty as accessory to a crime. If a state is satisfied that a body of insurgents, or a weak foreign state at war has right on its side, it may allow free export of arms and munitions and enlistment of volunteers to both sides, knowing that the weaker party will reap an advantage. But this is not neutrality. It is positive assistance, of a slight description perhaps, but still assistance. And the state so conducting itself must be prepared to take the consequences, just as if it had openly made an alliance. The word "neutrality" therefore, which is a survival of the old duelling conception of war, is quite misleading in modern practice. Pure neutrality is impossible now-a-days, and in consequence right is more certain to prevail immediately than in the olden time of brute force. Nations outside the quarrel will naturally throw their influence into the scale of right.

But the true laws of war are those which are dictated

by humanity in dealing with even the most abandoned criminals. No force must be used beyond what is necessary to accomplish the object in view, and so we should treat the most savage belligerents as we would the most civilised, if this were possible. No exception therefore can be taken to the laws of modern warfare, which forbid cruelty to non-belligerents, and provide for the treatment of the wounded; and perhaps neither to the rule which forbids plundering on land, just as we forbid policemen and jailers to practice cruelties on their prisoners. The horrors of war are sufficient without adding pillage to them, though no doubt the motive for its abolition is that it involves worse crimes and is demoralising to the army. But should we carry our individualism further, and abolish the right of capture of private property at sea? The severity of this rule has been much mitigated by the declaration of Paris of 1856, which practically transfers the commerce of the belligerents to neutrals. A state of war will thus derange entirely the commerce of a nation, and in many cases will operate as sufficient pressure to make it concede the remedy which its opponent justly demands. It is generally observed that the capture of private property at sea causes a loss chiefly to underwriters, and, as we shall see hereafter, the contract of insurance assists to spread the loss equally over the community. If a war is just on one side, it will presumably be unjust on the other (unless the whole affair is a huge mistake), and the sooner it is finished the better. It is more likely to be quickly finished, if it bears harshly and severely on the offending community. It is as much out of place to carry on war with kid gloves, as it is to feed criminals on partridges and champagne, and lodge them in luxurious palaces.

We see then the limits within which it is possible to abolish war. If the dispute between two nations is of the nature of a civil one, negotiation and arbitration are appropriate, for the discovery of right. War is here as much out of place as duelling, or trial by ordeal in private life. If the question is as to crime, and one state is truly criminal, then war is the ultimate remedy. War will only be abolished when our criminal classes have disappeared, and we are able to dispense with police. To propose its abolition before that happy period has arrived is absurd, and so even the most extreme advocates of peace allow a few soldiers to be kept for the purpose of firing on riotous mobs, and a few ships of war for the extirpation of slave dealers and pirates.

It is obviously a physical impossibility to put down war by physical force, as we attempted to do in this country with duelling, because this would aggravate the evils complained of. And it is very questionable if law, apart from public opinion, has done much to suppress that fashion which, it should be noticed, is still recognised on the continent of Europe and in America. But the lesson it points to statesmen is this, that wars are to be abolished by the education and reformation of the shouting mobs who urge them on, and by the rational members of the community, on whom the disasters and expense of them principally fall, raising their voices emphatically on the side of right, so that unnecessary and unjust wars may be avoided. It is very generally ignored by peace-at-any-price enthusiasts, that the fundamental causes of war are frequently incapable of being formulated and put in a legal form. As litigation is often the result of a feud between neighbours in private life, nations often seize frivolous pretexts for going to war when they would be ashamed of stating the true ones.[1] For example, if our French neighbours would only make the Revolution more thorough, by abandoning the policy of the "Grand Monarque" and giving up absurd ideas of aggression, the world would be much nearer the realisation of the dream of universal peace.

But, though the subject of delict bulks so largely even in modern law, the great source of obligations at the present day is contract. Here, as we have seen, the person legislates for himself, and apparently creates arbitrary obligations. And at the same time we have the creation of multitudinous "police offences," and offences tried and punished in a summary manner. At first sight, these contracts and legislative enactments

[1] See De Quincey's essay *On War*; Sheldon Amos' *Remedies for War*, p. 73.

appear to be a mere negation of the rights of the person bound; but a closer examination convinces us that they are a mere expression of what otherwise would be implied in some form or other. And even police offences are seen to be mere crystallisations of a few of the "implied obligations" to which I referred at the outset of this lecture. A man of honour does not feel a contract to be a restraint. A good citizen does not feel himself ruled by police statutes. Society has, therefore, come back in idea to the state of primitive innocence. But, "through much tribulation," it has become conscious of the law. The individual performs his duties and obligations, not from mere instinct or habit, or from blind deference to tradition, nor because they are laid down for him and enforced by a higher and stronger power, but because their performance is a source of the highest gratification to a self-conscious being. To him obligations are no longer bonds.

LECTURE V.

MATERIAL RIGHTS—PERSON AND PROPERTY.

We have now seen that rights spring from obligations. But, after all, obligations, whether arising from delict or contract, are merely *forms* of right, and the questions already proposed may be put again :—Whence do rights arise ? What is the nature of the rights which spring from delict or contract ? Are there not rights *prior* to their violation by delict, or their constitution by contract ? Is there not something implied in each of those forms of creating right ? Yes ; there are the rights of person and property. Or, to put it conversely: Are men only *bound* when they do some wrong, or when they make a contract, or when the legislature passes an act ? Is there no duty *prior* to these explicit obligations ? The answer must be in the affirmative, that the abstract duty corresponds to the abstract right, and that the rights of person and property give rise to duties on the part of those who have them and those who recognise them.

It will be necessary hereafter to examine the idea of person more fully, and I therefore allude to it here only to mark its *material* aspect. We may pass over the stage when personality was felt in the same way as a healthy man feels the operations of respiration and digestion.

There may be a period when the idea is latent and is only brought to light by delict, as disease makes us conscious of the existence of various organs and functions of our bodies. Here the person may enjoy his rights fully without knowing them as such, and he only becomes truly conscious of them when they are assailed or contradicted. If we may use the expression, the first legal idea of person is one of property in the body and limbs. The elaborate valuations in the Anglo-Saxon codes of the various members of the body show this, and if any further corroboration is needed, we have it in the fact of slavery being a recognised institution. Whenever the true idea of *person* is attained, slavery is seen to be a violation of right, as was acknowledged by the Roman lawyers, though they admitted it as a custom. In like manner, the Roman lawyers declared that it was impossible to put a value on the limbs of a free man, and it may have been a vague notion of this kind which impelled primitive societies to legalise the law of retaliation. And on the side of the delinquent it has been clearly shown by Mr Holmes[1] that in early English law there is practically no distinction between an injury caused by an inanimate object, a beast, or a man. One legal conception, therefore, both on the side of right and of obligation, may once have comprehended what we now place under the distinct categories of person and property.

In the notion of person, free will has already been

[1] *The Common Law*, Lect. i.

externalised in the body, which is the instrument of the will. The body is so closely connected with the individual that it is called "the person," as when we speak of offences against the person. The personality has thus, as I have just observed, a material as well as a formal aspect. But the individual can attach things outside of his body, and put his will into them. These things are property. "Thing," in the general philosophical sense, is what is not person. It is irrational, unfree, devoid of right. A thing only exists in relation to a person as the object of a rational, conscious, spiritual activity. In law, however, a thing is only a *corporeal* object—the object of acquisition. It is something which may be in a state of dependence on a person, and accordingly be the object of an action at law. Therefore, the stars, which are things in the philosophical sense, are not such in the jural sense. We recognise as things in law things not in commerce (*extra commercium*) such as the air, sea, &c., which are incapable of appropriation, except in actual use. But even portions of the sea may be appropriated as harbours, or fishing ground. As a thing the surface of the earth is undoubtedly capable of appropriation. The peculiar difficulties in regard to property in land are not metaphysical, but ethical and economical; and so the distinction of heritable (real) and movable (personal) property is accidental. It has grown up with the history of particular countries, but is discarded in the modern Roman law. We extend the idea of things in law to include the rights, privileges, and obligations of a person. Thus, a bond or an obligation, or a debt, is treated as a thing. A thing, in law, is thus an external object which is wholly or partially capable of being reduced into possession, and it includes obligations which relate to such objects. It is through this appropriation that a person puts himself forward in the world of things. In contradistinction to a thing which is irrational and will-less, and in the philosophical sense, unfree, a person stands capable of will and allowed to exercise it, and for that reason his rights over things are absolute and unlimited. In regard to things, every man has the right of appropriating all things—*i.e.*, the capacity of acquisition as an original right—as a part of his personality. The notion of property is thus an extension of that of person in its material aspect.[1] A man's property is part of the clothing of his spirit trying to realise its free will. Our common language illustrates this idea: we have the words "vest," "investiture." We speak of persons being "clothed" with possession; and lastly, we speak of "personal" property, which a man can attach to his person. The sacredness of property is therefore an extension of the sacredness of the person. The two ideas have developed together, and they have culminated at the same time. If life is insecure, property is also endangered.

It is useless to discuss the origin of property, or the

[1] Trendelenburg, *Naturrecht*, p. 203.

various theories which make it depend on occupation, labour, convention, or arbitrary law. The history of property runs parallel with that of person. In early times, when the person was sunk in the family and identified with it, all property was family property. The things which no doubt formed the family stock remained a separate class in Roman law long afterwards—the *res mancipi*. These were horses, oxen, mules, slaves, rural servitudes on Italian soil, and, we may add, wives and children.[1] As the personality of the *paterfamilias* developed so would his proprietary rights. As he ceased to be a trustee for the family he would hold the property for his own behoof.

Neither the notion of person nor that of property would be originally abstract in the common sense of the word. In other words, property and possession were originally identical, and with loss of possession, property too would be gone. With loss of freedom personality was gone. The possession of land would be like the possession which a ship takes of water where it anchors—exclusive property while it lasts. The air we breathe or the ground we stand on are ours in use, and to the extent we use them, and are hardly property any more than our bodies themselves. To take them from us is to deprive us of physical existence. But food and water may be property before they are incorporated with our bodies. And so, even within the family,

[1] Maine's *Ancient Law*, p. 277. Gaius, bk. i., § 120.

the members might have a rudimentary idea of property *inter se* in the food and clothing appropriated to each. We see possession ripened into property when the Roman *familia* as such disappears, and the *paterfamilias*, as I have just indicated, becomes a trustee *in rem suam*. The process may be understood from what has happened with large landed estates in our own country, for this is the origin of the title of many of our nobility to their estates. They were trustees with large property in their hands. The beneficiaries, or *cestuis que trust*, were not in a position to claim any part of it, and their claims were therefore ignored. An analogous process took place with the public lands in Roman history. The possessors became proprietors. So in Ireland at the present day, the precarious tenure of the tenants was in practice seldom disturbed. The disturbance of it was regarded as a wrong, and hence the proprietary right given to the tenants. This process is an affirmation of the sacredness of person. I must revert to the subject of possession as legally distinguished from property.

Whatever is attached to the person—whatever thing has had the will of a person put into it is sacred. So with any object which has been altered or made by art. The thing in its essence is created by the artist. If his work is valuable you are infringing his personality if you deprive him of it. On the contrary, if the work were of small value, the owner of the material might claim the manufactured object, and claim reparation for the destruction of his material, for the spoiling of material which is the property of another is an attack on his personality. Thus, the labour expended in acquiring a piece of property may vary from the simple act of stooping to lift a precious stone, to moulding and engraving a plate of gold, or painting a picture, or draining a lake, so that all property ultimately represents the will of the owner.

But the highest development of the idea is when the mere marking of the object is a sufficient indication of property without possession. This is what is accomplished by our Sasine Registers. A man may possess lands, houses, and money, far beyond what he can use, and yet they are his property, and the law protects them because they are his.

Now, here again we see the metaphysical moments to which I have referred. We have, (1.) The physical appropriation by a person of a thing; (2.) the consciousness of the act; (3.) the state or some organic society;[1] and (4.) the recognition of these facts by the state, or other persons in an organic society. None of these moments can be abstracted without the whole idea falling to the ground. It is incorrect to define property as a relation of a person to a thing. It is also a relation to other persons. It is a conscious exclusion of the whole world. Besides, it involves a recognition of the relation and this exclusion by the rest

[1] See note, p. 91.

of society. In very early times the recognition may have been only of brute force. It might be only an assertion more or less explicit of a *de facto* relation, but in process of time, and certainly in our day, we have the idea that the relation is one of "right." A handful of men hold as property nearly the whole of the land in this country, and yet we speak of the sacredness of property, and no longer of the sacredness of person, when these come into conflict. But, as far as we can judge from various indications, it appears that future legislation on the land laws will be in the direction of subordinating abstract rights of property to rights of person.

These considerations explain literary and artistic property, and property in patents, and trade-marks, &c., Physically the thing is as objective as if it were an acre of land, and, as to the author, he feels himself proprietor of the ideas embodied in his work, and claims credit for them. Even if he has published or sold his work, the book, the picture, the statue is still *his* in popular language. All that is required to complete the truly legal notion of property is the recognition of his right by the state. This is done by the various legislative acts dealing with these subjects. Thus, it is true that the law does and does not create a proprietary relation. In point of fact the right of an author in his work is as real as that of a duke in the most extensive domains. It is as easy for the law to enforce and protect the one as the other. The physical possession is as impossible in the one case as in the other.[1]

The fact that law defines, and, in one sense, creates the notion of property, explains and justifies the law as to the compulsory purchase of lands by public companies. If a private individual refuses to sell, he exhibits not will but mere caprice. He says, "I am proprietor; I do not wish to sell. I give no reason. No amount of money will induce me to change my resolution." The position of such a man may arise from sheer obstinacy. Perhaps he objects to railways or gasworks, and other products of modern civilisation. In such a case, by compulsory sale we merely substitute the will of the community for the individual caprice, and, at the same time, satisfy the utmost claim he can make for compensation. In such cases payment is notoriously lavish. So much so, that most men anticipate compulsion by buying properties which they expect public companies will require. On the side of the private individual free will is thus substituted for caprice. But, on the side of the state, we observe that his right rests on recognition by it. If the state withdrew its recognition he could not himself maintain *de facto* possession for an hour. The

---

[1] This extension of an idea by analogy may be illustrated from the mathematical theory of indices. Starting from the idea of positive integral indices, we have now got negative and fractional ones, and the expression x^0. We have another example in space of n dimensions.—See Professor Cayley's address to British Association, 1883.

estate in question may be miles in extent, and quite beyond the physical possession of an individual. But even if it is only a few yards, it is still the law which protects him in his possession, not for his own sake alone, but as a member of the organic unity of the state. And so, if he sets himself to abuse this protection, and to place himself in antagonism to the just requirements of the other members of the community, the law justly and properly withdraws its recognition in this particular form, and at the same time deprives the owner of nothing which is truly property, as it awards him compensation.

In speaking of the relation of person and thing, I said it should be conscious. This, however, must be modified by what we shall see hereafter—that personality is attributed to infants, lunatics, and others. In like manner they are treated as proprietors by the law. Is this arbitrary? No. As to children we give them property as we give them food. It is in things they find their personality. In toys their childish wills may find ample scope, and in the development of children's toys along with their years, we see their own progressive development. Through the years of minority they grow into their property, and when they attain majority their education is complete, and they enter upon possession of what has all along been called theirs. It was theirs by anticipation. It is now theirs in enjoyment. Such a process is inexplicable, if we abstract man from the

K

organism of society. This being, now clothed with the full rights of property, has been created by external forces: his rights have been created and given him by law; but, when he becomes a man, the law is no longer external—it is a part of himself. In the case of lunatics, the state merely defers the distribution of the estate which is called his until his death.

In last lecture we saw there was a standing dispute between the lawyers and the doctors on the question as to what amount of consciousness should ground responsibility for crime. It appears that there is a similar feud between the lawyers and the economists, with a similar tendency to call each other names.[1] The point in dispute is the same as to the meaning to be attributed to mere *formal* consciousness, in constituting a right of property, and the lawyers again tend to make all depend on mere form. It is the same spirit which advocated non-resistance in constitutional law, and non-intervention in international law, though these tendencies have generally been aggravated by selfish material interests. If a man has mere *formal* consciousness, the lawyers will make him responsible for all his acts, whether he actually foresees their consequences or not. And so, if a man is *conscious*, lawyers will defend his right of property, however extensive. In point of *form*, no lawyer would hesitate to complete his client's title to any number of counties, or perhaps even to the

[1] George, *Progress and Poverty*, bk. viii., chap. i., &c.

kingdom of Scotland itself. I am not aware that the deed by which Charles V. conveyed Burgundy and the Netherlands to Philip II. struck any of the lawyers who were present at the memorable ceremony, in the great hall of the palace at Brussels, as outrageously absurd. The soil of the Burgundian domains, including the Netherlands, their cities, castles, counties, baronies, and inhabitants were described with as great minuteness as if they had been a tenement in the Trongate of Glasgow.[1] This deed casts a lurid light on Philip's subsequent conduct in those unhappy countries. He thought himself as much proprietor of that territory as a Highland "laird" is of his glens and straths. He thought he was as much entitled to clear his land of Protestants as they are to clear theirs of paupers, and it took half a century of war and bloodshed to show him that he was not entitled "to do as he liked with his own."[2] But this is merely an example of *summum jus* being *summa injuria*. There is no need of going to the extreme of sacrificing matter to form, as in that case, or abolishing form by rushing into communism. Matter and form cannot be separated without the destruction of the whole idea of property, and so land reformers, like Mr. Wallace, are as strong upholders of the principle of property in land as the most extreme formalist. And

[1] *Dumont*, vol. iv., supplement, p. 93. Motley's *Dutch Republic*, part I., chap. i.
[2] Motley's *United Netherlands*, vol. i., p. 243, *et passim*.

we must bear in mind that we cannot identify law with the doings of lawyers any more than we can identify religion with the doings of priests. As great crimes have been committed in the name of law as in the name of religion. The cloak of law or religion is often adopted, because it appears to justify a course of conduct prompted by the grossest selfishness.

When the conception of property has once been grasped, the transition to such an idea as that of joint property (*condominium*) is not difficult. At first sight it looks strange that exclusive possession should belong to *two* persons in *one* thing. But all practical difficulty is overcome by appointing one person to manage the object (as a ship or a house) for the joint interest, and dividing the revenue equally. Again, it may be got over by actually dividing it or transforming it into something divisible, such as money.

But such abstract rights have been developed in further directions. As soon as it is seen that a person can be proprietor of property far beyond what he can physically occupy, by publication of his title, or that two persons can have a joint interest in one piece of property, it is not a great step to the modern definition of rights by written titles.[1] This is well illustrated in the practice

[1] As to the development of the idea of property in England, reference may be made to Digby's *History of the Law of Real Property* (Macmillan), 1877. The subject of equitable estates is particularly interesting to the Scotch lawyer, as Scotch law looks at these from quite another stand-point—from that of obligation rather than of property.

of subinfeudation. We may have a dozen people, all drawing a feu-duty or ground-annual in succession from one piece of ground, and then a bondholder or mortgagee, and then a proprietor, and lastly a tenant. The tenant has actual physical corporeal possession, or he may sublet to another who actually possesses. However, each of these persons may be described in his registered title as in the actual possession of the ground, while the last in the list (the tenant) may be able to defy them all and retain possession while his right lasts. The rights of the holders of the feu-duties or ground-annuals and the mortgagee are those of limited proprietors. The former may, in certain circumstances, become absolute proprietors. The latter (the mortgagee) in Scotland can only sell or administer the property as trustee for the other proprietors. In England, by foreclosing the mortgage, he may become proprietor. But, if things proceed in a regular manner, it is merely a case of joint property, in which certain persons receive a fixed sum, and the nominal proprietor draws the balance of profit for himself; or, if there is a loss, it must fall on him alone. In effect, the rights of all the parties except the last tenant depend on his obligation, or on the obligations of each other, but they are capable of being transformed by some legal process into a true real right—*i.e.*, into actual possession of the ground. I may observe that legal forms, which encourage the creation of co-ordinate proprietors are preferable to those which place them in even a nominal position of inferiority. These place the parties in a position of antagonism, which is unnecessary, and may even become dangerous.[1] Again: such an abstract right, as that in a feu-duty or ground-rent, can only very remotely satisfy the idea of property, and hence the tendency of our law to increase the rights of the feuar by enabling him to compel the superior to commute casualties.[2] After the passing of the last Scotch Conveyancing Act, superiors were much less proprietors than formerly, and the rights of the feuars were correspondingly increased. It is such considerations which point to the expediency of authorising the sale of encumbered lands, held under an entail, in order to pay off the debts. The personality of the present possessor is recognised, and provision is made for *persons* in existence. It is better that the holder of the land should be a proprietor; and, while the rights of the heir in possession are increased, the sub-division of the land enables a much larger number of persons to realise their personality in landed property, and so contribute to the stability of the state.

While we must recognise the advisability of getting rid of purely artificial notions of property, it must be acknowledged that the entire prohibition of the acquisition of rights short of absolute property would be

---

[1] M. Laveleye's essay on *Systems of Land Tenure in different Countries* (Cobden Club Essays), p. 444.
[2] Conveyancing Act, 37 and 38 Vict., cap. 94, § 15.

an unwarrantable interference with the right of contract. If I can enjoy fully a piece of property—a house or an estate, and also employ beneficially its value, advanced in the form of a loan, I am conferring a benefit on the lender as well as on myself. The abolition of such a right would be the sacrifice of one of the most useful devices of modern commerce to an abstract theory.

Another class of real rights is that of servitudes.[1] It is obvious that this is a modified right of property, in the case of drawing water, or pasturage, or cutting fuel, or a right of way. These are adjuncts of the principal or dominant tenement, and are possessed along with it. In negative servitudes it is hardly accurate to say that the owner of the dominant tenement has a modified right of property in the servient. But there is a modification of the nature of the servient, *e.g.*, as a general rule, a proprietor has right *a centro usque ad cœlum;* but his right may clearly be restricted to the surface and upwards, as where minerals are reserved; and, in like manner, it may be restricted in the other direction, if he cannot build on it at all. In this case the proprietor, in consideration of a payment, perhaps, agrees to abandon part of his right as a proprietor. He restricts his use to the surface, and gives up the right of going *ad centrum* or *ad cœlum.*

In property are involved the right of absolute use of the thing; its consumption, if necessary and possible, as

[1] See Austin's *Jurisprudence*, p. 383; and *Lectures*, xlviii. and xlix.

in the case of food, air, &c., or a right of transformation into something else; and further, a right of disposal for price or other objects. This right of disposal may be for the material benefit of the proprietor, or it may be a right of donation, which subserves moral ends. But, as *summum jus est summa injuria*, a person has no right to divest himself of all his property unless those who receive it undertake at least the burden of his maintenance. This is provided for in the *Code Civil*, which allows revocation of the donation, in case the donee refuses to maintain the donor.[1] Lastly, the proprietor can vindicate his possession against any possessor who holds without the consent either of him or the law. The right of testing, as we shall see hereafter, is not one of the rights of property as such.[2]

We have seen already that, in their first conception, possession and property are undistinguishable. We must now see how they come to be separated. If we conceive the right of a first proprietor and possessor as once established over a thing, it follows at once that no second person can obtain a similar right, and that for no other reason than this—that he is not the first occupant. In attempting to establish such a relation as I have spoken of in regard to the first occupant, a second person comes into contact, not with a thing merely, but with another person as well. There must, therefore, be something more than person *plus*

[1] Code Civil, § 955. [2] See *Lecture* xi., *infra*.

thing in the relation. This new element brings us to the borders of contract. But, suppose again that the second person establishes a physical relation between himself and the thing, such as the first occupant established, then it follows, from the fact that the first relation was legal and recognised by the law, this second must be illegal and prohibited by the law. It is thus that theft and robbery appear so early in ancient codes. They are the first contradiction of the right of property; they first show the distinction between possession and property. And this distinction in its first aspect is this— that property is possession, *plus* a right of exclusion recognised in law. Possession is, so to speak, merely a physical relation, or, as the Roman lawyers have it, "*possessio est facti, dominium est juris.*"[1] It is, however, incorrect to say that possession is merely a relation of fact, because we get possession without property in loan, pledge, life-rents, and in many other cases. In these cases possession is recognised by the law. It is legal possession—*justa possessio*. Again, we must not define possession as *mere* detention *plus* a right to possessory interdicts and a right of usucaption. We are forced to ask the questions we asked before. Is there nothing behind the right of interdict? Is it merely an arbitrary act of the state? Why speak of them as "possessory" interdicts, if they constitute the whole of

[1] On the whole subject reference may be made to Savigny *On Possession*, translated by Sir Erskine Perry.

the right? Are they not intended to maintain the possession (in a jural sense) of one who has begun to prescribe a proprietary title? In truth, the relation of person and thing is as organic in possession as in property. They are fundamentally identical, for in both we respect the personality of the owner or possessor who has put his will into the external thing. The law recognises a difference in the rights, and gives different remedies, because there is already a difference in the rights themselves. The old paradox thus recurs that law creates and does not create the right of possession as well as that of property. For practical purposes we may treat the rights quantitatively, and say that there are *two* rights of possession; but beyond the region of formal law this notion is entirely misleading.[1] And at the present stage of legal science and practice, it is very doubtful if practical effect could be given to such a view.

There may be many varieties of *justa possessio*, and so in like manner there may be different kinds of unjust possession. It may be by theft or robbery, theft including all the varieties of that crime—finding and appropriating lost goods, keeping goods lent, or changing the purpose for which possession was acquired. The distinction of *justa* and *injusta possessio* is thus quite objective. It depends on whether the possessor has a *jus possidendi*—a right recognised by law, a title to

[1] See Savigny, by Perry, p. 5.

possess or not. If he has, his possession is just; if he has not, it is unjust. But, introduce the subjective element. Suppose the possessor *thinks* he has a just right and title, does this alter the case? He then becomes a *bonæ fidei possessor*. He has perhaps bought for a full price from a person who thought he was proprietor, and who was not. His case is distinguished from that of the *malæ fidei possessor*, such as a thief, in this, that he has a good title and possession, if the thing were capable of being acquired—if his author had been the true owner instead of a mere holder of the thing. This leads us to consider how possession is changed into ownership—the laws of prescription and usucaption. From its conception mere physical possession, or *possessio injusta*, is not an absolute wrong, but only a relative one. It is only a wrong against the former proprietor—the *dominus* or the *justus possessor*, unless a criminal element enters into the case. But it will be remembered that under the old Roman law no one but the owner could vindicate against a thief, and that a thief had a good defence against every one but the *dominus*. And even, after the introduction of the *actio Publiciana*, it was only a preferable legal possessor who could claim the possession as against a thief. A thief accordingly had a good title against third parties, for he did no wrong to the thing. From these examples we see that any possessor has in his favour the presumption that his title is good until it is proved to be defective. He has all the rights of a possessor until that is done. There are sometimes modifications of this introduced in positive law—*e.g.*, in Roman law the interdict, *utrubi*, as to movables was given only to persons who had possessed for the greater part of the preceding year.[1] And with us the sheriff gives a possessory judgment, only if a party has been in possession, on a written title, for seven years without interruption.[2] Otherwise, the presumption of actual possession must hold. To such an extent did the Romans carry this presumption that they actually allowed the possessory interdicts to *malæ fidei* possessors.[3] But a *bonæ fidei* possessor stands on a much higher ground, and is generally regarded in the light of a *justus possessor*. His possession is regarded as property, until it is shewn to be wrong. Accordingly, in Roman law, the *bonæ fidei possessor* had a right to the fruits which he had consumed, and he had a *utilis vindicatio rei*, the *actio Publiciana*, to recover his possession, just as if he were proprietor.

The most rudimentary idea of prescription is that of a right which has existed from time immemorial. It is possession which dates so far back that it is presumed absolutely to have had a title for its foundation which has been lost. There is no time fixed for the presumption, but the oldest inhabitant

---

[1] See Puchta, *Cursus der Inst.*, vol. ii., p. 139.
[2] Dove Wilson, *Sheriff Court Practice*, p. 50 (2d ed.)
[3] Puchta, *Ib.*, vol. ii., p. 145.

remembers that this property has always been in the possession of the present possessor, and perhaps remembers his father or grandfather speaking of the ancestors of the present possessor as being proprietors. On general grounds of evidence there is here a strong case of ownership, and we require no definite law of prescription.

The next stage is when the right of a *bonæ fidei* possessor is made perfect by possession for a certain definite time fixed by law. This arises in the legislative stage of law. The time of prescription was remarkably short in the old Roman law, but this is explained by the habits of the people, and the fact that communication with foreign parts of the world was difficult. This prescription was only allowed to *bonæ fidei* possessors. If no definite prescription had been introduced, or if the period had been very long, a *bonæ fidei* possessor might have been changed into a *malæ fidei* one, and so he would have been incapable of acquiring a title by prescription. The effect on property would have been most disastrous, for a man might possess for fifty years and then discover a latent claim which would have changed him into a *malæ fidei* possessor. He would be in constant apprehension of a representative of the true owner claiming the subject, and he might be apt to neglect it, and allow it to go to waste. A definite prescription was therefore soon recognised in the Roman law as a necessary part of the law of property. It was a *modus acquirendi civilis*, as opposed to *modus acquirendi naturalis*, and as the prescription applied only to *bona fides*, it was necessarily short if it was to be of any use.

The next stage is the lengthening of the period of prescription. This took place to a considerable extent in the Roman law. With ourselves we have the forty years' prescription, positive and negative—the one establishing a right and the other cutting off a remedy. The positive prescription is, in fact, the recognition of the evidence of *animus* and *factum* (the physical possession of an object by a self-conscious subject) for forty years. The negative is the absolute presumption of the absence of *animus*, founded on the actual absence of the *factum* for that period. Our positive prescription of title of forty years, which was abolished a few years ago, was really longer than forty years, since it allowed the deduction of minorities. But by the Conveyancing Act of 1874, which came into operation on 1st January, 1879, this was reduced to twenty years. This is quite proper, because, just as among the Romans, when their empire extended, a person might be away from his property for several years without abandoning it, and they accordingly gradually extended the period of their prescriptions; so with us, owing to improvements in locomotion and the extension of the electric telegraph, no man requires to leave his property for such a length of time in the hands of strangers; and it is, therefore, not unjust that the period of prescription should be shortened. Another improvement, and one which we have borrowed from Germany, is the thirty years' prescription, without the deduction of minorities. This is equally just, and quite in accordance with the circumstances of the age.

In leaving the subject of property, I would point out that, beyond what is required for the natural sustenance and development of the person, it can only be held as a trust for the state. This was clearly the condition of primitive society. But the state has now absorbed the clan and the family, and recreated them in a higher unity. In early times it might be possible to bring this idea under the scope of law, but it is evidently impossible to enforce this in modern, as in ancient times, by a periodical redistribution of the land. But, if any person tried to exceed the bounds of reason, either in his attempts to appropriate things, or in his dealing with them, the legislature would undoubtedly interfere on behalf of society, and prevent the wrong which would be done by caricaturing an abstract right,—the *injuria* arising from *summum jus*. This was done in one direction by the Thellusson Act. But happily such interference is not required. In modern taxation, imposed by the free will of national representatives, we have a voluntary devotion of individual property to the benefit of the state. Every calamity which happens, either in our own country or even in foreign lands, evokes among us sympathy in a tangible form. Our voluntary missions to the heathen at home and abroad are examples of the same. In this view, it is the duty of every man to al with his property during his life, rather than at his death, and at the expense of his heirs. If such a view were clearly acknowledged and acted on, the tying up of property in mortmain would become unnecessary, and it would then be possible to maintain churches, universities, schools, art galleries, and libraries from voluntary contributions, or from the rates, which, as I have just indicated, are voluntary contributions placed on a legal basis. It is for this reason, that owners of valuable collections of paintings and works of art frequently afford the public opportunities of viewing and studying them.[1] And the owners of valuable manuscripts are in general only too glad to find some one who is able to appreciate and use them.

But the principle applies just as strongly to property in land. In one view it is absurd to speak of one man as proprietor of a large mountain, or a lake, or a great waterfall. But a proprietor can protect these in a manner that the general public could not do against the ignorant or the malicious. He can preserve ancient monuments, though it is to be regretted he often fails in his duty. And, even when lands are laid out as pleasure grounds or planted as gardens, the proprietor should regard it as a duty, to allow the

[1] Perhaps here as elsewhere there are too many failures in duty; but the extent to which a man appreciates such possessions, *i.e.*, is the *true owner* of them, may be estimated by the manner in which he fulfils this duty.

public occasional access for purposes of education and recreation. It is difficult to attach the notion of *right* in any individual to such a privilege, but there can be no doubt that the practice of enclosing fields, and excluding the public from innocent recreation in them has gone too far in this country. The liberty which is allowed in this respect in some parts of the Continent, cannot but strike a native of this country when he goes abroad. When ground is not in the actual use of the owner, it seems the sheerest caprice to exclude the public. If the same freedom of wandering over fields were allowed here as in some parts of Europe, one grievance which gives some point to land nationalisation schemes would be swept away. The same remarks apply of course to land enclosed for sporting purposes, if it is incapable of supporting human beings. But it seems intolerable that sporting ground should be artificially created by removing human beings, without the express consent of parliament. Private proprietors are thus enabled to do with natives in time of peace what the Crown could hardly dare to do with foreigners in time of war—namely, expel them from our shores though guilty of no crime.

But, on the other hand, the abolition of private property, even in land, would involve a return to barbarism. There are some classes who do not require property to any great extent to develop their personality: seamen, who possess the world, men of science and letters, the professional classes, whose heritage is the universe. But, for the lower orders, it would seem desirable that they should have a clear and determinate interest in the country, and so the ownership of small landed properties should be encouraged and extended. Land is as necessary for them as food, for every one must have a home. And yet, though the population of England is six or sevenfold greater than it was in the time of Elizabeth, the land it occupies is very much less now than then. Communism would be a mistake, for it is an attempt to grasp an abstract universal. It would be a serious blow to the personality of the individual, and through him, to the state and humanity itself. In organic society there is a truer communism than human ingenuity could invent. And so with land; it will only be "nationalised" when it is held by individuals in private property, for behoof of the nation, and its utmost capacity is developed. The practical discussion of how this is to be done belongs to economics. The aim of economists should be to reduce large estates, and set property free for other individuals by freedom of commerce. Confiscation would do irreparable injury, not only to the material interests, but to the moral sense of the community which adopted such a course. We do not reduce the superfluous fat of an athlete with a surgeon's knife, but by judicious training and natural means. We must, therefore, reject Mr. George's proposal to confiscate rents,[1] as this would reduce land-

[1] *Progress and Poverty*, bk. viii., chap. ii.

owners to the position of farmers of a land-tax. This would merely aggravate the evils of which he complains, and deprive the state of all benefit it presently derives from the social influence of the landowners. Besides, land has so long been treated as an investment in this country, that it would be unfair to deprive the landowners of their property, without paying them all they have expended on it. And so, even ardent land reformers, like Mr. Wallace, propose compensation.[1] It is impossible to discuss his scheme here, but I may point out one objection to it, which I cannot overcome, and that is, that he treats a man who has made an investment in land, as if he were a mere donee of the Crown.

But, if economists fail to devise a remedy, it may be necessary for law to interfere with some rougher means of adjusting the rights of individuals. There is no doubt, nature will cure all in the end, either by exterminating the inhabitants of the land, or by depriving the landowners of their exclusive rights by a revolution. Every patriot must desire to avoid both of those painful extremes, and we cannot, therefore, wonder at the attention which this subject is attracting at present. In a century which has witnessed a revival of mediævalism in religious worship, we cannot be surprised to find advocates of mediæval revivals in law. But, while revivals, such as Gothic architecture, Gregorian music,

[1] *Land Nationalisation* (2nd ed.), p. 197.

and Eastern postures, may appear ridiculous to the impartial spectator, they do no particular harm to any one, except perhaps to those immediately concerned. A similar revival of mediaeval law — such as the Anglo-Saxon land-laws, would lead to practical absurdities. But, is there no honest and thorough-going conservative, who can suggest a remedy? We "restore" with pious hands our ancient cathedrals, and make them serviceable for the present day. Are our old legal customs not as valuable? Can the Anglo-Saxon land-laws not be "restored" in spirit, by adapting them to the circumstances of the present age? Is our modern conservatism as great a sham as our modern aestheticism? Do we merely admire antiquity when it happens to coincide with our present interests or some passing whim? Is patriotism only a cloak for unadulterated selfishness? It is hard to imagine that this should be so. I refuse to believe that the great bulk of those who claim to represent at the present day our old historical parties, are merely two sets of selfish, grasping hypocrites, and that their professions are utterly hollow. The day of reform cannot long be delayed, and surely the times will call forth some statesman of commanding influence, who will be able to devise and carry some radical conservative measure of reform which will satisfy, not only the abstract form of law, but also every material interest involved.[1]

[1] See Maine's *Village Communities;* Laveleye's *Primitive Property* (translated by Marriot); Seebohm, *The English Village Community.*

In the ultimate and highest conception of property, we return to the old idea of property in the body, but in a higher form. In contract, a freeman is arbiter of his own conduct, and has full power, not only over his body, but also over his mental powers and their products. Thus, property in works of art, the laws of patent and copyright, rights in obligations of others—*i.e.*, rights over the bodies of others, but not slavery, bonds, paper-money, and such things; in short, our modern system of credit—all involve the highest organic development of society, simultaneously with the greatest possible expansion of the powers and rights of the individual. Property and possession can no longer be identified. Persons express their personality in *things;* but, as wealth becomes expressed by written titles, things appear as if no longer necessary, for the same gold stored in some bank's coffers will serve to embody the personality of thousands of individuals. Proprietors are no longer exclusive and isolated. In the organism of society all men possess all things, and each man regards himself as only a temporary trustee for the whole. Mankind do not live *on* the earth. They are its soul.

LECTURE VI.

THE FAMILY.

We have now seen that rights are declared and enforced in the legal forms of legislation, judgment, and execution; that their infringements are treated under the forms of crime and civil injury; and that the matter of those rights is person and property. But, still the questions may be asked, Whence do those rights arise? By whom, in favour of whom, and against whom, are the rights enforced? In answer, it may be said that the rights discussed arise from the *necessary relations* of human beings in society. These relations are not merely between isolated individuals, but also between individuals and groups of which they form a part, and from which they are yet distinguished. We have seen that the group, as representing and embodying the "universal," has taken into its own hands the *enforcement of right* by its judges and legislators, and also the *repression of wrong* by the same means under the category of crime. But, while it has been so doing, it has been, perhaps unconsciously, creating the rights of person and property, by defining the wrongs which it would repress, and the rights which it would protect. So prominent has this "universal" become, that many people seem to think anything can be done by an act of parliament. The state is omnipotent. All that it requires to do is to command temperance and virtue, with an equal distribution of property, and the millennium will have begun. But, on the other hand, in legal discussions we are apt at the present day to look on man only as an individual, and if we deal with the state, to treat it also as an isolated individual, forgetting that the subjects of the state form the state. Even in the private law of individuals, man is essentially a social animal. Person implies the existence of other persons, who recognise the personality, as well as of persons in relation to whom or against whom (if necessary) it is asserted. Property implies the exclusion of other persons, as well as the manifestation of the subjective personality. We must therefore push our investigation a stage further back, and seek the reason of person and property in the social groups which have generated those ideas.

In early law the individual was regarded not as " a man," but as a member of a family, or as " a citizen "— a member of the state. The individual had no personal private rights apart from the state or family. From this circumstance it has been assumed that the family is the true unit of society; but this is not so. The individual is the unit, though his life is imperfect and incomplete apart from the group. The species can only progress through individuals, but individuals can only progress in so far as they partake of and embody the whole life of the species. It is not I who live, but man that liveth in me. We have therefore subordinate natural groups of men, which train and form the individual, and enable him to partake of the larger life of humanity itself. Such groups are the family, the tribe, the state in its various forms—the free town, the burgh, the county, the kingdom, the empire, and the various confederations of these. The ultimate unit is humanity itself.

For the same reason as I refused to discuss the origin of property, I think it useless to discuss the origin of the family or state. As Mr. Spencer points out,[1] Sir Henry Maine does not go far enough back in his investigation of early law. Before man was a social animal, he was a merely gregarious animal. We may even conceive an epoch when men merely co-existed, but if we call such beings men, it would only be in consequence of their potentiality of becoming such. To themselves they would not be human. In such a condition it would be impossible for man as such to attain perfection, and so we could only call them men by anticipation.

The first of those groups which we meet is the family, for every man is born in a family, more or less perfect. Thus, the mere birth of a helpless infant creates a physical relation between it and its mother, which generates obligations and rights. These rights are

[1] *Sociology*, vol. i., p. 714.

purely *personal*, that is to say, they spring from the physical nature of the bodies of the beings involved. The relation becomes legal when the mother becomes conscious of it as implying a duty, and the state recognises it by punishing any breach of the duty, or taking steps to supply the mother's place by such institutions as foundling hospitals. In like manner, rights and obligations spring from the mere physical relations of the sexes. These, when recognised and formulated by the state, and deliberately and freely undertaken by the parties, create the law of the family. This relation, as recognised by the state, is marriage. The foundation of the family is thus marriage, and this subject must now occupy our attention.

It is apparently admitted by all authorities that the most rudimentary legal idea of marriage is that of *property* in a wife—she being a *res mancipi* in the *manus* of her husband.[1] And the same idea certainly existed in the case of children.[2] The relation of parent and child is still one of *status* modified to some extent by law; but marriage has shown a decided tendency to become contract. There is an arbitrary sphere, within which free-will may be exercised, for, as a general rule, persons are quite free in their

[1] Kant makes the person of each spouse the property of the other—*Metaphysic of Ethics, Works* (Hartenstein), vii., 76.

[2] The "genitive" case indicates possession. As to this blunder, see Max Müller's *Lectures on the Science of Language* (8th ed.), vol. i., p. 121. May the mistake not have arisen from Roman legal ideas?

choice of a partner, and they must judge as to the most appropriate time for entering into the relation. We must observe, however, that as in general no man is bound to enter into any particular contract, but, at the same time, no man is entitled to withdraw himself from society and refuse to have intercourse with his fellow-men; so in marriage, although there is no special obligation between any two persons, without the intervention of an act of will, yet there is a moral obligation to marry or remain celibate. It is not a matter of indifference. No healthy man with the means of providing for a family is entitled to remain single, unless he intends thus to devote himself more unreservedly to the service of the state and humanity, for a man is not entitled to live wholly for himself. Both of those sides of abstract morality have been formulated by the Roman law into positive laws. First, we have the *leges Juliæ* in the time of Augustus against celibates, and next we have the laws prescribing celibacy for the clergy argued out in the compilations of Justinian on utilitarian grounds, which apply with equal force to all professional men. But with us the question is decided as one purely of morality. The same reasoning throughout applies to women, but the weakness of the sex will explain why the subject has generally been dealt with from the legal point of view of the man. The ordinary rules of law as to force, fraud, and fear, apply here as in contracts in general. But, as we shall see presently, in modern practice specific performance of the agreement to marry will not be enforced, though damages will be given for the breach. The rise of the idea of marriage is coincident with the growth of the idea of person in woman. There could be no true marriage while the woman was the property of her husband. But, while the tendency towards "contract" is a tendency towards freedom, the later Roman law shows us an example of *summum jus* becoming *summa injuria*. The complete recognition of the personality of woman involved the practical abolition of marriage. If the union of the sexes is reduced to a temporary one, or one dissoluble at pleasure, there is no marriage. We come then to the difficulty to be noticed hereafter in contract. Can a person alienate his freedom for ever for the future? As we shall see, this question must be answered in the negative, because it appears to involve an abandonment of personality—a sort of moral suicide—and the law, therefore, refuses to recognise the transaction. But does the same reasoning not condemn marriage? If the end is merely physical, this would be the case; but the essential end of marriage is ethical. It is the development of the individual spouses in the intimate bond of the family, that they may be fitted to fulfil their functions in the state and in the world. Marriage is not essential for the mere propagation of the race, and so, in some ideal states, like Plato's, its abolition has been proposed. We shall see hereafter the difficulty of reducing æsthetic relations, and the higher professions to the sphere of contract. But the difficulty of formulating some ethical duties in a legal form is as great. Paper contracts to keep the peace, to abstain from strong drink, to refrain from beating a wife, and such like, are worthless. If the duties are not observed apart from the contract, it will have very little influence on them. It is thus absurd for Kant to define marriage as a contract of hiring between a man and a woman. The physical relation existed long before the idea of contract. Marriage is this relation *plus* an idea added by the law: and that idea is certainly not contract in the ordinary sense. This legal conception is as much out of place as those attributed to the plants by Dr. Darwin. Before the relation is entered into, it may, as we have just seen, have some analogies with contract. But, when marriage takes place, there is no place for contract—the relation is one of status. Law does not permit the parties then to regulate their relations by contract. This is strongly exemplified in the law of ante-nuptial settlements, which cannot be altered subsequently to marriage. An ordinary contract is of course open to alteration and annulment: but even in an ordinary contract there are ethical ends. Man is more dependent on his fellows as he becomes more civilised; and as society approaches perfection, it becomes more highly organised. But the distinction between an ordinary contract and marriage (besides the duration) is that in the former every detail may be laid down, in the latter, after it is once entered into, nothing is left to arbitrary determination, except within certain limits—arrangements as to aliment and property.

That the physical relation in marriage is subordinate to the ethical is shown by several doctrines in modern law. Thus, marriage is permitted to women beyond the age of child-bearing. Impotent persons may contract marriage, and the union will be dissolved only on the petition of one of the spouses: but delay in applying for this remedy will prevent their obtaining it. Such a physical defect may involve a serious injury to one of the spouses, and as a result the ethical element would certainly disappear: and hence it would be absurd for law to recognise the union, and insist on its continuance if one party objected. But if there is delay, the presumption is strong that the ethical aim is achieved, and law will not interfere. All this tends to show that the ethical aim of society is paramount. But, while law applies an apparently external bond, this is not really so. The motives which prompted such a union at first should be strengthened by their continuance, and, even if the parties were free to separate, they would be more likely to re-unite. Even divorced persons marry again. It is a well-known fact that in unions not recognised by the law, there are the same feelings of love and mutual self-sacrifice, and even jealousy, as in married life.[1] It is these sentiments

[1] See Dickens' character of Nancy, in *Oliver Twist*, and Preface.

which are recognised and developed by law and morality. The question may then be asked, If this is so, why not leave the relation entirely to morality? Why should law compel parties to keep up a union which is obnoxious perhaps to both? The answer is that law merely enforces the union, in so far as ethical ends are in view. It adopts external and physical force, in the belief that the ethical moment will appear later, just as a gardener fastens a branch to an apple-tree, in order that it may become a branch of the tree. But I must return to this in discussing the nature of divorce and the relation of law and morality.

The close connection between marriage and religion is an historical fact. By the Roman *confarreatio* the wife became a member of the husband's family, and adopted his ancestors as her own. The Church of Rome, and churches descended from it, make a religious ceremony essential. The Roman Catholic sacrament of marriage makes the husband and wife one flesh, and the relation becomes, therefore, indissoluble. Here the church was practically the state in defining and recognising marriage. The tendency of the state to oust the church from the position it had before the Reformation, has made the external religious element gradually disappear, and has substituted for it a civil consent, the common continental procedure being to have a civil ceremony first, and then the religious benediction. The partial withdrawal of the publication of banns from the Church of Scotland is another step in the same direction.[1] This does not necessarily imply the exclusion of religion from the union, but it is a most important advance in the idea of law. While law is revealed in outward acts, religion is a concern of the spirit. Law recognises the union when made; but it is only morality and religion which can elevate it, and make the physical union subservient to the spiritual life of the spouses. As Kant's discussion of the subject shows, abstract law is out of place in determining or explaining the marriage relationship.[2]

From the ethical aim of marriage it follows that it must be between only one man and one woman. Mr. Spencer points out that polygyny can never have been a usual form of union among the bulk of mankind. It is generally regarded solely as an indication of wealth and power, and so was permitted to the Merovingian kings. After a long discussion, he lays down the order of the development of sexual relations as follows: (1.) Promiscuity; (2.) Polyandry, ultimately taking the form of one woman being married into a family; (3.) Polygyny among chiefs and wealthy men. Gradually a preference would be given to one wife, and the others would be merely slaves; (4.) Monogyny, "which has long been growing innate in the civilised man."[3] The recognition

[1] 41 and 42 Vict., cap. 43.
[2] See Stirling's *Lectures on Philosophy of Law*, p. 51.
[3] *Sociology*, vol. i., p. 704. The leading authorities on the subject are referred to by Mr. Spencer.

of woman as a person would tend powerfully to make marriage monogynous. The allotment of more than one woman to one man implies their inferiority; but as soon as woman is taken out of the category of "things," and put into that of "persons," plurality of *wives* becomes an impossibility[1].

The advance in the personality of women is curiously illustrated by the law and practice in actions for breach of promise to marry. There is here a strange admixture of the purely legal and the purely ethical view of marriage. As is well known, actions by men against women are practically unknown, and when brought, juries are very prone to refuse redress. The confusion is very similar to that which exists in the law of reparation, whereby masters are held liable for their servants, as if they were still slaves. A woman used to be the property of her husband or guardian. Now she is a free person, and owns her own body, but it is treated as a marketable commodity, and the damages are given for "loss of market."[2] But the relation in question is an ethical one, and so specific implement is not asked or decreed; and in the case of a man, the sensible view is taken that the ethical aim would be defeated by the attempt to compel marriage; and, so far from suffering a loss, he has made a great gain in getting rid of a woman

[1] Kant's theory is that in polygyny the bargain is not fair, as the one side gets a whole in exchange for only a part.

[2] Guthrie Smith on *Reparation*, p. 53; Fraser, *Husband and Wife* (2nd ed.), p. 487 and foll.

who had little affection for him, and might have made his whole life miserable. Such actions have been abolished in Italy,[1] and several unsuccessful attempts to carry this reform have been made in this country. The subject is well worthy of the attention of advocates of Women's Rights. If they have a true sense of the dignity of woman as a person, the public will not be scandalised much longer with such exhibitions of weakness and cupidity. These remarks do not, of course, apply to actions for seduction. Such cases may approach very closely to a criminal complaint, and as there is here a most grievous wrong to the person offended, exemplary damages are not out of place. And if a deliberate course of fraud can be established, there is no reason why the act should not be placed in the criminal category.

Among the ethical ends of marriage we must reckon the procreation and education of children. The mutual love and impulse to self-sacrifice which formerly existed between the spouses—almost a kind of selfishness—is now directed to other objects. With the birth of children they are taught that they cannot live only for themselves. They feel their organic relation to the world in a way they never realised it before, for they have now a hope of immortality. And not only do the children constitute a bond between the parents, but the rapid and progressive development of the same beings from unconsciousness to a state perhaps far beyond that

[1] See *Codice Civile*, §§ 53 and 54.

of the parents themselves, is a valuable education *for the parents*. It is well known that perpetual intercourse with children has a tendency to narrow the intellect of elementary schoolmasters, unless they take measures to counteract its effects; but the intercourse of parents and children has quite a contrary effect. The continuous and rapid growth of the infant mind to maturity reproduces a process which went on unconsciously in his own case, and in his children the parent can live his own life over again. Besides, the paterfamilias, as the head of a small state, gains experience in ruling and directing his children. And on the side of the children the aim is beyond doubt ethical. The state cannot be satisfied with the unconscious multiplication of mere physical being. It demands persons as its units, and hence it requires the ethical training of its citizens in the family. Apart from this, mere physical being is a very doubtful gift. In the modern family, this "delightful task" of forming and developing the character is the peculiar function of the mother; and it is to be regretted if the development of the idea of person in woman should deprive the state of her services, and leave this duty to hirelings. Surely there are still noble women who would be content with, nay, would be proud of, the title "The Mother of the Gracchi!"

The procreation of children being one of the aims of marriage, we are led to consider the subject of the degrees within which marriage is prohibited by the state.

From all the information we can gather, it appears that the prohibition of marriage within certain degrees is a comparatively late institution.[1] Some hold that the rules laid down are quite artificial, and are merely for the purpose of maintaining the breed and promoting chastity. But if we start with the admitted fact that incestuous marriages aggravate hereditary diseases and insanity,[2] and are ultimately sterile, it is hard to see how the *horror sanguinis* can be a mere idea or superstition. It may be quite true that we can trace our present rules to the practice of some tribes stealing wives from strange tribes, and the custom becoming so fashionable that it was a disgrace to be married without stealing a foreign wife. It may also be quite true that the weak tribes which confined their marriages to their own limited circle have disappeared partly from disease and partly through sterility, and so the fittest have survived and carried their custom with them, and it has now become ethical, law and morality having elevated the animal instinct into a duty. The question here raised is very much wider than the subject of marriage; but it may be sufficient to note again, what I pointed out in referring to Mr. Spencer's system generally, that the external source of a custom gives no clue to the *thought* involved in it. So with the legal institution of marriage. It does not matter how instinct dealt with the question; but now

[1] Spencer, *Sociology*, vol. i., part II., chap. iii.
[2] Maudsley, *Responsibility in Mental Disease*, p. 279 and foll.

that society has become conscious of the relation, it prohibits as illegal and immoral certain unions which would result in pain and suffering to the individuals concerned, and ultimately in the extinction of the race itself. This regulation of degrees within which marriage is prohibited may be cited as an example of law being founded on physical fact; but the history of the restriction shows rather that the rule existed first, and the reason was discovered afterwards. This is an idea added by law to the mere physical relation. That this restriction is rather a creation of law and custom than of deliberate reason is shown by the rule that the relatives of the one spouse become corresponding relations of the other; which prohibits, for example, a marriage between a man and his deceased wife's sister. It has been abundantly proved that this prejudice has no foundation in Scripture. Indeed, it is very probable that the scriptural authority is an afterthought to explain the rule. It is not unlikely that it took its rise in the Roman law, which made the wife of the same blood as her husband, and that this doctrine was subsequently transformed into its present shape by the Latin Church. Like the popular prejudice against marrying in May, which has come down for 2000 years at least, and receives new explanations from each generation, or the custom of throwing slippers and rice at weddings, which Sir John Lubbock traces to the ancient struggle in capturing a wife, the objections urged against marrying a deceased wife's sister are evidently modern inventions, which may never have occurred to those who first formulated the rule. At the same time, the piecemeal discussion of this subject is much to be deprecated. The marriages between all *constructive* relations should be discussed and settled at the same time; and it would then be discovered that many people, who on theoretical grounds have no objections to marriages between brothers-in-law and sisters-in-law, would be shocked by marriages between a man and his step-daughter, or his mother-in-law, and many other such unions. Other legal systems extend constructive relationships further, as the French and Italian codes, which prohibit marriages between adopted children, or between the adopting parent and the adopted child, or the spouse of such child. It seems probable that marriages between brothers and sisters-in-law will be permitted by our Legislature in compliance with the demand of a determined body of agitators; and it might be worthy of the consideration of their opponents whether marriages between first cousins should not be prohibited. They are prohibited in Portugal, and there are strong utilitarian grounds for adopting this prohibition as a universal rule.

It is unnecessary to refer at length to the question of age in marriage. Marriage is both physically and ethically impossible below a certain age; but we see the function of law in the relation by the arbitrary age at which the union is permitted in this country. The letter of the Roman law has been followed, and its spirit ignored. In England, however, there has always been a tendency to deal specially and severely with attempts to entrap into matrimony women who are minors or heiresses.[1] If law does not interfere in such cases, it may be indirectly sanctioning and aiding fraud. It is, therefore, a step in the right direction to raise the age of female irresponsibility to fourteen or sixteen, as recently proposed by the select committee of the House of Lords on the law relating to the protection of young girls.

But, while law interferes to define the relationship of the parties who propose to marry, and fixes an age under which it will not recognise the union, it may allow absolute freedom to persons diseased, in body or mind, to enter into matrimony, if they are so disposed. We have already noticed the case of impotency. In this case, as well as in that of total mental alienation, our law will interfere only on the application of one of the parties. This question raises the difficulty of the relation of law to morality. Law can only lay down broad general rules, and even in the case of insanity it is well known that these can be formulated only to a limited extent. The matter must therefore be left for judicial determination in each particular case. With disease it is more difficult to deal. As everybody is more or less insane, so everybody is more or less diseased. The question of degree is therefore left to the feelings of propriety of the persons concerned; while law indirectly prevents

[1] Addison on *Torts* (4th edition), p. 915.

the transmission of hereditary disease, by preventing marriages of near relations. This is an additional proof that law now regards marriage from an ethical rather than a physical point of view.

We may now notice shortly in succession the various legal results—rights and obligations—which flow from marriage:—

(1.) The mere fact of marriage establishes a relationship between each spouse and the family of the other. Brothers and sisters become brothers and sisters *in law*. I have already sufficiently referred to this.

(2.) The right and duty of mutual aliment between husband and wife, and parents and children. In the corporate unity of the family, each member is bound to contribute to the common support, or rather does so, without any particular external obligation being enforced: but, in Scots law, between brothers and sisters, this applies only to the extent of compelling a brother who has legally carried away the whole family property, *e.g.*, an heir of entail, to contribute a reasonable amount to the support of his younger brothers and sisters.[1] In the case of illegitimate children, the idea of the family can hardly be said to be recognised by law. Aliment is given only until the child can provide for itself. The father may claim the custody of it after a certain age; but, otherwise, the relations of the parties are determined as if they were constituted by delict.

[1] Erskine, *Inst.*, i., 6, 58.

(3.) The curatorial power of the husband over his wife—in the law of Scotland, the *jus mariti*, and right of administration, now abolished in marriages contracted subsequently to 18th July, 1881.[1] By the *jus mariti*, the whole movable property of the wife was transferred to what was nominally a common fund, of which the husband had absolute control. In practice, the wife's property became his. Again, she could not, until the passing of the act above referred to, exercise any right whatever over her heritable (real) property without his consent. She could not sue without his consent. So far was this carried, that in many cases of injury to the wife, the husband appears to have had a better right to sue, *e.g.*, a person who seduced the wife.

(4.) The curatorial and tutorial power over the children. While the mother is entitled to the custody of young infants for their own sake, the father is entitled to their custody whenever her services can be dispensed with, and in early years—pupilarity, which extends to the age of fourteen in males, and twelve in females—he represents them, as they have no *persona* in law. After that age, and until majority, he is their legal guardian without any title or express appointment. He is the only one who can make provision for the continuance of the family, by appointment of curators and tutors to his children. Guardians so appointed have special privileges, and do not require to find caution

[1] 44 and 45 Vict., cap. 21.

(security) for their actings. The recent Married Women's Property Act virtually gives this power to the wife also.

(5.) The rights of the mother over the children are in other respects quite inferior. The tendency is to treat the children as belonging only to the father; and, as I have just indicated, to leave the children with the mother only so long as her assistance is indispensable. For many purposes they are the father's property.[1]

(6.) Rights of Succession. The idea at the root of our present law of succession is joint property of the family. Hence the *jus relictæ*, or widow's third, the *legitim*, or children's third, and the *dead's part*, on which the deceased is entitled to test. So with the rights of terce and courtesy in heritage (real property). But this subject will be dealt with in a future lecture.

The family is dissolved, (1.) in point of *fact*, when there are no children, by the death of one of the spouses; (2.) if there are children, by the death of both parents, when the children become *sui juris* and independent; (3.) by the emancipation of the children. This happens in the forisfamiliation of sons, and the marriage of daughters. This is with particular reference to the father, for the death of a mother, as a general rule, has no effect on the corporate life of the family. The precise effect will depend on the view taken in the particular legal system of the personality of women, and the precise position allotted to her in the family. (4.) The marriage is dissolved by

[1] This is perhaps more observable in English than in Scotch law.

operation of *law*, by the divorce of one of the spouses, if there are no children. The law here withdraws its recognition of the union; but, if there are children, some provision must be made for the continuation of the family by appointing guardians, or giving the children to one of the spouses for custody.

As to the dissolution of marriage by divorce, I would only remark, further, that, whenever the ethical side of marriage has disappeared, law has no interest in insisting on the physical side, and therefore divorce for adultery on the part of either spouse should be allowed.[1] Perhaps divorce for desertion may be justified on the ground that the physical side of the relation has disappeared, and it may be absolutely presumed that the ethical is gone also. Supervening insanity (even incurable) is, however, in our law, no ground for divorce. This rule is founded on ethical grounds, but it may be doubtful if it would not be better to permit such divorces. The chief aim of marriage is defeated, and it could surely be left to the other spouse to determine whether the continuance of the union was beneficial. Provision would require to be made for the future support of the divorced spouse, and of the children of the marriage. We may also regard as a modified species of divorce, allowed

[1] The Scotch marriage laws are regarded by some Englishmen with feelings of horror. But the English law, which practically permits a husband to live in adultery if he does not assault his wife, inspires similar feelings on this side of the Border.

"for the hardness of men's hearts," the deeds of separation recognised in English law.

Nothing is so striking in the history of law as the gradual absorption of the family in the state, partly by the supersession of the paternal power, and chiefly by the operation of contract.[1] The power of direct infanticide has long disappeared in modern Europe. Child-killing or neglect is a crime, and may be punishable with death. The maxim, that the "Paterfamilias can do no wrong," has almost disappeared from family law. A judge may enquire if a punishment has been excessive, and a father is punishable for an assault on his own child, or a husband for an assault on his own wife.

A parent does not now educate his child, he hires a schoolmaster to do it for him. The tutor who was a slave has disappeared, and so here *status* has given way to contract. Even the ultra-orthodox people of our day do not observe that they are assisting in the disintegration of the family, when they insist on the schoolmaster teaching religion. Things must be very bad, if parents cannot be trusted to do even this. I shall refer hereafter to the proposal to make education a burden on the rates.

It is notorious that this process of disintegration has been aggravated by the practice of employing young persons, and particularly young women, in mills and other public works, where they may earn considerable wages. They feel their individuality, and are free from the re-

[1] Montesquieu, *Esprit des lois*, L. vii., ch. xi.

straint of the family before they are ready to take their place in the state. Such a process is disastrous to the individual, as well as to the state. If the parallel is allowable, it may be said that the life in the family is like the life of the child prior to birth, and a premature birth is as dangerous in the one case as in the other.

In the case of guardianship, we may note, in passing, the tendency to substitute factors directly responsible to the state, for the usual tutor-dative or tutor-at-law.[1]

It is in the relation of husband and wife that most examples of the tendency will be found. As the Roman *familia* was broken up partly by the doctrine of the *peculium*, which gave individual property to the children, so the modern family is being further disintegrated by the wife's property being made an independent estate in her person. Thus the Intestate Succession Act of 1855 (18 Vict., cap. 23) abolished the communion of goods between husband and wife, but reconstituted the communion in the case of children on a different basis. To the Conjugal Rights Acts of 1861 and 1874 (24 and 25 Vict., cap. 86, and 37 and 38 Vict., cap. 31) no exception can be taken. They are intended to meet the case of the family having ceased to exist through the delinquency of its head, and the state interferes to assist the wife to take his place and exercise his functions. But the Married Women's Property Acts of 1877 and 1881 (40 and 41 Vict., cap. 29, and 44 and 45 Vict., cap. 21) are

[1] Pupils' Protection Act (1849), 12 and 13 Vict., cap. 51.

examples in point. The former of these acts provides that the husband is not to be liable for the ante-nuptial debts of his wife, except to the extent of the fortune she brings to him. This is very just, as the spouses are separate persons with separate interests up to the date of marriage. But another section of that act contemplates the wife earning a livelihood independently of her husband, and withdraws it from his control.[1] The act of 1881 goes further. It makes the funds of the husband and wife two separate estates, in which the surviving spouse and the children of the predeceasing one have a community of interest. The husband is deprived of all control of his wife's property; but, strange to say, while he is bound to maintain his wife and children, no corresponding obligation is laid upon her. Without this provision the law is quite unjust, and at the same time the symmetry of the rights in the respective estates of the spouses is marred. If this act was necessary, it throws a sad light on the state of modern society. It implies that as a rule husbands could not be trusted; or, it means that men are to be allowed to speculate with their own money as they please, and ruin everybody except their own families. It is possible, however, that these acts may enable a lower class of men to realise that their wives are persons and not chattels. It will not sensibly affect those who realise by their own free

[1] The same objection applies to the Policies of Assurance of 1880, 43 and 44 Vict., cap. 26.

will the duties of a husband and father. There is, nevertheless, a danger of injuring the power and freedom of a person, by taking out of his hands the means of attaining freedom. Many people who have great objections to deprive a man of the opportunity of getting drunk because it would interfere with his freedom, appear to have no scruples at depriving him of the control of his wife and family, and thus curtail his freedom in another direction. The objections just urged against the Married Women's Property Act of 1881 apply with equal force to the common form of marriage settlement. The Act, it may be said, merely made the law the same for the poor, who could not afford to make a settlement, as for the rich, who uniformly made one before marriage. But it is evidently a weakening of the family tie, for trustees to manage the property of the wife and children independently of the husband and wife. The fact of a provision being secured, is apt to make the husband reckless in his speculations, and hence the regulation of the right of settlement in Dutch law by Charles V.[1] It is perhaps too late to go back on it now, and provide that ordinary creditors must be satisfied before the wife's provisions come into operation, but it might have been better to have dealt with the power of making settlements, than to extend their disadvantages to all classes of the community. These acts have been passed for *women*, without giving adequate consideration to the fact that they were *wives* and *mothers*.

[1] See Thurburn v. Stewart, L.R. 3 P.C. 478.

But these atomic, individualistic relations of husband and wife and children do not truly constitute the family, any more than the prior stage in which the wife and children were the property of the *paterfamilias*. Marriage settlements, or the Married Women's Property Acts, are merely an expression of the feeling of the community that women are persons and not things. They really affect the constitution of very few families, for they only apply when relations become strained, and domestic discord enters. In the ideal family, where mutual love and confidence prevail, there is a true community of goods; the husband is still supreme, but the wife and children are no longer property. There may be a *constitutional* family, as well as a constitutional state.[1]

[1] See Spencer's *Sociology*, vol. i., p. 705 to end, as to the change which has recently taken place in the constitution of the family.

LECTURE VII.

THE STATE.

The family is the first concrete realisation of the universal. But true life in the family is conscious. The members must think themselves in the family, and the family recognises every member as such by sustaining and protecting it. If we can conceive true family groups existing in a state of isolation, or even of hostility, this is not an epoch of law, and need not detain us any more than a conception of isolated individuals. For the true existence of the family there is necessary a higher realisation of the universal—the state, or group of families, which recognises, and in one sense creates the individual family. The family soon becomes too narrow for the development of the capacities of the individual. If it were nothing else, it comes to an end by the death of its head, and the scattering of its members. In early Roman history ancestor worship, and the idea of community of blood of the *gens* or tribe at once enlarged and kept together the social group, while the fiction of adoption proves that the group was everything and the individual nothing apart from it. With the Jews, in like manner, the annual religious rites at Jerusalem were the real bond of union between the members of the nation. The whole religious polity carried the memory back to the family of Jacob, which had expanded into the nation of Israel. So strong was this feeling that, when Jeroboam founded the northern kingdom, he instituted religious rites at a different place, in order to unite his portion of the kingdom, and to place a barrier between it and the remaining tribes. The state is extended by the idea of race, and this idea is strengthened by community of language. The notion of an original ancestor gives way ultimately to the spirit of patriotism, arising from birth in a particular country—a Fatherland. The ideas of "race" and "Fatherland," along with the common language, have had an immense influence in the unification of Germany, even where a difference of religion would have been expected to stand in the way.

So the family externally grows into the state. But where the state consists of a group of families, the heads of which are directly or indirectly represented in the government, there is a tendency in the larger body to crush the smaller ones out of existence, and to supersede their functions. This is again a struggle between the form (the family) and the matter (the individual person). When the state becomes conscious of its existence, it feels the antagonism of such subordinate groups. It recognises the individual, and gives him rights. It formulates the duties of the *paterfamilias*. When once the law has given a *name* to the family group, it lays down the duties and rights of all the members, as members not of the family but of the state. Recognition of the family thus implies its ultimate annihilation.

We cannot reduce the state any more than the family to contract. Just as a man, when he first becomes conscious finds himself a member of a family, so every man finds himself also a member of a state. It is true that in modern practice any man not criminal, and sometimes even then, can take up his residence in any state, and generally can become a member of it, and so his relation to the state is apparently constituted by contract. But if a man tried to cut himself off from society by leaving the state in which he found himself, and entering no other, and founding no new one for himself, he must be either "a god or a brute." Every man must belong to some state. And men must group themselves in some such form.[1] Even a nest of pirates partakes in some measure of the character of a state, for the state is more than the individuals composing it. If, then, the state is the family "writ large," it follows that its functions are *mutatis mutandis* the same,[2] and the analogies between them may now be noticed. The size of the state is unimportant, and, therefore, the subordinate groups of burghs, &c., may be treated under the same title.

(1.) The first result of the existence of the state is

[1] Examples of some uncouth groups will be found in Mr. Bret Harte's works.

[2] See Professor Caird's *Hegel* (Blackwood's Philosophical Classics), p. 81, as to the reservations under which this statement must be made.

relationship between the members. They are fellow-citizens, and by birth on the soil of the fatherland, or by being descended from native parents, they are assumed to belong to the same nation. The ancient law of adoption still survives here, and in some cases naturalisation puts foreigners on the same footing as natives.

(2.) In the next place, we have the duty of mutual aid and protection. This is recognised in police arrangements for the defence of the citizens against internal or external violence. But is it restricted to the mere keeping of order? The state being an extension of the family, we must answer this question in the negative. While negatively the state must protect the citizen from external force, it may positively assist him to higher freedom when necessary. On the one hand it would secure order, with freedom as the ultimate end in view; and on the other it would promote freedom, which involves order. The state, being an assemblage of conscious moral beings, is itself a conscious and moral being. It has an ethical and spiritual, as well as a physical side. And the philosophy which would confine the state to the functions of a policeman ignores altogether its ethical and spiritual side. The danger against which the school of Kant was a protest was the destruction of the individual freedom by centralisation, and the consequent destruction of the freedom and the existence of the state itself.

It is this idea of the state which justifies our poor laws. The state (in the widest sense of the word) has brought those persons into existence for its own purposes, and it is bound to see that they do not starve, while it insists on able-bodied men working for their own support, and so adding to the wealth of the community. The individuals in the state have reaped the benefit of those persons' labour, and so they are bound to contribute to the common fund by paying the rates. There is no obligation enforcible by law between an individual beggar and a man in the street. There is a general moral obligation to attend to the poor, which is generally satisfied by a payment of rates, but the state only goes the length of compelling charity to prevent starvation. I say compelling, but the compulsion is only apparent. The acts of Parliament passed on the subject are only another form of making an agreement to pay a subscription. A gentleman who subscribes to an hospital feels himself *bound* to pay his *voluntary* subscription. The difficulty of collecting those subscriptions has led to proposals as to imposing a rate for hospitals; but this would merely put the ethical act on a legal basis.

In times of great distress it is often maintained as an abstract proposition that the state is bound to provide work for its members. The state does provide work through the individuals of whom it is composed, if there is freedom of contract. The question rather is, Is the state in its corporate capacity bound to provide work? When the state requires public offices, or law courts, or a mint, and makes a contract with a private individual to build them, it becomes a private citizen, and is subject to the law like any other person. If it goes further, it is on entirely different grounds, and any step must be taken with caution. The practical solution seems to be that if a temporary crisis is in progress, and the state *must* support a large number of working men who have been and will afterwards be useful to it, and who, if neglected, will become useless or dangerous members of the community, it may try to recoup itself for the loss by getting the men to perform work for the benefit of the community which is supporting them. The work must be secondary, and merely to recompense the individual members of the state who subscribe to the rates, or the temporary relief fund. Otherwise the state would be encumbered with parasites who had no share in its organic life. The measure of giving work must, therefore, be temporary and remedial, or perhaps, preventative, or the paupers relieved will kill the state. This question is rather one of political economy, or practical politics, than of law, for feeding or refusing to feed paupers is a question of self-preservation for the state. The state will only interfere in its corporate capacity, where the machinery at the disposal of private persons is too limited for the purpose, and where there is practical unanimity as to the remedy required. The important point to notice is that the idea of personality forbids the direct extermination of paupers, and suggests such remedies as government emigration schemes, whereby men, who may be only vermin in one country, become in another useful citizens.

In a free country the state affords facilities for joint action, which are quite beyond the powers of individuals; and there is a strong tendency to call in its aid even where it is unnecessary. We have just seen this illustrated in the relief of the poor. Thus, again, the state may found art galleries and museums, theatres, musical colleges, and universities. It may promote science, geographical discovery, and literature. It may endow churches; but, if there is more than one sect, they must all participate in the state fund, unless the state wishes to discourage one sect as dangerous, while it is averse to actual suppression. The state is thus in its aggregate coming back to the rudimentary family. It manages commercial concerns, like the post-office, gas-works, water-works, and, in some cases, railways. Nowhere have Kant's doctrines[1] been so defied as in his own country. The practical problem we are working out is to reconcile this activity of the state with private freedom.

(3.) So far we have been dealing with the relation of the state to its members, who are *sui juris*. We shall see hereafter that the state recognises potential personality in children by forbidding infanticide, and even the procuring of abortion. It also exerts a curatorial

[1] See *The Sphere and Duties of Government*, by Baron Humboldt, translated by J. Coulthard, jr. London: Trübner & Co.

power over the property of children in certain cases through judicial factors. But it now carries its curatorial duties further. In the Act for the protection of infant life,[1] it takes to some extent the place of the mother, and in the Education Acts it takes the place of the father. The state is bound for its own protection to give to children, who are neglected by their parents, education both secular and religious. The duty of supplying food is recognised in the poor laws; and if we were to stop here it would have been better not to have begun at all. Food without education is insufficient for a human being, and the probability, nay, the certainty, is that the state would simply manufacture criminals, if it did not give also education. This again is an act tending to the direct preservation of the state, since it tries to create good citizens for itself. And as the charity required is on too large a scale for private enterprise, the state undertakes it as it does the commercial and other operations above referred to.

But we go further, and now insist on the education of all children. The difficulty is as to where are we to draw the line (1.) in the children to be included, and (2.) in the subjects taught. The solution presently adopted is to make elementary education universally compulsory. All the state does in this respect is to insist on the father doing his duty and educating his child. But some would go further. There is at present an agitation

[1] 35 and 36 Vict., cap. 38.

going on for what is called free education. The agitators say that if we compel people to educate their children, we should pay for the education, as if a man has a right to bring children into the world and then leave them without the conditions of human existence. They might as well say if we compel parents to feed and clothe their children, we should supply the necessary food and clothing. This is a perfectly legitimate idea pushed to an absurd extreme. State interference weakens individual responsibility and individual freedom. If effect were given to such a proposal, the relation of parent and child would be entirely abolished. We should no longer possess the educating power of the family—an education, as we have seen, for the head as well as for the lower members. The power of the state in the matter of education, as in that of maintenance, should be exerted *through* the head of the family, and should only give pecuniary aid when his power actually fails. This is the idea at the basis of the present system, and no paltry saving of a few miserable pounds should induce us to alter it. We cannot afford to lose the ethical unit of the family altogether. And, until we are prepared to allow the improvident part of the community to procreate children, which the provident part must feed, clothe, and educate, we must give this proposal the most strenuous opposition.[1]

We may notice, in passing, that the idea of the family

[1] Spencer, *Study of Sociology*, p. 368 and foll.

(and, perhaps, ancestor worship) still applies in the law which allows children to be brought up in the faith which their father professed. Where a child has no father or mother, the state must choose a religion for it, and, even if there were no established religion, this would be done directly or indirectly.

The curatorial power of the state is also exercised in the case of lunatics, but this subject is usually put on the same basis as pauperism. The state respects the potential personality of the pauper lunatic, and so preserves his life.

(4.) The last point in which the state now represents the family is in the law of Succession, which will form the subject of a future lecture.

So far I have spoken of the members of the state as being subjects of it. We need not here concern ourselves with the form of the government of the state, which is often referred to as the form of the state itself. It is immaterial whether it is a despotism, or a limited monarchy, or a republic, or a pure democracy, like the small Swiss cantons. If the despot is a native, he may content himself with levying taxes and keeping external order, and let municipal law and customs alone. If he interferes with them, it is more than likely he will conform to native custom, as it will be difficult to rid himself of native associations and education. If it is a *constitutional* despotism,[1] like our rule in India, an attempt will be made to develop the customs of the people in certain directions, and so to educate them. Again, in this country the relations of the crown and the people are bridged over by means of legal fictions, which make the government nominally a despotism and really a republic. It is the government which gives form to the state, but, unless it interferes arbitrarily with native ideas, it is truly the people who rule themselves, even under a despotism.

The collision between the particular and universal is thus seen clearly in constitutional law. I am subject to the laws of the state, but I myself form the state. I am then subject to my own laws. The striving after a universal has caused the exclusion of the weaker, poorer, and more irrational element in the population from sharing in legislative work. It has resulted in the divine right of kings, and the corresponding theories of the divine right of men. Every human being in the state participates in its organic life, not only as a subject, but also as a ruler, if we may so call him. This is undoubted as to the nobility, the clergy, judges, magistrates, persons assisting in the interpretation or application of the law, as barristers or solicitors, newspaper editors and correspondents, and the literary world generally; but it is also true of every one who can influence his neighbour in a discussion. Every expression of opinion, if rational, is an element in the spirit of the state, which tends to promote its growth and strength, and, if irrational, correspondingly weakens it.[1] A demand for a franchise or voting power, is then of little importance. If a man now wishes to exert an influence in the state, a vote is perhaps the last thing he would think of asking. He would try to get others to use their votes for his purposes, and hence the development of newspapers of a certain class where there is great political activity. In politics, as well as religion, the idea has long been abandoned in modern progressive states that there is any specially consecrated caste from which the common people are to receive their laws or their beliefs.

In the family, as the members grow older, their influence increases and is exerted directly, until, as I have already suggested, we may conceive the family organised after the fashion of a constitutional state. In small states, such as some of the Swiss republics,[2] the whole of the male heads of families act directly in legislation. This was also the rule in the ancient Venetian constitution. We have traces of this in our modern law, for it is evident that the present suffrage in this country carries us back to a period when families were represented by their heads as plenipotentiaries. Even in a case like this, children and weak-minded persons, and even women, are excluded. The universal is not, for it cannot possibly be, the opinion of every being in the state. It is the rational part of the community

---

[1] Ruskin, *Munera Pulveris*, 127 and foll.
[2] Freeman, *The Growth of the English Constitution*, chap. i.

which acts for the whole. In larger states, where it would be impossible for the members to meet and deliberate, a committee is appointed. This is a parliament.[1] Strictly speaking, every one who has the power of voting for the members of committee should have the power of sitting in it, but this is departed from in modern usage. Who, then, have the right of voting? The most extreme of radicals advocate manhood suffrage, but this is a most dangerous concession to those who would restrict the suffrage. They ought, if they would be consistent, to advocate a womanhood, a childhood, if not an animalhood, suffrage. If all the stories are true that Americans give us of the practical working of their constitution, they have already advanced a long way towards this undesirable consummation. Their electoral rolls are said to be swollen with the names of children and dead men! The moment we admit that manhood suffrage is the extreme limit to which we can go, we admit that not *all* men have the power of voting. We must exclude criminals, lunatics, and also those who do not contribute to the taxation of the state. In this

---

[1] It is evidently the same process which has created the "caucus," which is an abuse of a very useful and quite legitimate idea. Electors should see that they rule their electoral committee, and not their committee them. They should see that the committee is representative, and confines itself to the duty of looking for suitable candidates. The intolerance of the "caucus" is shown in this, that they refuse to members of parliament, and sometimes even to the cabinet, the powers which they arrogate to themselves of judging what is for the good of a constituency, or the country at large.

country it must be admitted that the rating franchise of Mr. Disraeli was an admirable settlement of the question. It defines a citizen as a native subject who has a moderately permanent residence, and contributes to the rates.

A vote is spoken of as a right, but the right is precisely the same as that of the monarch to the throne, or of a peer to a seat in the House of Lords. It is not private property. It is *a trust for the state*. The constitutional idea involves this, that no one should use his vote for his own private purposes or ends, but should give it for the benefit of the state at large. And those men who get into parliament by promising to vote for what their own constituency wishes, are not only unfit to sit in parliament, but are unfit to exercise the franchise. They ought to appear at the bar of the house as advocates, and to abstain from voting. If an advocate is entitled to disregard his client's instructions, and is protected by the law in so doing, is it not a thousand-fold more important that the right of a legislator to do so should be recognised, and, if necessary, acted on? Men who act as mere delegates represent the mere particular and not the universal. Parliament is then transformed into a congress of delegates of bodies, which are not states or separate communities as formerly, but chaotic collections of individuals. It is not, then, a body of legislators striving to discover right and do justly, but a congeries of mechanical delegates. People often speak as if a number of individuals had only to make a demand sufficiently loud in order to receive its gratification by the legislature. "Whenever the people of Scotland ask disestablishment they will get it," is the fashionable formula. But this involves in the minds of many people a confusion of the particular and the universal. When such a statement is made, the question of justice or injustice is already implicitly settled. It merely proves that the principle of disestablishment is conceded, and that the carrying of it out is a mere matter of "local option," like the adoption or non-adoption of the Libraries Act or the Police Act. A certain locality can provide for its own religious wants, as it does for its literary or sanitary wants, and does not require a state church. There is no question of *religion* at stake. It is merely a question as to its practical embodiment. But the point causes practical difficulty elsewhere. We do not and will not apply the same principle in India. We there carry out British and not Indian ideas as to the relation of church and state.[1] It does not matter how loud the clamour for any change is, if the legislature thinks it is *unjust* it is bound, as representing the universal, to refuse it, and it should take means for educating the opinion of the people. No man can be *judge* in his own cause, but the parallel incongruity of a man being *legislator* in

[1] See as to the relation of church and state in India, Lyall's *Asiatic Studies*, chaps. vi., ix., x., xi.

his own cause does not seem to be so thoroughly recognised. From the highest peer to the lowest labourer, no one seems to be ashamed of using or claiming a vote for his own ends; not that there is any intentional corruption, but the judgment cannot be free from prejudice, and the principle of declinature which prevails on the bench might surely have some place in the legislature.

It is this fact of a vote being a trust which alone justifies secret voting; and here, also, we find a justification of the most stringent penalties on corruption and bribery. If we are shocked to see how kingdoms were bartered, sold, settled, bequeathed, and stolen in the middle ages, we cannot help condemning as emphatically the man who would give a vote merely to please a friend or a landlord, or who would sell it for anything whatever.

The fact of a franchise being a trust, excludes all idea of proportioning the number of votes to the amount of property possessed or the amount of taxes paid. Such a proposal proceeds on a complete misconception of the nature of a vote. We might as well propose to proportion voting power to the physical rotundity of the voter, and give double votes to fat members of parliament. I do not think it has ever been suggested that the political power of the *peers* in the House of Lords should be graduated, and any attempt to carry out such a change would aggravate the evils of physical majorities and carry us further from the universal which we seek.

In connection with this, I may observe that a numerical majority does not overrule a minority on account of its physical power, but because the minority adopts the view of the majority as presumably right. If it believes the majority to be wrong, it may resist physically to the extent of war. Mere numbers never have ruled, and never will rule the world. The battles of Marathon, Tours, Morgarten, and Plassey were not decided by the counting of heads. The rights and powers of a majority depend *ultimately* on the ideas it embodies, as well as on those of its opponents. The "clôture" recently adopted in the procedure of the House of Commons appears to be a deviation from this principle, and the necessity of its adoption is to be regretted. But it seems to be well understood that it will never be put in force against the constitutional "Opposition." "Her Majesty's Opposition," when beaten acknowledges defeat, and sometimes even assists in carrying out a policy of which it formerly disapproved. But when a minority opposes legislation mechanically, it must be met with mechanical weapons.

The breaking up of the family raises difficulties in the question of the franchise. In the Reform Acts of 1867-68, lodgers are treated as heads of families. The admission of such persons to the franchise makes it logically impossible to exclude unmarried women, who are otherwise qualified. The married woman and her children are all represented through the husband and father, and, if the vote is honestly given, it will be a deliberate resolution of the family council. Women have been ambassadors, and have done their work successfully, and there seems to be no reason why the wife's name should not appear on the roll, if necessary, as the representative of the family. But in the case of unmarried persons, the family is a single individual, and hence, since 1867, unmarried women have received the franchise in school board elections, and also in municipal elections. It is somewhat inconsistent with this position that married women, who have broken up the family and are living apart from their husbands, should receive the franchise. But the last place where we expect to find scientific consistency is an act of parliament. The opposition to female suffrage is therefore becoming weaker, and there is a possibility that the present parliament will carry a measure for the purpose of giving women the parliamentary franchise.

We have seen that in some small states all the heads of families act directly in legislation. In this country this privilege is confined to the male heads of noble houses. It is not absolutely correct to speak of the House of Lords as a body of hereditary legislators. We might as well speak of the Commoners as hereditary legislators, because their fathers either sat in parliament or had votes. It is a single class in the state, which acts directly without representation in the government of the country.[1] In the case of Irish and Scotch peers the doctrine of representation is carried out. We cannot, however, help observing that the power of the peers is on the wane. They have lost their judicial functions. The hereditary jurisdictions have been entirely superseded by the king's courts, and now even the king must bow to the law. They have still legislative functions; but, if the House of Lords is a mere collection of inferior potentates who legislate for themselves, its abolition would be urgently demanded in the interests of the state; but the constitutional idea applies here also. As the king does not rule for himself, and the people do not vote for themselves, it is a gross dereliction of duty if the peers legislate for themselves. And when collisions between the houses become a contest between a rabble of selfish demagogues and a rabble of equally selfish autocrats, the end of all things is surely at hand. It is said that reform of the House of Lords is to be taken up as a question by the liberal party. It may be that property, as a purely selfish extension of personality, is too much represented in both houses; but this will not be cured—the disease will only be aggravated by putting in their place men who are deficient in respect of property. The abolition of the House of Lords is out of the question; but a beneficial change would be to extend the power of creating life-peers so as to include other classes than lawyers, and

[1] See Ruskin, *The Crown of Wild Olive*, p. 153.

increase the number of the members, so as to make it equal to the House of Commons. We regret the loss of pocket-burghs, because they enabled men of ability to find a seat, who were, perhaps, too honest to catch the popular ear. This change would enable men who think more than speak, to benefit the state as legislators. And, in cases of difference between the houses, if it was found inconvenient for them to meet together in the style of the old Scottish Parliament, one-half of the members of each house, chosen by ballot, would serve for a committee to settle the question. This change would be a thoroughly conservative one. The House of Lords has been much weakened by the exclusion of the abbots, who formerly were largely in the majority, and were practically life-members. Prior to the Reformation, when learning was monopolised by churchmen, it would always be the most talented commoners, who were not soldiers, who thus found their way into the upper house as spiritual peers; and so, if life-peerages were instituted as proposed some years ago, it would merely be a restoration of the House of Lords to the condition in which it was prior to the Reformation. It is purely by accident that the Lords temporal have attained their present invidious position.

Some persons are dismayed by the progress of democracy. But the doctrines of Christianity, the invention of printing, of the steam engine, of the electric telegraph, the extension of commerce, and the institution of the newspaper press have made it inevitable. A common workman may now have a larger library at his command than Bacon or Leibnitz; he may have seen more works of art than Lorenzo di Medici; he may know more about the world than Marco Polo; he may be better acquainted with the world's political affairs than Philip of Spain; and why should he not have a vote? As in the case of the family, which we saw was an invaluable ethical training for its head, so in the state the exercise of the franchise is an invaluable education for the citizens. To delay giving it until a man is capable of using it properly, is like forbidding him to enter the water until he has learned to swim. If he realises the sacredness of the trust reposed in him, he adds immensely to the stability of the state. But he must feel his personality to some extent at least before the suffrage is given, and hence it would be desirable to see some real demand for it on the part of the inhabitants of counties before it is granted to them. The present movement appears to be confined to theoretical and professional agitators. But the fact is realised by every statesman that the wider the basis on which the state rests, the greater the number of members *organically* connected with it, the greater will be its strength. Union is strength. On any other condition the prospects of a large state are dismal. It contains within itself hordes of barbarians, worse than Goths and Vandals, because they do not possess their virtues, who may at any moment overturn its constitution and obliterate its civilisation.

The only danger from a premature extension of the franchise is that the new members of the state may imitate the vices of a former age, and, like mediæval monarchs and nobles, use their political power as if it were only their own private property. We should then have deposed an unconstitutional king only to subject ourselves to an unconstitutional people. The idea of property and right in political duties are distinctly present in the Ballot Act. This act, as we have seen, was specially intended to assist individuals in the execution of their duty of trust; and it at the same time afforded an opportunity of cutting off a residuum of ignorance which should never have been enfranchised. All the arguments for extending the franchise to the lower orders of society, except that a vote is a right—and, perhaps, also a saleable commodity—are against such a provision as that enabling illiterates to vote. A man who cannot learn reading for the purpose of voting is unworthy of the suffrage.

Before leaving this subject, I would refer to the idea of party—a subject which is generally thought to be outside of the sphere of law.[1] The attitude of a party towards the state depends on the idea involved in it, and this constitutes the principal difficulty in understanding the position of foreign political parties and even of parties bearing the same name in different divisions of the kingdom. If it is a mere selfish faction, fighting for its

[1] See Amos, *Science of Politics*, p. 61.

own ends, and careless of the state's welfare, it may ultimately destroy the state. But if it truly represents the universal, and honestly believes that it contains the *whole reason* embodied in the state, it may save the state from destruction. It is in this latter sense that party has been regarded by the greatest statesmen in this country. Party, in the other sense, has always been subordinated to the state's highest interests, and this explains the comparative continuity and stability of British politics. It is evidently the same causes which have been at work in splitting up the state into small parties, as have split the church into so many sects. Many analogies in this respect between church and state at once suggest themselves. But it matters little to what sect of religion or politics a man belongs if he is a good Christian and a good citizen. If the sect is not a mere faction, it enables a man to find scope for his zeal in church or state.

We have now seen how the state has transformed the family, until the latter is no longer a distinct unit in law. This process was traced at some length in last lecture; but the same process has been proceeding in other directions. We see throughout Europe a few crowned heads have deprived of their power their former vassals, who were often rivals. The little close towns and burghs are all absorbed in the greater unity of the state or empire. I have already referred to the change which has taken place in the constitution of the Netherlands. Under Charles V. the cities and towns of Antwerp, Mechlin, Bruges, Ghent, Brussels, Amsterdam, Rotterdam, Dort, &c., were little independent commonwealths. The states-general were a meeting of delegates with special powers, and the constitutional law of the United Netherlands was inter-state law. Those cities are at present only cities in the kingdoms of Holland and Belgium. The same process has been carried out in France, which has absorbed Normandy, Burgundy, and other duchies and provinces. In Italy the Venetian Republic, the Genoese Republic, the kingdoms of Sardinia and Naples, the duchies of Milan, Parma, &c., are all absorbed in the unity of the kingdom of Italy. The three towns of Hamburg, Bremen, and Lübeck still maintain their independence, but it is evident from recent events that they must eventually yield to the digestive capacity of the Germanic Empire. We may see the vitality of the corporate life in the struggle which the city of London is making to perpetuate what reformers call abuses. Provincial cities and towns have corporate existence, but it is quite subordinate to the state. Their freedom gives no privilege. Their members may ebb and flow, like the tide, or rise and fall, like a stream. The legislative powers of their councils are restricted to making by-laws for parks, and regulating the order of cabs at public balls. A city in Great Britain is a private corporation. Politically this has been a gain to the state. The cities have lost their power, but the citizens are freemen of a much larger city. And in like manner the nobility in our country and in Germany have a higher and better freedom than when they nominally ruled a small tract of country, and could at pleasure lead a few soldiers to battle. And this applies also to kings such as those of Bavaria and Saxony. Their vassals have a higher freedom, because they are subjects of a higher power, and have a wider field in which to display and develop their energies. Even the crown has come under the same influence. The state is above the king, and he swears obedience to the constitution.

The same process may be observed in the overthrow of the monasteries and other religious bodies. The entire subjection, and, if it offers resistance, the disestablishment of the church are results of the same movement. The ancients, of course, drew no distinction between church and state. During the middle ages the church became supreme, but at the Reformation the tide turned. The state (in the sense of the government) has often striven to govern the church; but its success would be a direct loss both to church and state, and hence a cry for their separation. But it is difficult to define exactly what is wanted. The church is already disestablished. It has no more power to pass a Patronage Act or a Worship Regulation Act, or even alter its creed, than the City of Glasgow has to make a Police Act. The church and the municipalities are on the same basis, and must get the state's consent to any change in the law which governs their members. The whole object of the present agitation, for pecuniary considerations are not generally referred to, seems to be to get the relation changed from *status* to *contract*. The church is to make a contract of copartnery instead of the common law the basis of its existence on earth. But on its face the proposal to separate church and state is absurd. The most voluntary religious association depends on law (the state) for recognition and protection. The conduct of the members towards each other, and towards the outside public, must be judged by the ordinary tribunals and by the ordinary standards of right and wrong. The plea of spiritual independence, in this form, is as meaningless to the state as municipal or artistic independence. It merely means freedom of contract within the law. And if with Hegel we define the state as the realisation of concrete freedom, every individual who is a member of the church is a member of the state. Church and state can only be separated by man ceasing to be a religious and legal animal. And the solution to which we seem rapidly tending is the complete freedom of the church *in* the state. Ahrens[1] objects to this phrase as implying an inferiority in the church, whereas, he says, the state can no more contain the church than the church the state; but the state is much more than the government, and

[1] *Droit Naturel*, vol. ii., p. 473.

the church much more than the dignitaries or ministers who rule it. As we shall see hereafter, nations are becoming bound into a unity by the mediation of law, and the same tendency of the human spirit is healing the wounds of the catholic church, and reconstructing it on a spiritual basis. The age of universal monarchy in church or state is past, and not even the genius of a Hildebrand or a Napoleon could now revive it. What mankind is striving after is *organic* unity in both religion and politics. It is perhaps unnecessary to point out that, if a body of individuals place their church before the state, the latter, in self-defence, may be justified in treating them as foreigners. This is the ground of the former legislation against Roman Catholics.

It should be observed that the mediæval church had many characteristics of the state, and supplied the functions of the state in many respects (*e.g.*, poor law, executry matters, actions of divorce, and slander); and it is only a very few years ago that the sheriff court (the state) absorbed finally the Scotch commissary court representing the church. The same fact is abundantly illustrated by the history of the papacy and the ecclesiastical electorates in Germany, and the exclusion of ecclesiastics from the legislative bodies in England, Scotland, and France, and the appropriation of their lands by the temporal nobility.

We may note that the same tendency has superseded the old trade guilds, which occupied such a prominent position in old burgher life, and the system of apprenticeship has in consequence almost entirely disappeared. In many respects the master and his apprentices formed a small artificial family.

The universities have been treated in the same way. There is a tradition that a Lord Rector of this university once presided at a trial for murder; and the Senate has still considerable power in the way of discipline, but its powers in this respect are very much inferior to those of the governing authorities in the universities of Germany, where the state appears not to be so jealous of them as in Great Britain.

In our own profession, the Law-Agents' Act, 1873, overthrew the local and weaker legal bodies, and substituted for their examining boards a central state body of examiners. And projected reforms in medicine would probably result in the suppression of medical graduation in the universities, when medical degrees would become honorary, or would be obtained like the freedom of the neighbouring cities and towns.

Parallel with this movement, we have a reconstructive process of voluntary associations for the promotion of science, art, music, religion, and other objects; and so even the state is becoming restricted by the operation of contract, and this subject must now occupy our attention.

LECTURE VIII.

CONTRACT.

IF any one were asked what had been the most powerful factor in breaking down national exclusiveness, if not the feeling of nationality, his answer undoubtedly would be commerce. The *jus gentium* broke down the exclusiveness of the old Roman civil law. The law merchant and the exigencies of commerce have completely transformed the old English common law handed down by tradition from Anglo-Saxon times. But this cause was at work long before, transforming the family from a small self-sufficient state into a temporary collection of individuals—from an universal into a particular—from being an end in itself to being a means to something higher. When families are broken up, therefore, it is impossible for rights to arise between the members as such. The relation is looser—the individuals appear at first sight to be isolated atoms—and an artificial *bond* is required to create rights anew. The place of the *paterfamilias* is taken by the government of the state, the members of which are now the family. And whereas, formerly, there was no question as to keeping the poor, educating children, and general police arrangements, for the *paterfamilias* was nominally at least an absolute despot, we now require acts of parliament—poor-law acts, education acts, &c.—to lay down and enforce duties, which in the family were assumed as a matter of course. I have already referred to such legislation as a source of obligations, and I therefore pass on to the other great source of them—contract. It should, however, be noted that it is impossible in an ultimate analysis to draw a distinction between a contract and an act of parliament. Mere numbers make no difference, for there are joint-stock companies larger than some European states. Acts passed for the purposes above indicated are truly contracts or agreements between those who first make them. Those who succeed are bound on the principle of implied assent, for they may get them repealed if they have any objections to them. It is the same in entering a new state or municipal community, and in like manner the buying of shares in a joint-stock company is held to be an express undertaking of obligations the person may never have heard of. And the same principle applies to the purchase of land, with conditions, servitudes, and real burdens, which *run with the land*. So in modern practice what formerly were the indeterminate, incoherent relations of men, are determined by enactments which have branched off into the departments of legislation and contract.

I have already alluded to contract (first) as a means of legislating for individuals and states; (secondly) as a source of obligations deliberately undertaken by self-conscious beings; and (thirdly) as the highest form of ideal property in bonds and written obligations. I wish now to examine contract a little more fully *as a means of creating relations between persons.*

Bargain (*conventio, pactum*), what is now commonly called contract, has been defined as a free and voluntary, and therefore a legal, determination by will, by several persons called the contractors, as to the founding of a right of obligation (*mutuus consensus de obligatione constituendâ*). The idea involved in the words contract, obligation, and the Latin *nexum* and *nexus* is the same, viz., that of a relation formed between two or more persons. There is always the idea of voluntarily, and to some extent arbitrarily, *tying* them together. They voluntarily come into connection with one another. Previously they are understood to have been in no way related. It is the new *bond* which makes the relation for the first time, and it is thus in one view artificial. But it expresses a right in the same way as a word does a thought. Another word might do as well, but the particular one has grown out of the feelings and associations of the people. But the relation of two persons, even in contract, is truly organic, for they live in the atmosphere of law in the state. A porter hired to carry a letter, an agent instructed to sell goods, a broker empowered to dispose of stock, a factor authorised to collect rents, a commissioner representing a landed proprietor, a physician called in to prescribe for a patient, an advocate retained to debate a case, a member sent to parliament, a plenipotentiary despatched as ambassador —all represent their constituents, and act for them, but even in the simplest case the relation is not merely artificial and mechanical. In the lower there is less discretion allowed to the representative. But in the higher ones, the representatives are often independent of their constituents. And so Rousseau and the "social contract" theorists made a double blunder. They degraded the state, and they failed to recognise the essential nature of contract. Notwithstanding the unprecedented legislative activity of this age, and the extension of the idea of contract, *status* plays a much greater part in human society than many people imagine. Witness not only such legal institutions as marriage, guardianship, and state law, but the whole law of servitudes, real rights, and other implied obligations.[1]

If we consider the state of early society, judging from what it was among the Romans in historical times, we see at once that there was no place for contract. If the Romans, during the latter period of the Republic and in the empire, had no working-classes and only hordes of slaves to take their place, we have no difficulty in affirming that the contract of service would not exist in any shape in very early times. The list of *res mancipi*, given by Gaius, shows that the old Roman *familia* was self-sufficient. They had their land, and beasts of burden and slaves, and their wives and children. These were

[1] See Holmes, *The Common Law*, Lect. xi.

really all *res mancipi*—the property of the *paterfamilias*. If work was to be done the *paterfamilias* could not *hire* persons to do it, he must do it himself or get his slaves or family to do it. This is involved in what Maine says, that in an early stage of society *status* is everything.

There seems to be no doubt that there is an intimate connection between the ideas of property and contract, but it is not quite clear how the one has sprung from the other. We saw that the mere fact of two persons co-existing, such as a mother and child, or two persons of opposite sex, gives rise to *personal* relations. But as the person grows by attaching property to himself, his relations extend. These relations give rise to contract. It was the acquiring of a *peculium* which enabled the inferior members of the family to trade beyond the circle on their own account, and so break up that unit. It is sometimes said that the obligation in the abstract is regarded as property—an asset of the creditor. But this is a very late idea, and implies a complete development of the idea and associations of property, and of the right of succession. Three points may be taken for granted. In the first place, persons would only become truly conscious of their personality—their dignity as persons—through property. In the second place, long before such contracts as hiring of service and executory contracts could be conceived, we would have contracts in regard to property, including, of course, slaves. And lastly, we must observe that all those words, *nexus, nexum, contractus, obligatio, religio,* and *jus,* evidently involve the idea of "tying." They all point to the relation of one man to another generally by some religious oath or vow. The transition from property to contract would then be this: A man might require to leave his goods in charge of a friend. He would hand them over, and his friend would swear that he would restore them. In a sale there would be also tradition, and besides, an oath by the seller that he would never re-demand possession, and that he would warrant the possession of the purchaser; and any other stipulations of a similar description would be made at the time of delivery, just as in England we may have an elaborate covenant to produce or exhibit titles, over and above the conveyance. And even in Scotland many obligations are usually inserted in conveyances, though now they might be held as implied. So in the old Roman law, we would have simply tradition of property and a solemn bargain, with the usual apparatus of oaths. There would be only one kind of transaction—the *nexum.* As yet no contracts would have separate names. The forms of stipulation would be indefinite and infinite, and could be suited to any circumstances. "*Uti lingua nuncupássit ita jus esto.*" Thus two persons who were related in this way would be *nexi. Nexus* might refer to the hirer or lessee, purchaser or seller, or in fact, to any person who had made a contract. If the contractor failed to perform his contract, he had violated an oath

P

to the gods. He was *nexus* in an especial sense. The difference between the former and the latter state was that between a debtor, who owes an open account, and is solvent, and one against whom a decree has been obtained, and is insolvent. The word "debtor" is often applied to an insolvent debtor *par excellence*. He was *religiosus*—accursed by the gods, and hence the severity with which he was treated. No treatment could be too severe for a man who was condemned by Heaven. This form of contract would supply the wants of a primitive people for many ages. It would be a perfect sale, loan, location, pledge, deposit, these contracts all dealing with property, and the *verba nuncupata* being varied in each case. It is easy to see how the Roman contracts developed from this state of protoplasm. The first contracts were both real and verbal.[1] When writing became common, witnesses could be dispensed with, and hence a written paction would be more explicit and stand in higher favour. The old *nexum* would split into two divisions, each forming a separate kind of contract, and being gradually restricted to one kind of transaction, the real contracts being those where the delivery of an article was the evidence of the transaction. And lastly, when people came to realise that a man was as good as his word, and that an oath made a

---

[1] See Hunter's *Roman Law*, p. 364, where all the theories are discussed; Lightwood's *Positive Law*, p. 156; and Maine's *Ancient Law*, p. 320. Maine's theory is rejected by Hunter.

worthless man's word no better than it was alone, we reach the stage of consensual contracts—a full recognition of the dignity of the person as such. So far we may have conceived that contract has only to do with property; but with the clear recognition of the idea of freedom of the person there is recognised the fact that the body is the instrument of the free will, and so the contracts of hiring—*locatio operis* and *locatio operarum* —would be later than the others. The last would only become really important as slavery disappeared.

In contract as in property there are four moments present: (1.) The agreement on the one side to deliver a thing or perform something to the other, and the acceptance of the undertaking on the other side—an external physical act; (2.) consciousness of the parties of the relation; (3.) the state;[1] and (4.) a recognition by the state of the transaction as legal. There is a free self-determined relation of the parties. They are conscious of it, and the state recognises it. If any of these elements is withdrawn, the whole relation falls to the ground. The first two points I shall refer to presently; but as to the third and fourth, I would point out that the interference of the state is express when it is called upon to enforce the contract, as law. Or, again, it may interfere by reducing contracts obtained by force or fraud, or by preventing their fulfilment, or by prohibiting whole classes of contracts. In early times

[1] See note, p. 91.

again it was only the external form which was regarded, and not the matter. If there was a correct use of certain words and forms, the contract was complete. So in the old Roman law *written* contracts could not be set aside for fraud. And conversely, in England at the present day we may have an absolute undertaking on the part of one person, and a corresponding acceptance on the part of another, but if there be no consideration the law does not recognise the contract, unless it has been reduced to the form of a deed. But the law does not concern itself merely with form. It deals with the matter of contracts when it sets them aside for fraud or error. It does not recognise slavery, which may be looked upon as a caricature of contract, as well as of property. Therefore, a contract to serve for life may be broken at any moment, for the law will not enforce it beyond the point that pleases the person bound, such a contract being an entire alienation of the personality. I shall refer hereafter to contracts dealing with the limbs.

So far the interference of law is very clear. It does not and cannot restrict itself to the mere recognition and enforcement of the agreement of parties. But the most important part which the law plays is the interpretation of the contract. Interpretation here must mean a great deal more than merely reading the contract. Even that could not be done without the judge as representing the state—the embodiment of the universal—adding something to the document or circumstances presented. But in the general case, some emergency quite unlooked for has arisen. It might have been provided for if it had been foreseen. By a fiction it is said the common law applies. But in point of fact the judge must add a stipulation to the contract and enforce it. Certainly this addition must not be arbitrary, but must harmonise with the rest of the bargain. It is and it is not deduced from the bargain. Perhaps the most striking example of this principle will be found when people enter into simple consensual contracts. Their consent plays a very subordinate part. The whole of their rights and duties, which may be very far-reaching, are determined by the law. The mere knowledge of the transaction is held in law to make them liable for the most unforeseen liabilities, and this is justified by saying *ignorantia juris neminem excusat*.

In order to make a complete contract, which the law will recognise, four things are commonly said to be requisite: (1.) Capacity on the part of the contracting parties; (2.) possibility and legality in the act to be done; (3.) definiteness in the object; and (4.) free absolute consent. And (1.) as to the contractors, it is necessary that they should be persons capable of entering into a contract, *i.e.*, capable of having rights. They must, by hypothesis, from the very notion of contract, be persons: they must have the physical and mental properties necessary for free determination and expression of their will. Thus, children and persons of weak intellect of all grades, and perhaps also persons intoxicated are not fully persons in the eye of the law, and are, therefore, incapable of contract. Intoxication of the party defrauded is a frequent accompaniment of a scheme of fraud. If both parties were intoxicated, the contract should be void. (2.) As to the object of the contract, the thing to be done must be a physical possibility, and it must relate to something within the power of the contracting party. An undertaking that the sun shall rise in the west and set in the east in the course of one day is a joke, and not a contract. An undertaking that the tide shall rise to a certain possible height, and a bargain for a penalty if it does not, is a bet and not a contract. The broad distinction between a bet and a contract is that by the former one loses what the other gains, by the latter both parties gain, if it is a fair bargain. For the same reason gaming must be excluded from the sphere of contract. A contract, therefore, which provides for the performance of anything which is physically impossible is null. It is simply nothing. The same remark applies to contracts which the law expressly forbids or regards as immoral. And it is only a corollary from this position that if such a transaction has been, in the language of Scotch law, implemented, the law will not decree restitution because the transaction is meaningless, and, therefore, the law cannot recognise it. If a man pays a gaming debt, it may be regarded as a donation. (3.) The person being capable of contract, and the object being legal and possible, the resolution of the will must be positively expressed. The *genus* and *species* of the contract must be unambiguously laid down, *e.g.*, it must be clear whether a gift or a sale is intended. At an early stage this is provided for by insisting on the observance of certain forms. But in Scotch law all that is now required is the final and determinate resolution of the will, except in reference to the conveyance of heritage, and undertakings to pay money, and some other cases where writing is required. (4.) The representations which have led up to the contract must be correct. The basis on which the parties proceed must be such that they are free. A contract, therefore, is null, if even on one side there is essential error, *i.e.*, error as to the essence of the transaction; or if there is fraud, which may be accompanied with intoxication on the part of the defrauded party. Error or fraud clearly excludes freedom of consent, and the transaction (by definition) cannot be contract. Much more is this the case when "force and fear" have been used. The transaction here is only apparently bilateral. It is really the act of one person who extorts the apparent consent. The personality of the second party appears only negatively. It is violated by the other. He is conditioned by an external force, and, therefore, the transaction again is not contract.

I have said that the consent must be final; but this does

not prevent conditions being attached. If they are impossible the whole contract may be looked upon as a joke, or held to be void. But, as a general rule, conditions are not something added to a contract; they are part of the contract itself. For example, it requires no argument to show that in a document such as this—"I promise to pay you £10 on 1st prox., if A. B. shall fail to pay the same on the previous day," the contract is complete at once, though the condition prevents it being enforced at once. If the condition were absent it would be a totally different kind of contract. And if we examine so-called conditions attached to any contracts, we shall see that they all belong to the essence of the contract, and are not merely superinduced upon it.

I have observed the important part that contract fills in modern life. It is the last product of the perfect idea of personality in the individual, especially when it is permitted among members of different states, and the individuals who enter into the relation are truly free. It is through contract that man attains freedom. Although it appears to be the subordination of one man's will to that of another, the former gains more than he loses. It is painful to hear people speaking of the rights of servants, or masters, or tenants, or landlords, as if these were independent individuals. They cannot be so abstracted without destroying the relation. It will be found in an ultimate analysis that the rights of master and servant, landlord and tenant, are the same.

In ancient times great works were achieved by the collection of great bands of slaves, merely held together by external physical force. But now works as great are accomplished by the exertions of freemen. It may be noticed that this is one of the weaknesses of trades' unions, that they sink the power of contracting, and consequently, the human personality, in another power. The working classes thus escape one slavery to fall into another. Such tutelage by trades' unions must be only temporary, until working men have been educated beyond the helpless state in which they are into a power of using their freedom. The trades' unions seem thus to represent a stage between slavery and freedom. If they are permanent their influence will be pernicious, but the more advanced members of the working classes will rise above them. Much will, however, depend on how the union is worked. If the individuals have truly a deliberative voice, and if they are free to leave the society, they may have much freedom, and their power of contracting will scarcely be curtailed. If individuals are compelled to join, and an oligarchy rules the union, it will be otherwise.

It is a subject of common remark that many acts of the present parliament—the most liberal which this country has ever seen—show a tendency to interfere with freedom of contract. In the Ground Game Act[1] it recognised and

---

[1] 43 and 44 Vict., cap. 47, § 3. See also the *Agricultural Holdings Act*, 1883, 46 and 47 Vict., cap. 62, § 36.

affirmed the weakness of farmers by prohibiting contracts in which the game should not be let to them along with their farms. The fashionable excuse is, that hares and rabbits were consuming the food supplies of the country! This is a mere pretext. The true reason was, that the farmer was a *rusticus*, easily imposed upon, and he required protection by the law. He is put under a guardian. Rustics and soldiers were similarly favoured by the Roman law,[1] and in our own law sailors are a familiar example of the same principle. Owing to their childish simplicity, their power of contracting is curtailed. Their personality is defective, and the defect is recognised and provided for by the state. Another example, where freedom of contract has been taken from persons by the present parliament, is in Ireland. I have already spoken of the Coercion Act as being evidence that the Irish people were behind the rest of Europe in civilisation, since we required to revive for them a rude and primitive form of law. But the Land Act is another and even sadder proof of their backwardness. They are attached to the soil like wild animals. They cannot exercise will in making a contract. Like the poor farmer or sailor, it is "their poverty and not their will which consents." In many cases the relation is as truly constituted by fraud or force as in cases which come before our courts of law. They are entirely helpless in the hands of a grasping landlord, and hence the

[1] Hunter's *Roman Law*, p. 591.

state has to undertake their tutelage by instituting a landcourt to make contracts for them. If the reductions recently made in Irish rents are just, they show a deplorable state of affairs both in regard to landlords and tenants, the former pushing their abstract rights to an extreme until they become wrongs, and the latter without conscious personality, except to cry like children for external help. And the patriots who might have remedied this by sending the helpless creatures to take possession of new lands and there develop their personality, have assisted to thrust them back some centuries in the development of civilisation by an insane agitation for what they have not the power to take, and are incapable of using even if given them, viz., the right to rule themselves. A people who cannot contract cannot legislate. Such acts as the Land Act must be but temporary in their operation, and must be repealed as soon as the subjects whom they are intended to protect feel the dignity of persons. And as soon as an agitation is begun for the repeal of that act, we may listen to an appeal for the extension of the franchise.

It is obvious that the struggle between the supporters and opponents of the principle of *laissez-faire* is merely another example of the opposition between form and matter, to which I have again and again referred. The legal mind tends to support contracts if they are *formally* correct. If a human being has a spark of self-consciousness, give him freedom of contract and it will do the rest. Thus the Romans were a long time in discovering that fraudulent contracts, however solemnly made, should be set aside. And we ourselves, at the end of the nineteenth century, are only now awakening to the fact that freedom of contract is not much more than a theory. If the matter is closely looked into, it will be found there has been not only much less freedom of contract, but much less contract than is generally supposed to be the case. Our present danger is rushing to the opposite extreme. *Vitia dum vitant stulti, in contraria currunt.* This error of excessive state interference corresponds to communism in the institution of property, and is as disastrous in its results to the state.[1]

Contract has expanded in other ways. The onerous have all but completely swallowed up the gratuitous ones. Thus mandate has given way to factory and commission; deposit, to the hiring of storage room; mutuum in money, to the practice of discounting bills and pawnbroking; commodate, to the extension of hiring, as in sack-hiring companies, circulating libraries, the hiring of agricultural implements, musical instruments, furniture, sewing-machines, &c. So with advocates and physicians. Their services were originally gratuitous, and the former even now cannot sue for their fees; but in a short time they began to get *honoraria*, and these are now as obligatory

[1] See on this whole subject Mills' *Political Economy*, bk. v., chap. xi.; Ruskin's *Unto this Last*, *Munera Pulveris*, &c.; Mr. Goschen's Address to the Philosophical Society of Edinburgh on 2d November, 1883.

as "tips" to waiters in hotels, cabmen, and other menials. Even the sacred office of the ministry has been brought within the scope of contract. Whereas the early Christian ministers supported themselves, the office is now a means of livelihood. And the latest development of independentism or voluntaryism is the hiring of a man of letters, to deliver two sermons per week to a number of persons who can afford to pay for his ministrations. Individually, they cannot afford to keep a private chaplain, but they combine to hire one jointly. The hiring of a body of musicians completes the modern conception of a church. Poets write for so much per line. Philosophers write for enterprising publishers at so much per page. Artists are hired for illustrated journals. Music, classical and other; dramas, high and low, are supplied to a public demand on the principle of contract—*locatio operarum* of the performers, and *locatio rei* in the case of the auditory, the theatrical manager being the intermediate contractor between the performers and the public. It may be interesting to note that the gradual rise of the freedom of person has caused a gradual lowering of the status of the followers of art in all its forms. And so there is a risk of professions becoming trades, the distinction being that in the latter remuneration is the first object, in the former the work done is alone of importance, and that for its own sake. In the one case, it is a means to an end; in the other, it is an end in itself. In like manner, any merchant or shopkeeper, or tradesman, may make his trade a profession, if he conducts it in the proper spirit.[1] It is with art as with morals. The work of the artist or the act of the individual must be the spontaneous outcome of his spirit. No great work of art, no heroic deed, was ever done by contract. And so on every side we are reminded that, although such relations as that of a musician and his audience, of a soldier and his government, of a husband and his wife, are commonly placed under the head of contract, that idea cannot be present to the parties in the performance of their duties without destroying the relation.

The most extraordinary extension of the idea of contract in recent times is the law of insurance. Marine insurance is not older than the fourteenth century. At first it took the form of a mutual insurance against risks of sea, but the modern form is in consideration of a payment for a number of persons to undertake to make good the loss. They undertake absolutely *to raise a subscription*.

So in fire insurance, it may also be in the form of mutual insurance. The people in a square or street may undertake to rebuild each other's houses if they are burned down, or they may contribute periodically to a fund for that purpose, but the common form is to obtain for a present payment, an obligation from a person to make good the loss by fire. Here again, the insurers undertake

[1] *Unto this Last*, p. 32.

to make a subscription for that purpose. In life insurance, again, instead of a man's friends requiring to raise a subscription for his wife and family, a company undertakes to pay a sum to them at his death in consideration of a payment during his life. We have the same idea in accident insurance. It is a contract superseding the necessity of Christian charity.

In very recent times the insurance principle has been extended to steam-boilers, plate-glass windows, horses and cattle, though in country districts a subscription is still raised for a poor man who loses a horse or a cow. Even honesty may be insured. A person whose character is good may find companies who for a small premium will guarantee his delinquencies, if he should succumb to temptation in a position of trust. In fine, wherever loss falls upon individuals, and an estimate may be made of an average by spreading it over a large number of persons, insurance becomes possible as a mercantile transaction by making the premiums sufficient to pay (1.) the average losses, and (2.) a remuneration to the persons concerned in the transaction as insurers, with interest on their capital. The *Code Civil* has classed insurance contracts with wagers under a common class—"aleatory contracts."[1] But the similarity is only superficial. In a wager one loses,

---

[1] *Code Civil*, § 1964; Holland's *Jurisprudence* (1st ed.), p. 199. The idea is elaborated by Sir W. R. Anson on *Contracts*, p. 166. See also Holmes, *The Common Law*, Lect. vii., viii., and ix. Mr. Holmes seems to reduce all contracts to wagers.

another gains, and herein, as we have seen, lies its objective immorality, unless the payment of stakes is a voluntary donation, and by this means ethical ends are subserved. In a contract, even of insurance, *both* parties gain. Insurance-broking and underwriting are profitable undertakings. All insurers pay losses which are accidental *to the insured as individuals*. But to the insurers the losses are periodical and certain, and if there were no losses to pay, there would soon be no business to do. Life insurance only provides for the accident of premature death. If a man were certain to live a long time, an insurance on his life would be a very bad investment, unless he were of improvident habits, and required an external stimulus to make him save money. The balance of premiums over what is necessary to pay the sum insured goes to pay losses and expenses. A moment's consideration will show that an insurance broker or agent, who collects premiums from large classes of the community, pays losses to a few unfortunate individuals, and gets a small balance for his trouble, is not very unlike a merchant who purchases large quantities of goods and retails them for use. The two cases are exactly converse. A man says—"By paying a small subscription each year, I may secure indemnity in certain circumstances, if I lose my property; if I do not make this payment, the loss will ruin me." A thousand are in the same position. One or two are burned out, for example, every year, and would be ruined, unless their neighbours indemnified them. This is accomplished by spreading the annual loss over the thousand. They pay their subscriptions in the form of premiums; the person who collects the subscriptions and pays the losses is the insurance company. No doubt, there may be gambling in insurance, but there is often gambling in stocks, or grain, or iron, or anything else; and yet we do not class the transactions of a wholesale merchant among " aleatory contracts." There is great risk in shipping a cargo across the Atlantic, for it may be lost, or in selling goods on credit, for the purchaser may become bankrupt, but that does not entitle us to stigmatise the merchant as a gambler. If he is wise, the ordinary profits of his trade will enable him to meet such losses; in other words, he will spread it over the general community in the persons of his customers, as is done by the insurance company.

The classification of contracts is a matter of especial difficulty. It is a matter that belongs to the theory of positive law, and yet most codes possess the most illogical classifications. They may be classified as to their form, as in the Roman code, but forms are of no importance in the philosophy of law. All contracts are ultimately consensual. The weakness of this division is shown in the Roman texts, which added innominate contracts, or an *et cetera*, which was larger than the principal classes. The division of onerous and gratuitous is useless, because the two classes are identical in all respects,

Q

except as to "consideration." The idea of primary and secondary is also accidental from a philosophical point of view. An obligation is an obligation whether it refers to a preceding one or not. Thus marine insurance is a primary contract. The insurance of a person's honesty is a secondary one, because it is a contract of surety. If we try to classify them according to their objects, it is impossible, for this implies an enumeration of all the possible modes of human activity. According to their objects, they may be reduced to (1.) contracts as to the person, and (2.) contracts as to external things. Any further classification involves an enumeration of the ways in which the body or mind can be made subject to the will of another for a temporary purpose, *i.e.*, without absolute alienation of the will and personality of the subject, and it involves also a complete list of the external objects which may be matter of an obligation. In modern practice the variety of contracts is legion. In other words, freemen legislate for themselves by contract. They establish thereby a particular law for the regulation of their affairs.

And now I would notice shortly the extinction of obligations under contract. It is obvious that they may be extinguished by (1.) fulfilment, or (2.) by a counter contract, or (3.) by the death of the obligant, where the contract is purely personal to him, or (4.) by some cause which makes fulfilment impossible, without the fault of the person bound. In all such cases one or more of the essential moments of the notion are withdrawn, and the whole relation falls. In like manner, a contract may be terminated by operation of law. Here the state withdraws its recognition of the legal character of the debt. This is illustrated by the various prescriptions. Putting the matter generally, the law presumes a *person* to be free, and so it presumes that all contracts which are not enforced in due course, are discharged or were never entered into. This presumption may be absolute, or it may be only *prima facie*. For example, in the triennial prescription of tradesmen's accounts, the law presumes that the contract was never entered into, or, if it was, that it has been satisfied, and that the person is thus free unless he admits the existence of his obligation. The English Statute of Limitations presumes absolutely that the debt is discharged.

Another mode of extinction is bankruptcy. Here a person owes debts to a greater amount than he can satisfy at the moment they are due. If his creditor agrees to give him time, or to take a composition, there is a new contract, and the law will recognise it as such. But a bankruptcy law is a declaration that a partial payment must be taken for the whole. This is for the benefit of the debtor, and, through him, of the state itself; for a person overwhelmed with debts which he will never likely be able to pay, is far from being free— from realising his personality as free-will. The law, therefore, while endeavouring to pay the creditors as much as possible, gives the insolvent debtor freedom—power to make a fresh start in life. The contracts of the bankrupt are terminated by the law withdrawing its recognition. A proper bankruptcy law, therefore, strives at once to protect the debtor and secure the creditors, but punishes fraud, instead of dealing with all insolvents alike *in point of form*. We must, therefore, recognise in the legislation of 1880 and 1881 as to small debtors another step in the direction of freedom of the "person."[1]

[1] 43 and 44 Vict., cap. 34, and 44 and 45 Vict., cap. 22.

LECTURE IX.

THE COMMUNITY OF STATES.

WE have now seen that what at first sight appear to be the merely physical relations of individuals in the family give rise to personal rights. When the state becomes conscious of its own existence, and important enough to recognise the individual, it enlarges enormously those rights, and affirms his personality, even against the *paterfamilias*, if necessary. Relations with other individuals outside of the family and within the state extend the idea of person, and create the notion of property, apart from the family property. It is through property that men contract with each other, and it is in contracts that they find the highest realisation of property. The *filiusfamilias* gets a *peculium*. The mere fact of the *peculium* being recognised by the law shows the interference of the state in creating the notion of property in the time of the Romans, as the passing of the Married Women's Property Acts shows it in our own day. In like manner, the high organisation which we see reflected in police acts, education acts, poor law acts, and so forth, is due to the fact of men co-existing in circumstances only slightly removed from those of parent and child, and husband and wife.

That is to say, *physical* relations involve and generate *jural* relations, in the case of self-conscious beings. Rights of person and property are here again created. It may be noted, too, that the principle that action and re-action are equal and opposite applies here as in the material world. Person and property have created the state just as truly as the state has created them. Or rather, as in an organic body, each part is a means and at the same time an end.

But the process does not end with the state. As the *filiusfamilias* acquired property and made contracts outside of the family, so the native merchant acquires property and makes contracts abroad. Foreigners gradually come to do the same in this country. Can we recognise the personal right of freedom in a foreigner? Can we recognise his right of property? Passages will be found in Justinian's Digest, showing that these questions were not long before his day answered in the negative.[1] And the same doctrine has been maintained as orthodox between Europeans and European colonists on the one hand, and savages on the other, down to this very day.[2] But when we rise to a higher universal than the state, we recognise the ideas of person and property in foreigners, and even in savages, and attribute them to an individual who is not a *citizen*.

[1] The title, *De Captivis et de Postliminis*, &c. (49, 15), is a most valuable contribution to the history of international law.

[2] See Ward's *History of the Law of Nations*, vol. ii., p. 111 and foll.; and daily newspapers, *passim*.

The external embodiment of the universal has thus been expanding, and the larger bodies have been absorbing the smaller units. As I indicated at the close of a previous lecture, we find in the history of England, France, Spain, the Netherlands, Switzerland, and Germany, examples of this process of progressing integration. Compare, again, the relations of the towns forming the Hanseatic League, at the height of its power, with their relations at the present day. Then they were formally bound by a treaty. Now they are apparently unconnected, but their relation is closer and more organic.

During the middle ages a higher embodiment of the universal was to some extent presented by the Emperor and the Pope. The Reformation broke the power of the latter, and the French Revolution abolished the shadow of the former. Both of these events gave a distinct impulse to international law. For the moment there was an apparent destruction of existing institutions, but it was immediately followed by reconstruction on a wider basis.

One idea which has had a most important influence on the development of the modern notion of a state and of international law is that of property. Just as we saw the legal notion of the family had its rise in the wife and children becoming the property of the *paterfamilias*, and thus enabling him to realise and display his personality, so the idea of property in their states and the whole of their inhabitants was distinctly present to the minds of the petty counts and nobles of Germany and France during the middle ages, and even to monarchs like Charles V. of Germany. States were bequeathed, settled, sold, and even stolen. Examples are familiar to every student of European history, and can be found on every page of Dumont.[1] But the successive revolutions in Switzerland, Holland, England, America, and France (for men are always slow to learn) showed that if the states were property, they were only held in trust for the beneficiaries, and that even more emphatically than ordinary private property. But the advantage of the idea of property was that mankind got accustomed to look upon the state as a unity. It had an actual physical (though abstract) existence in the body of one man. He truly held his power by divine right. Ambassadors were his representatives. An insult to him was an insult to the state. War by him was a national matter.[2]

Thus we see that as the idea of person has developed, it has burst the bonds of the family, and then those of the burgh or the province, and now it transcends the state. This was the significance of the great American civil war.

[1] See Ward's *History of the Law of Nations*, vol. ii., p. 256 and foll.; Grotius, *de J. B. & P.*, I., iii., 12.

[2] And so in religion, anthropomorphic conceptions may enable men to rise to the idea of God. It may be noted that the religious development of Comtism in abandoning the popular religion and ultimately deifying Humanity, is parallel to the French political movement which led the Republic and liberty to become the Empire and a despotism.

If the Confederates had succeeded, it would have been a backward step towards individualism. But the Federals fought not for a particular state or states, but for *The Union*. They recognised a higher unity than the single individual state. Their citizenship, though nominally in a particular state, was really in the larger federal union. And it is interesting to note that those who fought for The Union were the New England states—members of the same race who have created the largest and greatest Empire the world has yet seen.[1] But the idea goes further. Even such state-groups as the United States of America, Austria-Hungary, and the Germanic Empire, are only units in our modern system of states. An individual belongs to them—is a member of them, by being a member of a smaller unit; and in like manner an individual can only become truly a citizen of the world by being recognised as a citizen of one particular group.

Now, as attraction and cohesion among the units of the family can only co-exist with repulsion of other families, so the cohesion and attraction of the members of the state-unit can only co-exist with the repulsion of other state-units. In order to exist, the state must become conscious of itself, not as the ultimate unit of society, but as one of many states. And so, as in the case of the individual, we have (1.) a *de facto* existence of a group of persons on a definite territory,

[1] See Professor Seeley's *The Expansion of England*.

with independence and a regular settled government, and power to enforce recognition, or dispense with express recognition; (2.) a consciousness of this existence, and, therefore, a demand for recognition; (3.) the existence of other similar states in an organic society; and (4.) the recognition, express or tacit, of humanity as a whole through the other states. None of these elements can be abstracted without detracting from the position of the state. If, as has been suggested, the whole function of law is to affirm the *de facto* existence of certain objective qualities, it appears very strange that insurgents should always be so anxious to obtain recognition, and that neutral states should be so unwilling to give it.[1] But, as was pointed out in a previous lecture, the subjective and objective sides here coincide. It is as true to say that the state only exists as recognised, as to say that it is only recognised to the extent it exists.

If we keep this essential fact in view, we at once get a philosophical explanation of the doctrine of intervention which is such a sore trouble to publicists. Independence is only guaranteed to states, as freedom is guaranteed to individuals, so long as, and only so long as, that independence and that freedom are employed in the pursuit of higher social aims. If a state fails to fulfil the purpose of its existence, recognition may be withdrawn, and it has then no longer a claim to independence.

[1] See Correspondence as to Recognition of the Confederate States, Parliamentary Papers, North America, No. 2, 1863, p. 12.

If other states can interfere with effect, and by doing so can advance the cause of humanity, they are bound to do so. The questions raised are essentially casuistical in their nature, and bring us to the boundary line between law and morality. Are neutral states *bound* to interfere in every quarrel? Are they *bound* to interfere in any? May they lawfully abstain from *all* interference? The questions are, however, not so difficult as they appear at first sight to be. We must remember that in the modern world neutrality is impossible,[1] and that a bald rule of perpetual intervention is as true as the usual one of non-intervention, "*nam tua res agitur, paries quum proximus ardet.*" And if we follow out the analogy, and consider the conduct of a fireman in such circumstances, we may see how common sense deals with the matter. If the fire is small, he intervenes, throws water on it, and puts it out. If it is too great for him, he adopts a policy of non-intervention—lets it alone, and allows it to burn out, and he may even go the length of pulling down adjoining buildings to prevent it spreading. It is right to observe that in some recent discussions the right and duty of intervention have been founded on ancient treaties or contracts.[2] But there is an instinctive tendency to

---

[1] See p. 115, *supra*.

[2] See speech of Sir Charles Dilke in House of Commons, 25th July, 1882.—Hansard, 3rd ser., v. 272, c. 1720. This speech is worthy of note as containing an express disavowal of any connection between the Liberal or even the Radical party, and the doctrine of absolute non-intervention. This disavowal was somewhat required.

intervention in some cases quite independently of such express obligations as, for example, in the recent examples of Poland and Bulgaria. If the foreign state cannot be recognised, conquest or pacific annexation may be necessary, perhaps in self-defence, or perhaps in the interests of the freedom of the individuals forming the state annexed. We may notice also that when a tyrant is oppressing a people, intervention may be as justifiable as it would be with a private citizen assaulting or murdering his family. "A man's house is his castle;" "The king can do no wrong;"[1] "A sovereign state is independent," are abstract propositions which can only be accepted as true *along with their contradiction*. But men, as a general rule, only discover the falsity of such propositions when they are used as an excuse for freaks of caprice or malice.

Nations have thus in spite of themselves been brought into contact by war and commerce—institutions which were regarded by the Romans as equally sinful. Hence the institution of ambassadors and consuls. The establishment of permanent embassies indicates an organic and not an occasional union, for by them governments may more frequently and more freely exchange their views. As I have indicated already, a congress of ambassadors may be regarded as a legislative body, and

---

[1] This maxim has been applied in international as well as in constitutional law.—See Sir Walter Scott's *Quentin Durward*, chap. xiii.

a treaty is truly a legislative act for several states, or it may be a bill drafted for several states.

The tendency of modern states to obliterate the distinction between them is shown in such international arrangements as "the general postal union," international railways and telegraphs, customs unions, monetary unions, combinations to suppress the slave trade or piracy, to stop plagues, to open up the navigation of rivers, and lastly, in congresses to suppress war between minor states. Such legislation as that for suppressing outrages on fishermen on the North Sea,[1] or the proposed legislation on submarine telegraph cables, are merely extensions to international law of the idea of police regulation.[2] Since the abolition of the passport system an individual may go from the one end of Europe to the other with almost as much ease as from Glasgow or Edinburgh to London. The different governments to which he becomes subject in the former case may not be so diverse as those of the counties through which he passes in the latter. The world, in one aspect, has become a large nation divided into counties, called kingdoms and empires. This process of state obliteration has been caused by the expansion of the individual person. Commerce has always been cosmopolitan. If there is a *jus gentium* at the present day in the old Roman sense, it is commercial law. We now allow foreigners to possess land in this country, and we

[1] 46 and 47 Vict., cap. 22.   [2] See p. 106, *supra*.

reprobate as inhuman laws which forbid foreigners to succeed to property left by a deceased person belonging to another nation.

The doctrine of free-trade is simply another step in the same direction. The abolition of monopolies allows all the individuals within the state to find the occupations and pursuits most suitable for themselves. The recognition of the rights of outside persons to trade destroyed the old guilds. In like manner, free-trade allows individuals belonging to foreign states to supply the wants of other states than their own, if they can do so, whereas the contrary doctrine tends to separate states into small perfect entities, each self-sufficient. Aristotle's remark as to the individual applies to such states. They must be composed of either gods or brutes. If they do not require to import anything, if they have nothing to export, they must be either above or below humanity. As the doctrine of protection thus sets itself in antagonism to the unity of humanity, it is philosophically unsound. It takes for granted that the limited circle within which free-trade is permitted is the unit of society. But the nation which supplies its own and its neighbours' wants by imports from and exports to every part of the world, has taken largest advantage of the heritage of the earth, is nearest the ideal of humanity, and has already made its citizens citizens of the world. Of course, this does not affect the economic question. If protection is economically effectual—and this appears more than doubtful—it may be necessary to consolidate an imperfectly developed state, but it cannot form a basis for the ultimate ideal of society.

It is in what is commonly called private international law, however, that we see the union of the two ideas of the importance of the individual and the ultimate unity of humanity. This department of jurisprudence has taken its rise at once from the recognition of the dignity of the person and the recognition of the jurisdiction of a foreign government over a particular territory. A foreigner is a person, and as such is entitled to justice. In an empire such as ours we see very strongly the objections to calling this subject a branch of "international" law. The disputes with us, as in America, arise in cases of conflict between different systems of law prevailing in different parts of the same nation. Such problems are now dealt with by our courts on much the same principle as they deal with questions of local customs, or customs of trade. A similar question might be raised even as to the application of the rules of one or other stock exchange as ruling a particular bargain. If proved, the local customs, the rules of the exchange, or the foreign laws are recognised by the court and applied as law to the case. The foreign law is thus, in one sense, personal to the litigants, and recognised and applied as such. The recognition of the foreign state is only implicit in the recognition of its subjects. It has even happened that the court has, with consent of parties, discovered and applied the foreign law without asking proof of it.[1] It may thus be said that it is quite accidental that our courts administer native law. They do so because the jural relations which come before them involve that law. But if, as with the Judicial Committee of the Privy Council, the majority of the cases involved some foreign law, then our courts would habitually administer foreign law. What the courts of all civilised countries strive to do is to secure that the decision in any particular case will be identical wherever it is tried. It is then merely a matter of convenience to decide whether it is better to try a case in London, Paris, Berlin, or New York, if there is jurisdiction in the respective courts.[2] To ask that judges should know the laws of all civilised countries, is only an extension of the movement which first made judges lawyers.[3]

But though the individual may travel, may trade, may possess land, may take up his domicile in a foreign

---

[1] Bradlaugh v. De Rin, L. R. 5 C. P., 473.

[2] It is right to warn the student that this doctrine is extremely unorthodox. It has been laid down by Lord Westbury in *Cookney v. Anderson* (1863), 1 D. J. & S. 379, that the English courts are intended to administer only English municipal law, and this doctrine is quoted with approval by Vice-Chancellor Kay in *In re Hawthorne* (1883), L. R. 23 Ch. D. 748. But it will be noticed that Lord Westbury restores by a legal fiction what he has taken away. It appears that the doctrines of private international law are *part* of the municipal law of England, and so we may reach the law of any part of the world. Is it not better to state the fact directly without the interposition of a fiction?

[3] See p. 56, *supra*.

country, and receive the same justice as natives, there is still a link wanting. He may not be allowed to become a member of the foreign state. This has been met by modern naturalisation laws. In every European state and nearly all those of America, a person who will make a useful citizen can by residence, and by going through certain formalities, obtain almost all the privileges of a native born citizen. In some states, by certain services, he may acquire full rights. The transaction is as nearly as may be a social contract, and again we observe the four moments—(1.) physical, *de facto* residence; (2.) a claim for recognition; (3.) the state physically existing; and (4.) recognition of his status by the state which adopts him as a citizen. By this means the United States of America are effecting a slow and silent conquest of Germany and Scandinavia, and perhaps of Great Britain also. In passing, we may note an extension of the doctrine of manhood suffrage which has been made by Professor Laurent of Ghent. He holds that every man is entitled to demand naturalisation in any country in which he may choose to take up his residence. Such a doctrine would only result in society uniting to extirpate political agitators, who fled from a state when they found themselves uncomfortable. This view shows the tendency of some modern thinkers to exaggerate individual freedom.

It has been said that the individualistic tendencies of

[1] *Revue de Droit International*, vol. xiii., p. 537.

modern politics threaten to destroy society. This statement ignores the fact that society is becoming highly organic. We see this very clearly in international relations. Thus down to comparatively modern times the Swiss and many petty princes in the Empire made a trade of war, hiring themselves or their subjects as soldiers. In the days of Elizabeth the great English naval heroes were as much pirates as anything else. In such times it might be possible for a private individual to carry on war without involving his state. But now piracy is a crime against the laws of every country. Nearly all civilised states prohibit their subjects from trading in warlike materials, especially during war, or waging or taking part in war without the consent of their government. The American and British Foreign Enlistment Acts show the direction of the current. But in the Alabama arbitration a step in advance of this was taken, by making the state liable for the warlike acts of its subjects. It was taken for granted that neutral states could control such traffic. We see, however, the individualistic tendency in other directions. The laws of contraband, and especially of blockade as now worked out, are distinctly favourable to individual private trade, and are a concession to the person of the individual trader; and the question now appears to be, if we are to extend this privilege, and exempt from capture the goods of all private individuals on the high seas.[1] Such a proposition could only be made after a clear

[1] See above, p. 116.

distinction had been drawn between the government and the individual in the social organism, and implies that war is an amusement of governments, with which the citizens as individuals have nothing to do!

And here, again, the question forces itself on us—If we have succeeded so far in repressing individualism, can we not secure the total abolition of war? The progressive integration of states is clearly a step in this direction. I pointed out before that the species of war, which may be reduced to international duelling, may be abolished in course of time. The spread of a rational public opinion, and the existence of a free and enlightened newspaper press, will make it more and more difficult to initiate such wars. But man is man, and while human depravity exists war must exist, for the enforcement of right. For this reason no project of perpetual peace, by means of international councils or arbitration boards, has succeeded, or can succeed. They are merely revivals in international law of the exploded doctrine of "the social contract." They would weaken individual states both morally and physically, and in effect it is very probable they would be alternately inefficient and unjust, as was the Amphiktyonic Council in Greece. As I have already observed, we cannot dispense with the family-unit as a training-school for the individual, and still less can we dispense with the state-unit, for the sentiment of patriotism will enable a man to do deeds he would not do merely for humanity as a whole, just as the descendants of a noble house will strive to preserve the family reputation. But, further, we cannot bind international law by the forms of a summary court, for if we are to do justly we must often rise above precedent, though not above law. We have succeeded in taking war out of the hands of private individuals. Responsible statesmen have all but abandoned it. But we cannot otherwise control mobs within or without the state, and war must be reserved as a last resource against them.[1]

Whither then is modern democracy tending? Is it the destruction of society by the exaggeration of the individual freedom? If we study the constitutional history of particular individual states, we may adduce facts which lend colour to such a statement. But the teaching of the history of international law and international relations is quite different. It is only when we separate the individual from the organism of humanity that our doctrines become one-sided and dangerous. In this country many politicians, calling themselves conservatives, advocate the protection of one class against another, and native industries against foreign ones. In America we have demagogues and radicals the most strenuous supporters of the same exclusive and protective principles. In France, again, Sir T. E. May mentions one communist

[1] While Rousseau and Kant were reducing the state and the family to mere contract, they were logically working out their principles in international affairs by schemes of perpetual peace. At the same time Paley was proposing to abolish duelling by establishing courts of honour!—*Moral Philosophy*, bk. iii., chap. ix.

who objected altogether to international intercourse as dangerous to principles of equality.[1] It was another phase of the same idea which made Bentham propose that European states should give up their colonies.

But the truth is that individualism is not so strong at the present day as it was in the middle ages. Of Feudalism in mediæval Europe, Professor Laurent says:[2]—
"Dans l'Europe féodale, l'élément dominant, c'est l'individu; tout est particulier, local. La féodalité a son principe dans la décadence de l'unité carlovingienne; loin de tendre à l'unité, elle aspire à une division infinie. Au moment où le régime féodal s'établit, l'anarchie paraît complète. Chaque propriétaire est souverain dans ses domaines; on croirait que la société va se réduire en atomes: pour mieux dire, il n'y a plus de société politique. La royauté, seul lien des hommes, disparait; il n'y a plus de relations de citoyen à État: il n'y a pas d'État, il n'y a que des individus: ce qu'on appelle institutions féodales, n'a pour but que le libre développement de l'individu et la garantie de son indépendance."

So in modern communism. It was proposed by the French communists to divide France into 37,000 little sovereign states or communes.[3] The small feudal baron is to be supplanted by an infinitesimal commune, the relations of which to similar bodies would be voluntary.

---

[1] *Democracy in Europe*, Int. p. lxvi.
[2] *Histoire du droit des gens*, tome vii., Int.
[3] May, *Democracy in Europe*, ii., 326.

Thus feudalism—the extremest conservatism,—and communism—the extremest radicalism,—meet. They are both pure abstractions, and they equally ignore the fact that man can only exist as a member of Humanity. The family, the commune, the burgh, the state, the empire, a federal union, however wide, is still short of humanity. Nothing less can satisfy human needs and cravings. Humanity must become conscious of its unity, and this can only be attained when each individual feels himself a man.

This expansion of the idea of the state has had a corresponding influence on the idea of party. There are missionary parties as well as missionary religions. Foreign politics and foreign relations bulk largely in the present day. Many people, and people who ought to know better, complain of this, and say we ought to confine our attention to domestic concerns. When I listen to such complaints, I begin to wonder if there may not, after all, be something in the transmigration of souls; or whether we have not got the soul of some ancient Egyptian or Hindoo, or early Greek or Roman, speaking through the body of a modern member of the British parliament. If we are to give up our interest in foreign politics, we must tear up our railways, cut our telegraph cables, and sink all our ships. It is amusing to watch theory bending to the stern logic of facts. For the last half century each successive British government has preached non-intervention in foreign politics, and practised intervention. If a distinction is to be drawn between our political parties in this respect, it is in the aims and manner of the intervention, and not in the act itself.

And whereas our first conception of human society was one of purely physical relation, then of relation in the family, and lastly of relations as citizens or members of a state, now we must conceive men related only as *men*. "There is neither Jew nor Greek; there is neither bond nor free; there is neither male nor female." Foreigners can claim the benefit of our poor-laws. They can now possess land in this country. Their contracts are recognised and enforced. Their laws are carefully observed. Such devices as treaties of commerce and friendship will soon be as antiquated as the *tessera hospitalis* of the Romans. We sometimes hear a plaintive lament from a certain class of politicians that Great Britain is without allies. They might as well lament that they have no compacts of hospitality with persons in France or America. Treaties of alliance must disappear as nations and states realise their rights and duties. All the world should be Britain's friends. The question should be not, Have we allies? but, Have we enemies? Confederation is thus not the highest form of political organisation. It can only be admitted as a stage preparatory to something higher. The union of the various groups of men must either become closer or looser; but, if it does become apparently looser, it only means a truer and more intimate union. And the true end of treaties of commerce is to determine matters which must be arbitrarily settled—the colour of postage stamps, the number of coins to be made from a kilogramme of metal, the number of cruisers to be contributed to watch a slave station, the powers of the officers, and such matters. Men associate and trade without inquiring as to each other's nationality. And here the relations are truly physical and personal, though now spiritual. In the physical division of labour men supply each other's wants as certainly as in the case of mother and child, with which we started. The preacher, the poet, the artist, the musician, are *physically* related to the rest of mankind, and hence the origin of their rights and duties. The notions of person and property have thus developed in a direction exactly parallel to that of the relations between men. Spiritual relations create spiritual, and at the same time material, rights.

And whereas, men were first divided into freemen and slaves, the latter ministering to the wants of the former, and even Aristotle could not rise above the conception of lower classes—hewers of wood and drawers of water—who promoted the interests and attended to the physical comfort of upper classes who truly formed the state, the idea is now reversed. The greatest politician, the most erudite lawyer, the most devoted preacher, the most gifted scientist, the most consummate artist, are all the servants of the public—the so-called lower classes, not merely in one state but in the World.

The hard-working men of the present day are the professional classes. It is no exaggeration to say that the manual labourers, at least in this country, are the leisured classes. But in an ideal society there are no upper and no lower classes. Each man is proud of his position in the social organism, and each man fulfils his duty.

And so with government. In some small states where the members could meet and talk to each other, each man could legislate directly; but now, the world, through the newspaper press, is one vast legislative assembly. The electric telegraph has again brought men into contact, and nations now speak and act with the eyes of the world turned upon them. Debates are carried on between newspapers within and without the state, while legislative assemblies and cabinets merely formulate and express the national resolutions. And so the world is one state, with one government and one legislature.

LECTURE X.

SUCCESSION.

Hitherto I have regarded rights as bound up with life and self-consciousness, and the different subjects of right as coexisting in *space*, without any special reference to *time*. But death is an event, the effects of which must be anticipated before it occurs, or remedied after it has taken place. Hence arise laws of succession.

If it were possible to conceive mankind coexisting as separate independent units in space, then the only succession possible in time would be mere " one-after-the-other-ness." But when we speak of succession we mean *organic* succession, by which, while the individual is lost, the organism of which he is a part still lives. If a community is not organised, no law of succession is possible. A flock of sheep or a herd of cattle will graze over a field for generation after generation, and there will be no distinction between the group now existing and one existing twenty years ago, though each individual is changed. But, whenever humanity reaches the stage of having a division of functions and offices, and whenever property becomes recognised, then a law of succession springs into existence. The village baker or smith dies, and some one *must* take his place. It may be a stranger who steps in and is adopted, so to speak. It may be an apprentice, who continues his master's work as a matter of course, and no break is felt. It may be a son who assisted him during his life, and steps into his father's shoes without any question. If ever there was a *natural law* (in the jural sense)—a law adopted unconsciously from pure convenience—this surely is one. All that is required is a recognition and fossilisation of this idea by law and custom, and we have the hereditary trade castes of India recruited naturally by children, and artificially by adoption (apprenticeship). The only relic of this artificial succession in this country is the rule of succession to the crown and to titles of nobility—hereditary rulers and leaders.[1] The constitutional idea of ruling through ministers, which has hitherto worked so admirably, will prevent the theoretical question being made even a matter of discussion. I have already referred to the House of Lords as a legislative body.[2] But the members of that House have other important social duties to perform, and it is interesting to note how, by a *natural law* of succession, they succeed to all the social rights and obligations of their predecessors. Even the Lord Mayor of London, or the Lord Provost of Glasgow, besides succeeding to the honours and rights of his office, succeeds to the obligation of paying many

---

[1] As to how the law of succession to titles came to be rule of succession in property in this country, see Maine's *Ancient Law*, p. 237, and *History of Institutions*, p. 202.

[2] P. 193, *supra*.

thousands of pounds *in voluntary subscriptions*. These considerations point to the organic relations of *personal* rights and duties of individuals in society.

But we observe the same in property. Wealth accumulated is a means of enabling a person to display his personality. When an owner dies, some one *must* take up his property if it is tangible. And the possession of property implies obligations. Two houses stand side by side. The lower one must receive the water flowing from the higher. Access to the one can only be got through the other. Such obligations *run with the land*. Whoever is owner must be liable personally to make them good, and so mere possession implies obligation. Such cases point to organic relations *in respect of property* between successive proprietors, apart altogether from the question of death.[1]

Laws of succession may be regarded (1) from the point of view of the state, or society which recognises rights, as representing the universal; (2) from the point of view of the predecessor who may be deceased; (3) from the point of view of the individual or individuals who succeed; and (4) with reference to the rights which are transferred from the predecessor to his successor. These are generally material rights of person and property (implying obligations), and in general they are translated into an expression of relation of the successor to persons to whom the predecessor was related. If we view succession entirely from one of

---

[1] Holmes, *The Common Law*, p. 353.

those points of view, without keeping the others at the same time before us, we shall get only a partial and distorted aspect of the subject. The only possible means of avoiding the errors which are so common in discussing this topic, is to remember that those elements are combined in point of fact, and each must receive due weight in any attempt to connect succession with other legal institutions. As to the order of discussion of the subject, it is advisable to commence with *testate* succession, as this is a deliberate conscious attempt to heal the wound to society caused by death. The justification of this order will appear in the course of my discussion.

And (first) we must reject such theories as found testate succession on the right of property in the deceased. This is the theory of Grotius,[1] and the common English theory, and that which has most profoundly affected English legislation on the subject.[2] The assumption made by those who adopt this theory is, that a *mortis causâ* conveyance is exactly the same as a donation *inter vivos*. Now this is not so. In the latter case the person conveying does not lose the power of enjoyment, while he does so in the case of a testamentary conveyance. The right of disposal is undoubtedly a

[1] *De J. B. et P.*, II., vi, 14, 1.
[2] See Ahrens, vol. ii., p. 298, where the supporters of this view are referred to, and the subject fully discussed. This is also Prof. Lorimer's view, *Institutes of Law* (1st ed.), p. 181 (2nd ed.), p. 234. Compare Puffendorff, *De Jure Naturæ et Gentium*, bk. iv., chap. x., and Barbeyrac's notes thereon.

result of the right of property. But how far does this go? I have already pointed out that a man has no right to give away his whole property and leave himself an object of charity in the world, and yet we must maintain this if we say that a testamentary conveyance is a transaction *inter vivos*. Writers adopting this view have no doubt been misled by the fact, to which I shall allude presently, that in early Roman law *mortis causâ* conveyances, as we understand them, were unknown, and also that in Scotland a conveyance of heritable (real) property was unknown till 1868. Before that date it was necessary that a testator should convey *de presenti*. And when we consider the old law against death-bed deeds repealed in 1871, it is evident that a truly *mortis causâ* conveyance of heritage was, if not prohibited, discouraged by the law as far as possible. In practice, however, lawyers overcame those restrictions by granting absolute conveyances, with a reservation of life-rent, and a dispensation with delivery of the deed. As soon as this device was hit upon, we had *mortis causâ* settlements in fact, and the Titles to Land Act of 1868 only logically carried out what was the common practice by changing the form of conveyance into one purely testamentary— another example of the amendment of legal forms by legal fiction prior to legislation. But if we take *mortis causâ* donation, where the corporeal transference is complete, we shall see it is essentially different from an *inter vivos* conveyance. A man conveys his property *mortis causâ*, or by will, for the very reason that he can no longer use it. He gives it away because he is no longer proprietor. If he could keep it for ever he would, and it is very much against his will that he parts with it. A man often dies to all intents and purposes long before the breath leaves his body, and so among the Hindoos old men were expected to retire into a private religious life. Our own laws recognised that fact in the law of death-bed, and the English law of Mortmain and the Roman laws, which forbade men to squander their property in prospect of death, to the prejudice of their heirs, all point in the same direction. There is an essential difference between an unconditional conveyance by a man in health and vigour, and a conveyance by a man who lets a thing drop from his fingers because he can no longer hold it. We may admit that figuratively in both cases, the one proprietor expires, *quâ* proprietor, before the other comes into life; but there is this essential difference that in the case of conveyance *intuitu mortis*, the *person* as well as the proprietor expires, and he can never be proprietor again, and he knows and feels this too. The mere fact of the breath leaving a man's body has little to do with the question. Take the two following cases:—A man, after making a gift of a ring to a friend, suddenly falls down and expires. The man was apparently in perfect health, and if he had lived for fifty years could not have revoked that gift. Again, suppose a man dying, gives a ring to his friend *mortis causâ*, or tells him to take it in the event of his death. Here the recovery of the man would revoke the gift. If the man dies, just as he hands over the ring, we have a case apparently similar to the last, but only *apparently*. And the distinction is this, that the former conveyance was made without reference to death; the latter was caused by death, and but for death would never have taken place. Barbeyrac quotes a passage from Pindar, where he very candidly states that it is "very detestable" for a dying man to see his wealth passing to another owner.[1]

It is objected that a testamentary deed refers to the future, and it is only by a fiction it can be made *de presenti*. But a will should always be executed with reference to the state of a man's affairs at his death, and when a great change takes place in his affairs, every sensible man makes a new will. Thus a rational will, instead of being a future deed, will always be the most reasonable and wise provisions the deceased would have made if he could have given a clear judgment in *articulo mortis*. We must beware of confusing a will with a contract, to pay or convey at a future time certain to come; and much more with a contract which, though present in form, may have to be performed at a future date. As to this, it is sufficient to point out that in an *inter*

---

[1] ἐπεὶ πλοῦτος ὁ λαχὼν ποιμένα
ἐπακτὸν ἀλλότριον,
θνάσκοντι στυγερώτατος.
                Pindar, *Olymp.* 10, 106.

vivos transaction, which is not to be executed at a future date, the present is of the essence of the transaction, while in a *mortis causâ* transaction the future is of the essence. In the former case the transaction would be carried out at once if it were possible, and in any event at the date fixed. In the latter the performance is put off as long as possible, and, as far as the granter of the deed is concerned, may never come, because "*nemo tam senex est, quin putet se annum vivere posse;*" and if he could so arrange, the period of execution would never come. In obligations undertaken at a date long distant, or which in modern law do not fall by the death of the obligant, there is implied a highly developed law of succession. *If the estate of the obligant is solvent*, his heir undertakes liability; and if it is not so, the obligation will rank on the estate as a debt. If there is no estate the obligation is valueless. It is, therefore, reasoning in a circle to explain the law of succession by saying that every obligation may possibly be carried out after death. Such a statement presupposes the law of succession. We are, therefore, compelled to accept the emphatic statement of Hegel that "the mere direct caprice of the deceased cannot be made the ground of the right of testing."[1] Before leaving this I may note Leibnitz's most ingenious theory that as the soul is immortal, the deceased still continues proprietor, and we, therefore, pay deference

[1] *Naturrecht*, § 180. See Trendelenburg, *Naturrecht*, p. 306, and foll.

to his wishes expressed in a will. But Gundling's objection seems fatal—"Non constat utrum anima sit damnata an secus: quis autem damnatæ animæ voluntatem censeat exequendam?"[1] It must be admitted, however, that there is some historical foundation for Leibnitz's view. The modern will seems to owe its origin to the church; and its principal object was to make provision for the saying of masses for the soul of the deceased.[2]

For the same reasons we must reject theories[3] which found the rules of *intestate* succession on the presumed intentions of the deceased if he had made a will. This case is *a fortiori* of the last. If we do not respect a man's will merely on the ground of his being proprietor, much less do we consult his presumed wishes when he is dead. He can do nothing for his successors. All they can do for him is to bury him, "for we brought nothing into this world, and it is certain we can carry nothing out." The only point of dispute appears to be as to the rate at which his mortal remains should be oxidised. It is even a question if he is entitled to bequeath his body for scientific purposes. The division of his property is the concern of his successors, and not of the deceased. This is recognised by the Movable Succession (Scotland) Act of 1855, as well as by the

[1] Ahrens, ii., p. 301; Puffendorf, *Le Droit de la Nature, &c.*—Note by Barbeyrac, iv., 10, 4, n. (4).

[2] Maine, *Law and Custom*, p. 79.

[3] *E.g.*, Grotius, *de J. B. et P.*, ii., 7, 3—criticised by Bynkershoek, *Observationes Juris Romani*, ii., 1.

English Statute of Distributions. These acts were intended to make a more just distribution of the estate of a deceased person, and the whole scope of the acts has reference to the claims of the survivors, and not to the presumed wishes of the deceased.

We must also reject the old theory which made a man's property at his death a *res nullius*, which the first occupier would then be entitled to step in and appropriate. The objections to this theory are historical. It does not explain why the nearest relatives are preferred. But it has been observed that there are traces of this idea in the Roman *possessio pro herede*, and the custom which is said to prevail in Rome when a cardinal dies, of the common people rushing into his house and taking away anything that is not previously set aside.[1] The first interference of the state in point of form might be to protect this occupier—to prohibit others from interfering with him, in order merely to preserve "the king's peace." But, as in other cases, this external form must ultimately yield to forms which attempt to determine the substantial rights of parties on some other ground.

In point of fact our modern law of succession has taken its rise in the family.[2] In early times the family was a corporation, and there would be no change in the possession. The property would be the same, and the members

---

[1] Zoepfl, *Rechtsphilosophie*, p. 212.
[2] Mr. Morgan shows this connection of the family and succession to have been universal.—*Ancient Society*, pp. 75, 526, &c.

would have the same relation to it as they had during the lifetime of their ancestor. This has been abundantly illustrated by Sir Henry Maine. And so at an earlier stage, when children were regarded as related only to their mother, at her death her property, being ownerless, would go to her tribe or her children. But as we have seen already, the true modern family only appears when the children are recognised as belonging to the father, even though it is merely as property. A fine example of how naturally this state of society would arise is furnished by the Scotch case of *Aitchison v. Aitchison*, in 1877,[1] where a family carried on a confectionery business for a great number of years, just as their father had done, and continued to live together without dividing their father's means. In such a case there is no real change of possession. Each member of the family is a *pro indiviso* proprietor. When he dies his rights accresce to the rest. In the modern Scottish rules of intestate succession we have still traces of this common-property idea. The *communio bonorum* is expressly abolished, but when a paterfamilias dies his wife gets one-third, or one-half, if there are no children—the *jus relictæ*—the share which she presumably enjoyed during her husband's life. The children, in like manner, get another third under the name of *legitim;* and lastly, the third, or half, which the deceased presumably enjoyed, and significantly called *the dead's part*, is the share of which alone he is entitled to dispose by will. The widow's

[1] Court of Session Cases (4th ser.) iv., 899.

third, under the English Statute of Distributions, is evidently borrowed from the same source. I have already pointed out that, while recent legislation has tended to break up the family, by making the wife independent of her husband, the Married Woman's Property (Scotland) Act of 1881 has created a new family with the wife at its head, by giving the husband and the children, on her decease, the same rights as she and they would have on his decease.

A law of succession in its primary aspect is an attempt to reconstruct the family when broken by the death of the paterfamilias. This is accomplished by the appointment of guardians (tutors and curators) to the children, and in earlier times to the wife also. We sometimes find an attempt to anticipate death by breaking up the family during the father's lifetime, as in the parable of the Prodigal Son given by St. Luke. Among the Hindus it appears customary for the father to retire into religious life.[1] This is a means of obviating the necessity of a law of succession; but it is apparent it can only apply where sons have grown to manhood, and it cannot apply to infant children. It is a similar principle which applies in the contracts of modern mercantile firms which provide for the capital of a retiring or insolvent partner being paid out. When an aged man retires, and leaves his sons in a business, under an obligation gradually to pay out his capital, it is thus only another phase of the law of succession.

[1] Maine, *Law and Custom*, p. 122.

The distribution of an estate, as I have observed, is a matter which belongs to the survivors and to the state, and not to the deceased. Property, as we have seen, enables the individual to realise his personality, and if a person has been in joint possession of property, it would be a grievous wrong to deprive him of it, on the death of another, who was nominally sole proprietor, but really only a joint owner. The state, therefore, divides the property among (1) those who stand in need of property for physical subsistence, as infant children and aged parents; and (2) those who will most miss the presence of the deceased, and who in his lifetime presumably enjoyed his property along with him. It is evidently a mistake to put the rights of infant children and foris-familiated children on the same basis. In the case of helpless dependents the state may impose an obligation on the heir who takes the estate—a sort of implied *fidei commissum*—to support them in so far as he is benefited. Such is the rule as to the support of unmarried sisters by an heir, and this is truly a part of the law of succession. But the rules of distribution among foris-familiated children and strangers rest on a similar ground, which is not so much the necessities of the persons in themselves, as the necessity of disposing of unoccupied property. And here we may conceive the two theories of the family occupation of property, and the occupation of the deceased's property as a *res nullius* to coincide. The state divides the property. The near relatives of the deceased are probably present at his death. As the individual members of the family recede from the deceased in relationship, the probability of intimate intercourse is more distant, and the public can fairly claim a larger share of the property. Hence legacy and succession duties, which are merely a means of giving the state a share of the succession, vary from nothing in the case of a husband or wife, to ten per cent. in the case of strangers. The propriety of dividing property as widely as possible explains why a share is given to descendants of deceased representatives. But this idea is modified in practice by feudal traditions, and by the transmission of titles of rank. In such cases the association of the transmission of land along with the title taken from it, as we shall see, gives rise to the law of primogeniture and the exclusion of females. We may here note that the inheriting of property carries with it the inheritance of debts and obligations. The state here creates a new obligation in the person of the heir, in consequence of his acceptance of his ancestor's property,[1] with the obvious exception of cases where the obligation is entirely personal, such as painting a picture, or performing a part in a play.

It has been proposed to exclude collaterals from succession, and allow it only to ascendants and descendants.[2] But there is often as much reason for the succession of a brother or a sister as for that of a foris-familiated child.

[1] See the Scotch Act, 1695, cap. 24, as an example of this.
[2] Mill's *Political Economy*, II., ii., 3.

Cousins might be excluded, or put on the same footing as bastard children by the present law. That is to say, they might apply to the crown for a gift on good grounds being shown, such as that the petitioner and the deceased had lived in family, and the petitioner was dependent on the deceased for maintenance.

The interest of the state in disposing of ownerless property is shown by the provisions of the French Code and codes founded on it as to the property of absent persons, and more recently by the Presumption of Life Limitation (Scotland) Act, 1881. It is highly inexpedient that property should be allowed to go to waste, while persons who could use it beneficially are perhaps in need of it. Hence the state gives them the present enjoyment of the fruits, under certain guarantees as to the substance of the property itself, if it should be claimed; and, after the lapse of a certain period, it gives them the complete rights of owners.

The ancient family, as we have seen, has expanded into the state, and this conception has now given way to the idea that the human race is one family. The law of succession has progressed in a corresponding manner. The state in succession has thus come into the place of the family. In legal language the crown is now *ultimus hæres*, in default of heirs. But even here the state implicitly recognises a trust, by making a gift to illegitimate children, or those who are otherwise incapable of succeeding by the common rules of succession. But the most interesting illustration of this fact is to be found in the extension of the idea of succession to relations between members of different states, in the application of the law of domicile, and the rule *mobilia sequuntur personam*. Here not only the particular state to which the deceased belonged, but all civilised states, join in the reconstruction of the particular family. Instead of each state distributing the funds among its own citizens, it allows them to be collected and sent to a foreign country for distribution among foreigners.[1] German civilians extend this principle even to land, and Savigny pushes the rule so far as to recognise a foreign fisc, in case the deceased died without heirs.[2]

The view of the right of succession above indicated justifies the doctrine of *ipso jure* investiture, which has long been recognised in England, but only recently in Scotland. The doctrine is embodied in the brocard "*mortuus sasit vivum.*" The right of property, which is vested in this manner may be as real as that formed by first occupation, if the proprietor is *sui juris* and enters on active possession. But the doctrine just referred to goes much further, and gives the right of property to unconscious infants, who are incapable of conscious possession, and to persons absent who perhaps

---

[1] Must England be made an exception? See the decision of the House of Lords in the case of *Orr Ewing* (Decr., 1883).
[2] Guthrie's *Savigny* (2nd ed.), p. 285.

die before they are aware of their rights, and therefore have neither the *animus habendi* nor the requisite *factum*. Is the doctrine of *ipso jure* investiture therefore unsound? By no means. We attribute the right of property to such persons as the infant or the absentee as a matter of convenience and merely by analogy. What we really do is to make his person another centre for the distribution of the succession. It is essential to the well-being of society that property should be as widely distributed as possible, since persons can only display their energies and powers through it. With this view society distributes the deceased's estate the moment the breath leaves his body, in order that as little loss as possible may be felt by the community. If actual possession were necessary to complete a title to the succession, then it might happen that the circle in which the property should be divided would become gradually narrower; but as the law now stands, the circle is a perpetually widening one. Our legislature has thus perhaps unconsciously adopted communistic principles, but to this extent, at least, their operation must be highly beneficial.

What, then, is the position of testate succession? If succession is the concern of the state, why should it not lay down a rigid rule, and compel every one to obey it? And why, on the contrary, is such deference paid to the wishes of a dead man, embodied in a testament? As Sir Henry Maine points out, our notion of a will is quite different from the ancient Roman one. With the Romans it was used for the purpose of naming and pointing out the legal heir; with us it is intended to modify and change the regular rule of succession. The Roman testator was not allowed to disinherit his heir. The modern testator has absolute power, except within certain narrow limits. But though they appear to be so different in their aim, the result is the same. It is the state which regulates and divides the succession. The Romans pointed out the natural heir and protected him. The moderns assume that each individual in the state who has amassed a fortune, or who has the power of holding it rationally, is a competent judge as to who should have the power of possessing it after his death. The state asks his opinion. He expresses it in the form of a will. It in general pays so much respect to his opinion, that it will refuse to interfere with it. But in order to have a reliable judgment, the testator must be free from the influence of fraud and violence. He must be sane, and in possession of his faculties, and the test of sanity which is required for making a will is much more strict than that applied in criminal law.[1] In Scotch law the legislative powers of the deceased are restricted in movables to the one-third or one-half, called the dead's part—the share which we have seen is set free by the owner's death. In England, however, the freedom of testing is much greater. The idea of property is carried much further than in Scotland, where we have still a tradition of the

[1] Maudsley, *Responsibility in Mental Disease*, p. 111.

common-property idea, which was the basis of the Roman law.[1]

Looking at a will from this point of view, the making of one appears to be an important public duty. It is a right which every person enjoys not merely because he is proprietor, but much more because he is a person, endowed with rational will, and a judgment which the state can entrust with legislative functions. If the ancient *arrogatio*, done in presence of the assembled *comitia*, was a legislative act, no less is every will now-a-days equivalent to an act of parliament laying down the rule of succession for the special case in question. It is such considerations which justified the recently abolished differentiation of rates of duties on testate and intestate succession, to compel a man as far as possible to make a will. There is always a possibility of the ordinary rules of succession being inapplicable to special cases, but if a person makes a will, there is a strong presumption in favour of his judgment. It is the experience of every practising lawyer that intestate succession is often unsatisfactory. There seems always to be some claimant who has a legal, but no equitable claim, and

---

[1] Mr. Digby quotes an example of a will of *folcland* in England, in the form of a nomination of an heir, and a request to the king that he would allow him to hold the property.—*History of the Law of Real Property*, p. 7. This is the form adopted for testaments dealing with moneys payable by friendly societies, deposits in savings banks, &c. See The Provident Nominations Act (1883), 46 and 47 Vict., cap. 47, §§ 5 and 8.

who would have been passed over in a will. Many people get money by intestate succession who would be better without it, and to whom no one would have left it by will. It has sometimes happened that a sudden windfall of fortune has transformed an honest and useful day-labourer into a dissipated and pernicious idler. A judicious and justly framed will should, therefore, carry out the Roman ideal, and favour *the true heir*, instead of disinheriting him. It is only where a will is arbitrary, and is an abuse of the privilege, that it can give rise to heart-burnings and disputes.

The law of entail is an extension of the right of testing. It had its origin in personal vanity—in a desire to attain immortality. It is the modern counterpart of the ancient Egyptian practice of embalming the body of the deceased. Entails were only recognised by the legislature on false theories as to the nature and rights of property, and from the moment the law was recognised, lawyers set themselves to defeat it by every means which their ingenuity could invent. And lastly, the legislature has stepped in and has been gradually relaxing the fetters imposed on property by this means. The principal objections to the law of entail are the following : (First) It attaches undue importance to the wishes and aspirations of testators. It recognises deeds which go quite beyond the legitimate functions of testaments, because men can only pass a judgment on people whom they know. Further than that their views are worthless, and the state is not bound to pay any deference to them. Thus the provision of the Entail Amendment (Scotland) Act of 1868, restricting the life-rents of movables which may be created to persons in life at the date of the deeds creating them, is quite in accordance with the views I have laid down. But (secondly) an entail is an insult to the successors of the entailer. It limits their personality and reduces them to the status of infants. At the best it is an attempt to create a permanent endowment for persons who may turn out worthless members of society. If there were no fears as to their worthlessness, an entail would be unnecessary. But the entailer cannot trust his posterity to remember and perpetuate his good name, and he therefore trusts to his land to do it. A common charitable institution, since it affects a wider class, often does good. But when we see the abuses which creep in even there, and what unworthy characters often receive the bounty of the testator, we must admit how much greater is the danger when the object of charity is a single individual.[1] (Thirdly) Closely connected with this is the objection that entails are a wrong to the state. The property which should enable the members of the state to energise is thus cut off from commerce. The state loses not only the full benefit of the services of the heir of entail, but also of those who are debarred from

---

[1] If out-door relief under the Poor-Law Act pauperises the muscle, entailed estates pauperise the brain of the country. Both might therefore be abolished in one Act.

utilising their full energy from want of property. Property is not only a result but also a condition of personality, and every obstacle put in the way of human beings acquiring property prevents some one from attaining perfection as a human being, and inflicts injury on the human race. The law of entail, which owes its existence merely to a false analogy, is thus unsound in its origin and pernicious in its effects; and it is satisfactory to see that the struggle against it, which has been carried on so long both by common law and statute, will soon result in its complete abolition.

Many of these objections apply to the tying up of property in mortmain for particular objects. I have already indicated that it would be more satisfactory if public institutions could be maintained by subscription or taxation (legalised subscription) than by endowment.[1] In the former case the public, either directly or through Parliament, has more control over the institution. In the latter it may become a close corporation living on its property and defying public opinion. Wills leaving endowments should, therefore, always make provision for their revisal from time to time. Our present tendency is to show too great deference to foolish wills.

The law of primogeniture and the preference of males over females in succession in land are generally associated with the law of entail. It has been attempted to justify these rules on the ground that men have more power and

[1] P. 144, *supra*.

capacity than women, and the eldest son has more power and capacity than the younger ones. But this explanation fails when we apply it to the case of a son of an eldest son excluding his uncles, or the daughters of an eldest son succeeding in the same circumstances. We cannot explain those rules without reference to their history. As an historical fact, property in land is a very late idea, and as Sir Henry Maine has shown, the rules of succession referred to have been borrowed from the rules of succession to titles. This may enable us to see some reason in primogeniture and the exclusion of females—which are an entail *ex lege*—as well as in entail proper which arises *ex contractu* or *ex testamento*. If the law of succession is to repair the loss inflicted upon a community by the loss of one of its members, then these rules would be necessary for the nobility and holders of hereditary titles, otherwise we might have a very poor nobleman succeeding a very wealthy one. The estate might be divided or sold, and there would be no continuity in the position of the holders of the title. Such considerations have in recent times weighed with persons to whom titles were offered. If the younger members of the family get a good education, and a profession, or a provision of some kind, they may have a more enviable position than the eldest son. It would be most unfair to him to give him the burden of keeping up a position, and give him only such a provision as his younger brothers and sisters, who had no similar position to sustain.

Paine's tirades against primogeniture,[1] apart from his attacks on the House of Lords itself, are thus for the most part out of place. If the rule in its present form were abolished, it would be necessary either to make a special provision for the eldest son, if an hereditary aristocracy continued to exist, or it might be found necessary to enforce more strictly a rule that a peer who did not possess a certain income should be suspended from sitting in the House of Peers.[2] The law of entail is a proof that the right of testing would obviate many of those disadvantages. As for commoners, it is so very unusual for them to die intestate, that the law of primogeniture can hardly cause any inconvenience. But to adopt a law which would compel subdivision would be absurd. In France the rule of subdivision is evidently a part of a system in a highly centralised state, which cannot trust the freedom of its individual citizens. But in this country, where each citizen has a share in imperial and municipal legislation, his legislative powers are completed by the right of testing or legislating for his family.

It is interesting to note simultaneously with the development of the interest of the state in succession, the gradual exclusion of the rights of the church. In ancient Roman Paganism and mediæval Catholicism the claims of the church were paramount, but now the church is altogether ousted by the state, and the last vestige of its

[1] *Rights of Man* (9th ed.), part i., p. 45.
[2] Stephen's *Commentaries*, vol. ii., p. 617.

former authority in Scotland was obliterated by the merging of the duties of the Commissary Clerk in those of the Sheriff Clerk by the Sheriff Courts Act of 1876.

In passing I would observe that in the law of succession we have the four moments to which I have so often referred :—(1) A *de facto* existence of a person, who must survive the testator or predecessor for a moment at least; (2) consciousness, which is absolutely presumed; (3) the state; and (4) a right conferred by the state, or recognised by it—even apart from the actual consciousness of the individual in certain cases.

In conclusion, I would point out that we cannot now regard succession as merely a transference of *property* from one man to others. Property, as we have seen, is merely a form in which personality clothes itself. We can no more regard the man who enjoys the wealth of a dead man as his "successor" than we can regard a man as the successor of the sheep and oxen he eats, or the peasants who eat the grain which grows on the fields of Waterloo or Gravelotte as the successors of the soldiers who fell there. Modern law strives to make the law of succession a succession to rights and obligations—a reconstruction of *relations*,[1] of which property is merely an accidental concomitant. This is the explanation of the fact alluded to above, that laws of succession, such as

---

[1] Is this not the import of the old form of assignation which "assigned the person into" the right, and "surrogated and substituted" him for the assigner?

primogeniture and the exclusion of females, which are primarily laws of succession to *offices*, become subsequently laws of succession to *property*.¹ And further, in the reverence paid to a man's will for centuries after his death, and in the rights attributed to future generations of beneficiaries, we see another example of the recognised dignity of person in the individual.

In this view the law of succession is only a phase of a wider movement which has been going on from time immemorial even between nations. A nation like England must change, but there is a unity in its history for many centuries. The succession here is the same as that of any living organism. But nations may die, like ancient Greece, or Rome, or Judea, and leave behind them a rich heritage to be taken up by other nations in the world. The bodies politic are decomposed, and their names only are left. But their literature, their art, their laws, their religion, embodied in external forms, have become the property of other nations, and have awakened in them a new life. There may be nations which possess such things in the same sense as the earth, in which treasures of art are buried, possesses them. But the true possessors are the true successors—those whose spirit finds some expression of its inmost thought in such remains of antiquity—those who feel themselves at one with the past, and yet look forward to the goal of human

---

¹ See Coulanges, *La Cité Antique*, bk. ii., chap. vii., as to the relation between worship and the transmission of property.

perfection; who not only reverently preserve the remains of the past, but hand down to their posterity a still more glorious heritage. In its lowest form it is a transmission of mere physical existence, with a gradually accumulating store of instincts and habits. The transmission of accumulated material wealth indicates a higher stage. In its highest development the succession becomes spiritual, until it appears to transcend material things. The most precious bequest to posterity is a higher civilisation than the predecessor received. Law, however, deals with this movement only between individuals, and small groups of individuals, and in general only with reference to property and material rights. Mankind, in development and as coexisting, is a unity. International law strives completely to formulate the unity of mankind in *space;* the law of succession strives partially to do the same in *time*.

LECTURE XI.

PERSON.

WHAT is the idea of right? In the five preceding lectures I have been examining the answer, that rights and obligations spring from the relations of men. We have seen men are related as individuals, then in families, clans, tribes, and states; and finally, as an organic whole, in the conception of humanity, in which each individual is both ruler and ruled—both master and servant. We have seen each of those groups in succession asserting and enforcing the rights of the individual, either against other groups or in relation to his own group. We might thus construct a complete code of positive law by showing what rights the state or humanity—I might almost say the *jus gentium*—will *recognise*. But there is a converse side. We may regard the individual as expanding and bursting the fetters of the lower groups—freeing himself from the family and appealing to the state, rebelling against the state and appealing to humanity. And in this way we might make a code of the rights *claimed* by the individual which would correspond exactly, like the counterpart of a seal, to the former code constructed from the side of the universal. The question is not finally answered by saying rights spring from relations, because a further question suggests itself. Is there not something *in the nature of the individual* which generates law? Yes; the individuals must be self-conscious *persons,* and this element is as essential as the relation. The persons are nothing apart from the relation, but the relation is nothing unless those related are persons.

We may regard the group as *the form*, and the individuals as *the matter*. The group is merely the shell with which the living organism within has clothed itself. The human spirit has recorded its progress in material things —buildings, literature, works of art; and similarly in the history of the material rights of person and property, and in the history of the family and the state, we may read the history of the human spirit. The history of law is thus a struggle between form and matter. The person in his striving after freedom would destroy the family, allow free divorce, obliterate states, abolish property. On the other hand, the abstract forms of the state, the family and property, tend to crush the individual out of existence. It is only a living organism which can practically reconcile this contradiction. The view which has sometimes prevailed is, that man is an existence with certain rights tacked on, or attributed to him. Personality in such a view may be merely implicitly recognised, but it is apt to be regarded as merely the *unity* of the rights or as the *cause* of them. But it is in truth both the beginning and the end of all right.

Law starts from the self-consciousness of the individual, and it cannot rest satisfied till the whole human race, including each individual member, becomes conscious of its unity.[1]

The idea of person, though implicit in the whole progress of law, is always the last to be formulated. This process of self-realisation has been going on both in the race and in the individual. It is a struggle of nations and individuals for freedom, self-government, autonomy. In municipal law this is the peculiar value of the history of Roman law. For example, in Rome the plebeians had no *connubium* with the patricians, and later the Latins had none with the *cives Romani;* in fact we may read the whole history of Roman law as a struggle for a wider meaning of the word "person," which only reached something like our modern idea in the days of Justinian. Again, in old German law there was a doctrine as to misalliances similar to the Roman one just referred to. The German serfs, in the times of the *Leges Barbarorum,* could not enter into the contract of deposit, and in very recent times the privilege of drawing a bill of exchange was restricted to special privileged classes,[2] while in our own country, down to about the beginning of this

---

[1] It is only the other day (November, 1883) that the Chinese government issued a manifesto to the world that France was wrong in the quarrel then pending. Truly a revolution since 1856, but it is a little humiliating that a European state should be the aggressor.

[2] Zœpfl, *Rechtsphilosophie,* p. 94.

century, we had miners astricted, like slaves, to the soil. Until within the last two years, the legal ideas which regulated the relation of husband and wife were originally drawn from the law of property. Again, we may find an illustration of the same progress in the history of our constitution. The Revolution settled finally the question as to the king being the state, while the Catholic Emancipation and Jewish Disabilities Acts, the Reform Acts of 1832 and 1867-68, and the Naturalisation Act of 1870, each gave a wider signification to the word "citizen." In like manner we have the creation of the new Germanic Empire, and the kingdom of Italy, and the recent movements in the East of Europe, all illustrating the same tendency of nations to become conscious of unity, and realise their freedom. Law is thus a realisation of free-will. It is the idea of freedom clothing itself in a sensuous form, which, in the individual, becomes the idea of *person*, and, in the group of individuals, becomes that of *the state*.

As this is a process, it is quite incompetent to arrest the individual or the group at any stage, and analyse this entity as if it contained its whole nature. This is what Austin has done on the universal side. He takes modern law as a complete entity, and analyses it without asking how it has arrived at this stage, and so the historical jurists have been compelled to reject or modify his theoretical conclusions. It is just as fallacious to analyse psychologically the individual consciousness, and stop when we have discovered that certain ideas are found in it. A full-grown man is more than a mere being now and here: he is a product of past education. From his birth, and even before it, he has been moulded into his present shape.[1] The child derives its notion of right from the persons who educate it. Just as a child becomes rational because it is addressed as a rational being before it has become such, so it gradually becomes conscious of its rights. He comes of age; he is then a person *sui juris*. His will is a law to himself. He has now identified right with what before appeared to be merely might; and later, as a law-abiding citizen and himself the father of a family, he is prepared to enforce his will on his own children, and so prepare them to take his place as members of the community. It is therefore too late to examine his consciousness for information as to the individual nature. Exception must thus be taken to the method of the analytical jurists as a means of reaching the idea of law. We might as well cut up a body in order to find the life in it, for the life disappears in the analysis. Their work can only be preliminary to the study of the living organism.

Personality is the legal aspect of a self-conscious being. To affirm that any being has rights is to affirm that he is a person, for a sensuous being is a person by being able to have and to be conscious of rights. Personality is

[1] See on this subject Mr. Bagehot's *Physics and Politics*.

the common ground (the *titulus generalis*) implied in all acquisition of particular rights. A man's personality does not consist in his reason or in his will alone. It is the unity of his body and spirit. But it is only through his body that his right can be displayed, though his body is more than a mere condition of personality or substratum to which it is attached. The right of personality is the consequence of the fact of existence as a rational being in the world of sense, and to be a person is the potential condition by nature of every human being as such. In positive law personality may be treated as a potentiality of having rights, because it is presupposed in the acquisition of every special right. But in truth it is much more than a potentiality, it is really a formal legal condition—a *status* in the eye of the law. The moments which are present in the conception of a person are thus—(1) a physical existence in space and time; (2) consciousness of the fact, which in earlier years is supplied by the consciousness of the parent or guardian; (3) the coexistence of other similar beings in an organic unity—the state, or it may be other states in a case of intervention;[1] and (4) implicit or explicit recognition by them in their corporate capacity of those elements.[2]

[1] See pp. 91, and 234, *supra*.

[2] It may be questioned whether it is not possible for a person to exist in relation to things without the coexistence of other persons, but it is evident he could not be a person in the legal sense. The theological doctrine of the Trinity shows the speculative difficulty felt in conceiving a person unrelated to *other persons* as equals.

In positive law personality has a content in the physical body, and the rights which flow from its existence. These have been alluded to in a former lecture.[1] In an early age the fact of unconscious being implied no right to exist. Infanticide was not only a custom, but it was a *legal* one. In such a state of society it might be a crime to kill a full-grown conscious man, and a duty to kill a weak or deformed infant. The change in our modern ideas is due partly to Christianity, and partly to Germanic tradition, and it illustrates clearly that law (in the jural sense) is something more than a mere statement of a physical fact.[2] When we trace the stages of the physical existence of a human being, we find he is now recognised by the law, long before he appears in the world as an independent existence. Formerly in English law, though a child *in utero* could not be technically " murdered," the crime of procuring abortion was more severely punished when the woman was "quick with child."[3] The execution of a capital sentence will, in

---

[1] Lect. v.

[2] Trendelenburg, *Naturrecht*, p. 201. As to the amazing amount of infanticide which prevails in this country, see Jevon's *Methods of Social Reform*, p. 157. It might be plausibly argued that in legalising infanticide we should only be following *a law of nature*.

[3] Russell on *Crimes* (3rd ed.), vol. i., pp. 485, 671. Recent legislation looks at this crime from the point of view of the woman only. Perhaps this was found a more effectual mode of protecting the child. It will be remembered that this question as to the personality of a child is raised in *Tristram Shandy*, where it is discussed whether a child can be baptized before it is born.

some cases, be deferred in order to save the life of a potential human being. A child *in utero* has rights, or at least a succession will be kept in suspense until it has been seen whether it will come to maturity. There is here no self-consciousness, but the law recognises and attributes the rights, and maintains them by physical force in order to create personality, which will appear later. After birth the rights become more definite, though the right of custody of the child is discussed not very differently from that of a thing. But the state may interfere in certain circumstances to secure its due physical and intellectual development, as in regulating which spouse should have the possession of it in case of divorce. Again, by our Education Acts children, as members of the state, are protected against worthless parents, to whom their existence is an accident, or an intolerable burden. As the child progresses, his rights emerge by positive law at various fixed dates. The law recognises the change which popular language marks by changing the pronoun. The child ceases to be a *thing*. At an early age the law vindicates for him the right of elementary education, and until the age of thirteen, and in some cases longer, he can claim education and aliment from those who brought him into the world. But up to the age of minority (in our law, fourteen in the case of boys, twelve in girls) he has no true personality, and hence the maxim, *Tutor datur personæ.* Any legal act is done for him as if he were entirely unconscious of rights. But the process of education proceeds. At another epoch, varying in different systems from eighteen to twenty-five, and even thirty, he gradually acquires greater rights and powers until he reaches majority. He is then *sui juris*—autonomous: he has his rights complete, and he is conscious of them, and the law recognises and vindicates his condition and status. He is then a *Person*. In the intermediate stage of minority, up to the age of twenty-one, his reason is growing, and he has the assistance of legal guardians, while he acts in his own name. In England the system is more rigid, and the process of development not so gradual; while in France we may say a man does not attain freedom until he is thirty, for up to that age he cannot marry without consent of his parents or certain relatives. Now, throughout this process we see that the two elements of a subjective claim and an objective recognition of the claim are present. The presence of physical qualities *de facto* without recognition by law is useless. The legal notion without the *de facto* existence is void. The recognition by the state may, however, be really implicit; because, as I have observed, the development of abstract personality comes late. At an early stage an individual would be represented in the law-courts by the *paterfamilias* or *patronus*, his person being sunk in the *familia* or *gens*, but as soon as he is allowed a *persona standi* he becomes a person. This is explicit recognition.

I may further illustrate the process of the development of the idea of person from the history of the disabilities of women. They may have all the physical qualities required in a man, but the law denies them rights, in some cases absolutely, and in others if they are married. By the laws of Manu a woman was subject to her sons after the death of her husband. The Grecian women were kept in tutelage; but under the Roman Empire women, according to Mr. Lecky, arrived at a point of freedom and dignity which they subsequently lost, and have never altogether regained.[1] But in our own day we have seen a distinct advance in the notion of person as applied to this sex. Instead of a woman's person being sunk in that of her husband, she is, by recent acts, made almost entirely independent of him. In school board and in municipal elections she has the suffrage, so that no argument, even of a sentimental character, can be advanced against her right to the parliamentary suffrage, even if we refuse her admission to parliament itself. In all this there is a distinct growth of the notion of personality in a self-conscious being. It will be observed, however, that the giving of the suffrage to married women as well as to their husbands would involve the disappearance from our law of another trace of *the family* as a legal unit.

So, too, in the case of fatuous or imbecile persons, or of those who are mentally affected, the physical existence

[1] *History of Morals*, ii., 304.

is present only in a modified state, and the law accordingly attributes to them only modified rights. They are children in intellect, and treated as such. Their want of personality in mind is supplied by guardians. It is not strictly accurate to speak of them as persons. In many cases they are merely kept alive because the state does not feel inclined to take the responsibility of destroying them. If they succeed to property, it is administered for their support, and the division postponed till their death.

Again, difficulties may arise as to the physical conformation of beings—hermaphrodites, and such like. It may be questioned if a monster is human. But here positive law must decide on the report of experts as to the physical facts. A court will decide if the facts presented are or are not in agreement with the notion of personality. Here also the recognition is by the state, through its law-courts.

I may notice here the extension of the idea of person to corporations, firms, and such bodies of men. All the elements of personality are present, but as these have a perpetual succession, they cannot die, and grave abuses may result. These arise chiefly in connection with the right of property, which may enable strong corporations to defy the state. But in recent acts for the revisal of educational foundations, we see the state asserting its power.[1]

---

[1] See The Conveyancing Act, 1874, § 5, as to payment of casualties by corporations.

The body being the instrument of the free-will of the person, the notion of slavery is excluded. My body is mine, and no other person can appropriate it and display his will in it. Anyone who can appropriate the body of another is himself only imperfectly a person, and the moral effect of the attempt is as disastrous to the owner as to the slave. The right of personality is inalienable, because from its very nature it cannot be transferred. No one requires to get it from another; every one has it for himself. As a possession it may be defended, and hence arises the right of self-defence in case of sudden assault. But the questions have been raised: Can a man legally authorise another to injure or kill him? Can a man legally injure or kill himself?[1] In other words, does the maxim, "*Volenti non fit injuria*," satisfy us as a foundation of such a right? I think not. As to the man himself we cannot abstract him from society. In most cases his cowardly desertion of his station and its duties will throw additional burdens on others as little able, or perhaps less able, to bear them. Such conduct, then, deserves punishment. For this reason self-maiming, attempted suicide, and many other acts which appear at first sight to affect the guilty parties alone, are acts which the state is interested in preventing, if it is not disposed to undertake the burden of maintaining the maimed person or getting rid of him by death.

[1] Kant (Semple's tr.), *Metaphysic of Ethics*, pp. 238, 230 (Hartenstein's ed.), vol. vii, p. 227.

In like manner the law refuses to recognise and enforce all contracts which treat the body as a mere *thing*—such as an undertaking to allow blood to be drawn or skin to be taken for a surgical operation on another individual. The bill which was introduced into Parliament lately to protect young children who were being trained as gymnasts is founded on the same principle.

No higher proof of the dignity of the person in modern law can be given than the statutes for the relief of the poor. The mere fact of physical existence—conscious or unconscious—is recognised by the state, and is made to confer a right to demand physical sustenance or shelter. With lunatics the case is somewhat different, as society may be said to protect itself from them. But this is not a true explanation of the poor-law. The duty of charity to the poor has been transferred from the family to the state. The state has expanded into a large family. It has reaped the benefit of the pauper's labour, or it has given him birth. The duty of the individual is not to give alms to any haphazard beggar, but to pay the rates, and thus contribute to the support of all the poor. It would certainly be detrimental to the community if many poor were allowed to exist in a state of starvation. But apart from this the law recognises in a "person" an infinite potentiality, and hence it does not allow the needless sacrifice of a single human life.

On the other hand, the individual cannot be said to have a right to live unless it is for the benefit of the state and the world. Hence the most noble poor, whom most people would be anxious to succour, would rather starve than beg.[1] Those who are most ready to accept charity are the sturdy beggars, of whom by a sterner poor-law, in a former age, the state would have rid itself by hanging. Such individuals are merely parasites. They do not contribute to the life and strength of the organic body. Circumstances are conceivable in which a state for its own preservation might require to rid itself of paupers. If such an occasion occurs, as in a state of siege or during a severe famine, paupers have no rights against the state. On the contrary, they have a duty to relieve the state of their presence. This is evidently another example of the case of two drowning men on a plank which can save only one. Who is to die? The general impression is that the stronger should let the weaker live. The legal solution is that if the stronger push the weaker off, nobody can blame him.[2] But why should not the weaker be sufficiently noble to see that it is better that the fitter should survive? If the weaker required to be pushed off the plank, his life was probably not worth preserving. And so in all those cases of paupers and others, *dulce et decorum est pro patriâ mori*. If a man can do no good to his country by

---

[1] This is brought out by Dickens, in the character of Mrs. Betsy Higden, in *Our Mutual Friend*.

[2] See Broom's *Legal Maxims*, p. 11 (6th ed.); and Lorimer's *Institutes of Law* (2nd ed.), p. 331.

living, why should he be anxious to live? Or, does this maxim apply to all except paupers? It must be admitted that the existence of an individual raises a presumption in his favour of his right to exist; and it can only be the utmost necessity which can reverse such a presumption. But if the individual attempts to make the right absolute, then the answer is that the state exists, and has the same presumption in its favour. If the existence of the individual is dangerous to the state, as in the case of a murderer or traitor, he has no right to live, and, if necessary, the state is bound to kill him. But, as I have observed already, if the state requires the services of the individual, it must maintain him; and if the maintenance cannot be otherwise given, the obligation may lie on the corporate body as such.[1] Rights and duties are thus reciprocal throughout.

So with children and aged persons. Apart altogether from the fact that children supply the waste of life, both they and aged people have a position of the utmost importance in the organism of society. Their removal would take from life all its poetry and romance. To many the prattling and romping of children are the only relief from the monotony of life. And a society, which had no aged men to guide it with wisdom, or entertain it with the adventures of times long past, would feel a want which no literature could supply. A community, therefore, which contains no children or no aged men

[1] See p. 179 and foll., *supra*.

is necessarily imperfect, and such a state of society is a clear indication of a low condition of barbarism. It could only be the most desperate straits which could prompt the able-bodied members of a community to rid themselves of such encumbrances.[1]

The rights of man cannot be estimated quantitatively. We cannot regard a person as a being who has a *jus connubii*, a *jus commercii*, and certain other rights in the abstract attributed to him. The American and the French revolutionists fell into this error when they attempted to enumerate the "rights of man." His rights as a person are infinite and unlimited. His actual *material* rights are limited by his own powers and activity, and the recognition accorded by the state. But the abstract right is inconceivable apart from material rights. If a man has no property, he has no *rights* of property, and so with all material rights.

The consciousness of the rights is a most important element in practical application. It justified the demand for an extended suffrage in 1832 and 1867, and the general absence of it tends to throw doubt on the expediency of enfranchising agricultural labourers or women just at present. The demand is confined to a very few individuals. On the other hand, as with children, the attributing of rights ultimately brings

[1] The same question arises between different races of men, and must be resolved on the same principle. The fittest physically and morally will always survive.

the power of using them; and as in the case of men, the mere fact of being born into or put into a responsible position entails nearly always the necessary capacity for filling it. The exceptions are so few that positive law cannot notice them. And if agricultural labourers and women were admitted to the full benefit of the franchise, the same result would no doubt follow.

Personality belongs only to man because he alone is self-conscious. It cannot be attributed to the lower animals, and with them slavery becomes a true freedom. They have no will, and man may put his will into them. An interesting question is much discussed at the present time as to man's right to use up the bodies of the lower animals for scientific purposes—vivisection.[1] The extreme views which prevail in some quarters at the present day will be found to have been anticipated by Bentham.[2] He projects his own personality into the lower animals, and passes a judgment on his own synthesis. But if we admit the right to use the lower animals for food, the whole question is admitted. The objection seems to be that the operations are accompanied with pain, but the administration of an anæsthetic, or the removal of a portion of the brain will prevent pain; and what more can the philozoist wish? If the animal were conscious, might it not sacrifice itself for the benefit of its fellow beings? It is the same as in the case of the

[1] Trendelenburg, *Naturrecht*, p. 201; Krause, *Rechtsph.*, 73.
[2] *Morals and Legislation* (Clarendon Press), 311 n.

two drowning men holding on by one plank. Some people seem to think that human beings must be sacrificed when their rights conflict with those of hares and rabbits! The suppression of bear-baiting and of cock-fighting was in the interest of the human spectators, but that is certainly not the case with the recent development of the movement. Up to this point no one can or does complain of the suppression of wanton cruelty, particularly to such of the lower animals as assist man in his daily toil. But the subsequent development of the idea affords strong proof of the fact that legislation is carried on in this country by instinctive and irrational impulses, rather than by the light of pure reason. A man of science may pursue a fox for hours over the open country and kill it at last through sheer exhaustion or congestion of the lungs, while if he inflicted but a tenth part of the pain in his own laboratory, he would be liable to an exorbitant fine.[1] That is to say he may use the animals for amusement, pure and simple, but not for science. The careful reservation of the rights of "legitimate" sport remind us of the Roman view of slavery, which was "contra naturam," but yet recognised as a "constitutio juris gentium." In sport, too, it should be observed, personality is in some sense attributed to the lower

---

[1] This point is well put by the late Professor Stanley Jevons in his essay on "Cruelty to Animals," in *Methods of Social Reform*, p. 221.

animals. It is a game between the hunter and an animal, in which the stake is the animal's life.[1] And so the sport is more noble where the hunter stakes his life too, and ignoble where the animal hunted is tame.

The only justification of acts against cruelty to animals is that the cruelty demoralises those who practise it. They are less than human. We have no guarantee that they will draw the line at the lower animals, and abstain from cruelties to their fellowmen. By such statutes we seek to complete their personality, and raise them to the ordinary standard of humanity. But when we go further and prohibit vivisection to men of science, it is a gross insult to them, as it distinctly implies that they are, as a general rule, inferior in moral feelings to the average members of the community. The proper mode of dealing with such a subject is to regard it from the *human* point of view. Positive law deals only with human relations and conduct, and when it goes beyond its proper limits and deals with the relations of man and God, as was done in much of the Canon law, or with the relations of man and things in themselves, as in the Anti-vivisection Act, the legislation becomes suicidal. Instead of promoting human progress, it retards it. In this case we have an example of a merely arbitrary subjective creation of law. There is no objective existence as there was in the case of slaves, corresponding to the subjective act of the state. The lower animals will never be any

[1] See this idea in *The Iliad*, xxii., 159, 161.

the better of such legislation, as it is not probable that they will give up torturing each other—in some cases quite unnecessarily. They can never become persons. It is the same superstitious reverence for life *in itself* which prompts other members of the Aryan race to abstain from killing even vermin. In the East the superstition takes a religious form; in the West it clothes itself in a legal shape. The same feeling may be extended to plants, and even to inanimate objects, but fortunately the legislature has not interfered with trees or ancient monuments, except from a *human* point of view. It is from this standpoint that recent legislation has taken place as to the destruction of wild birds.[1]

It will now be obvious why I insisted on the four moments in the idea of person, viz., the physical existence of the individual, and of a society, and the conscious recognition of that fact and its legal consequences both by the individual and by the society. Man cannot exist as such apart from society. If he is not recognised by his fellow beings, or expelled from their society, he may exist physically, but he can hardly be regarded as a "person" in the eye of the law. The Roman punishment of *capitis diminutio* and our outlawry are in effect a withdrawal of the recognition of personality to a greater or less extent by the state. And so, if a human being sink his moral nature entirely in the animal, it is possible the law may require

[1] 43 and 44 Vict., cap. 35.

to treat him accordingly, and make sanitary and other regulations as it would do for cows or pigs. It is this fact which has compelled our legislature reluctantly to enact and so long keep in force the Contagious Diseases Acts. The dignity of the person has been abandoned or lost, and it would be the sheerest affectation to keep up an appearance of respecting it. But such regulations must be carried out with the greatest care and soundest discretion. If there is a spark of personality left, it should not be quenched.

Personality is the last and highest form of right, and in all its fulness it is the latest product of law. It is interesting to note how, as each legal category comes to consciousness, it is exaggerated and caricatured till it distorts and even threatens to destroy society altogether. When a new idea possesses men's minds it becomes a kind of monomania. It is not more certain that the discovery of new gold and diamond fields will attract crowds of speculators hasting to be rich, or that the invention of a new legal device like that of "limited liability" or bills of exchange, will create an activity which would have previously been regarded as inconceivable, than that a legal category newly discovered will be done to death by the philosophers. It is only a few months ago that a company was formed for the purpose of floating limited liability companies! But in the moral domain the results are as striking. In the writings of Plato and Aristotle we see the dominant conception of "the state" elaborated and defined till the individual appears to be nothing. In the Roman law we see a legal conception of "property" applied to the ancient Aryan institution of the family, and the wife and children made *res mancipi* of the father. At a still later epoch we find the family shattered by "freedom of contract," and society reduced almost to individual atoms. In the middle ages we have the conception of "the church" so distorted that it had supplanted the state, and the vicar of Him who had not where to lay His head raised to a temporal throne—a temporal monarch above all other principalities and powers. The decline of the Papal power allowed temporal princes to arrogate rights which they had never possessed, and these were again clothed with the legal category of "property." But the struggle for freedom between the period of the Reformation and the French Revolution developed other ideas. The geographical discoveries of the previous age had opened up commerce, and "contract" for a time appeared to overshadow everything. "*Laissez-faire*" is the watchword. Hobbes and Rousseau reduce the state, Kant reduces the family to contract. International law is regarded by them as only a heterogeneous mass of treaties. We are only now working our way back. But a reaction has certainly set in. And now the legal idea which rules men's minds is that of personality—the rights of MAN.[1] All men are equal as men. All men are self-conscious beings.

[1] It is more fashionable in some quarters to sneer at Hegel than to understand him. But the fact of legal development in the order

But it is forgotten or ignored that the physical qualities of men, mental and bodily, are infinitely different. Their minds are as diversified as their bodies. What is meant, then, by saying that persons are equal? It is merely a *formal* abstraction, as true and as untrue as those which have been accepted at former stages of the world's history. The consciousness of self is alike in all men. Every man feels himself to be a self. It is this abstract, immaterialised, transcendental self, which the French philosophers emphasised last century. It could not be materialised or projected in matter without altering its character, and hence the havoc it made with French politics. The statement that all men are equal is only a half truth. That all men are utterly unequal and infinitely different is just as true; but as society can only be formed by a unity in differences, the contradiction is not felt in actual life. It is only a product of the understanding. So far from it being the normal condition of men to envy one another, it is a common-place to say that a man must be very miserable indeed if he would permanently change places with another. Person is thus not mere " being," for under this category a horse, a

---

above indicated—an historical fact which cannot be gainsaid—should be pondered by his critics. To complete the development of the notion, we require only to add at the commencement the notion of physical force—" might is right," and at the end the notion of " personality," as including and involving the whole of law in its multiplicity.

dog, a tree are all equal to man. They all equally "are." But as we cannot identify freedom with indifference, so we must not confound equality with identity. Men must be infinitely unequal, but they may all be equally men and realise their rights and duties as such. When, therefore, Proudhon said that property was theft, he should have gone on and said that material personality was theft, since the hydrogen, carbon, and phosphates which made one big man might make two little ones, or a host of little animals. Perhaps his ideal of the universe was *a plenum* composed of a perfectly homogeneous fluid of perfectly uniform temperature!

And here again the question presents itself—Must this individualistic tendency be stopped? If the reference is to *mere* individualism, the answer must be emphatically, Yes. But as I pointed out, when we met the same question on the side of humanity, it is a mistake to imagine individualism is more rampant now than in the middle ages. The number of individuals who commit the wrong may be greater, but the offence is not new. And no remedy will be found in the mechanical balancing of the powers of the state and of the person. The greatest freedom of *each* is involved in the greatest freedom of *both*. As there is no refuge from religious difficulties in an infallible church, there is no refuge from political ones in a tyranny, or a feudal aristocracy. However much we may dread the progress of democracy, it is as impossible to revive the Greek state, as it would be to get modern Europeans to adopt the Greek language. But the world has survived the barbarous cruelties and excesses of the ancient and the middle ages, and carried away some valuable lessons. It may be that it is about to go through a similar experience from the opposite quarter, but the result will unquestionably in the end benefit humanity. It is very doubtful if mankind can learn by anything else than examples. And so a people who are unfit for liberty, and who cannot be taught by the experience of others, may have to go back a few centuries and commence their political training anew. The experiments which are being carried on in various countries of the world at the present moment will affect the weal of untold myriads in the American and Australian continents when Europe is perhaps the most insignificant part of the globe. In the laboratory of nature the destruction of a few nations is a matter of indifference, and no efforts of an anti-vivisection league will avail to stop the suffering which must ensue. Our difficulty in passing an opinion on the tendency of events is that we do not see them as a whole. We should, as Solon advised Crœsus, suspend our judgment until we see the end of all things.

But the salvation of the world depends on individuals. At great crises in the world's history all seems often to depend on one man. The question every man should ask himself is—Can I be a hero if occasion demands it? And no individual can rise to the true dignity of humanity, unless he feels proud of being a man, however humble his lot. If the least in the kingdom of heaven is greater than John the Baptist, the least in the kingdom of humanity is greater than anything in the world. But the individual must *consciously* live for society, and he must be proud of playing the most subordinate part in the great drama of life.

Christianity made the individual christian a priest in the church. In the state it is making him a king. And if, as Plato wished, every king became a philosopher, we might almost realise on earth that the voice of the people was the voice of God. But this consummation can only be reached by a thoroughgoing recognition and practical application of the constitutional idea, whereby the greatest become the servants of the least, and no one lives for himself, but every one not only for the state, but also for humanity, and every one is ready " to lay down his life for the brethren." And as the greatest men are those who represent in their persons all that is good and noble of preceding generations, so the highest ideal of man which humanity can form is One who sacrificed Himself for all preceding and succeeding generations.

LECTURE XII.

RETROSPECT OF THE DEVELOPMENT OF LAW THROUGH THE CATEGORIES.

I HAVE now exhausted the various forms which legal judgments, as historically developed, have assumed. If this development is looked at as a whole, it will be seen that as law became scientific, lawyers were empirically deducing the categories. In other words, men at different stages of legal history looked at legal phenomena from different points of view. And when the Roman lawyers gave the names of property, person, contract, or obligation, to certain relations or transactions, they were merely naming in a special class of cases the categories which logicians were discovering in a more general form, as the necessary forms of thought. If we lay the forms of legal judgments, as developed in the foregoing lectures, alongside the forms of logical judgments, we shall discover that there is a legal institution corresponding to each logical form, which may be set forth in the following table, taking them in the order in which they have already been treated :—

Logical forms of propositions in respect of—				The corresponding forms of legal judgments are—
1. Modality,	are	Problematical,	=	Legalised violence—(Lynch Law);
		or Assertory,	=	Judicial Decision and Legislation.[1]
2. Quality,	,,	Affirmative,	=	Civil Injury;
		or Negative,	=	Crime.[2]
3. Quantity,	,,	Universal,	=	Person;
		or Particular,	=	Property.[3]
4. Relation,	,,	Categorical,	=	Social Relations;[4]
		or Hypothetical,	=	Contract.[5]

But we have discovered, further, that thought does not rest with the categories as given by formal logic. To each pair already mentioned under each class, we must add a third, as was done by Kant, when he constructed the following list of categories :—[6]

I. Of Quantity: Unity, Plurality, Totality.
II. Of Quality: Reality, Negation, Limitation.
III. Of Relation: Inherence and Subsistence (Substance and Accident), Causality and Dependence (Cause and Effect); Community (Reciprocity between the Active and the Passive).
IV. Of Modality: Possibility—Impossibility; Existence (Actuality)—Non-existence; Necessity—Contingency.

Thus, under the head of *quantity* we saw that the

---

[1] Lectures ii. and iii.   [2] Lecture iv.   [3] Lecture v.
[4] Lectures vi., vii., ix., and x.   [5] Lecture viii.
[6] The list of categories is here given in Kant's order, which is more convenient when we are merely analysing the idea of right, for we advance from quantity to relation on the part of the individual, and from quality to modality on the part of the state. See p. 308, *infra;* also *Critique of Pure Reason* (Max Müller), vol. ii., p. 71; Caird's *Kant,* p. 306, &c.; Stirling's *Kant,* pp. 69, 193.

first rude notion of right was of property in one's body. This was all a man possessed. It was property and person in one. The man's rights were regarded under the category of *unity*. But, as the individual progressed in his struggle for freedom, he got single rights one after the other conceded to him—the *jus commercii*, the *jus connubii*, the *jus suffragii*, and so forth. Man's rights were regarded as a mere quantity which could be added to or subtracted from. They were regarded under the category of *plurality*. But the modern conception of a person is an individual with an infinite potentiality of rights. In the modern view of personality, men's rights are regarded under the category of *totality*.[1]

In like manner, under the categories of *quality*, we observed that the state began by asserting its own existence, and enforcing rights as a matter of course, without considering the rights or the character of the person offending. The judgments may be placed under the category of *reality* (*affirmation*). But at a later stage it is seen there is something wrong with the delinquent. His acts are crimes, and are treated as such. They are dealt with apart from the question of reparation to the person wronged. They are placed under the category of *negation*. But, as we have seen, every crime involves a civil injury, and every civil injury,

---

[1] It must be borne in mind that this idea of progress from lower to higher categories here sketched, does not belong properly to the Kantian system, but is the product of later philosophy

if deliberately and consciously done, is a crime.[1] That is to say, there can be no affirmation without negation, and no negation without affirmation.[2] And so, in an extreme view, the mere existence of a person is a crime against society, if we push Proudhon's idea to its logical conclusion.[3] But in an ideal state, where the government exists but needs not put forth its power, or where men legislate for themselves individually, no one encroaches on his neighbour, no one refuses what his neighbour claims, and no one claims what he should not have. "Juris præcepta sunt hæc: honeste vivere, alterum non lædere, suum cuique tribuere." The two previous categories are merged in that of *limitation*.

So with the categories of relation. As Sir Henry Maine has pointed out, society has progressed *from status to contract*,[4] or in Kantian language, the rights of men are classed under the category of *substantiality* before they are treated under that of *causality*. In other words, the family or the state is looked upon as "substance," while the individuals (the wife, the child, the slave, or the citizen), are merely "accidents." And in like manner, the individual is regarded as "substance," and his rights as mere "accidents." But, at a later stage, the state is regarded as *creating* rights by legislation, while the individual does the same for himself by contracts and other private transactions. The

---

[1] Pp. 92 and 93, *supra*.
[2] Caird's *Kant*, p. 313.
[3] P. 300, *supra*.
[4] *Ancient Law*, p. 170.

relation of the state or the individual to rights is regarded as one of "cause and effect." But we have seen further, that law does not stop with contract (causality). We have seen that in the reaction against *laissez-faire*, it has come to be discovered that freedom of contract is not the ultimate idea of human relations. Contracts between individuals and treaties between nations can determine arbitrary points only, for men are organically connected even before they enter into contracts. We have seen that in legislation and contract no one can be called ruler or subject, master or servant. In other words, we must extend Sir Henry Maine's formula by saying that society has progressed *from contract (causality) to reciprocity*.

And lastly, under the categories of *modality*, we saw that at an early stage the existence of rights depended on the possession of a strong arm. Might was right. When the state did interfere, it was to stop disputes and not to enforce rights. A man might thus have a right one day and not have it in similar circumstances the next. There was merely in some cases the *possibility* of right, and in others the *impossibility*. Each particular right would depend on whether the individual could enforce it himself, or get his tribe or family to assist him in so doing. And even in historical times, the possession of rights depended on whether a man happened to be born in a particular state. If he fell into the hands of strangers he had no rights. In the next stage rights fell under the category of *actuality*. Rights actually existed, defined in codes, recognised by judges, and enforced by rulers. This is the epoch of *positive law* in an especial sense. If rights are not so recognised and enforced, they are *non-existent*. Right is might. The particular rights are determinate, and each one has the might of an empire to maintain it. But law does not rest here. As we have seen, law is not an arbitrary creation of rulers, judges, or even of legislators. It is something eternal and independent of human judgment. It is now regarded under the category of *necessity*. Might and right are identified. The might is not that of a tribe or nation, or even of an empire, or of the world. The laws of " Nature " are seen to be self-avenging. And yet at the same time, legislation and contract are now more active than they have ever been in defining the *contingent* matter of right—in *making* laws.

And yet further, we have seen that law does not rise only from lower to higher categories, but from lower to higher classes of categories—from the categories of quality to those of modality, from the categories of quantity to those of relation. It is only for a temporary purpose that it appears to be satisfied with one category. Its point of view is perpetually shifting, if it is not progressing. Thus the state first makes law by attempting to put down violence. It treats a number of acts as crimes on the one hand, and enforces particular rights on the other, without considering anything beyond the isolated act. The distinction of the acts is quite arbitrary, as in the *Regiam Majestatem*, which defines criminal causes as being "quhen controversie is anent the paine of blude, or of life and limme,"[1] or in the Summary Procedure Act, which draws the line where imprisonment is competent,[2] or once more in the desperate statement that a crime is an act which the state, for purposes of its own absolutely prohibits. The acts are regarded under the categories of quality. But it is found that there is something deeper in the declaration of the state. If it enforces the right of one man, it represses the wrong of another. If it punishes a criminal, it declares that another man has rights which have been infringed. Each judgment is no longer one but two. And, instead of dealing with the acts of a wrong-doer, it examines and classifies the *rights* of the individuals involved. It appeals in the first instance to the immemorial customs of the realm, or to the codes and laws, and says one has a right and another has no right. In other words, the rights are regarded under the categories of modality. This transition from quality to modality is shown in the rejection of the view that the distinction between crime and civil injury is merely a matter of procedure.[3]

And so with the categories of quantity. If we turn to

[1] Bk. I., chap. i., § 3.
[2] 27 and 28 Vict., cap. 53, § 28.
[3] See Holland's *Jurisprudence*, p. 218.

any legal treatise which enumerates the rights of person or property, we shall find them stated in the form of relations of the owner to other persons. Personality is a right of self-defence against assault, a right to one's good name and so forth. Property is a right of vindication against thieves, a right of transfer or conveyance to other persons—a right of donation or sale, &c., &c. Conveyance and contract always tend to interchange. The Roman conveyance *(mancipatio)* became a contract. The theoretical treatment of the preparation of contracts we now call conveyancing. Land is now transferred by leases, feu-contracts, contracts of ground-annual. In England the contract of sale transfers goods. Scotch law still holds nominally to the doctrine that property can only be transferred by tradition, but it now accomplishes the same end as English law by imposing an *obligation* on the representatives of a bankrupt seller to transfer the goods, and conferring *a right* on purchasers or their representatives to demand them. In other words, in all those cases the right of property is looked at from the standpoint of relation. In like manner with the idea of person, rights and duties are formulated apart from their infringement, and it is even maintained that the mere existence of beings in society, such as paupers, confers rights on them and imposes duties on their neighbours. The whole law may thus be laid down in propositions setting forth the relations between persons in respect of (1) their material personality, and (2) their property which is an extension of that personality.

It will be remembered that the same tendency of thought was found in the law of succession. As mere coexistence in space (*i.e.*, rights of person and property in their baldest form) presupposes and involves *relation*, so mere one-after-the-other-ness implicitly involves relation. But succession is not merely one man taking a thing which another formerly possessed, or fulfilling a function which was formerly fulfilled by another. Nor is it merely a capricious nomination of a successor by a person about to die (causality). It is a conscious effort of society to repair the ravages of death by a reconstruction or continuation of relations. And in these the rights of husband and wife, parents and children, brothers and sisters are determined on the principle of reciprocity. Moreover, in the absolute freedom of testing allowed in English law, we see the idea that the members of the state are all reciprocally related as individuals.

It will be remembered that each jural relation involves two pairs of moments—one pair on the side of the state, and the other pair on the side of the individual. (1.) The individual *de facto* exists; (2.) is conscious of and claims a right; (3.) the state exists; and, (4.) as representing the universal, recognises, and if necessary, enforces the right. It will be seen that the categories of quality and modality regard legal phenomena from the point of view of the state, and those of quantity and relation from the point of view of the persons subject to it. We cannot separate the two moments without destroying the whole conception, and so the progress under the categories of quality and modality has been simultaneous and parallel with that under the categories of quantity and relation. Thus, we cannot say that law begins when individuals or families claim to have rights of person and property, any more than that it begins when the state first consciously represses individualism and takes the enforcement of right into its own hands. At first sight, law makes its appearance by the state prohibiting in various successive forms the individual caprice, first prohibiting indiscriminate self-redress, then superseding judges by appointing popular juries to try offenders and popular legislative assemblies to enact laws. At first, all it demands is that the parties shall formally keep "the king's peace." It does not attempt to discover who began the quarrel or who is in the right. When, however, it begins to discriminate and analyse acts, it punishes some and merely gives reparation in others. And, finally, the state recognises the rights of the individual as necessary, and in some cases exerts its influence for his reformation. On the other hand the individual struggles for freedom, expressing his claim first in the ideas of material person and property. But, in the process of acquiring freedom, he discovers his organic relations to other men in the family, in the state, and lastly, in humanity as a whole. The state in asserting its existence discovered that it must deal with, protect, and reform individuals. The individual in asserting his existence discovered that he must uphold and, if necessary, sacrifice himself for the state. The two complementary movements have filled up the details of our conception of humanity.

It may be noted, too, that the categories of modality are truly the counterpart of those of relation. In the former, the individuals involved are regarded from the point of view of the spectator who, in this case, is the legislator—the state;[1] in the latter there is an attempt to determine the characteristics of persons as members of particular groups. Thus, when the relations of men could be described by substance and accident, there was from the point of view of the state only a possibility of rights on the part of some individuals, an impossibility on the part of others. But when the individual has asserted his rights, and these have been recognised by the state, it does not matter whether we describe the relations as falling under the categories of cause and effect, or of actuality and non-existence, or, rather we should say, they fall under both. And so, finally, with reciprocity on the one hand, and necessity and contingency on the other. This fact throws a new light on Montesquieu's definition of law—"Les lois dans la signification la plus étendue sont les rapports nécessaires qui dérivent de la nature des choses."

[1] See Caird's *Kant*, p. 468.

If we substitute "persons" for "things" in this statement, we have a combination of the two categories of necessity and reciprocity (modality and relation), for the rights are reciprocally created by the individuals involved, and the state recognises and enforces these rights as necessary. And we are now in a position to expand the definition of positive law with which we started provisionally.[1] Combining the highest categories of each class, we may say that positive laws are the contingent expression of the material rights and mutual limitations of individuals arising necessarily from the reciprocal relations of human beings in society.

In tracing the relations between men, we found that we were led to regard each individual as related to the whole of humanity, the members of which are regarded as a unity, both in coexistence and in succession. But as succession is merely a means of reconstructing relations, and rights of succession are determined only as between the survivors, we must neglect our predecessors and our successors in discussing *abstract law*. Looking then at mankind as presently existing on the earth, we found there were two ideas involved in our relations, namely—(1) the individual person; and (2) the unity of humanity. These ideas severally suggest the two sciences of natural law, and the law of nature and nations corresponding to the two sciences of empirical psychology and rational cosmology, attacked and exploded by Kant.[2] The third

---

[1] See p. 9, *supra*. [2] These two sciences are not clearly distinguished in theory, but they arise in the mode of treating the subject.

science of rational theology holds the same relation to law as to physical science, and it may therefore be neglected in our present discussion.[1] In natural law it has often been asked, what are the rights of man—of the individual as such? The answer is that such a being is inconceivable apart from society, and if a categorical answer is pressed for, it must be "none." But again, when we attempt to construct an abstract ideal society, in which each member shall have certain *natural* rights, it will be found that we arrive at two sets of contradictory propositions, which appear equally axiomatic— the antinomies of pure reason. Whichever side is adopted by an opponent, it is easy to show its absurdity; and hence, as Kant points out, the victory is always with the attacking party. Very often all that is meant by a political reaction is the adoption of one side of the antinomy—the antithesis for the thesis, or *vice versâ*. And it is not improbable some political sceptic might suggest that some of the theses or antitheses of these antinomies are among the permanent members of the civil service.

To illustrate this I shall take the antinomies as given by Kant, paraphrase them as applied to law, and then add a number of corollaries or propositions, in which the various sides of the contradiction are generally embodied.

[1] Caird's *Kant*, p. 623, and Principal Caird's *Philosophy of Religion*, chap. v., may be consulted on this subject.

FIRST ANTINOMY.

Thesis.

"The world has a beginning in time, and is limited also with regard to space." (Max Müller's *Kant*, ii., 368), or—

The world of mankind, as subject to law, has a beginning in time, and is limited also with regard to space.

Antithesis.

"The world has no beginning and no limits in space, but is infinite in respect both to time and space." (*Ibid.*, p. 369), or—

The world of mankind, as subject to law, has no beginning and no limits in space, but is infinite, in respect both to time and space.

Corollaries.

1. Man has no rights against God. (Lorimer's *Institutes of Law*, 2nd ed., p. 205.)

2. Law begins when men become civilised, and applies only to them. Savages are ruled by instinct and physical laws.

3. Animals and vegetables have no rights. (See p. 293, *supra.*)

4. A person has rights only to the extent he can physically take them—(Might is Right).

Corollaries.

1. "La Divinité a ses lois." (Montesquieu, *De l'Esprit des lois*, I. i.; see also Lorimer, *l. c.*)

2. Law begins with Being. Every being has his rights.

3. Animals have rights. "The last rose of summer is entitled to equality before the law." (Lorimer's *Inst. of Laws*, 2nd ed., p. 406.)
"The poor beetle, that we tread upon,
In corporal sufferance finds a pang as great
As when a giant dies."—Shakspere,
(*Measure for Measure*, act iii., sc. i.)

4. All persons have a right to the conditions of human existence—(Right is Might).

Corollaries—continued.

5. A person has rights only when he comes of age. (See p. 285, *supra*.)

6. The rights of a person cease at death. (See pp. 258 and 314, *supra*.)

7. The average "Eternity" of Napoleon's treaties of peace was about two years.

8. "Culpa tenet suos auctores."

9. A person has rights only within his own state, and it is only by comity he can have rights outside of it. (Story's *Conflict of Laws*, chaps. i. and ii., *passim*.)

10. It is unfair to ennoble future generations for ever for the act of one man. It is absurd to deify dead ancestors, as the Chinese do, for the same reason.

11. It is unfair to deprive future generations of titles and property for the crime of one individual.

Corollaries—continued.

5. A person may have rights reserved for centuries before he is born.

6. The will of a person should be respected for ever after his death, in spirit, if not in letter.

7. In assenting to the Irish Church Disestablishment Act, Her Majesty violated her coronation oath.

8. Every wrong affects the universe.
"Earth felt the wound, and nature from her seat, Sighing through all her works, gave signs of woe, That all was lost."—Milton, *P. L.*, bk. ix.

9. Every person is entitled to claim as a matter of justice, that he should have the same rights in a foreign state as in his own. (See Lorimer's *Law of Nations*, i., 370; also p. 241, *supra*.)

10. Heredity is a law of nature. The same idea as to the individual is expressed in the Scotch proverb, "Ance a bailie, aye a bailie."

11. God "visits the iniquity of the fathers upon the children unto the third and fourth generation."

COROLLARIES—*continued*.

12. What has posterity done for us? It has no rights against the present generation.

13. The right of ruling belongs to the upper classes alone.

14. Majorities are always right.[1]

15. Minorities are always right.[1] "God speaks not by the many, but the few."

16. The state has no right of interference with the private conduct of citizens. "An Englishman's house is his castle."

17. The state has no right to interfere with the affairs of the church.

18. The church has no right to interfere with the affairs of the state.

COROLLARIES—*continued*.

12. It is unjust to hand down debt to posterity. Each year's revenue should defray its own expenditure.

13. All citizens have a right by themselves, or their representatives, to concur in the making of the laws. (Declaration of French National Assembly; Paine, *Rights of Man*, 9th ed., p. 74.)

14. } Vox populi (*i.e.*, the voice
15. } of humanity), vox Dei.

16. The state's right of interference extends to every part of the citizen's conduct.

17. } Church and state cannot
18. } be distinguished. (See *Natural Religion*, by the author of *Ecce Homo*, p. 180 and foll.)

---

[1] It will be observed that in this and some other cases opponents do not always maintain a thesis and its corresponding antithesis. It frequently happens that they support only different applications of the same thesis.

COROLLARIES—*continued.*

19. A subject has no rights against the crown, for "the king can do no wrong," and "Tempus non occurrit regi." (Broom's *Legal Maxims*, 5th ed., pp. 52, 65.)

20. No state has any right to interfere in the internal affairs of any other state; sovereign states are independent. (Wheaton's *Elements*, § 72.)

21. "Sic utere tuo ut alienum non lædas."

COROLLARIES—*continued.*

19. Every member of the state has rights against the crown. The king swears obedience to the constitution and the law.

20. States cannot cut themselves off from the rest of mankind, and intervention may be a duty. (See Lorimer's *Law of Nations*, i., 139.)

21. A man can do what he likes with his own.

For the general thesis[1] that the world of men as subject to law is limited in time and space, we may argue that if it is not so, then we must conceive law existing when there were only animals on the earth, and even prior to that epoch. We must conceive under a legal aspect two trees struggling for one particle of carbon or nitrogen. Must we not even go further and conceive the convection of a fluid caused by heat as a legal process? The denial of the thesis is therefore absurd, and we must hold that law commences only when men become self-conscious, and applies only to men who are

---

[1] The arguments here given are intended rather as illustrations for the general reader. The student of Kant will have no difficulty in applying Kant's arguments as given in the *Critique*. Reference should be made to Professor Caird's *Kant* on this subject.

conscious of right. The same argument applies generally to the corollaries.

For the general antithesis that the world of men as subject to law is infinite in respect of space, we may argue that we cannot conceive law stopping abruptly with Europe and America. We must extend it to other continents. Wherever there is man, he must be brought within the domain of law. If it is to be restricted to civilised and intelligent men, who is to judge? We must cut off children, lunatics, women, and the large majority of men. If intelligence is to be the criterion, how many members of parliament, magistrates, rulers and kings will remain, after we have eliminated the unintelligent? Again, if there were only two men in the world, one would not thereby acquire a right to destroy anything wantonly, for he might interfere with a potential right of the other. The rights of each extend over the whole universe. Even a solitary being in the world would injure himself if he wronged anything. The highest men are those who would not tread on a worm, and who would respect even a daisy. And so with God. If we deny that God must be just to men, we deny His existence. We cannot conceive Him merely as a capricious tyrant.

The same arguments apply to time. If we do not admit that law has existed from all eternity, then it must be a capricious or accidental addition to the universe at some period of its history. What we now call law (in the jural sense) is organically connected with what appeared to be mere physical law in long distant ages. We must therefore hold that law is eternal and infinite.

SECOND ANTINOMY.

Thesis.

"Every compound substance in the world consists of simple parts, and nothing exists anywhere but the simple or what is composed of it." (Max Müller's *Kant*, ii., 376), or—

Every state or social group consists of mere individuals, and there exists nowhere anything but individuals, or groups of individuals.

Antithesis.

"No compound thing in the world consists of simple parts, and there exists nowhere in the world anything simple." (*Ibid.*, 377), or—

No state or social group consists of mere individuals, and there exist nowhere in the world any solitary individuals.

Corollaries.

1. "Law, or The Law, taken indefinitely is an abstract or collective term, which, when it means anything, can mean neither more nor less than the sum total of a number of individual laws taken together." (Bentham; see Holland's *Jurisprudence*, p. 12.)

2. Every general right may be divided into a number of simple rights.

Corollaries.

1. "Lex est ratio summa, insita in naturâ, quæ jubet ea, quæ facienda sunt, prohibetque contraria: eadem enim ratio cum est in hominis mente confirmata et perfecta, lex est." (Cicero, *De Leg.* i., 18.)

2. No general right can be resolved into a number of merely simple rights.

COROLLARIES—*contd.*

3. "Person is merely a collective term for personal qualities." (Lorimer's *Law of Nations,* i., 413.)

4. Property = the following rights—"utendi, fruendi, abutendi, fructus percipiendi, possidendi, alienandi, et vindicandi." (See Holland's *Jurisprudence,* pp. 132, 133.)

COROLLARIES—*contd.*

3. "In personality . . . I know myself even in my finitude, as what is infinite, universal and free." (Hegel's *Naturrecht,* § 35; Stirling's *Lectures,* p. 30.)

4. Property is a plenary control over an object: (Das Eigenthum ist eine totale Herrschaft über eine Sache). (Holland, *Ibid.*)

For the thesis that a state consists merely of individuals, we may point out that the Jews have ceased to be a state, while the individuals who might have formed a Jewish state have become English, French, German, &c. In like manner Poland has disappeared, and the Poles are either Russian, Prussian, or Austrian, while a few exiles have become English and American. In like manner Great Britain might be cleared of all its inhabitants, who might become citizens of Canada, Victoria, South Australia, Western Australia, and New South Wales. This island might then again be inhabited by colonists from all the countries of Europe, who might form another state. The world, therefore, consists of individuals grouped accidentally into states.

And when we take an individual and analyse his rights, we find that there are only certain determinate rights which he can enforce in courts of law. He has a right of personality and a right of property. These enable him to do certain determinate things. He enforces one single right at a time as it is assailed, or he exercises one right at a time. As these rights all cluster round person, in relation to determinate things, personality is evidently a compound right composed of simple ones. And as a complement of this proposition there must be a number of single simple laws, each of which enforces a right and corresponds to it.

For the antithesis that a nation is more than a collection of individuals, it may be pointed out that England is still the England of Queen Elizabeth, though there are as many people now in London as there were then in the whole kingdom. Protestant Germany has been celebrating the birth of Martin Luther, although those who took part in the Reformation have been dead for centuries. We do not recognise any change in France after the absorption of Savoy and Nice or the cession of Alsace and Lorraine. The individuals who compose the United States of America are much more numerous, and great numbers of them differ widely in nationality from those who threw off the British yoke in 1783, and yet they speak and act as if they themselves had fought for their freedom. There is, therefore, more in a nation than mere individual men.

And in dealing with the individual we need not try to enumerate his rights. He is perhaps the proprietor of a ship. Has he a right in each mast and each life-boat? Has he property in each rope, in each strand of each rope, in each thread of each strand? His right is to the ship as a whole, and it is absurd to subdivide his right quantitatively. As a person he feels his rights over it to be infinite, and they cannot therefore be analysed and enumerated. There may be moreover a *pretium affectionis* which no law can estimate.

Now, it may be said generally that all these contradictions arise from the fact of man—in one aspect an infinite being—being placed in a finite world, and being able to realise his personality only in things. If we abstract the infinite side of man's nature, and ignore the finite, we get one set of propositions apparently axiomatic. If we abstract the finite and ignore the infinite, we get a similar contradictory set equally axiomatic. Thus, to begin with the individual, property is essential to realise personality, and wealth is undoubtedly an element in the perfect life. But, how much is necessary or how little will suffice? A man's possessions may possess him. A miser is no better proprietor because he can count his bags of gold each day, than a man who has daily wages sufficient for all his wants. If the miser converted his sovereigns into farthings he would have more to count, but would he feel himself richer? A man might own the Koh-i-Noor, and yet be poorer than another who could only gaze at Jupiter or Venus through a hole in his cottage roof. Nor does the power of touching the object bring the man spiritually any nearer to it. He may know as much chemically of the planet as of the diamond. The one may be as useful or as useless, as beautiful or as commonplace as the other. He may be proprietor of the one as much as of the other. In short, while man must exist in relation to things, things cannot embody the fulness and infinitude of his nature. If a man could conquer the world, he could only sit down and weep because there were no more worlds to conquer. A man may "gain the whole world and yet lose his life." Material property is therefore nothing. Nor is material personality more. The greatest men are the most ready to lay down their lives as a voluntary sacrifice. Thus man possesses all things and even his own life in a sense in which he could not when it was merely property.[1] Our Lord's statement, therefore, "Blessed are the poor in spirit," is not a religious platitude, but a literal fact, established by the experience of humanity.

And so with nations. They must exist in space. They must consist of individual men, but each nation in turn appears to regard itself as the centre of humanity, round which other nations ought to revolve. Each nation strives, as it were, for universal dominion. When once a nation feels its power, and has set out on this career of expansion, no line can be drawn until it embraces the whole earth. But, as in the case of the individual,

[1] See p. 121, *supra*.

mere territorial aggrandisement is unsatisfying. There is one idea—one spirit—which animates the nation, and it is utterly impossible to estimate its power by so many square miles of area, so many millions of a population, so many thousands of a standing army, so much accumulated wealth. These are elements in the nation's existence, but they are still accidents. It may happen that the life of a nation may ebb, until one man—some patriot or hero—arises to rouse the spirit of his fellow-countrymen. For the moment the nation may be only the one man, but he creates it anew. Other individuals catch the fire of his inspiration and feel themselves organically related to the nation. Outlying provinces, differing in language religion and customs feel bound up into a unity which throbs with one life. This is a nation.[1] But as a living organism it cannot be confined to one portion of space. It may overflow by conquest or trade. Individuals migrate. And if this process of change and aggression were to cease the nation would languish and die. Is then the struggle for existence incompatible with "peace on earth and good-will among men?" Not necessarily. We must find some conception of human coexistence which will allow each nation to possess *universal* dominion, and yet at the same time restrain it to a determinate portion of the earth's surface. Such an

---

[1] See M. Renan's tract, *Que ce que c'est qu'une Nation?* France is an excellent specimen of heterogeneous elements bound up into a true unity. There are many loyal Frenchmen who cannot speak a word of the language.

idea is no novelty in modern thought. The Jewish kingdom, even in the time of Solomon was small and insignificant, but a descendant of that king has founded a spiritual kingdom which is destined to be universal. The empire of Alexander has crumbled into atoms, but Greek civilisation and literature have conquered the world. The Roman empire has passed away for ever, but its laws are obeyed, consciously or unconsciously, by all civilised nations.[1] The French nation has more influence and a wider dominion at the present moment than it had after the sham conquests of Napoleon. Germany, when it was little more than a geographical expression, dominated the thought of those who ruled the world. And England owes its power, not so much to the fact that its mercantile marine penetrates every quarter of the habitable globe, as to this that its constitution is the admiration and envy of every civilised state, and has served as a model after which the constitutions of her numerous colonies are framed. In the course of a few centuries English respect for order and love of constitutional liberty will be the predominant qualities in the world. The world may then learn to despise the Revolution.

We speak of one world, but there are many worlds. It was a religious world superimposed on the civil world

[1] This is true in one sense even of England and America in their municipal law, but it applies literally to international law. Last year (1883) saw Wheaton's *Elements* translated into Chinese!

that the Catholic church tried to create on earth. The division of bishoprics and parishes clashed with that of counties and burghs. It was, however, the most gigantic mistake ever made by Christianity to imagine that Christ's kingdom was of this world, for in the spiritual world we may have many bishops and archbishops of the same place, with the same territorial title.[1] When persecution as a part of state policy was abandoned external uniformity of creed disappeared, and with it the ecclesiastical divisions of the country. Each dissenting church divides the country as it chooses, and now the established churches are finding that the old divisions, especially in towns, are useless.

And not only is there a religious world; there is a scientific world. The British association is a parliament or a church council in science. The small scientific bodies are councils, presbyteries or synods. There is a world of trade and commerce with its chambers of commerce and associated chambers of commerce—its trades' unions

---

[1] Not long ago the bishops of the Scottish Episcopalian Church protested against the restoration of the Roman hierarchy in Scotland, on the ground that one bishop had no right to thrust himself into the diocese of another. The ludicrousness of the protest was only equalled by the ludicrousness of the assumption of the territorial titles. The Ecclesiastical Titles Act is repealed, because the titles may be legitimately required for purposes of description, but they should not be recognised, except as titles of mere description, beyond the circle of the particular communion, any more than the high-sounding titles of freemasons, or of the officers of the Salvation Army.

and relative congresses. There is a literary world, an artistic world, a philosophical world. The modes in which men may be combined are infinite. We are therefore constrained to abandon such views of the individual and of nations as regard them as separate and independent entities, coexisting in space and following each other in time. We must rise to the higher categories of relation and modality.

Before mentioning the antinomies of causality I would observe that many of the statements placed under the first antinomy might have been placed here, and in like manner some of those placed here might have found a place as appropriately under the first as some which are there. The obvious reason of this is that mere coexistence in space, like figures in a waxwork—an impossible conception in the case of men—implies relation of one space to many spaces, and one time to many times.[1] I have allowed the statements to remain, as in this arrangement they may bring the fact more clearly before the mind of the student.

THIRD ANTINOMY.

Thesis.	Antithesis.
"Causality according to the laws of nature is not the only causality from which all the	"There is no freedom, but everything in the world takes place entirely according to the

[1] Caird's *Kant*, pp. 458, 601 and foll.

THESIS.	ANTITHESIS.
phenomena of the world can be deduced. In order to account for these phenomena it is necessary also to admit another causality, that of freedom." (Max Müller's *Kant*, ii., 386), or—	laws of nature." (*Ibid.*, 387), or—
Custom and convenience are not the only sources from which rights can be deduced. In order to account for these it is necessary to admit the function of legislative acts, judicial decisions, and contracts.	There is no right created by legislators and judges, or private persons, but all rights spring from the nature of things.

COROLLARIES.	COROLLARIES.
1. Law is a command of a ruler, express or implied.	1. "All human laws are, properly speaking, only declaratory."
2. Rights emerge by entering into contracts or committing delicts.	2. There are natural rights of man prior to such acts.
3. "The real foundation of our right (of property) is the law of the land." (Paley, *Moral Philosophy*, bk. III., pt. I., chap. i., and foll.)	3. Law cannot create a right property. (See Lorimer's *Institutes of Law*, p. 259.)
4. "Property is theft."	4. Property is merely an extension of personality.
5. Marriage is a voluntary relation, and should be dissoluble at pleasure.	5. A true marriage is made in heaven, is indissoluble, and lasts through eternity. (These state-

Corollaries—contd.

6. The form of government is a matter wholly at the will of a nation at all times. It may say to a king, "We have no longer any occasion for you." (Paine's *Rights of Man*, 9th ed., p. 83.)

7. It is recognition which makes a state in international law. (See the discussion on the whole subject in Lorimer's *Law of Nations*, bk. II., and the review of that work by Professor Holland in the *Revue de Droit International*, t. xv., p. 200.)

8. Paupers derive their rights only from charity and the Poor Law. (See pp. 181 and 289, *supra*.)

Corollaries—contd.

ments are both examples of the sacredness of the marriage tie. (See Hepworth Dixon's *Spiritual Wives*, vol. II., chap. xxvii., to end; see also Comte's *Positive Polity*, i., 192.)

6. "He rules by right Divine, and his Majesty's heirs and successors, each in their time and order will come to the crown with the same contempt of their choice, with which his Majesty has succeeded to that he wears." (Quoted by Paine, *Ibid.*)

7. A state must exist before it can be recognised.

8. Mere being involves the right to continue to be, and a right to the conditions of human existence. (See Lorimer's *Institutes of Law*, pp. 212, 213, 323, 324.)

For the general thesis that the state makes law it may be argued that if a man's rights are not recognised and enforced by the state, how can he be said to have them?

We may as well say that a blind man can see, or a lame man walk, as maintain that a slave or a person labouring under particular disabilities has rights. An individual by himself can do nothing without the help of his fellows, and hence it is absurd to say he has rights before the state exists and enforces them by legislation and judicial establishments. For example take the pauper. Can an African wander to Greenland and demand a share of his food and shelter from some one there? Is a man, who might get work sufficient to maintain him abroad, entitled to refuse to go and to demand maintenance from the state at home? Surely it depends on the views of the state whether it will consent to undertake such a responsibility. If England exports paupers to America, America is entitled to return them. The rights of a pauper, therefore, are created by the state which supports him or receives him. The same may be argued of the law of property, and in particular with respect to patent and copyright. If the populace combined to destroy property, rights of property could not last for an hour. It must therefore be by their consent that the institution was originally created and by their tacit consent it still exists.

For the general antithesis it may be argued that legislators do not make law, because, if their subjects did not claim rights and demand justice, there would be no need of it. We may make any laws we please, but unless they are addressed to self-conscious beings at a certain stage of their history, they are useless. There must be a demand for justice before the judge acts. The legislator and the judge merely enforce and declare rights already existing. What would be the use of a law of copyright if there were no books, or of a law of property if men had not already put their personality into things? How could there be a poor-law, if persons did not recognise the duty of charity and the claims of poverty?

It may be noted in passing that when the attention of "common-sense" people is called to these contradictions, they practically adopt Kant's distinction of *noumenon* and *phenomenon*.[1] They will say that they admit one view in theory to be perfectly sound, but that it is quite impossible to apply it in practice to actual life. And, in like manner, they say in dealing with the first two antinomies that *both* statements are false; and so the great bulk of reasonable politicians call themselves liberal-conservatives, or conservative-liberals.

FOURTH ANTINOMY.

Thesis.	Antithesis.
"There exists an absolutely necessary Being, belonging to the world either as a part or as the cause of it." (Max Müller's *Kant*, iii., 394), or—	"There nowhere exists an absolutely necessary Being, either within or without the world as the cause of it." (*Ibid.*, p. 395), or—

---

[1] Caird's *Kant*, pp. 586 and 587.

Thesis.	Antithesis.
There exists an absolutely necessary Being, belonging to the world, as the source of law and right.	There nowhere exists an absolutely necessary Being, either within or without the world, as the source of law and right.

This subject has already been alluded to.[1] It has been observed that this antinomy is merely a phase of the third.[2] It was added by Kant merely to preserve the symmetry of having a set of antinomies applicable to each class of categories, for Kant did not see what was pointed out afterwards by Hegel, that antinomies "appear in all objects of every kind, in all conceptions, notions, and ideas."[3] We have seen in the course of our present discussion that they may be multiplied indefinitely in law and politics. But the third of the Kantian antinomies arises when we look at law as developing in the individuals who are subject to it, whereas the fourth arises when we look at it from the side of the universal which recognises and declares the law—a distinction corresponding to the distinction between the categories of relation and modality. When we have pushed our question as to the origin of the idea of law as far back as we can go, when we have reached the conception of mankind as a unity subject to one law, there still remains the question—Whence has mankind got this idea? Each state recognises and enforces the rights of its own citizens.

[1] See p. 10, *supra*.
[2] Wallace's *Kant* (Blackwood's Philosophical Classics), p. 186.
[3] Wallace's *Logic of Hegel*, p. 84.

The community of nations recognises and enforces the rights of particular states, or of individuals as members of humanity. But who recognises and enforces the rights of humanity? In attempting to answer these questions we are again placed on the horns of a dilemma. We cannot, on the one hand, conceive law without a legislator, and we cannot, on the other, conceive law as an arbitrary creation even by God. The idea of God is therefore the last to which we are led by our investigation of the idea of law. It cannot be the postulate with which we start. It is only in the idea of God that might and right are ultimately and absolutely identified. We cannot regard God as merely a great architect of the universe. Nor can we regard Him as merely a great king or a great legislator.

> "Regum timendorum in proprios greges,
> Reges in ipsos imperium est Iovis."

It is this conception which gives rise to the absolute contradiction of the fourth antinomy. For example, the maxim, "the king can do no wrong," is often deliberately applied to God, as an excuse for such doctrines as the damnation of infants. But here, as in many other cases, it will be found that the current orthodox theology is a hideous misapplication of legal doctrines now discarded. God can do no wrong, not because He is a capricious tyrant with no political superior, and because human beings are impotent to oppose His will, but because He is the embodiment of Right.[1] He is Law itself. We cannot therefore admit such a conception of God as is conveyed in the following lines of Milton's *Samson Agonistes* :—

> "As if they would confine the Interminable,
> And tie him to his own prescript,
> Who made our laws to bind us, not himself,
> And hath full right to exempt
> Whom so it pleases him by choice
> From national obstriction, without taint
> Of sin or legal debt:
> For with his own laws he can best dispense."

This is merely an adaptation of the Jove of Horace.

We saw that we could not stop short with the categories of relation and modality.[2] It was only half an answer to the question, What is the idea of right? to say that rights spring necessarily from relations. We saw that in the self-consciousness of the individual person there was implied all that actually exists in humanity. We saw that humanity, as conceived by international law, is a unity in space, and as treated by the law of succession, a unity in time. But this unity is a growing organism, beginning apparently with mere physical coexistence in space, and mere physical succession in time, but evolving new ideas as it advanced. The idea of right has become the multiplicity of positive law, and this has again returned into the unity of the idea of

---

[1] See Leibnitz, *Théodicée, Discours de la conformité de la foi avec la raison*, § 37.
[2] See pp. 277, 278, *supra*.

self-conscious personality, which was truly implicit in the whole process. Humanity as now conceived is a unity in an infinity of diversity. This idea of right must now be extended to include the whole universe and God himself. The individual, in claiming and vindicating his rights, is only thinking God's thoughts after Him. In making a demand on his fellowman he is only anticipating what the latter was ready to give. And so in the unity of the self-conscious individual with the infinite idea of right—God himself, we have a solution of all contradiction. But here we leave space and time and their categories of quantity, quality, relation, and modality. We rise above law to morality and religion.

The two sets of antinomies represent generally two distinct political parties, and all the theses on one side are generally adopted by the adherents of one party,[1] though, as has been recently remarked with respect to theological discussions, the most violent conflicts in politics are often between men who do not differ at all—"when men fall out, they know not why." They may be making only different applications of the same thesis. Hence politicians, who claim to think for themselves, often refuse to be bound by party ties, and, as we have just seen, describe themselves as liberal-conservatives or conservative-liberals. And when an extreme politician on either side finds himself accidentally included in a ministry, he feels at once bound to resign, for a

[1] This is also the case in philosophy. See Caird's *Kant*, p. 574.

merely mechanical compromise is no solution of the contradictions. Such men are useful as advocates of their own views in their position as private members of parliament. But in actual life all these antinomies are practically solved by systems of morality and religion. Men recognise that *summum jus* becomes *summa injuria*—i.e., that a right abstracted from its relation to others, caricatured, and exaggerated, becomes a wrong, and they try to find a higher principle by which the contradiction disclosed will be obviated. This may be done with the idea of reciprocity—"Do unto others as ye would that others should do unto you." A partial solution may be found by creating an ideal society of gentlemen subject to the laws of honour. A still wider reconstruction is generally made by creating a society subject to a higher equity or morality; or finally, all contradiction may be made to disappear by treating all men as fellow-subjects in a spiritual realm—the Kingdom of Heaven. As these forms of relation all exist in the modern world, I shall devote my concluding lecture to a short consideration of some of their leading analogies and points of distinction.

LECTURE XIII.

LAW, MORALITY, RELIGION.[1]

When the unity of man's life has been broken up into physical and spiritual sides, the process of differentiation still continues. On the one side we have divisions of races, nations, trades, professions, castes, ranks of nobility, and so forth. On the other we have the ethical life in its widest sense distinguished from the artistic, the scientific, and the intellectual generally. The ethical, again, branches out into the forms of law, customs, fashions, rules of etiquette, morality, and religion. To trace this process would involve an historical examination of man's spiritual development; but in this lecture I purpose to confine myself to indicating briefly some of the relations between the three leading ideas of law, morality, and religion.

We have already seen that in their first conception,

---

[1] On the subject of the relation of morality and religion, reference may be made to Principal Caird's *Philosophy of Religion*, chap. ix.; Drummond's *Natural Law in the Spiritual World*, p. 373; Matthew Arnold's *Literature and Dogma* (5th ed.), p. 51, as well as to Ahrens, Trendelenburg, &c.

ethics and law are practical arts.[1] The same appears to be true of theology. Sir Alfred Lyall[2] says, "If primitive men were asked the use of their beliefs, they might in substance reply that theology is like navigation or astrology, or any other empiric art, which helps one through the risks and chances of the voyage through sensitive existence; that it is the profession of interpreting signs and tokens of the divine caprice, and of propitiating powerful deities who take a sort of blackmail upon human prosperity." It may be that this idea still survives. Certainly Paley's moral doctrine looks very like it, when he defines virtue as "the doing of good to mankind, in obedience to the will of God, and for the sake of everlasting happiness."[3]

A very obvious and striking example of how a subject may be treated from each of these points of view is afforded in the case of the rest required by man to recruit his body after physical toil. In the Mosaic legislation this demand of man's physical and intellectual nature took the form of a religious observance, and was embodied in the fourth commandment of the Decalogue. But in the nineteenth century, for workers in factories and workshops, and especially for women and children, one day in seven, which sufficed for an agricultural people four thousand years ago, is quite inadequate. And, hence, in our day the fourth commandment appears

---

[1] Pp. 4 and 5, *supra*.   [2] *Asiatic Studies*, p. 55.
[3] *Moral Philosophy*, bk. I., chap. vii.

in the form of the Factory Acts, and acts restricting the hours of labour for women and children.[1] Here law has in one sense superseded religion. And in other trades and professions, with which parliament has refused to deal, social morality is tending to shorten the hours of labour, and has already succeeded to an enormous extent in so doing, while, at the same time, parallel with this movement, the Christian religion teaches that the whole life and not merely one day in seven is to be devoted to God.

The present agitation for disestablishment is another phase of the same differentiation. It is only an episode in a wider movement, but, being concrete, it has a firmer hold on the vulgar mind. The actual tendency is towards the complete freedom of the religious spirit from external forms and external legislators, whether bishops, priests, general assemblies, or synods. The Pope has been stripped of his temporal power and in the process has both lost and gained spiritual power. Protestant Prussia has swallowed up the territories of the ecclesiastical electors and deprived them of their power. And while the ultramontanes in Europe are sighing for the restoration of the temporal power, the high church parties in this country, and especially in Scotland, with a keener sense of the power of true religion, are urging disestablishment in order that a greater share

[1] These will be found collected in the Appendix to Fraser on *Master and Servant*.

of the spiritual power may eventually fall into their hands. But recent events which have taken place in the established church of England, and in the dissenting churches of Scotland, all teach the same lesson—that it is no longer possible to trammel religion by external bonds of creeds and confessions. The age of excommunication and fulmination, whether by pope or general assembly, is past. Law and religion are now separated, and yet are more strongly united than they ever have been. Even the abolition of parliamentary oaths can be urged, *because of* the sacredness of the oath, and *because* the religious tone of parliament is higher than it has ever been in our history.

One very obvious point of contact between the three ideas is their relation to custom. Precedents in law, fashions, usages, etiquette, customs in social morality, and rites and ceremonies in religion have all a peculiar sacredness from their antiquity. The very words morality (from *mos*), ethics (from $\mathring{\eta}\theta o\varsigma$), and the German *Sittlichkeit* (from *Sitte*), all illustrate a transition from the lower to the higher idea—from mere external custom to the ideas of duty and obligation. Even the word "manners" has been rising, for it now appplies to *good* manners *par excellence*.[1] The first step is the conscious adoption of the custom because it is old. This is an advance on the merely unconscious animal instinct of the utter

[1] Montesquieu discusses the relation of morals and manners to laws in the 19th book of the *Esprit des Lois*.

savage. When any act takes place at variance with usage, the popular conscience is wronged and endeavours to find a remedy in the form of punishment.[1] Variations from the ordinary type are put down with unrelenting vigour, for modern conservatism is anarchy compared with that of the primitive savage. But this is only a negative movement. It is merely a negation of the particular negation of some individual. A further step must be taken, and from a higher point of view it must be seen that both the custom and its contradiction are equally imperfect, and that the idea which transcends and explains them both is a positive idea.

Thus, in religion we have some persons who insist on the observance of ceremonies and of feast days, and on the wearing of vestments, which have been in use from time immemorial. Others hold these to be in great measure immaterial, but declare that religion consists in the belief, if not the understanding of certain philosophic dogmas, which are as venerable as the ceremonies insisted on by their neighbours. In the one case religion is regarded as merely an art, and in the other as merely a science. The one side say "religion is habit;"[2] the other "religion is knowledge."[3] But in each of these cases the religion is external to the man and quite inconsistent with later

---

[1] See Bagehot's *Physics and Politics*, p. 25, and foll.

[2] The unpremeditated pun is significant.

[3] As to the reconciliation of these statements, see Zeller's *Plato and the older Academy* (trans.), p. 448; Ferrier's *Greek Philosophy*, p. 384.

Jewish and Christian ideas. "The sacrifices of God are a pure and contrite heart." "Your new moons and your appointed feasts my soul hateth." " I beseech you, brethren, that ye present your bodies a living sacrifice to God, which is your reasonable service." "Pure religion and undefiled before our God and Father is this, to visit the fatherless and widows in their affliction, and to keep himself unspotted from the world." Passages such as these reveal clearly the contradiction between an external pharisaical religion and true piety. But while the nature of religion in itself is thus set forth, a difficulty at once arises as to the relation of the religious man to what was his former custom. Is he to set it at defiance or is he to follow it? This difficulty, which was propounded by Naaman, the Syrian, to the prophet Elisha, is resolved by St. Paul in a rough and ready way by making it a question of circumstances, depending on the effect it will have on the faith of a brother, with this important proviso, to which I must allude again, that the custom to be followed must not be positively wrong. "It is good not to eat flesh, nor to drink wine, nor to do anything whereby thy brother stumbleth."

The same question may be raised, though not so explicitly, in morality. In some countries it is thought to be scandalous for a lady to go abroad unveiled. If such an act cause pain to her friends, although in other circumstances it might be quite innocent, common sense says that it is her duty to comply with the demands of the current morality. In many of our popular fashions we see an exemplification of the same difficulty. It is a superstition of very old standing that marriages in May are unlucky; but any man who would insist on being married in that month against the remonstrances of his bride or his friends would be guilty of a wrong act. So we may have objections to dresses of ceremony, to forms of address and to a thousand little things which go to make up etiquette; but if they do no harm to anyone, it is only foolishness or malice which could prompt us to run counter to the current fashion. All sound moralists in such cases would tell us that it is our duty to obey, because otherwise we should "offend the brethren."[1]

And finally, in the domain of law, the distinction between law and justice is perpetually reappearing. Rights which have lasted from time immemorial, fortified by prescription, legal forms which have been in use for ages acquire a peculiar sacredness in the eyes of those who are familiar with them. But a period arrives when they are seen to be cumbersome, if not unjust, and the same difficulty arises of a contradiction between the established custom and the ideal right. The practical solution is really St. Paul's. We may individually disapprove of the law but we must obey it. A good man will obey it *because it is the law*. For the sake of his weaker brethren, he will submit to what he feels to be an injustice. And so in changes of the law, if the movement

[1] See Stirling's *Secret of Hegel*, vol. ii., p. 621.

is merely negative, and the new law is only an arbitrary enactment substituted for the old one, not because the new one is just, but because it is the contradiction of the old, the result can only be confusion and anarchy. The only satisfactory changes in the law are those which adopt and develop, and so transcend the ancient institutions of the people to whom they apply. The arbitrary adoption of foreign customs is often absurd in its results. It is a favourite source of amusement with travellers to describe the manner in which barbarians wear European clothes, as when they put stockings upon their hands. The results of adopting foreign law are not less ludicrous. Witness our fixing the age of marriage for women in Scotland at the same period as that of Italian women.[1] And in religion it is to be feared that the efforts of missionaries have frequently had results not widely different.

But, while in each case the *prima facie* duty of the individual is to obey the custom or the law, as the case may be, circumstances may arise which impose a higher duty. If a man is satisfied that his idea represents the true universal, and that it ought to be carried out, and that he would be wronging the world by concealing it, then it may be his duty to declare his views and meet martyrdom and death, ostracism from society, or the

[1] In India it is well known that the legal system introduced by us has made it much more difficult to recover debts than the old system, which was one of morality, and left the payment of the debt to the honour of the debtor. It seems to be admitted that Ireland, in the same way, has been unable to assimilate English law.

extremest penalty the law can devise. This is a question for the individual himself to solve, and he must look to God and to posterity for condemnation or justification. No code of law or morality can guide him to a decision.

Before passing from this I may point out that in each of these three spheres, the development of the individual is first negative and then positive. Religion first appears to a child as the negation of sin, morality as the negation of wrong, and law as the negation of crime. This negation disappears when the individual becomes a true child of God, a conscious member of the family, and a true citizen of the state.

So far we have been looking at external acts; but the difficulty of distinguishing law, morality, and religion is greater when we look to motives. If a man is about to do an act, he may ask, Will the law punish this? Will my friends disapprove of it? Shall I be expelled from my club, or from the exchange? Shall I be reprimanded by my ecclesiastical guardians? Shall I be excommunicated? Will it haunt me with the terrors of a guilty conscience? Shall I be consigned to temporary punishment in a future state? Shall I be condemned to eternal perdition? It surely requires no argument to show that each of those questions is in effect the same.[1] Whether

[1] Every student of the Roman law knows that at even the time of Cicero much of what afterwards became the *law* of obligations was dealt with by the priests as a matter of *religion*, or by the Censors as a matter of *morality*. In our own country before the Reformation the ecclesiastical courts in Edinburgh, St. Andrews,

the sanction is legal, moral, social, or religious, it is still an external motive, and the individual who regulates his conduct by it alone is at the lowest stage of *law*. If therefore a course of conduct is laid down in a code, and a sanction is added for cases of infringement, it is quite erroneous to call the system a religion or system of morality or even law. It is a stage which law has been striving to transcend and in all stable and civilised societies has actually transcended. In like manner a person may so deal with rewards. Instead of considering his abstract duty, he may consider the pecuniary reward he will obtain for doing the act, or the approbation of his fellows, or of his own conscience, or the sensual rewards of a heaven of oriental grandeur in a future state. Here again the external conduct may be correct, but the motive is only accidentally connected with it. The individual is at a low stage of development. It must be admitted, however, that in practice, in cases of difficulty, such utilitarian considerations often determine our conduct. In law, as in ethics, this is particularly the case where common sense fails and where perhaps a general rule has been established from considerations of conveni-

---

and Glasgow, completely eclipsed the civil courts. Every legal wrong was treated as a sin.—See Innes' *Scotch Legal Antiquities*, p. 239. The modern kirk-sessions and presbyteries have still jurisdiction to deal with *sins*, but their procedure is merely an imperfect survival of the old ideas.—See note p. 353, *infra*; also Cook's *Church Styles*, and Moncreiff's *Practice of the Free Church of Scotland*.

ence. But the tendency is to rise above such external rules and to regulate our conduct by the dictates of reason.

In drawing a distinction between law and morality, it is often observed (1) that an act may be legal and yet not moral *(non omne quod licet honestum est)*; and (2) that a moral act may yet be illegal. Ahrens[1] points out that the first maxim does not imply any complicity between law and immorality. It merely means that the act referred to cannot be affected by law, and law therefore ignores its existence, and if possible, refuses to enforce the apparent rights arising.[2] But there is something more in the statement. When it was first made by Paul[3] and his contemporaries, it signified that the Roman lawyers had begun to criticise the later law from the standpoint of morality, as their predecessors had criticised the old civil law from the standpoint of the *jus gentium* and equity.

In like manner we criticise ordinary popular customs from the standpoint of a higher "morality," and pass a judgment on such practices as adulteration in trade, which traders frequently excuse by saying it enables

---

[1] *Droit Naturel* (7me éd.), vol. i., p. 163.

[2] *Punch* (12th Jany., 1884) appears to hold an opposite view when it says on the subject of adulteration:—

"And men who honest trade pursue,
 Will poison gaily—if it pay.
 The kindly laws such things allow."

[3] L. 144 D. *De reg. jur.* (50, 17).

them to supply classes of goods for which the public are willing to pay; conventional falsehoods, such as that a person is "not in" when he does not wish to see the particular visitor; the conduct of soldiers who fight for what they believe to be an unjust cause; of lawyers who plead for a client they believe to be in the wrong; of clergymen who preach doctrines they do not believe; or such forms of art in painting, or the drama as would not be tolerated in the homes of the people. In all those cases there are two or more distinct codes of morality.

And once more, in the sphere of religion, the Greek philosophers criticised the old religions from the point of view of a higher morality. So in India we have suppressed the Suttee and such barbarous religious rites. But when we deal with the conduct of a priest who might administer extreme unction to a person who merely required care and nourishment to make him recover; or that of a woman, like Mrs. Jellyby, who neglected her family and her domestic duties for what she was pleased to deem religious calls, we cannot do much more than criticise and condemn from the point of view just indicated.

If the statement that a moral act may be illegal means that in the identical circumstances the act may be prohibited by law when it would be enjoined by morality, it merely shows that a breach has been made between law and morality, and the preceding remarks apply. Morality here supplies an ideal which mere custom or law strives to reach. The statement referred to may also mean that the act is indifferent, but if it is forbidden or commanded by law, it is no longer indifferent to morality, for it is immoral to break the law.

Again, St. Paul shows clearly that many acts in themselves perfectly innocent may in certain circumstances become irreligious. Thus we may expand the two statements that an act may be legal and not moral, and that a moral act may yet be illegal, and say: (1.) an act may be approved by conventional morality, and yet not be moral; and (2.) a moral act may be prohibited by conventional morality; and in the sphere of religion: (1.) an act may be religious and yet not moral—" Tantum religio potuit suadere malorum!" and (2.) a moral act may yet be forbidden by religion.

The whole difficulty, as we have seen, is caused by our laying down absolutely *general rules*, whether legal moral or religious, which are mere abstractions. Such rules at once raise practical difficulties of a casuistical character. The difficulties raised in morality are very familiar. All men should always speak the truth, seems a very plain and very sound rule; but ought a physician to tell the truth, if so doing will kill his patient, when a lie would save his life? Men ought to pay their lawful debts, but should they do so, if their creditors would injure themselves by their use of the money? And so forth *ad infinitum.* We do require general rules to a certain extent in all three spheres. We must have uniform religious rites, uniform beliefs, uniform procedure in church courts. But when any of these uniformities is violated, a *legal* question is raised. The fundamental idea may be religious, but the form is legal. There may be an admonition to conform to the rite, or punishment in the form of expulsion from the body. This was the mistake in the persecuting policy which was so common two centuries ago, and which still survives in a modified form. Religion was absorbed in law. An external rite and an external belief were laid down in a code and enforced by physical sanctions. But Protestantism declared that every Christian was a priest, and the whole earth was consecrated ground. Uniformity of rite was thus rudely shaken. And now within the bosom of Protestantism the same struggle is going on against external uniformity of belief. The old mechanical theories of inspiration are exploded. Each Christian must now be a prophet as well as a priest and receive his inspiration direct from the Eternal Spirit.

In practice the difficulties of general rules are obviated in various ways. We have already seen St. Paul's solution in the case of meats. Another example may be taken from the sacrament of baptism, which is enjoined in nearly all Christian churches. The church of Rome requires a priest to perform the ceremony with consecrated water; but if this cannot be done, anyone in an emergency may perform the ceremony with any water. In other churches, again, the ceremony may be validly dispensed with in such circumstances.

The system of casuistry in morals is quite analogous to the one just referred to in religion. Here morality is absorbed in law. The confessional is a spiritual court in which the confessor is judge.[1] Codes too have been compiled to cover the whole of possible human relations. If such an idea could have been successfully carried out, it would have transformed human society into an arrangement of moving puppets. But the ideas of freedom which led to the Reformation made it impossible for such systems to endure.[2]

Is law, then, the appropriate sphere of general rules? We can hardly say so in the face of modern legal phenomena. If our examination of current forms of positive law has shown us anything, it is this, that law has always struggled to free itself from a rigid uniformity, in order to realise the idea of justice. We leave to judges the greatest latitude in opening up and adjusting

---

[1] See Dens, tom. vi., p. 155; *De Sacramento Penitentiae; N.* 114, *De Officio Confessarii tanquam Judicis.*

[2] These statements are amply borne out by the ethical portions of St. Thomas Aquinas' *Summa*, and Peter Dens' *Theologia Moralis et Dogmatica.* To a people who could endure such a system, free parliaments and trial by jury must have appeared supremely ridiculous. Such institutions can be given with safety only to persons who demand them. Blunders of British rule in Ireland and India seem to be very similar, and have arisen from the same causes, viz., differences of race and religion, and different conceptions of the relation of law and religion, church and state.

2 A

pleadings. We have juries to assist in determining civil damages, or the precise amount of guilt of a criminal. The punishment is almost entirely left to the discretion of the judge and after all there remains an appeal to the clemency of the Crown. And so, equally in positive law, positive morality and positive religion, there is a struggle for freedom, against antiquated forms of process and conveyance, servile forms of dress and speech, and obsolete rites and creeds.

But in each of the three spheres there must be a line drawn where general rules must apply. This line may be found by experience, while it is hard to define it theoretically. Within this line the common usage must be followed "for the sake of the brethren." Any other course would involve anarchy and the destruction of society. Any violation of these rules involves legal punishment, ostracism from society, or ecclesiastical censure or excommunication. Here, then, law, morality and religion are practically distinguished by their sanctions, and in an early state of society these would coincide.

As another point of contact between these three ideas we may notice that positive law, positive morality, and positive religions always fall short of their ideals, and cannot in this world attain to them; and, again, in both morality and religion there are divisions corresponding to common and statute law, the one floating about in the common consciousness of the community, and to some extent revealed in its literature, while the other is fixed in sacred codes, creeds, and articles. The one is regarded as a fair subject for discussion, while the other can only be elaborated and interpreted, but not abrogated or repealed. The declaration, *Leges Angliæ nolumus mutare* has been discarded in law, but it still survives in morality, and specially in religion. But in these spheres we can see the operation of the same processes as have completely altered law. Legal fictions, as in the case of baptism given above, and judicial interpretations are at work altering the creeds, and from various indications on the ecclesiastical horizon we may say that the epoch of legislation in this country cannot be long deferred. And if we are to judge from parallel cases in the civil world, no new creeds will be enacted. Some of the most orthodox bodies in this country have no apparent creed!

The conclusion to which these considerations lead is that law, morality and religion are ultimately identical. Stahl complains that Hegel confounds morality and religion, but he forgets that they are not distinguished by the authors of the Jewish Scriptures, nor by Plato and Aristotle. In the development of the human consciousness we can clearly trace these different stages. The age prior to birth is one of purely physical law, both in the individual and in the race.[1] The age of childhood is certainly one of law in the jural sense. So is the infancy of the race. Law is then a few simple rules rigidly enforced. We see the same in the history of art.

[1] Bagehot's *Physics and Politics*, essay I.

The distinction between Greek and Egyptian sculpture was that the latter looked at nature through the medium of rigid rules; the former was as free and varied as nature itself. It was the appeal to nature which separated Giotto from the earlier Italian painters. And in music Wagner, Berlioz and even Beethoven shocked the orthodox musicians of their day as much as Haydn did the old contrapuntists. The age of childhood cannot progress unless it submits to rigid laws.[1] The rule of conduct is laid down by an external power and enforced by a physical sanction. This is satisfactory to a certain extent; but if the process is continued too long it becomes destructive of its object. If the man is to use his limbs, he must throw his crutches away. Or, to use the Platonic simile, law is medicine, but if it is too long used, it becomes poisonous to the system. Law is thus, in the words of St. Paul, the *paidagogos* that leads us to Christ. It is merely preliminary and supplementary to social morality. Law deals only with the external and physical relations of men; and it strives to effect its purpose by physical sanctions—by operating on the person and property of individuals. It deals only with overt acts, and with intentions and motives only in so far as they are evidenced by such acts. The moment that law tries to change opinions or beliefs for their own sake, it enters on a struggle in which it must be defeated.

[1] This is the only hope Mr. Ruskin has of seeing a healthy school of architecture in this country.—*Seven Lamps*, chap. vii.

We may then define law as a portion of social morality recognised by the state through its organised tribunals, and enforced, if necessary, by physical means. Kant's definition of law as an institution for protecting the individual from external interference is quite inadequate. We must even go further than Trendelenburg, who holds that law tries to secure the external conditions for the realisation of human perfection. Law uses external means, but its ends are positive as well as negative, and if it could teach and enforce the complete duty of man, it would not feel debarred from so doing.

How, then, is the transition to morality made? Here, again, Kant is merely negative. Morality frees us from internal impediments to freedom, as law does from external.[1] Stahl defines law as a command of God addressed to the state; morality as a similar command addressed to the individual.[2] Again, it has been suggested that the maxim *summum jus est summa injuria* indicates a point where law ends and morality begins; but this maxim can be slightly altered so as to apply to positive morality itself. It merely means that a general rule pushed to an extreme becomes transformed into its opposite, for such an abstraction raises antinomies such as were noticed in last lecture.

It must be noted that in its abstract form law has never served to keep a society together. This has

---

[1] *Metaphysic of Ethics* (Semple tr.), pp. 179 and 195.
[2] *Philosophie des Rechts*, vol. ii., pt. i., p. 195.

been observed by Sir Henry Maine in India; and in some parts of that empire it will be found that law (in its abstract form) did not exist till it was introduced by the British. The relations of men were ruled by morality and custom. And in our day and in modern states, how few men regulate their conduct by law! There are 14,000 penal statutes in England from the time of Edward III. to 1844—too many for any judge to know. But what Englishman regulated his conduct by them? How many Englishmen have never heard of the Criminal Law Consolidation Acts! What Scotchman going to England or the Continent ever thinks of purchasing a code of the laws prevailing there in order to see how he should act? In fact, any man who regulated his conduct merely by law, who never paid his debts unless he were sent to prison or until his goods were attached, would be rightly shunned by his fellowmen. The recent abolition of imprisonment for debt shows that even law is getting beyond the stage of mere physical sanctions. If a man cannot pay his debts, the presumption is that his inability is owing to misfortune and not to a deliberate intention of defeating the law.

But in other directions we see the impotence of law. We have hardly yet recovered from the hideous nightmare which hung over us, while the secret societies in Ireland had formulated wrong as right, and enforced it by sanctions. As a result, the machinery of law proper was brought to a stand-still, and for a moment appeared to be utterly powerless. And how often in our own experience do we find dishonest debtors legally defeat the claims of their creditors and ultimately defy all attempts to punish them. When Austin said that international law was only morality he was unconsciously uttering a deeper truth than he intended. But if he had been a practising lawyer he could never have fallen into the mistake of supposing that the sanctions of municipal law were more potent than those of international law. The legal remedies of punishment, reparation by awarding damages and divorce are a poor substitute for the doing of right. Law appears to feel its own weakness, because the tendency of modern law is to abolish physical sanctions and avoid general rules—what some would say were its most prominent characteristics. Law is thus again becoming identified with morality, with this difference, that the ancients made law the predicate and said, "morality is law;" while we make morality the predicate and say, "law is morality." They identified morality and law with stern unbending custom, while we are striving to identify them like the body and soul of man, by making law as free and infinite as morality. This change precisely corresponds to that which has taken place in the position of the governing and the governed classes. In the Greek state only the philosopher had to do with morality. He discovered the right and the just and gave it to the people as law. In the Jewish state the will of God was revealed by prophets as law. But the whole relations of those classes are now reversed.

Christianity has now made philosophy and morality the heritage of the vulgar. Statesmen have long since abandoned the idea of forcing a nation into a higher morality by means of law, for both law and morality must be a spontaneous growth of the community. Even when we try to educate, it must be by adopting the idea of development and not that of creation.

Social morality must be realised in space and time, as is done in our daily life. But law tries to realise the ideal in space without reference to time. Even the law of succession is no exception, for it is an attempt to translate relations of time into relations of space. It is quite true that space cannot exist without time, for the mere synthesis of space takes place in time, but when a legal point is presented it is abstracted from time and determined at a particular moment. And when a law is made with reference to a future time, this is a device for the ethical development of society. The question of law can arise only when the time appointed has arrived, and is decided from moment to moment as it arises. As we have seen, there is a tendency in law to regard all rights, in the first instance, as rights of merely person and property. But person and property, looked at abstractly, are merely coexistence in space, and to say that law develops through the categories which were examined in last lecture is just another way of saying that legal rights can exist only in space and time. It must be noted, however, that the antinomies of time, such as those referring to the rights of predecessors and successors, are moral rather than legal in their nature. As in the case of succession, men put themselves forward as voluntary trustees for their ancestors. And, as in the development of the person,[1] they put themselves forward as voluntary guardians (in legal language tutors and curators) of the interests of their unborn posterity. The persons living here and now have the *legal* title, and claim the rights as their own; but an *equitable* title is recognised in their dead ancestors or their remote successors—an ethical movement, which is partially crystallised into the law of trusts and guardianship.

But, again, religion deals with time as law does with space. It aims at man's perfection in time, or perhaps out of time and space altogether. And so in many systems of religion and morality, as among the early Christians, we find ideas quite inconsistent with the legal ideas of person and property. Again, in some religious systems the idea of human perfection on earth is abandoned and perfection is postponed till man attains an existence in a remote eternity. Others again anticipate a millennium on earth. But however this future is regarded, the Christian world looks forward to a time when, just as morality has at present almost superseded law, religion will supersede both—a golden age in the future, like that of the Roman poet in the past,

"Quæ, vindice nullo,
Sponte sua, sine lege, fidem rectumque colebat."

[1] See p. 284, *supra*.

We may express this distinction between abstract law and morality by saying that law is statuesque, morality picturesque. Law abstracts a single relation and expresses it in a formula without any reference to the surroundings. It enacts that a man shall pay his debt without considering whether he is a poor man who will be overwhelmed by it, or a rich one to whom the amount is a matter of indifference. In morality, again, the artist endeavours to fill up all the details and give a complete picture of human life. And in like manner, religion is dramatic. It is law and morality taught by examples. All the greatest religions have been religions of humanity. The example may be a divine being a saint or a martyr, as in the various aspects of Christianity. And in the living church, the most effectual preaching is the life of the man of piety. Men such as he are "the salt of the earth." Without this the whole apparatus of sacraments, preaching and prayer is an empty mockery.[1] Thus in the

[1] It appears doubtful if Mohammedanism should be classed as a religion. It is undoubtedly a system of law, with the religious element subordinated. On the other hand, some Greek philosophies, and particularly Stoicism, may fairly be ranked among religions. The same difficulty presents itself in the classifying of religions bearing the same name, as in the classifying of political parties. (See p. 197, *supra*.) Thus, in the Christian church, there are high dignitaries whose religion is not much removed from fetichism—who are more heathen than the heathen for whom they pray. Again, religious bodies which confine themselves mainly to the didactic mode of influencing men are more nearly allied to philosophical schools of morality. But, as religion transcends and embodies both law and morality, it may at different stages of its

lowest and the highest stages of human development, progress is caused by conformity to *type*;[1] but in the last stage it is self-conscious. We might pursue the analogy between the ethical and the æsthetical ideas by showing the close relation of painting, sculpture, and the drama at an early stage of their history and the strivings of them to realise life.

What then is the relation of law to morality and religion in the state? Law can and does promote morality. It may be by refusing to recognise immoral transactions or immoral foreign laws. Such a rule is very elastic, because it depends on the view taken by society at the time the question arises. We may prohibit immoral exhibitions, because they obtrude themselves on the public, and there is no reason why law should extend its protection to institutions which will ultimately injure the state itself. It may even go so far as to make donations revocable for ingratitude, as in the ancient Roman law and some modern systems. Again, if any particular vice is wide-spread, and by some clear and simple means the young and ignorant can be protected against temptation, the state may wisely interfere, provided the remedy does not cause greater injury than the disease. This last is the objection taken to the Permissive Bill by its most honest oppo-

---

history present closer analogies to them than it does in its highest development.

[1] Bagehot's *Physics and Politics*, p. 90.

nents, and we may take this measure as a type of all those intended to suppress vice.

Such proposals will always be discussed on utilitarian grounds, with an implicit reference to a higher standard of morality. Apart from the view that such legislation encourages secret vice and hypocrisy, we may ask, Is drunkenness really so wide-spread? Is it not the gradual disappearance of the vice which has brought into greater prominence the few who are still addicted to it? Should the training in the family and the church not suffice? Is it not better to allow a few to fall, in order that the morality of the many may be more robust? Is the drink question not merely a branch of a more general temperance problem, and is it not dangerous to exaggerate it as if it were the whole? It would carry me beyond my purpose to discuss these questions, but I think we must draw the line at external conduct. It is no doubt absurd to speak of a man having the *right* to drink all his wages and leave his wife and children to be supported by the parish. If he has such a right, the state has as good a right to take his wages from him and spend them for his behoof. The problem is one of immense difficulty, but theoretically we can have no hesitation in approving of legislation whereby habitual drunkards are dealt with as partially insane persons.[1] And whenever it can be shown that the drunken habits of any one interfere with society, then the state

[1] See the Act 42 and 43 Vict., cap. 19.

may interfere for its own protection. If it goes further it it must still be for its own ultimate benefit. If there is any prospect of restoring pauper dipsomaniacs to society as moral or even externally law-abiding citizens, there is no reason why the state should ignore that form of insanity while dealing with other forms, and that for the benefit of the person treated, because the result would benefit the state itself by giving it another citizen. It might even be found more economical to treat such cases at an earlier stage of the disease.[1] A very good specimen of wise temperance legislation is afforded by the act prohibiting the sale of liquors in Sunday steamers.[2] From the circumstances of the country these vessels became in many cases floating pandemoniums. The conduct of the passengers was dangerous to their neighbours, and the law found it easier to cope with the evil before rather than after irreparable injury had been done.

So with religion. The state, as I have remarked before, should protect all positive forms of religion. It may be found practically impossible to accomplish this where the church and the state are identical, as in Mohammedan countries. Persons of a different faith may be treated as aliens. But in a modern Christian state its own laws

---

[1] Of course the Scotch and the Irish Sunday closing and the early closing Acts may be regarded as being for the benefit of the publicans.

[2] 45 and 46 Vict., cap. 66.

will, without doubt, be in accordance with the fundamental doctrines of Christianity. This does not involve the maintaining of any positive form of religion, though there is no objection to the government paying the ministers of all religions, if the doctrines they teach are not subversive of the constitution of the state or dangerous to it. If they are, then punishment is competent, unless the sect is small and practically harmless, when any appearance of persecution may make it dangerous. Here, again, the test of the necessity for interference is the external conduct of the members of the sect.

Both morality and religion afford powerful aid to law; but in order to reap that benefit to its full extent the individual subject should be free to energise to the utmost of his capacity; and, hence, in the most advanced modern states there is either concurrent endowment of all important sects, or the greatest laxity in the enforcement of the nominal creed of the national church. Without freedom morality and religion cannot flourish; without morality and religion true freedom cannot exist. "Where the Spirit of the Lord is there is liberty." It is, therefore, incorrect to say that morality and religion are concerns of the individual, and not of the state. No one who understands what the state is could make such an assertion.[1] Law, morality, and religion are the forces which keep society together. And society is a

[1] See p. 201, *supra*; also *Natural Religion*, by the author of *Ecce Homo*, part II., chap. iv.

unity in differences—one state or one church, for either name is applicable, composed of individuals. No other bond is possible. Thus a scientific body like the British Association, or an artistic one like the Royal Academy, or a corporation like a university or a church, has a legal aspect in space and time. The members of whom they are composed are living human beings. They hold property; they enter into contracts of lease; they hire servants; in short, they are persons. It is this legal personality which enables them to perform their functions in the world. In like manner, they all have moral and religious functions, which are recognised when they subordinate themselves to the idea of human perfection, or look upon themselves as integral parts of the universe. And so with all the other associations of men which represent the infinite diversity of the human mind—they are merely the result of the nature of man, as an individual related to the universe, both in respect of his material body and his spiritual nature.

What, then, is the relation of the individual to the universe? In the age of infancy we have seen he is subject to physical law. His obedience to custom is almost a nervous involuntary reaction. His neighbours are pained with the violation of custom and correct the disturbance. The first consciousness of this process is law in the jural sense. Law is a practical art in which one part of society consciously and deliberately attempts to develop the whole. The unconscious stage is merely one of "eating and drinking, marrying and giving in marriage." The conscious stage is one of rule and government.

Morality is a higher stage. The individual rises above the unity of the family to that of the state, or even to that of humanity. This does not contradict the legal stage. It transcends and embodies all that is involved in it.

But man cannot rest with this world. He cannot conceive the earth as merely a plane of definite extent. He has learned that the physical universe is infinite, and he comes to believe that all the planets are inhabited. He feels himself related to a spiritual kingdom which transcends space and time. This highest synthesis is religion.

Now it cannot be said that science or art is religion. Science is merely a more correct perception than that of ordinary people. But seeing things in their true light, even when it results in the advancement of practical arts, is not a very great advance. The utmost advance of science, together with the perfection of practical arts would merely enable men to eat and drink, marry, and give in marriage with greater physical comfort. Nor is religion art. Art is higher than science, for it is a conscious expression of admiration of what is seen and what is known. Art is truly a part of worship, but not the whole of it.[1] Such admiration or contemplation should only be

---

[1] It may be noticed that music, the latest of the arts, and that which has been most developed by spiritual religions is an abstraction of *time*.

a precursor to sacrifice, which is true worship. And this sacrifice may involve even the laying down of one's life, as with the ancient Romans and religious martyrs. Our "reasonable service" is the conscious consecration of the whole life to God. Our knowledge of the external universe is then no longer mere science; our knowledge of men no longer mere history; our contemplation of men and things no mere admiration and wonder; our knowledge of God no mere theology. These sciences are again made the foundation of practical arts of living—arts of Life itself. Law, morality, and religion were all arts in their first conception, but they are now arts consciously founded on science, and filled with a richer and fuller content than when they were only empirical.

When a man becomes conscious, he demands a vote that he may have a share in the goverment of his country, and not merely that he may have the power of taxing others to supply pauper doles and music in the public parks. In a higher stage he takes a conscious part in the work of advancing human knowledge and promoting art, and in the philanthropic pursuits of missionary and civilising institutions. But in the highest stage he feels himself truly a "labourer together with God." His whole life is a service. There is no specially consecrated place of worship; the whole earth is God's temple. There are no sacred days; the whole of time belongs to God. There are no special rites and ceremonies; whether he eats or drinks, or whatsoever he does, all is done to the glory of God. There are no priests in this temple; each Christian is a priest, offering up himself as a living sacrifice. There are no preachers; each Christian in his life is a living gospel.

It is this consciousness under the name of religion, culture, or civilisation which is the life-spirit of society. But the truly religious spirit frequently inspires the individual with a sense of his own nothingness. The feeling of awe and wonder in the presence of the universe and God may paralyse such a man. He may abandon all interest in practical politics and let events take their course. He may declare it hopeless to attempt the regeneration of the world. Such fatalism is a sad result of self-consciousness. But it is more painful to see a hopeless conservatism, in which the individual is swept along by a rapid current of incessant change, against which he impotently struggles. Such a man is like the helpless savage who has not yet learned to cope with the power of the physical universe. On the other hand, the consciousness of power sometimes inflames the individual with the most aggressive zeal. It is often a mixture of zeal and ignorance which prompts men like the ancient giants, or the builders of Babel, to scale heaven itself and take it by storm.[1] Such undertakings must fail, not so much

[1] If the practice of rationalising old myths were not out of fashion, it might be suggested that the confusion of tongues is the first authentic example of the proverbial divisions in the Radical camp.

because they are impossible, as because the problem is misunderstood, the time selected is inopportune, and the means employed for its solution are inadequate. If the individual can become fully conscious of his function in the universe, if his zeal can be tempered with wisdom and discretion, no limits can be set to human achievement. If the individual can realise the honour of being a fellow-labourer with God, and at the same time remember that he can see only a small part of the process of development, for it is not granted to every man to have the keen eye of a Moses to see the promised land even from the top of some Pisgah, he will strive to act well his own part, and for the rest let " patience have her perfect work."

APPENDIX.

A.—NOTE ON THE USE AND MEANING OF THE TERMS "LAW," "POSITIVE LAW," "NATURAL LAW."

It may be found convenient to recapitulate some of the results of the foregoing lectures by discussing the various meanings in which the term "Law" is used. The words of Lord Stair are more true now than when they were written two hundred years ago:—"There is no term of which men have a more common but confused apprehension than what law is; and yet there be few terms harder to be distinctly conceived or described."

In English the word corresponds to two words in Latin and most European languages. These are *Lex* and *Jus* in Latin; *Loi* and *Droit* in French; *Legge* and *Diritto* in Italian; *Gesetz* and *Recht* in German, and similarly in the related languages. I begin with a Law:—

1. A LAW is a statute, and corresponds to the German *Gesetz*. It may be derived from the Anglo-Saxon *Laga* or the Latin *Lex*, through the Norman. Hallam uses the word in this sense—"We know not of any laws that were ever enacted by our kings without the assent and advice of their great council."[1] The Latin *Lex* was used in a narrow technical sense—"*Lex est generale jussum populi aut plebis, rogante magistratu.*" Later, it approaches the meaning of "law" in English. The modern French "*Loi*" is applied to an act of the legislature.

2. The next step is to assume the existence of such a rule from the fact of certain persons observing a certain course of conduct. A custom or usage is referred to an imaginary statute or law called a common law. So it has been said—"It would be most easy for the judges of the common laws of England, which are not written, but depend upon usage, to make a change in them."[2] This explains

---

[1] *Constitutional History*, chap. i. Elsewhere in that chapter he uses the words "law" and "statute" interchangeably.

[2] North, C. J., quoted by Dr. Broom, *Phil. of Law*, p. 7.

how the phrase "a law of nature" arose. Mankind generally act in a certain way. The existence of a law, as a rule or statute, was inferred *as a cause*.

3. A further step consists in the transfer of this idea to the physical world. A star or comet follows a certain course. The cause which impels it to follow this course is *a law*. The notion of legislation by God appears in the works of some early writers. So a modern writer says—"If God be the Ruler of the world, ... the laws of nature are the laws by which He rules it."[1] In one of Montgomery's hymns we have the lines—

> "Worlds His mighty voice obeyed:
> Laws that never shall be broken
> For their guidance He hath made."

And even at the present day a contrast is sometimes drawn in the pulpit between the obedience rendered by the planets and the tides to God's law, and that displayed in the conduct of men!

4. But it is found that further investigation simply pushes causes further and further back—that the scientific observer can only observe and record phenomena, and generalise them, and that the idea of cause does not belong to physical science. The name law is then transferred from the assumed cause to the generalisation. We then say, for example, that particles attract each other directly as their masses, and inversely as the square of their distance from each other, and stop here. We do not add that *gravity* or anything else *causes* this.[2]

5. The last development in this direction is well exemplified in the laws of mathematics, where the idea of cause is entirely eliminated. Thus, in the expansion of a binomial to a given power the number of terms is always one more than the index. The first term and the last are the two terms of the binomial raised to the power of the index, and so on. These are mere statements of facts, characteristics, qualities, or uniformities, with the idea of cause entirely eliminated.

It can hardly be disputed that the idea at the root of these

---

[1] *Natural Religion*, by the author of *Ecce Homo*, p. 56. See also Grotius, *De Jure Proelii*, chap. ii.

[2] The Duke of Argyle's *Reign of Law*, pp. 64 and foll.; Drummond's *Natural Law in the Spiritual World*—Introduction; Caird's *Hegel*, p. 170.

various meanings is that of *command*. But recently some other
analogies have been suggested. For example, Mr. Westlake hints[1]
that the only connection between them is the idea of *uniformity*.
But it is uniformity which suggested the law—the statute—to
which conduct has conformed. The cause is still kept in view in
this use of the word. And again, mere uniformity is no part of the
modern idea of justice. Law must embrace also infinite diversity.
The law applicable to each case must be discovered, and in theory
it is accidental that the same law is applied over and over again.
It is only so because the cases presented are the same. Once more,
Professor Huxley has laid it down that the analogy between the
different kinds of law consists in the effect of their violation. "The
law," he says, "is not the cause of a man's paying his taxes, nor
is it the cause of his abstaining from theft or murder. The law
is simply a statement of what will happen to a man if he does
not pay his taxes, and if he commits theft or murder."[2] But
the violation of a human law does not always imply detection and
punishment. The physical law on this subject is not that a thief will
be punished for his act, but that the chances are, say ten to one,
that he will be punished. Before we can say what will happen to
a thief we must have a sufficient number of cases for an induction:
and we must eliminate in some way the inefficiency of the police, of
the counsel who conduct the prosecution or defence, of the judge or
jury who try the prisoner. When we can estimate and measure all
those forces, we may arrive at *a law* in the sense indicated by
Professor Huxley. And, yet again, is the law not the cause of
the jailer or the hangman exercising their respective functions?
The truth is that the word was borrowed by physical science from
jurisprudence with the idea of command, to express the idea of
cause in the physical world. It has come back emptied of the
idea of cause, and as jurisprudence is now also a science, there is
a place for the word in its new meaning, as I hope to show
presently.

A Positive Law means, in the first place, a statute, an actually
enacted law. It may also be taken in the second sense above-men-

---

[1] *International Law*, p. 2.
[2] Quoted by Prof. Pollock, *Essays*, p. 45.

tioned, as a presumed statute, which has given rise to a custom, the law being the cause of the uniform custom.[1]

"A Natural Law," or "A Law of Nature," is used in several senses.

1. It is used by old writers to mean a rule of the code applicable to men in a state of nature, before the existence of civilisation. This is an historical absurdity which needs not detain us.

2. The phrase, A Natural Law (*lex naturalis*), as distinguished from Natural Law (*jus naturale*), is not common. But we meet frequently with the expression, "laws of nature," and that appears to refer to the rules of the systems, which are denoted by the phrase *Jus Naturale*.[2] Thus, some would say that each of the Ten Commandments is a law of nature, as being one of a body of rules laid down by Nature; while, in the following sentence from Cumberland,[3] the reference is to the mode of acquiring a knowledge of the law and not to the power which enacted it:—"Lex naturæ est propositio naturaliter cognita, actiones indicans effectrices communis boni." It is not likely that Cumberland identified Being and Knowing.

3. But the common use of this phrase refers to physical laws, going through the gradations above-mentioned in the third, fourth, and fifth senses of the word "law." There is no more abundant source of confusion in the jural meaning of the word than this. It is undoubted that there are natural (physical) laws of man, on which natural (jural) laws are founded. Thus, a person deprived of food will die, is a physical natural law. Parents are bound to support their infant children, is a jural natural law. In this way, all laws proper must be adapted to physical laws or characteristics. So, the law as to coinage must depend on the metals in existence, their characteristics and their value. We cannot make coins of quicksilver nor of iron. Laws as to protecting persons passing along the street from snow or rain falling from roofs, are unnecessary in a country where there is no rain. We may for many purposes regard a positive law as a mechanical contrivance, which adapts natural

---

[1] Professor Lorimer's use of this term has given some trouble to his critics. It has some analogy to the *Transcendental Schema* of Kant, and seems to correspond exactly to the Platonic "idea" of a law.

[2] Spinoza, *Tract. Pol.*, ii., 4.

[3] Holland's *Jurisprudence*, p. 29.

(physical) laws, and uses them for certain ends. Just as an engineer uses the force of a water-fall, or the explosive qualities of gas and air, or the expansive nature of steam, or the force of electricity to subserve certain ends, a legislator or a judge avails himself of the moral and intellectual qualities of men to attain certain ethical ends. When we say then that a legislator should have a knowledge of the laws of nature, we do not mean that he should know the philosophy of law, but that he should know the laws of trade and commerce—political economy—the history and character of the people for whom he is legislating and human nature in general; in a word, the nature and characteristics—the natural physical laws—of the subjects with which he deals. Without such knowledge, he might make such blunders as enacting the same regulations for the transit of cattle, grain, and nitroglycerine! No doubt a knowledge of the philosophy of law will be useful to the legislator, as theology may be useful to a preacher, but it is not necessary. The best legislators have been men who knew nothing of philosophy—who were guided by a practical tact, which in a rude age would be called inspiration. It may, however, be expected that in the future there will be a greater communication between the theoretical philosopher, who devotes himself to the science of law, and the practical lawyer who deals with it only as an art, as has recently taken place between pure science and practical art in the departments of dyeing and electricity.[1]

Now, if this idea is firmly grasped, it is at once evident that it is impossible for man to violate any of the laws of nature in this physical sense. If he can violate them, they cease to be laws. If men could go for a week without food, and do hard work, and yet remain comfortable and healthy, the laws of man's nature would be different from what they presently are. The violation of a law of nature in this physical sense, is vulgarly called a miracle, and not a crime. In short, throughout the whole domain of man's moral and intellectual nature, the laws of nature are as inflexible as in the physical universe. The examination and discovery of these laws is a legitimate field for empirical science, and to Mr. Herbert Spencer is due much credit for the manner in which he has worked out this

---

[1] See the late Dr. Siemen's Inaugural Address to the British Association at Southampton, 22nd August, 1882.

side of the subject. But the physical side of law and ethics cannot be separated from the ideal, and we cannot stop at the point at which Mr. Spencer leaves us. Whether we can answer them or not, questions are asked, and we must attempt an answer. In the opening of his *Metaphysic of Ethics*, Kant draws a distinction between physical and moral laws in this, that the former are laws of necessity and cannot be broken, and the latter are laws of freedom and may be violated![1] There are no moral laws if they can be violated with impunity. Without going fully into this matter, I would point out that we frequently find men apparently violating natural physical laws, while in reality they are only illustrating the same or other laws. For example, gardeners cultivate the stamens and pistils of flowers into leaves, and make the flowers barren. And so the whole art of breeding flowers and animals is at once a violation of, and an obedience to, the laws of nature.[2] The mistake made in assuming that moral laws may be broken is analogous to the confounding of freedom with the liberty of indifference. We are familiar with the views of the Roman poets, who condemned navigation and trade as unnatural and impious. Is our modern civilisation an example of obedience to, or violation of, the laws of nature? Our answer will depend to a great extent on how we define "natural law."

And yet again, in this sense, as I have already pointed out, we may have the laws of laws just as we have the laws of thought or the laws of language.[3] Many such laws have been observed, such as the increase of legislative enactments being a sign of decreasing morality, or perhaps, rather, of increase of sensitiveness of the national conscience. Such natural laws it is the function of jurisprudence to observe and record.

Turning now to the abstract use of the word Law, we notice that the meanings correspond somewhat to the concrete ones already mentioned.

1. The Law means the body of laws, whether statutory, customary, or judicial, actually or potentially prevailing in a state. It is not, however, true, as Bentham says, that "Law, or the law

---

[1] Abbot's *Kant's Theory of Ethics*, pp. 1 and 2.
[2] On this whole subject, reference may be made to *The Reign of Law*, by the Duke of Argyle.
[3] See p. 27, *supra*.

taken indefinitely is an abstract and collective term, which, when it means anything, can mean neither more nor less than the sum total of a number of individual laws taken together." If the law is dead, as the civil law of Rome, then this statement is approximately true. But applied, as Bentham applied it, to English law, it bears absurdity on its face. We might as well say that the English language is a collective term for all the words in the last edition of Johnson's Dictionary. But, as both language and law are living growing organisms, the statement is only true for an instant. It would be out of place here to discuss generally the nature of abstract terms; but it is quite obvious that the law of Scotland, the law of England, and the law of France are distinct organic entities, not to be identified with the individual legal rules of which they consist, and without which they would not exist.

2. It is also used in a narrow sense, as in the phrases, the law of contracts, the law of property, the law of merchant shipping, to denote the body of laws relating to those respective subjects. Bentham's statement and the criticism of it apply equally to the wider and narrower use of the word.

3. We may also put this abstract meaning into the word, as used in the following sentence quoted from the judgment of Lord Chancellor Cairns in the case of *The Phosphate Sewage Company* v. *Molleson* before referred to:[1]—" That is *res judicata* upon those facts, and upon those materials to which I have referred, and there is no question that it cannot now, in any way, be set aside; that decision stands as perfect and complete *law*." We may regard the decision as a concrete positive law, or on its abstract side as *law*.

The phrases, "natural law," "the law of nature," (jus naturale—jus naturæ) have corresponding variations.

1. The latter is used, as by Paley,[2] to denote the code prevailing when man was in a state of nature, anterior to the existence of society. This is simply an unhistorical body of positive law.

2. Another class of writers, of whom our Erskine may be taken as an example, uses the phrases as equivalent to the Law of God.[3] This aspect of the subject occupied largely the attention of the schoolmen. Thus Suarez, after a long discussion, holds that natural

---

[1] L. R. 4 App., Cas. 810.
[2] *Moral Philosophy*, book III., chap. xxiii.
[3] *Institutes of the Law of Scotland*, i., 1.

law is true law, and that God is the legislator of it.[1] He holds that there is a transcendental law, part of the being of God, of which the human mind can know nothing except through special enactments. This is eternal law.[2] But even eternal law is laid down by God.[3]

3. The necessary character of the law of nature is vindicated by Suarez, Soto, and others, by making law a part of the being of God; but there is an evident struggle to make law independent of the will of God. The phrase, "The law of nature," is used now as equivalent to morality,[4] or the moral law. So perhaps Milton—

> "If aught against my life
> Thy country sought of thee, it sought unjustly,
> Against the law of nature, law of nations."[5]

4. Erskine, again, uses the word as equivalent to a body of very vague positive law. He says,[6] "By one of the laws of nature, fathers are bound to leave, at their death, some part at least of their substance to their children; and by another, every man has a right to dispose of his property to whom he will. That neither of these laws may be stretched beyond its just limits, it is highly expedient that special rules be prescribed for fixing the particular proportions of the father's estate, which he is disabled from leaving to strangers to the prejudice of his own issue; that so every member of the state may be taught to give both of these laws their due weight.

. . . .

18. That law, which is thus superadded to the law of nature by the legislative power of any sovereign state is called civil, and sometimes positive or municipal." Now this natural law is a wide generalised positive law. It is as true positive law as an act of Parliament. In Erskine's view the human legislator holds to the

---

[1] *De Legibus*, &c., i., 6, 13.

[2] *Ib.*, ii., 4, 10. This is a common view of the schoolmen, and is set forth in Peter Dens' *Manual of Theology*, founded on St. Thomas Aquinas' great work.

[3] *Ib.*, ii., 2, 4.

[4] Kames, *Prins. of Equity*, *Prelim. Disc.*, chap. ii.; Paley, *Moral Phil.*, bk. I., chap. i.

[5] *Samson Agonistes*, 888.

[6] *Institutes*, I. i. 17 and 18. See Stair, *Inst.*, I. i. 3.

Divine the same relation as the Court of Session or the Privy Council to Parliament, when they issue Acts of Sederunt or Proclamations, in virtue of powers delegated to them. Human statutes are like Rules of Court issued by the judges, on general principles laid down by Parliament. God enacts the moral law, and leaves the details of working it out to kings and such as are in authority. The criticism under the next head will apply to this usage of the phrase.

5. A more modern use of the phrase is to denote an ideal law or body of laws. In this view every positive law is an attempt to reach a natural law, which serves as a model. Positive laws are asymptotes which approach, but do not ever reach, natural laws. M. Demangeat expresses this idea when he says,[1] "For us natural law (*le droit naturel*) is the beau ideal; it is the abstract type of perfection in the matter of law. Natural law is therefore before us and not behind us. Each time that the legislator modifies a rule of law, he thinks that the new rule which he establishes is more conform to natural law than the former one, which he supersedes; or, in other words, each time that we seek to perfect positive law (*droit positif*), by that very act we seek to bring it nearer to natural law." In concluding, he points out that human weakness will always prevent the complete realisation of this abstract ideal in human legislation. In regard to this I would only repeat that the natural law at which the legislator or judge aims cannot be realised apart from positive law. Such natural law is present in every positive law. And so it is the grossest absurdity for Erskine to call the right of testing a natural law. It is as much a positive law as the law "Thou shalt not steal." Mere generalisation of a positive law does not make a natural law. The blank schedule of the end of a conveyancing act is a positive law as much as the completed deed founded on it. We may go further, and say that the three precepts of the law—"Honeste vivere," "neminem lædere," "suum cuique tribuere," are also positive laws, highly sublimated, no doubt, but still positive laws. And suppose we go further and reduce our three precepts to one, say Kant's Categorical Imperative—"Act so that thy will may become a universal law," we are still in the region of positive law. What

[1] *Cours de droit romain*, vol. i., p. 7.

we are seeking is one transcendental statute or law, which includes and implies every conceivable positive law. Is this transcendental law not as much out of our reach as the transcendental, as distinguished from the phenomenal, universe? Can we know duty apart from particular single individual duties? or law apart from particular positive laws? Can we have rights in general without having particular rights? Can we have a right of property without possessing anything? The metaphysic of ethics should therefore bring us to a law, in the physical or mathematical sense, and not to a law in the jural sense. If we put our result in the form of an imperative law, we have gone a step beyond the sphere of pure reason. We make the law a positive law.[1]

6. On the physical side the phrases in question now approach Ulpian's idea—"Jus naturale est, quod natura omnia animalia docuit," and we may extend it to all animate and inanimate nature. This usage is now admitted to be undoubtedly a metaphor.

7. The last and certainly the best usage is to define natural law as the science of law.[2] This is the sense in which Ahrens uses the words when he says, "The philosophy of law, or natural law, is the science which discloses the first principles of right, conceived by reason, and founded on the nature of man, considered in itself, and in its relations with the universal order of things."[3] Trendelenburg uses the words in the same sense, but wisely leaves them on the title-page and in the preface. To attempt to put the new wine of modern philosophy into the old bottles of the scholastic terms, "natural law" and "laws of nature," can only result in the usual catastrophe. The experiment is so dangerous that it should be avoided. It is only by giving up the use of those words that we can give anything like satisfactory answers to the questions which so much occupied the schoolmen,[4] and which still divide the schools of philosophical jurists. Is law one or many? Is it created by God or men, or is it prior to and independent of them? Law is all of these at once. The thought which is at the foundation of positive law is

---

[1] See Green's *Ethics*, p. 206.

[2] The transition from the idea of natural law as the subject to the idea of natural law as the science of that subject is analogous to the confusion between religion and theology.

[3] *Cours de droit naturel*, vol. i., p. 1.

[4] See Thomas Aquinas, *Summa Theologiæ*, *Prima Secundæ*, Quæst. xciv.

one, but cannot be conceived by itself as an abstraction. Even for the idea of personality or being we must have the prior idea of right. The two sides are inseparable. It then becomes an historical question how men became acquainted with law. If it were revealed it must necessarily be in the form of positive law, but the positive law necessarily involves the idea of right. And so at the same time even man may create, and, after all, only declare law, which existed prior to him. He will only be "thinking God's thoughts after Him."

I would only observe further that, if we work out the ideas involved in the words "Right," "Rights," "Natural Right," "Rights of Nature," it will be found that they go through variations corresponding to those above indicated with reference to the word "Law;" but the subject is looked at from the point of view of the individuals subject to the law, instead of from that of the state enacting or recognising it.[1]

[1] On the subject here discussed reference may be further made to Professor Pollock's *Essays in Jurisprudence and Ethics*, essay II. I have thought it unnecessary to refer to the phrase the "law of nations," which is so intimately bound up with the "law of nature." That phrase denotes what is truly positive law, and this supports my contention that natural law, as commonly conceived, is only a generalised positive law.

B.—NOTE ON THE HISTORY OF SECONDARY RESPONSIBILITY FOR SERVANTS IN SCOTLAND.[1]

THE name "secondary responsibility" was applied in a recent case in the Court of Session[2] to the liability arising in cases where a person is held to be answerable for a wrong done by another person, thing, or animal belonging to him or in his possession. The chief exception down to the year 1881, was when one servant injured another servant in the same employment as himself, under the same master. The servants are then called "collaborateurs," and the doctrine in question is generally called "the doctrine of collaborateur."

A person may commit a wrong through another in various ways. The simplest case would be like this:—If a person put poison into a cup of tea which a servant has put down for a moment, and is about to take to his master, it is the first person and not the servant who is guilty of the crime. Here the maxim applies, *Qui facit per alium facit per se*. Again, if a person conspire with a servant to poison some person, both are equally guilty. This is recognised every day in the doctrine of art and part in Scots criminal law. And it is the most elementary view of the foundation of secondary responsibility for civil reparation. This is the sole ground of responsibility mentioned by Erskine in his *Institutes*, which were published after his death, in 1773. He says—"As to the persons liable to repair the damage, it is he who does the wrong that must repair it; and whoever gives a mandate or order for doing it is held as the doer," and he refers in support of this doctrine to L. 169 D., *de Reg. Jur.* (50, 17), where Paul says—"Is damnum dat, qui jubet dare: ejus vero nulla culpa est, cui parere necesse est."

[1] See p. 106, *supra*.
[2] *Woodhead* v. *The Gartness Mineral Company*, 10th Feb., 1877, 4 Rettie, 469.

SECONDARY RESPONSIBILITY.

We cannot understand the modern law on this subject without referring to the Roman law. I may state that, as a general rule, by that law one freeman would never be responsible for another, unless a mandate were given for the commission of the act. But the case was different with sons, slaves, and beasts. At an early period these, no doubt, stood on precisely the same level. They were all *mancipia*—all *in manu* of the *paterfamilias*. The paterfamilias was liable for them, because they were in his possession. By a law of the Twelve Tables it was competent to him, when sued for damages, to abandon his son, slave, or animal to the person suing. In other words, his liability was limited to the value of the person or animal doing the damage: just as in cases of collision, under the Merchant Shipping Act, liability is limited to so much per ton. The advance of civilisation raised sons to a higher level. It was not, however, until the time of Justinian that the old law as to sons was repealed. Under his legislation, since the paterfamilias had no longer the right to abandon his son, he was no longer liable for him. The person injured must sue the son, who would pay the damages if he had a sufficient *peculium*.[1]

Another noteworthy point in the Roman law was that, as the master was liable for his slave, it was the master alone who could recover the damages. A slave had no *persona* in a court, and therefore the master sued for injury to his property. The master could do no wrong to his servant, because he was simply a piece of property. Generally speaking, the law stood thus: (1.) There must be personal fault in order to create liability; (2.) Possession of a slave, or of an animal which did damage created liability, but this might be got rid of by surrendering the slave or the animal to the person injured. The chief exception to these rules was that by which a person inhabiting a house was liable for injury caused by something being thrown from the window, even though he was not aware of it. This was really a police regulation, and did not affect the general law. But even here, if a slave were the culprit and his master personally innocent, he could elude

---

[1] The codes of France, Belgium and Italy impose liability on parents for pupil children residing with them. See p. 113, *supra*.

liability by surrender of the slave. Another exception sometimes referred to is under the edict " Nautæ, caupones, &c."[1] But, as Ulpian points out, this is not so much a liability on the ground of delict as on the ground of contract—" quod cujusque *salvum fore* receperint." The undertaking of custody implied insurance, just as the sending of money in a properly registered letter now implies insurance to a certain amount by the Post Office. From what has been said it will be at once understood how the Romans dealt with injuries done by one servant to another. The liability of the master was the same as if one of his horses had kicked or bitten another. He was the only one who could claim damages, and if there was a claim, it was extinguished by the " *concursus debitoris et creditoris*" in his person.[2]

Such was the law which was to be applied in modern Europe when slavery was abolished, and it is hardly surprising that a blind devotion to the letter of the Roman law should have led to results which violate all our notions of justice, and would have shocked all the great Roman jurists. In our law, as a general rule, *culpa* must be proved in order to create liability. If you are bitten by a dog, you must aver and prove that the owner knew its vicious habit, and that he did not take care of it. If a pipe in a house bursts and floods the house with water, the tenant must prove negligence on the part of his landlord before he can obtain damages. As was said in a recent case in the Court of Session, there is no liability from the *mere* fact of ownership *per se*.[3] But the liability for servants has gone in quite a different direction. If we examine the cases reported in Morrison's Dictionary under the word " Reparation," sections 10 and 11, we shall find that lawyers, instead of trying to obtain reparation from the party guilty of a wrong, frequently sought out a person who could pay damages, and then exerted themselves by quibbles of all descriptions to bring

[1] See title in Digest (4, 9).
[2] The student who is interested in this subject should read carefully the ninth book of the Digest.
[3] See Moffat & Co. *v.* Park (1877), 5 Rettie, 13. This case shows a divergence of opinion in the Court, but even the Lord Justice-Clerk, who was in the minority, does not attach liability to *mere* ownership.

him within the power of the law. The early cases all point to a strong presumption of authority on the part of the master. We begin by noticing a *simple* presumption against him but it soon becomes an absolute *presumptio juris et de jure* which he is not allowed to redargue.

The doctrine of collaborateur is said to have been imported from England, if not from America. The law making a master liable for his servant is settled in England by a long series of decisions, beginning in the time of Charles II. and ending in 1850, when the law was finally settled.[1] In this way the law is only about two hundred years old. While the law was being matured as between third parties and the master, it did not occur to any one to bring an action by a servant for a wrong done by a fellow-servant until 1837, and the first attempt was checked in the case of *Priestley* v. *Fowler*.[2] The law was not made then for the first time. Chief Baron Pollock said in a later case that he always so understood the law. It is perfectly obvious that while there was any doubt of the master's liability to third parties, it would have been madness in a servant to sue for damages, and this will account for no attempt appearing in the books prior to *Priestley and Fowler's* case. Since that date the attempt was frequently made to fix liability on the master for a wrong done by one servant to his fellow-servant, but the attempts were always unsuccessful unless the servant injured was in the position of a stranger to the master.

In Scotland, as will be found in the old cases in Morrison's Dictionary, to which I have referred, there were several attempts to fasten on one person responsibility for another, *e.g.*, husbands for wives, owners for tenants, &c., &c.[3] But there is one specially interesting case in 1685—*Sibbald* v. *Lady Rosyth*; M. 13,976, where Dr. Sibbald sued Lady Rosyth for damage done to his house, which had been burned by the negligence of her servant. The case was debated in presence of the whole court on account of its novelty, but no decision was given. It is, however, evident from Fountainhall's report, given by Morrison, that that eminent judge

---

[1] See the Parliamentary Report on this subject, 1877.
[2] 3 M. and W. 1.
[3] See the recent attempts in *Barr* v. *Neilsons* (1868), 6 Macph. 651; and *Wardrope* v. *The Duke of Hamilton* (1876), 3 Rettie, 876.

and lawyer was of opinion that the Roman law, which was largely quoted, did not apply in a modern Christian state, in which slavery was not recognised. It is evident from this case, then, that the law was not fixed in 1685, nor was it well settled till within the last fifty years. In 1822 we find a case, *Fraser* v. *Dunlop and Montgomerie*, 1 Shaw, 258, where the pursuer, a child four years of age, was run over by a cart belonging to Dunlop, but which was under the charge of Montgomerie. The Lord Ordinary (Gillies) found the action relevant against the servant, but reported it to the Court as against the master. This shows clearly that the law was not firmly settled in 1822. The Court, however, held that the action was relevant against the master. It was of course possible that he might have been personally negligent, for example, by employing a negligent and incompetent servant.[1] In the same volume of Shaw's Reports, p. 367, we find another case which shows the logical character of the Scotch mind. It is *Waldie* v. *The Duke of Roxburgh*. In accordance with the tendency of the cases, the Sheriff in the inferior Court decided against Mr. Waldie for a breach of interdict, committed by his servants in his absence and without his knowledge. Though this was really a criminal offence, the Lord Ordinary (Pitmilly) adhered to the Sheriff's judgment. But the Inner House preferred justice to logic for once, altered the judgment by a majority, and assoilzied Waldie. In 1826, another case of a child being run over by a cart occurred, and the question was argued at full length.[2] The Lord Ordinary again reported the case, but the five judges were unanimous. The grounds of liability are interesting. Lord Glenlee seems to put it on the ground that the cart was the property of the defender, a principle which, as we have seen, has recently been repudiated by the Court. Lord Alloway partly confounded the case with one of contract. Lord Pitmilly went on the cases, and was thus the only member of the Court who gave a sound reason for his judgment. He had gone wrong in *Waldie's* case by so doing, but it was the only possible way out of the difficulty. Lord Robertson and the Lord Justice-Clerk seemed to make out some sort of constructive negligence on the part of the master.

---

[1] The general ground of liability put by Lord Stair is keeping "outrageous and pernicious servants or beasts."—*Inst.* i. 9. 5.

[2] Baird *v.* Hamilton, 4 S. 798.

The latter concluded his remarks by hoping that the decision "would lead to much greater caution on the part of owners of carts and carriages in the choice of those to whom they entrusted them." It is interesting to look at the authorities quoted, for not one of them bears out the law deduced from them. Even so lately as 1836, in a case where a woman was injured by the carelessness of a man who kept a bridge, two eminent lawyers like Mr. Hope, then Dean of Faculty, afterwards Lord Justice-Clerk, and Mr. More took the trouble to prove that the servant was generally careful and steady. In charging the jury, Lord President Hope remarked that the liability of the master for the servant was simply assumed.[1]

This series of decisions all proceeded on the ground that the modern servant took the place of an ancient slave, and they, in fact, ignored the change that had been made in the condition of a servant by Christianity and civilisation. They ignored the dignity of the person by ranking servants with cattle and things. They were not even put on the same level as domesticated animals, for which a master is not liable unless he has knowledge of their nature. They were treated as being animals *feræ naturæ*! Such a rule could not have stood for a moment unless there had been supposed to exist an equity in making the master, who, it was tacitly assumed, drew the *whole* profit from his servant's work, recompense third parties who were injured by his operations. These equitable considerations, hardly specious if they had been examined, but "nailed" with a text of "scripture," for the Bible and the *Corpus Juris Civilis* occupied in men's minds very much the position of the Pope and the Emperor in the political world, sufficed to carry conviction to most men, and have raised the principle under consideration almost to the dignity of a "law of nature."

But the dignity of the person was shown in another way. A servant may be injured, and the damages, which were formerly payable to his master, must now be paid to himself, for the wrong is now done to him and not to his master. This is all perfectly clear, if the wrong-doer is a free person and can make reparation, and even under the new rule which we have been considering, if the wrong-doer were a servant his master would be liable.

[1] *Hunter or Niven* v. *The Edinburgh and Glasgow Canal Co.* (1836), 14 S. 717.

But if one servant injured another in the same employment, who was under the same master, *quid juris*? If the Court gave damages it was because the one servant was a freeman and the other a slave—a mere thing, an animal. If they refused damages the general rule must be wrong. The Court took the first alternative, and with that love of logic which had made Lord Pitmilly give damages against a master for a servant's crime, they found the master liable. I am unable to find a case in our books earlier than 1839 where this was done. But in *Sword* v. *Cameron* (1839), 1 D., 493, it was assumed that the master was liable and the defenders did not dispute it. This state of the law was most illogically logical. If the master was liable for his servant, the master was the only one who could claim damages. The two claims were thus extinguished when one servant injured a fellow-servant. It is a mistake to say that it was ever in law in Scotland, that a master was bound to make reparation to a servant who was injured by a fellow-servant. If this was really decided in *Sword's* case, it was a blunder committed by the agents and counsel, if not by the judges, and persevered in until it was corrected in 1858, by the House of Lords in the well-known Bartonshill cases, where it was laid down broadly that a master is not liable to a servant who is injured by the negligence of a fellow-servant. These cases illustrate how great an influence the bar has on the development of the law, for the credit of these judgments is due to the eminent lawyer who advised the appeals, and who has since so long adorned the bench of the Supreme Court in Scotland.

The only unfortunate circumstance was that this rule of "collaborateur" was made an exception to the general rule. It seemed as if it was an exception made against the working-classes, and hence the agitation which has been so far successful to give the working-classes the benefit of the injustice while it lasts. In 1877 a Committee of the House of Commons took evidence on the subject, and made a report proposing to alter the law where large companies were concerned, or where a master delegated his authority. Two English judges were examined before this Committee, and both concurred in thinking that the rule making a master liable for his servant is an unjust one, but that it had too strong a hold on the popular mind by custom to be altered now. In the Scotch Courts the tendency certainly was to extend the exception of collaborateur as far as possible, and so destroy the injustice of the rule by the exceptions. In this state of the law the agitation by working-men's champions continued, not to have the personality and dignity of the working-man completely respected, but to have the injustice of secondary responsibility, logically or illogically, extended so as to give the working-classes the full benefit of it. Another step would give a careless servant compensation for injuring himself.

The Employers' Liability Act of 1880 was passed in consequence of this agitation. This Act created a liability of the master *quasi ex delicto* in certain cases and to a limited amount. The absurd compromises which are apparent on the face of the Act, and the limitation of the liability should surely convince us that the Act on its present basis is quite unjust. It would have been much more satisfactory to provide that every contract of service shall imply a contract of insurance on the part of the master towards his servant or his representatives. It would then have been possible for him to recover for injuries done to himself, if not done wilfully. The master would insure with an Accident Insurance Company, and retain the premiums from the servant's wages.[1] The present Act has already caused more litigation than it is worth.

I may remark in passing, that if the liability in such cases had been regarded as an implied obligation of indemnity or insurance, instead of being looked at as a sort of constructive culpability, the questions discussed in such cases as *The Mersey Dock Trustees* v. *Gibbs*,[2] and *Virtue* v. *The Alloa Police Commissioners*,[3] and the earlier case of *Findlater* v. *Duncan*, could hardly have arisen. The insurance of the public against accidents would then have been a legitimate part of the defenders' business. At all events a great part of the difficulty of such cases would have been avoided.

On the general question, the only change, if I might be allowed to suggest one, which would do justice to all, would be to make the

---

[1] Lord Shand, in an address to the Glasgow Juridical Society, strongly urged the general adoption of insurance as a solution of all those difficulties.
[2] L. R. 1. E. and I. App. 81.
[3] (1873) 1 Rettie, 285.

master in all cases responsible, *unless* he proved he was personally innocent. This would substitute a simple for an absolute presumption against him. This would secure at once the freedom of the public from the negligence of a servant, and at the same time avoid as far as possible doing injustice to the master. But perhaps, even here the extension of the principle of insurance against injuries to third parties would afford a satisfactory practical solution of the difficulty. An employer, whose servants are likely to injure third parties, might then insure himself against all risk, and the premiums being a charge on the business would ultimately fall on the public.

C.—NOTE AS TO THE HISTORY OF *IPSO JURE* INVESTITURE IN SCOTLAND.[1]

It was formerly held by our law that no property was transmitted by succession unless the successor *animo et facto* took possession. The possession might be constructive, but still there must be some act *as proprietor*, such as service or confirmation—some *aditio hereditatis*—before it could be said that the person had become proprietor with an *animus sibi habendi*. The idea was similar to that prevailing in the law of sale, that the contract merely gives a title, and that the title is "completed" by delivery, actual or constructive. The change in Scotland was introduced very gradually and extends over a period of about 200 years. The first innovation was in 1690. In that year an act was passed (cap. 26) whereby special assignations granted by the deceased, though unintimated, were made valid to carry the full right without confirmation. In other words, the state, instead of recognising such assignations in detail, recognised them all by anticipation *en bloc*. In 1729, in Gordon's case (Morr. Dict., 14,384) it was decided that special legacies fell under the statute of 1690, and that they vested without confirmation. The next change was in 1823, by the Act 4 George IV., cap. 98, which provided, that if any persons who would have succeeded to movable property of an *intestate* died before confirmation, the right should transmit to their representatives. Thus *ipso jure* investiture was the whole rule as to movables.

The changes as to heritable property have been somewhat different. Prior to the passing of the Act, 1695, cap. 24, an heir might succeed to an estate and sell it, but, if his title was not complete, the purchaser would have no claim against his heir who made up a title passing over his immediate ancestor. This was partially remedied by the Act just referred to, which provided that if an heir were three years in possession of an estate without

---

[1] See p. 265, *supra*.

having completed a title, it should be liable for his debts. Moreover, in 1850, an Act was passed (13 Vict., cap. 13),[1] by which it was provided that when once a title was recorded in favour of a body of trustees for such an institution as a church or school, their successors should not require to make up a title. The title simply flowed into the persons of their duly elected successors. Again, in 1868, it was provided by the Titles to Land Consolidation (Scotland) Act (§ 46), that a decree of service should vest a title equivalent to a conveyance by the deceased ancestor in favour of his heir. But it was not till 1874 that the complete change was made. The Conveyancing Act of that year made heritable property vest immediately on the death of a predecessor, adopting to its full extent the maxim *mortuus sasit vivum*. Prior to this at common law a *mortis causa* conveyance of land vested a right as a general rule on the death of the testator; but this was in consequence of the form of the deed, viz., a *de presenti* conveyance under reservation of liferent. And no question appears ever to have been raised as to the effect of the 20th section of the Titles' Act of 1868 on vesting. By that enactment it may be assumed that the decision in Gordon's case as to movables, above referred to, was simply extended to heritage. When may we expect *ipso jure* investiture to result from the mere contract of sale?

[1] This Act is repealed, but the provision is embodied in the Titles to Land Act, 1868, § 26.

D.—NOTE AS TO THE RELATION OF LAW AND HISTORY.[1]

The intimate relation of law and history is generally recognised. In constitutional and international law the cases with which we deal are generally great historical events. Thus, the transference of the crown from Harold to William of Normandy, the signing of Magna Charta, the summoning of Simon de Montfort's Parliament, the execution of Charles the First, the Revolution settlement, the Wilkes and the Bradlaugh agitations are matter of history, but to the constitutional lawyer they are merely "cases." He abstracts more or less consciously, and with greater or less success the purely *legal* aspects of these events, and confines his attention to these aspects, or in other words, he classifies the events under certain legal categories. And so in international law, the wars of Francis the First and Charles the Fifth, the wars of the French Revolution, European interventions in Turkey and Greece, the affair of the Trent, the Alabama Arbitration, are all historical events in the ordinary sense; but to the publicist who abstracts their legal points, they are merely "cases." It is thus obvious on the surface that it is impossible to study constitutional or international law without a previous knowledge of history, which supplies the facts of the cases with which the student deals.

When we deal with special separate doctrines it is not difficult to trace a progress; but serious difficulty arises when we attempt to trace an organic development in the whole body of law, and not merely in individual laws. The cases appear to arise without a connection much closer than that which we find in any odd volume of law reports, or of the statutes at large. The cases *A.* v. *B., C.* v. *D., E.* v. *F.*, and so on throughout the alphabet, are entirely unconnected. The chaotic arrangement of our statutes is frequent matter of comment. In one volume a money act is followed by one as to burials, and that by one as to the Privy Council, and that again by two Irish Acts, and so forth. If, however, we put our-

[1] Read to the Public Law Class, as an introductory lecture, 2nd Nov., 1883.

selves to the trouble of investigation, we should find that the current volume of law reports reflects with considerable accuracy the social condition of the people, or rather of the propertied classes at this particular date ; and that the statutes at large indicate generally the principal topics which from time to time exercise the public mind. But to the ordinary practising lawyer who is in search of a precedent for a case presented to him, this connection of law and history presents few attractions. In discussing a case he may be compelled to discover the history of a particular law, just as he may try to discover the etymology of a word, in order to apply it, or perhaps to show that it does not apply. But the question arises, Is there nothing more than this external connection of law and history? Is there no *organic* connection between them? This is a question of paramount importance, and deserves more than a mere passing notice. It is at present attracting much attention, and the answers recently given by two high authorities may be quoted.

Thus, Professor Holland, of Oxford, in reviewing Mr. Hosack's *History of the Law of Nations*, says,[1] "Il est fort douteux, selon nous, que le droit international puisse être traité dans l'ordre historique. Nous ne sommes donc nullement surpris que M. Hosack n'ait pas pu résoudre un problème peut-être insoluble."

Again, Mr. Justice Stephen, in his *History of the Criminal Law*,[2] says, "The law of England as a whole, or even the criminal law as a whole, can scarcely be said to have a history. There is no such series of continuous connected changes in the whole system as the use of the word 'history' implies. Each particular part of the law, however, has been the subject of such changes. The law as to perjury and the definition of the crime of murder, have each a history of their own, but the criminal law, regarded as a whole, is like a building the parts of which have been erected at different times, in different styles, and for different purposes. Each part has a history which begins at its foundation, and ends when it reaches its present shape, but the whole has no history, for it has no unity."

Each of these statements involves a deliberate abandonment of the problem to be solved. That the views here expressed are utterly and entirely unsound cannot for an instant be doubted. Professor

---

[1] *Revue de Droit International*, vol. xv., p. 195.
[2] Vol. i., p. 6.

Holland puts forward his statement with evident hesitation, and seems disposed to excuse the undoubted failure of the work under review. Perhaps the best comment on his statement is to show how the problem can be solved. With this view I shall offer a solution at the end of this note. And if we turn to the preface of Mr. Justice Stephen's work, we shall see that after he had finished his task he saw signs of unity which were not apparent before he commenced.

I have quoted the views of two lawyers. I may now refer to the opinion of an historian. The Scottish University Commissioners, in 1878, dealt with the subject, and recommended, amongst other things, the establishment of a chair of history in the Faculty of Arts in Glasgow, with a proviso that the professor should treat also constitutional law, while they proposed to separate the professorship of history from that of constitutional law in Edinburgh. Although he did not dissent, Mr. J. A. Froude, who was one of the Commissioners, thought the subject of sufficient importance to demand some special reference, and in a note appended to the report he gave some suggestions for the Law and History School in our Universities.

Mr. Froude says: "The Professor should direct the student always to original authorities. He must not let them content themselves with the ablest modern writers. Through contemporary writings only he can be introduced into the inner life of passion and conviction where the interest and the instructiveness really lie. It may be objected that trustworthy contemporary writings are not to be found except at intervals. For our knowledge of Scotland, as of most other European countries in early times, we depend chiefly on monks and poets, who are neither of them particularly reliable. But they are not our entire dependence. In the statutes of the Scottish Parliament we have a record of another kind growing steadily, generation after generation, in which the evolution of the national life can be distinctly traced— a sort of bony skeleton upon which flesh and blood and colour can be laid on from other authorities, with a certainty that the true proportions are still preserved. The law and history schools are combined. The two subjects can be carried on together and will mutually illustrate one another."

He then illustrates at length the proposed mode of procedure, and concludes thus :—

"The adventures of Queen Mary, the accession of James the

Sixth, the growth of the kirk, the struggles between the crown and the new spiritual authority which succeeded the Catholic Church, the Union of the Crowns, the fierce battle which Scotland had to fight for its freedom, the final union of the kingdoms—all can be traced in the same pages. The history of these events as there written or implied controls the narrative of partisans, and exhibits in authentic force, with an authority continuously contemporary the motives and passions which influenced opposing factions. Historians from the nature of things describe things from their own point of view. They distribute the lights and shadows according to their preconceptions. The result may be an interesting book, but it contains not the truth, but the truth as it represents itself to the historian's mind. In the statute-book, so far as it goes, we have the minds of the actors themselves, and that is the nearest approach to reality attainable in historical studies."

What might be done in this direction had previously been very well shown by the late Professor Cosmo Innes in his *Scottish Legal Antiquities*. Nor does that writer confine himself to the statutes, but draws his inferences from charters, records of courts, and other similar sources. With all deference to such an authority as Mr. Froude, I would observe (1) that he is here illustrating the study of history through law, and it is therefore quite a mistake to speak of the proposed combination as a school of law *and* history, for it is a school of history alone, and one which is only partially true to nature; and (2) the relation of law to history is exaggerated. In investigating history we must not neglect law, but as little should we neglect politics, literature, art, agriculture, trade, manufacturing industries, and all the elements which go to make up the sum total of a nation's life. In some nations legislative activity may have almost disappeared. Have they therefore no history? In the very example given by Mr. Froude we find trustworthy guides as to the condition of our forefathers in other directions than the Scots Acts. As an example I need only mention burgh accounts, minutes, and public accounts of expenditure. Such documents as the reports of the Venetian ambassadors are familiar to all historical students. Mr. Buckle has found ample material for historical purposes in old sermons. Mr. Motley has constructed his valuable histories almost wholly from private and diplomatic correspondence. De Tocqueville and Taine have written the history of the French Revolution from the reports of government officers. Dumont commenced his great collection of treaties for the benefit of historians. It is the obvious duty of the historical student to correct contemporary histories by what lawyers call *real* evidence, or original documentary evidence. It is a matter of every-day procedure with the practising lawyer to search for documentary evidence, and with it to correct mistakes in the oral evidence arising from prejudice or negligence. This is the sum and substance of Mr. Froude's suggestion, but this is not what we mean when we speak of the historical study of law.

This may be regarded from two points of view, *external* or *internal*. In the external history of law we find the sequence in time of the various bodies of positive law, and arrange them in chronological order. We ascertain the various causes which have effected the changes in the doctrines. It may be the effect of race, climate, geographical position, foreign conquest, emigration, religious or intellectual revival, manufactures, trade, amusements, and a thousand other things. It is almost unnecessary to illustrate this. One or two familiar examples will suffice. Thus the question why law and equity were never practically distinguished in Scotland, and why they subsisted so long side by side in England, can only be answered by a careful examination of the histories of the two nations. The friendly intercourse between Scotland and the Continent, and the custom which formerly prevailed to a great extent among our lawyers of resorting to France and Holland for their legal education, has made the Roman law almost a living system with us; while the hatred of the French, and generally the insular exclusiveness of our southern neighbours tended to exclude that same system. Again, the different direction taken by the law of divorce in the two countries can only be explained by reference to their religious history. And lastly, in the department of constitutional law, the modern constitutions of such states as Holland, Belgium, France, Spain, and England, can only be explained by a careful study of their history, and a just appreciation of the race of men with whom we are dealing, and their geographical position. The same remark applies to the United States of America. Why did the North fight for the Union? Why did the South fight for slavery? The constitutional law of the United States is unintelligible apart from the history, political and religious, of the races which inhabit that continent. And finally, the effects of apparently accidental events cannot be omitted—the Norman conquest and English land-tenure; the French wars of the Edwards and the increasing influence of parliament in England, simultaneously with its decay in France; the matrimonial affairs of Henry VIII. and the Reformation; the flirtations of Elizabeth and the wars which followed the Reformation; the weakness of Charles II. and James II., and the strength of will of William of Orange and the Revolution; the fact of the first two Georges being foreigners and the third one an Englishman, and the consolidation of the power of Parliament; the invention of steam-printing and parliamentary reports—these are merely a specimen of cases where our constitutional law can only be explained by referring to contemporary history.

It is unfortunate that constitutional law and history are so expressly associated in our academic course, as if constitutional law could be profitably taught apart from history, and as if there was any special relation between law and history in this special case. And it is still more unfortunate that Mr. Froude should have given the sanction of his name to the perpetuation of such a mistake. I have more than once in the foregoing lectures referred to the importance of the history of Roman law, but in private law we have advanced much since the days of Trebonian. New contracts—insurance—factory—joint-stock companies—bills of exchange—modern maritime law—certainly illustrate history, but their existence cannot be explained unless we have a knowledge of the events which have taken place, and which have given rise to such legal institutions. Sir Henry Maine's works and the lectures of Mr. Holmes, junior, are examples of how law and history should be combined. International law is also, as we have seen, essentially historical, and hence in some universities international law and history are associated in one professorship. But in all these cases we must observe the history is subordinate to the law, and we explain the law through the history.

But once more, we may study the internal development of legal ideas. We may say that the external history is the history of positive law; the internal history is the history of natural law. In the latter we trace the idea of right from the first glimmerings of consciousness to the full light of the present day. In each system and each succession of systems we can see the idea of personality expanding, and we can trace the growth of the family and the state, and the community of nations. This is the peculiar value of the study of Roman law. We can trace its rise, progress, and decay, and its rejuvenescence in the Dutch, French, German, Italian, and Scottish systems. In the Roman law we see the individual struggling for "personal" freedom. It is the history of the legal idea of person. In our own constitutional history we find another example of the same. Here it is the person demanding first freedom, and then citizenship. It has been said that we do not as yet know whether constitutionalism or the progress of democracy is a process of organisation or of disintegration. The fact appears to be that it is both. An exclusive study of the history of municipal and constitutional law might lead us to imagine that individualism was gradually destroying society, but such a notion would be corrected by a sound historical study of international law, where we see the perfection of the idea of the state in the community of nations. Such a study would convince us that the apparent disintegration is merely a preparation for a higher organisation. Accordingly in a thoroughly equipped faculty of law, the two great divisions of private and public law—including in the latter term both constitutional and international law, should be treated historically.

The confusion here indicated appears to be caused by the fact, that the word "History" has come to be applied specially to "Political History." It is impossible to understand law without reference to that history; and it is as impossible to understand that history without reference to law. But the two subjects are distinct, and there is no difficulty in distinguishing them. It is as erroneous to group law and history exclusively, as it would be to group religion and history, commerce and history, science and history, literature and history, or agriculture and history. A complete history of a nation should embrace all the elements of its progress and being.

If we make this correction on Mr. Froude's suggestion, the remaining points may be cordially approved of, except his sneer at the philosophy of history. If we had no philosophy of history, we should be compelled to approve of schemes which describe progress merely by centuries, and classify men merely by nationality.[1] It is to be hoped we have seen the last of such histories. I would therefore suggest that a professor of history (1) should presuppose a general knowledge of historical facts on the part of his students, and should lecture on the philosophy of history. Any theory—even an erroneous one—is better than none. Great progress has been made in physics on hypotheses, which subsequent investigation has shown to be utterly untenable, *e.g.*, the corpuscular theories of heat and light. Without some guiding principle history becomes a mere collection of facts like a Japanese picture, with the smallest and most distant objects on the same scale and the same plane as the greatest and nearest. To the ordinary historical student no one element must be exaggerated; but, when he comes to specialise and apply his historical knowledge to theology, law, or literature, he will be able to estimate the effects of the other forces on the particular one which he has abstracted for special study.[2] (2) The next duty of the professor should be to direct the student as to methods of historical investigation, the weighing of historical evidence, and the balancing of authorities. This department would correspond to the laboratory work in the physical, chemical, and other classes, and the excursions which are found so instructive to students in botany and geology. We should then find a use for the volumes of state-papers and blue-books which now encumber our library shelves as useless lumber. And (3) lastly, the professor might direct the student as to the principal sources of information for the history of particular epochs and nations, very much in the style adopted by Messrs. Gardiner and Mullinger in their well known and valuable "Introduction to the study of English History."

When a law student thus prepared came to the study of constitutional law, the professor of that subject might lecture on (1) the actual presently existing law as to the rights of the

[1] See Dugald Stewart's *Dissertation on the Progress of Metaphysical Philosophy*, and Heron's *History of Jurisprudence*, which show too great a tendency in this direction.

[2] Professor Seeley's *Expansion of England* is a good specimen of what may be done for the philosophy of history in a popular form.

crown, parliament, cabinet, &c., &c.; (2) the philosophical ideas implied in those institutions, in some such manner as these have been explained in the foregoing lectures ; and (3) the history of the law, showing how the ideas have developed, whence they have arisen, and how they have been affected by the other elements of national progress.

The subject of international law should be dealt with in precisely the same manner. To illustrate how the subject may be treated, I may give, in conclusion, a short sketch of the leading features of the history of international law, as I am in the habit of treating it in my lectures on that subject, forming the second portion of the course of Public Law in this university.

What we have to trace is the process by which mankind became divided into a number of groups called states; and at the same time became an organised unity under the domain of law. We must pass over the prehistoric stage as discussed by Sir John Lubbock, Mr. Tyler, Mr. Morgan, Mr. Bagehot, and others—a stage of almost unconscious subjection to physical law.

At the first dawn of history we find mankind divided into groups of tribes or families. These were bound together by religious ties; and if the families or tribes had intercourse with each other, it was through common religious rites, or mutual rites, which implied a higher bond than their particular religions. In a great measure personal safety was unknown outside of the special group.

In India we find a larger group of states, bound together by religion, and strictly separated from the rest of the world. If, as Professor Laurent thinks, caste had its origin in conquest, then this was an advance towards recognising the value of the individual life. But here international law of a limited description prevailed *within* the peninsula, while foreigners were ranked below the most degraded caste, along with worms and reptiles. In like manner it appears that a system of true international law flourished in China before the Christian era.

In Egypt we have a step in advance. The different classes are no longer strict castes, and the division is now into freemen and bondmen. Greece advances still further, for caste disappears altogether. Men are now divided into Greeks and Barbarians. The Homeric conception of humanity is like that of the world it inhabits. We have a small circle of Greeks and other human beings surrounded by savages and inhuman monsters outside of humanity, like the Cyclops and the Laestrygonians.

There is an Indian world, an Egyptian world, a Greek world, a Chinese world, all isolated and separate. Meanwhile the great military empires have been attempting to weld the known world into a physical unity. The maritime nations—the Phœnicians and Carthaginians,—are doing the same in another way, and by their explorations are adding to our knowledge of the earth; and beneath all, family customs and general trade are laying the foundations of our modern municipal and mercantile law.

In Palestine we have the Jews developing the religious idea for modern Christianity; and possessing a rude idea of a state, after the unification of the kingdom under David, and afterwards a kind of international law in the relations of the northern and the southern kingdom after the revolt of Jeroboam. And, lastly, when we come to the period of the Maccabees, with their extradition treaties with Rome, and treaties of neutrality defining contraband goods, the atmosphere is completely modernised.

In the Roman empire those elements all culminated. We have personal freedom and rights of citizenship extended to all but slaves. The world is absorbed into one immense unity. In some texts of the Digest we find reference to states which are friendly, hostile, and neutral; but there is no true international law.

The breaking up of the Empire into east and west, and the rise of the Italian republics and other free towns give rise to an international law. The law is externally represented by the Emperor or the Pope. Europe, after the breaking up of the empire of Charles the Great is one state-system. Christendom is now the unity, of which Christ's vicar on earth is the head, and the crusaders give a practical direction to this idea, while on the theoretical side, at a later date, it is worked out by the Spanish and Dutch jurists. They divide mankind into (1) believers, (2) infidels and heretics, and (3) heathens. International law, which is tacitly or expressly assumed to be the private civil law of Rome, applies to the first. Towards the second war is the normal and proper attitude; and as to the third, if they do not at once accept the Gospel when offered, war is justifiable. This is exactly the old Greek division, believers being put for Hellenes, infidels and heretics being equivalent to barbarians, and the heathen being outside monsters.

The Reformation wrought an immense change in those ideas. Protestants could not renounce commerce with Papists, and so the idea of Christendom was at once raised to a higher level. It is interesting to watch how the orthodoxy of Grotius yields under the influence of external pressure, and how he allows treaties between Christians and heathens, if the former are Dutch and the object is to oppose Spain. The peace of Westphalia closed a century of war. It put Protestants and Catholics on the same basis in the community of European states; and hence, it has been justly regarded as the foundation of modern international law. It was no longer religion, as then understood, but law which was to regulate the relations of states, and we now commence to hear of the idea of "the balance of power."

There was one important element to which I have not referred, and that was the introduction of Feudalism. As a result of this institution, the state was regarded as the property of the monarch. The law of succession applied as in property, and hence, by succession, purchase, gift, theft, and otherwise states or estates were becoming consolidated. But the establishment of Swiss independence, the revolt in the Netherlands, and the revolutions in England and America gave a rude shock to such a notion. In the century and a-half between the peace of Westphalia and the French Revolution, this idea of property in the state was at the root of the wars of Louis XIV. and Frederick the Great. The French Revolution reaffirmed the lessons which had been so often taught before, but had fallen on deaf ears. It was a truth "clad in Hell-fire, since men would have it so." We here see for the first time a crusade for a political idea and not for religion.

The Revolution ran into the empire of Napoleon, which was a caricature of the *ancien régime*. If Louis Capet, James Stewart, and Philip of Hapsburg, could traffic in states and their inhabitants, who could say that it was wrong for Napoleon Buonaparte to do so also? But the attempt to revive the empire of Karl der Grosse in the person of a Frenchman, was 1,000 years behind date. The problem of humanity could not be solved by arbitrarily dividing the world among the relatives of a Corsican adventurer, and physically uniting them under his suzerainty. The tyrant was overthrown by a coalition between the oppressed peoples and their former proprietors, and the Congress of Vienna tried to patch up the *ancien régime.* It was an expiring struggle. We have since heard no more of the *rights* of kings and princes, except in the paper protests of petty Italian dukes and such potentates. Belgium, Greece, Germany, Italy, Roumania, Servia, Montenegro, all point to another principle—the spirit of nationality. The Congress of Vienna tried to solder up the claims of princes and rulers. The Congress of Berlin discussed only questions of nationality. A state is now a free union of free men. And these states are now united by law. It is significant to note that the disgraceful squabbles among ambassadors as to precedence were put an end to at the Congress of Vienna. The kings were no longer the states.

The balance of power which was intended, and failed, to keep the conterminous proprietors within specific bounds, was spasmodically revived by the Russian war, but it has now disappeared from practical politics. The idea of law has given rise to the concert of Europe, and the practice, still somewhat unsettled, of authorising one power to carry out the decision of the whole. In this society of nations are now included American and Asiatic States, and though we still divide men into civilised, semi-civilised, and uncivilised, these distinctions will no doubt gradually disappear. It is a more humane division than the Greek or the Mediæval one; but in international intercourse, a tremendous responsibility is thrown on civilised states to see that their conduct towards their inferior neighbours is regulated by justice and morality, and not by cupidity and selfishness.

It is beyond my present purpose to discuss the effect of those ideas on the special doctrines of international law. I have already indicated the revolution which has taken place in our ideas of war, and particularly, in our ideas of neutrality, and it may be sufficient to note in addition, that nine-tenths of what is called international law in the books, is law of procedure and forms—adjective law—including laws of war, neutrality, contraband, blockade, treaties, ambassadors, &c. It is Professor Lorimer's great merit as a publicist that he has reminded lawyers that there is an idea of right underlying those forms—a substantive law, which they are intended to enforce.

Parallel to and simultaneously with this change in the idea of the state and of the relations between states, we have the progress formerly noticed in private and mercantile law, caused by the invention of the compass and steam navigation; and, as a necessary result, the doctrines of private international law.

But, while we are tracing the history of the legal idea of person in municipal law, and the corresponding idea of citizen in constitutional law which unites the individuals into a state, and also the prolongation of this process in international law—the "person" giving rise to private international law, and public law making the individual a member of a world-state—we must also trace the history of the individual states which now form this world-system. We must answer the question why England and not Ireland or Scotland became the leading power in the British islands. We have to show how Gaul became France and not Burgundy. We must explain how Russia rose and Poland fell. We must trace the union external and physical, of the small kingdoms in the Spanish peninsula; the disappearance of the small German principalities and ecclesiastical powers, and their absorption into Prussia and Austria; the division and subsequent union of Italy, and such changes. For this purpose, treaties and other legal documents form a veritable quarry of information; but this is not the history of law. It is the history of an organic self-conscious unity which is the subject of law, and originates law in and by the process of living and growing. These external changes have been brought about by associations of race, religion, and geographical position; by great inventions,—gun-powder, bayonets, rifled guns, breech-loaders, iron-clad ships, heavy artillery, steam, electricity; and by great preachers, statesmen, soldiers, and sailors. This history of the states actually existing, is a necessary complement to the history of the legal ideas which have been growing up along with them.

Law in this way supplies to some extent the place of a philosophy of history; but legal ideas are not the only ones involved in the growth and history of humanity, and if we would understand fully what is comprehended in civilisation, we must treat in the same way the history of religion, morals, science, art, practical industry, and commerce. But as lawyers we must rest content if we can contribute our share to the solution of the question:—What is the end of Humanity?

E. BIBLIOGRAPHY.[1]

I. ANCIENT WRITERS.

PLATO—The Republic and The Laws.
ARISTOTLE—The Ethics and The Politics.
CICERO—De Republica, De Legibus, De Officiis.

II. EARLY CHRISTIAN WRITERS.

LACTANTIUS—(330 A.D.) Institutiones Divinæ.
ST. AMBROSE—(387) De Officiis Ministrorum.
ST. AUGUSTIN—(354-430) De diversis Quæstionibus; De Civitate Dei.

III. THE SCHOOLMEN AND MEDIÆVAL WRITERS.

ST. THOMAS AQUINAS—(1225-1274) Summa Theologiæ; De Regimine Principis.

[1] This list is borrowed chiefly from Ahrens, omitting the special works on international law given by him. Of these a somewhat complete list will be found in Appendix I. to Woolsey's *Introduction to the Study of International Law.*

The subject of Law is often discussed in works on Morals under the idea of Justice. Down to a comparatively late period the legal works of Grotius and Pufendorf were used as ethical text-books, and both Ethics and Theology show decided traces of their treatment by lawyers; but I have generally omitted writers who have treated solely of Ethics. I have also omitted works on Political Economy. This science deals only with things which are the objects of rights, treating even the body as merely a machine—a supply of labour. But, as it is impossible entirely to abstract things from their relation to persons, writers on Economics frequently discuss ethical and political questions. This abstract science of things as property, corresponds to the equally abstract science of Natural Law which deals with individuals as persons.

Students commencing the study of the Philosophy of Law are recommended to read Maine's *Ancient Law* and Holland's *Jurisprudence*, along with either Trendelenburg's *Naturrecht*, Ahrens' *Cours de droit naturel*, or Lorimer's *Institutes of Law.*

DANTE—(1265-1321) De Monarchia.
ENGELBERT, of Admont, in Styria—(1331) De Ortu, Progressu, et Fine Romani Imperii.
MARSILIUS, of Padua—(1328) De Translatione Imperii.
WILLIAM, of Occam—(1347) Disputatio de Potestate Ecclesiastica et Seculari.
LUDOLF, of Bebenburg—(1354) Tractatus de Juribus Regni et Imperii Romanorum.
DOMINIC SOTO—De Justitia et Jure (1560).
FRANCISCO SUAREZ—(1548-1617) De Legibus ac Deo Legislatore.
PETER DENS—Theologia Moralis et Dogmatica, 8 vols. (2d ed.). Dublin, 1832.

IV. EARLY PROTESTANT WRITERS.

MELANCTHON—Epitome Philosophiæ Moralis (1538).
OLDENDORP—Elementaris Introductio Juris Naturæ, Civilis, et Gentium (1539).
HEMMING—(Danish), De Lege Naturæ (1562).
ALB. BOLOGNETUS—(1585) De Lege Jure et Æquitate Disputationes.
ALBERICO GENTILI—De Legationibus (1583); De Jure Belli (1588).
WINKLER—Principiorum Juris Libri V., Lipsiæ (1615).
The following writers of this period treated the subject of Monarchy:—
LANGUET (Junius Brutus)—Vindiciæ contra Tyrannos (1577).
BUCHANAN—(1582) De Jure Regni apud Scotos.
CLAUDIUS SALMASIUS—Defensio Regia pro Carolo I. (1649).
MILTON—Defensio pro Populo Anglicano (1650).
JUAN DE MARIANA (Jesuit)—(1536-1623) De Rege et Regis Institutione.
ALGERNON SIDNEY—(d. 1683) Discourses concerning Government.

V. THE SCHOOL OF GROTIUS.

HUGO GROTIUS—De Jure Belli ac Pacis Lib. iii. Parisiis (1625). Published, with an English translation, by Dr. Whewell, with Barbeyrac's notes: Bell & Co., Cambridge; De Jure Prædæ, Hagæ (1858). (The introductions to those works deal with the general subject.)

J. BARBEYRAC—Le Droit de la guerre et de la paix; translated from the Latin of H. Grotius, with notes. Amsterdam (1724); new ed., Basle (1768), 2 vols.

SAMUEL PUFENDORF—Elementa Juris Universalis Methodo Mathematica, Hagæ (1660); De Jure Naturæ et Gentium Libri viii. (1672); cum notis variorum, Francofurti et Lipsiæ (1744); De Officiis Hominis et Civis (1673); the same, cum notis Barbeyracii, Lugd. Bat. (1769); Le Droit de la nature et des gens, translated from the Latin of Samuel Pufendorf, by Jean Barbeyrac, Amsterdam (1706); new edition (1771), 2 vols.; translated into English, with Barbeyrac's notes, by Basil Kennett, London (1729); Des devoirs de l'homme et du citoyen, Amsterdam (1707); new edition, Paris (1830).

RICHARD CUMBERLAND—De Legibus Naturæ Disquisitio Philosophica, London, 1672; translated into English by Towers. Dublin (1750). "This work is particularly directed against Hobbes, and has exercised a great influence on subsequent English writers" (Ahrens).

HEINRICH VON COCCEJI—Grotius Illustratus, &c., 3 vols., published by his son (1744-1747).

SAMUEL VON COCCEJI—Tractatus Juris Gentium; De Principio Juris Naturalis unico, vero et adæquato (1699).

T. RUTHERFORTH — Institutes of Natural Law. Cambridge (1754-1756).

"The following works are specially directed against Pufendorf:—

"ALBERTI—Compendium Juris Naturæ orthodoxa theologia confirmatum. Lipsiæ (1678).

"RACHEL—Dissertationes de Jure Naturæ et Gentium (1676)." (Ahrens).

VI. THE SCHOOL OF THOMASIUS.

CHRISTIAN THOMASIUS—Fundamenta Juris Naturæ et Gentium (1605).

EPH. GERHARD—Delineatio Juris Naturalis, sive de Principiis Justi (1712).
GUNDLING—Jus Naturæ et Gentium.
H. KOEHLER—Juris Naturalis ejusque imprimis cogentis Exercitationes (1728).
ACHENWALL—Prolegomena Juris Naturalis, and Jus Naturæ (1781).

VII. THE SCHOOL OF LEIBNITZ.

LEIBNITZ—Nova Methodus discendæ docendæque Jurisprudentiæ, 1767; Observationes de Principio Juris; Works (ed. Dutens), iv., part 3; Codex Juris Gentium (with two prefaces), 1693-1700.
WOLFF—Jus Naturæ Methodo Scientifica pertractatum, Lipsiæ, 8 tomi in 4°, 1740-1748; Institutiones Juris Naturæ et Gentium, Halæ, 1754. (There is a French translation of this work by Luzac, Amsterdam, 1742, 4 vols.) Vernünftige Gedanken von der Menschen Thun und Lassen, 1720.
FORMEY—Principes du Droit de la nature et des gens; extracted from Wolff's great work, Amsterdam, 1758, 3 vols.
DARIES—Institutiones Jurisprudentiæ Naturalis, Jenæ, 1740; 7th ed., 1776.
NETTELBLADT—Systema Elementaris Jurisprudentiæ Naturalis, Halæ, 1784; 3rd ed., 1785.
VATTEL—Le Droit des gens, or the Principles of Natural Law applied to Nations, Leyden, 1758, 2 vols, edited by Royer-Collard, Paris, 1835; the last edition is by P. Pradier-Fodéré, Paris, 1863, 3 vols.; English translation 2 vols., 1760, and by Joseph Chitty, London, 1834.
MARTINI—De Lege Naturali Positiones, Viennæ, 1764, 6th ed., 1779, and Brussels, 1789; Lehrbegriff des Natur-, Staats-, und Völkerrechts; 4 vols., 1784 and 1787.
DE RAYNEVAL—Institutions du Droit de la nature et des gens. Paris, 1803.
J. CHR. FRIED. MEISTER—Lehrbuch des Naturrechts, 1809.
HOEPFNER—Naturrecht der einzelnen Menschen, der Gesellschaften, und der Völker, 1780. "The authors of the last two works have already begun to pay attention to the theory of Kant.

Among the *eclectic* writers who combine the doctrine of Wolff with the theories of Grotius and Thomasius, may be noticed

"BURLAMAQUI—Principes de Droit naturel, 1747; Principes du Droit de la nature et des gens, last edition by M. Dupin, Paris, 1820, 5 vols.; Éléments du Droit Naturel, posthumous work, 1775, several times reprinted;

"DE FELICE—Code d'humanité—a dictionary of natural and civil justice, Yverdon, 1778, 13 vols., in 4to" (Ahrens).

VIII. SCHOOL OF KANT.

IMMAN. KANT—Grundlegung zur Metaphysik der Sitten, 1787; Die Metaphysik der Sitten, (First part) Rechtslehre, 2nd ed., 1798 (Hartenstein, vol. vii.) The same in Latin, "Imm. Kantis Elementa Metaphysicæ Juris Doctrinæ Latine vertit L. Kœnig, Amstelodami, 1809;" Principes métaphysiques du droit de Kant, translated from the German by Tissot, Paris, 1837; translation of Jules Barni, Paris, 1854. (Portions of these are translated into English by Mr. J. W. Semple in his translation, entitled "Kant's Metaphysic of Ethics.")

G. HUFELAND—Lehrsätze des Naturrechts, 2nd ed., 1795.

PH. SCHMALZ—Recht der Natur, 1795; Erklärung der Rechte des Menschen und Bürgers, 1798.

CHR. HOFFBAUER—Naturrecht aus dem Begriffe des Rechts entwickelt; 3rd ed., 1804.

K. K. HEIDENREICH—System des Naturrechts nach kritischen Principien. Leipsic, 1795.

L. N. JACOB—Philosophische Rechtslehre; 2nd ed., 1802.

A. MELLIN—Grundlegung zur Metaphysik der Rechte oder der positiven Gesetzgebung, 1796.

H. STEPHANI—Grundlinien der Rechtswissenschaft oder des sogenannten Naturrechts, 1797.

L. BENDAVID—Versuch einer Rechtslehre, 1802.

J. CH. FR. MEISTER—Lehrbuch des Naturrechts, 1809. See head vii.

H. GROS—Lehrbuch der philosophischen Rechtswissenschaft oder des Naturrechts, 1802; 5th ed., 1829.

CHR. WEISS—Lehrbuch der Philosophie des Rechts, 1804.

ZEILLER—Naturrecht, 1813.

ZACHARIÆ—Philosophische Rechtslehre, oder Naturrecht und Staatslehre, 1819; 2nd ed., 1825. Vierzig Bücher vom Staate—Heidelberg, 1839-1843.

A. BAUER—Lehrbuch des Naturrechts, 1808; 3rd ed., 1825.

W. F. KRUG—Philosophische Rechtslehre, 1817.

S. BECK—Lehrbuch des Naturrechts, 1820.

J. HAUS—Elementa Doctrinæ Philosophicæ sive Juris Naturalis, Gandavi, 1824.

A. VON DROSTE-HULSHOFF—Lehrbuch des Naturrechts, 1831.

L. VON ROTTECK—Lehrbuch des Vernunftrechts und der Staatswissenschaften, 2 vols. 1829.

ANT. VIROZSIL—Epitome Juris Naturalis, Pesthini, 1839.

M. BUSSART—Éléments de droit naturel privé, Fribourg en Suisse, 1836.

HENRI JOUFFROY—Catéchisme de droit naturel. Leipsic and Paris, 1841.

V. BELIME—Philosophie du droit, 2 vols., 3rd ed., 1869; 4th ed., 1881.

SORIA DI CRISPAN—Philosophie du droit public, 1853.

IX. SCHOOL OF KRAUSE.

C. CHR. KRAUSE—Grundlage des Naturrechts oder philosophischer Grundriss des Ideals des Rechts, 1st vol. 1803; Abriss des Systems der Rechtsphilosophie oder des Naturrechts, 1825; Das System der Rechtsphilosophie, Leipsic, 1873.

HEINRICH AHRENS—Cours de droit naturel ou de philosophie du droit; 7th (French) ed., Leipsic, 1875; 6th (German) ed., Vienna, 1870; and translated into English, Boston, U.S.A., 1880; Organische Staatslehre; vol. i., 1851.

K. D. A. ROEDER—Grundzüge des Naturrechts, 1846; 2nd ed., 1860.

JAMES LORIMER—The Institutes of Law, Edinburgh, 1872; (2nd ed.), 1880; Institutes of the Law of Nations, vol. i., Edinburgh, 1883.

X. LATER GERMAN SCHOOLS.

J. G. FICHTE—Grundlage des Naturrechts nach Principien der Wissenschaftslehre, 2 vols. 1792; 2nd ed., 1797.

J. H. Abicht—Neues System eines aus der Menschheit entwickelten Naturrechts; Kurze Darstelling des Natur-und Völkerrechts zum Gebrauche bei Vorlesungen, 1795. "The author comes near the doctrine of Krause" (Ahrens).

G. Hugo—Lehrbuch des Naturrechts als einer Philosophie des positiven Rechts, 1799; 3rd ed., 1820.

G. E. Schulze—Leitfaden der Entwickelung der philosophischen Principien des bürgerlichen und peinlichen Rechts, 1813.

F. Bouterweck—The Division on "Naturrecht" in his "Lehrbuch der philosophischen Wissenschaften;" 2nd ed., 1820.

G. W. Gerlach—Grundriss der philosophischen Rechtslehre, 1824. "The last three writers have sought to place natural law in a more intimate relation with morality" (Ahrens).

G. W. F. Hegel—Grundlinien der Philosophie des Rechts, oder Naturrecht und Staatswissenschaft, Berlin, 1840.

Marrast—La Philosophie du Droit de Hégel, Paris, 1869.

J. Hutchison Stirling—Lectures on the Philosophy of Law, London, 1873. This is an outline of Hegel's Naturrecht.

v. Hasner—Philosophie des Rechts und seiner Geschichte, 1851.

E. v. Moy—Grundlinien des Rechts, vol. i., 1854.

A. Geyer—Die Rechtsphilosophie in Grundzügen, 1863.

Albert Hermann Post—Das Naturgesetz des Rechts. Bremen, 1867.

Adolf Trendelenburg—Naturrecht auf dem Grunde der Ethik; 2nd ed., Berlin, 1868.

Heinrich Zoepfl—Grundriss zu Vorlesungen über Rechtsphilosophie (Naturrecht), Berlin, 1878.

XI. EMPIRICAL SCHOOL (ZOEPFL).[1]

Welcker—Die letzten Gründe von Staat, Recht und Strafe. philosophisch und nach den Rechten der anerkennungswürdigsten Völker rechtshistorisch entwickelt; Giessen, 1813.

L. A. Warnkœnig—Die Rechtsphilosophie als Naturlehre des Rechts, Freiburg, 1839; and Philosophia Juris, editio altera; Tübingen, 1855.

[1] This school and the following one may be considered to be philosophically identical.—See p. 46, *supra*.

F. A. Schilling—Lehrbuch des Naturrechts oder der philosophischen Rechtswissenschaft mit vergleichender Rücksicht auf positive Rechtsbestimmungen; 2 vols, Leipsic, 1859-1863.

Vollgraff—Erster Versuch einer wissenschaftlichen Begründung, sowohl der allgemeinen Ethnologie wie auch der Staats-und Rechtsphilosophie durch die Ethnologie oder Nationalität der Völker; 3 vols., Marburg, 1853-1856.

Dimitry de Glinka—La philosophie du droit ou explication des rapports sociaux. Paris, 1842; 3rd ed., Paris, 1863.

Helfferich—Die Kategorien des Rechts auf geschichtlicher Grundlage. Berlin, 1863.

W. Arnold—Cultur und Rechtsleben. Berlin, 1865.

XII. HISTORICAL SCHOOL.

Vico—See head xviii.

Montesquieu—De l'Esprit des Lois, 1748; translated into English; 2 vols., London, 1750.

Antione-Yves Goguet—De l'origine des lois, &c., 1758; (6th ed.), Paris, 1820.

Friedrich Carl von Savigny—Geschichte des römischen Rechts im Mittelalter, Heidelberg, 1815-1829; Vom Beruf unserer Zeit für Gesetzgebung und Rechtswissenschaft, Heidelberg, 1814; (translated for private circulation by Abraham Hayward, and printed by Littlewood & Co., Old Bailey, London).

Gustavus Hugo—Lehrbuch der Geschichte des römischen Rechts. Berlin, 1826—See head x.

Sir Henry Sumner Maine—Ancient Law, London, 1861, 7th ed., 1880; Village Communities in the East and West, London, 1871, 4th ed., 1881; The early History of Institutions, London, 1874; Dissertations on early Law and Custom, London, 1883.

Lerminier—Cours d'histoire des législations comparées, 1837; Introduction générale à l'histoire du Droit, 2nd ed., 1835; Influence de la philosophie du xviiie siècle sur la législation et la sociabilité du xixe, 1833: Philosophie du Droit, 3rd ed., 1853; Histoire des législateurs et des constitutions de la Grèce antique, 1852, 2 vols.

EDWARD GANS—Das Erbrecht in Weltgeschichtlichen Entwickelung, 4 vols. Berlin, Stuttgart, and Tübingen, 1824–1835.

CARL VON KALTENBORN—Die Vorläufer des Hugo Grotius auf dem Gebiete des Natur und Völkerrechts. Leipsic, 1848.

FUSTEL DE COULANGES—La cité antique (10th ed.), Paris, 1883; Histoire des institutions politiques de la France (2nd ed.)

EMILE DE LAVELEYE—Primitive Property; translated from the French by G. R. L. Marriott, with introduction by T. E. Cliffe Leslie. London, 1878.

OTTO GIERKE—Das deutsche Genossenschaftsrecht, 3 vols. Berlin, 1868, 1873, 1881.

KENELON EDWARD DIGBY—An introduction to the history of the Law of Real Property. Oxford, 1875.

WILLIAM EDWARD HEARN—The Aryan Household. London, 1879.

WILLIAM FORSYTH—History of Trial by Jury. London, 1852.

MELVILLE MADISON BIGELOW—History of Procedure in England (the Norman Period). London, 1880.

ERNEST NYS—Le droit de la guerre et les précurseurs de Grotius. Brussels and Leipsic, 1882.

O. W. HOLMES, jr.—The Common Law. London, 1882.

SIR JAMES FITZJAMES STEPHEN—A History of the Criminal Law of England. London, 1883.

HERBERT SPENCER—The Principles of Sociology, 2 vols., 1876–1883; The Data of Ethics, 1879; Social Statics, 1851; Essays (three series), 1858–1874; The Study of Sociology (2nd ed.), 1874; Descriptive Sociology (eight parts), 1873–1881.

XIII. THEOLOGICAL SCHOOL.

FRIEDRICH JULIUS STAHL—Die Philosophie des Rechts, 3 vols.; 4th ed., Heidelberg, 1870. (Vol. i. (History), is translated into French by Chauffard; Paris, 1880).

CHALYBÆUS—System der speculativen Ethik, oder Philosophie der Familie, des Staates, und der religiösen Sitte. Leipsic, 1850.

HEINRICH LAUER—Philosophie des Rechts, Mainz, 1846.

FERDINAND WALTER—Naturrecht und Politik im Lichte der Gegenwart, Bonn, 1862; 2nd ed., 1871.

Zoepfl observes that the last two look at the subject from the standpoint of the Catholic Church. He classes Krause and his followers (ix., *supra*) with the Theological School. But as to this, see Lorimer's *Institutes of Law* (2nd ed.), p. 21, note, and p. 12, *supra*.

XIV. THE SCHOOL OF HOBBES, AND THE ENGLISH UTILITARIAN SCHOOL.[1]

THOMAS HOBBES—De Cive, 1642; Leviathan seu de Civitate Ecclesiastica et Civili, 1651; (Molesworth's Edition, 1839-1845).

BENEDICT DE SPINOZA — Tractatus Politicus, 1677; Tractatus Theologico-Politicus, 1670; Bruder's edition, Leipsic, 1844.

WILLIAM PALEY—Moral and Political Philosophy, 1785.

JEREMY BENTHAM—Principles of Morals and Legislation, 1789; 2nd ed., 1823 (reprinted at the Clarendon Press, Oxford, 1879), and other works.

JOHN AUSTIN—The Province of Jurisprudence determined; Lectures on Jurisprudence, 2 vols.; 4th ed. London, 1879.

WILLIAM MARKBY—Elements of Law. Oxford, 1871.

DAVID NASMITH—The Institutes of English Public Law, embracing an Outline of General Jurisprudence. London, 1873.

HERBERT BROOM—Philosophy of Law. London, 1876. (This is merely an elementary outline of English Law.)

[1] Any claim that the writers from Bentham downwards have to be ranked as a School of Legal Philosophy is to be attributed to the fact that they, with one or two exceptions, tacitly adopt the philosophical views of Hobbes, and of Spinoza who is so closely associated with him (Maine's *History of Institutions*, p. 354). This school, as developed by Bentham and Austin, owes its existence to the accident that English law at the end of last century was, as a science, and perhaps still is, in a state of chaos. The soil was therefore favourable for the development of the doctrines of Bentham in legislation, and of Austin in the interpretation and application of the common law. Although, therefore, their doctrines cannot pretend to be a system of philosophy, it is impossible to deny their value in the special circumstances for the reform of the system with which they had to deal. The fact of the divisions and arrangement of the Roman law being adopted on the Continent and in Scotland accounts for Austin being at once unknown in Germany, and ignored in Scotland. There was no place for his system where the Roman law prevailed—see Phillimore's *Principles of Jurisprudence*, Introduction. The later writers, and particularly Professor Amos, show decided leanings towards the Historical School, while Professor Pollock connects the school directly with Spinoza.

SHELDON AMOS—A Systematic view of the Science of Jurisprudence. London, 1872; The Science of Law. London, 1877; Political and Legal Remedies for War. London, 1880; The Science of Politics. London, 1883; The History and Principles of the Civil Law of Rome. London, 1883.

THOMAS ERSKINE HOLLAND—The Elements of Jurisprudence. Oxford, 1880; (2nd ed.), 1882.

FREDERICK POLLOCK—Essays in Jurisprudence and Ethics. London, 1882.

JOHN M. LIGHTWOOD—The Nature of Positive Law. London, 1883.

E. C. CLARK—Practical Jurisprudence. Cambridge, 1883.

XV. ENGLISH WRITERS OF VARIOUS SCHOOLS (GENERALLY ECLECTIC).

SIR THOMAS MORE—(1516) Utopia; translated into English by Ralph Robinson (1556); Arber's Reprints, London, 1869.

RICHARD HOOKER—Ecclesiastical Polity, book I. (1594); Keble's edition, Oxford, 1863.

JOHN SELDEN—De Jure Naturali et Gentium juxta Disciplinam Ebræorum, Libb. vii., London, 1640; Mare Clausum, 1635.

RICHARD ZOUCH—Elementa Jurisprudentiæ, &c., Oxford, 1629; Juris et Judicii Fecialis, sive Juris inter Gentes, &c. explicatio. Oxford, 1650.

NATHANAEL CULVERWELL—An elegant and learned Discourse of the Light of Nature, London, 1652; edited by Dr. Brown, Edinburgh, 1857.

GEORGE DAWSON—Origo Legum: or a Treatise on the Origin of Laws and their obliging Power. London, 1694.

FETTIPLACE BELLERS—A Delineation of Universal Law. London, 1750. (This is merely a sketch of an extensive work, but the writer rejects the mythical state of nature, and adopts the idea of development.)

RICHARD WOODDESON—Elements of Jurisprudence treated of in the Preliminary part of a Course of Lectures on the Laws of England. London, 1783; (2nd ed.), London, 1834.

DAVID ROWLAND—Laws of Nature the foundation of Morals. London, 1863.

BIBLIOGRAPHY. 419

JOHN GEORGE PHILLIMORE—Principles and Maxims of Jurisprudence. London, 1856.

JOHN RUSKIN—Unto this Last, 2nd ed., 1877; Munera Pulveris, 1880; Time and Tide, 1868.

XVI. SCOTTISH WRITERS (ECLECTIC, COMBINING THE METAPHYSICAL AND HISTORICAL METHODS).

GERSCHOM CARMICHAEL published with notes, an edition of Pufendorf De Officio Hominis et Civis (2nd ed., 1724). (Hutcheson declares the notes to be more valuable than the text.)

FRANCIS HUTCHESON—A short Introduction to Moral Philosophy, in three books, containing the Elements of Ethics and the Law of Nature; translated from the Latin (4th ed.) Glasgow, 1772.

DAVID HUME—Essays, Moral, Political, and Literary (1742); Green and Grose's edition, vol. i. London, 1875.

HENRY HOME (LORD KAMES)—Principles of Equity (2nd ed.), Edinburgh, 1767; Historical Law Tracts, Edinburgh, 1758; Sketches of the History of Man (new edition). Glasgow, 1819.

JOHN MILLAR- The Origin of the distinction of ranks, or an inquiry into the circumstances which give rise to influence and authority in the different members of Society. London, 1779; 4th ed., Edinburgh, 1806.

JAMES GRANT—Essays on the Origin of Society, . . . Property. . . . Contracts, and Marriage. London, 1785.

ADAM FERGUSON—Institutes of Moral Philosophy (3rd ed.), Edinburgh, 1785; Principles of Moral and Political Science, Edinburgh, 1792; Essay on the history of Civil Society, Edinburgh, 1767; History of the Progress and Termination of the Roman Republic, London, 1783.

THOMAS REID—Essays on the Active Powers; Essay v., chap. iii., on Systems of Natural Jurisprudence.

THOMAS BROWN—Lectures on Ethics (Lectures 18 and 19). Edinburgh, 1846.

SIR JAMES MACKINTOSH—A Discourse on the Study of the Law of Nature and Nations. Edinburgh, 1835.

JAMES REDDIE—Historical Notices of the Roman Law, Edinburgh, 1826; Enquiries, Elementary and Historical, in the Science of Law, London, 1840; An Historical View of the Law of Maritime Commerce, Edinburgh, 1841; Enquiries in International Law, Edinburgh, 1842; 2nd edition, Edinburgh, 1851; Researches, Historical and Critical, in Maritime International Law, 2 vols., Edinburgh, 1844–45.

LORD MACKENZIE—Studies in Roman Law, Edinburgh, 1862; (5th ed.), by John Kirkpatrick.

COSMO INNES—Lectures on Scotch Legal Antiquities. Edinburgh, 1872.

ALEXANDER ROBERTSON—The Constitution and Laws of Scotland. London, 1878.

JAMES LORIMER—See head ix.

XVII. ITALIAN WRITERS.

"In Italy the philosophy of law has been cultivated in modern times with great zeal and with understanding of the high practical importance of this science. Röder has given a review of the modern works on the philosophy of law in Italy, in several very instructive articles inserted in the Critical Review for Jurisprudence (Kritische Zeitschrift für Rechtswissenschaft), vol. xxv., parts 1, 2, and 3. Several authors of these works, as Baroli, Tolomei, lay down principles analagous to those of Kant; others, as Mancini, Poli, Dalluschek, have pointed out their defects; some others adopt the principles of Krause or approach them, as Melchiorre, Boncompagni, and others" (Ahrens).

BAROLI—Diritto naturale privato e publico; 6 vols., Cremona, 1837.

ROMAGNOSI—Assunto primo della scienza del diritto naturale, 1820.

ROSMINI DE SARBATI (The Abbé)—Filosofia del diritto, Milan, 1841; La società e il suo fine, Milan, 1839.

TAPARELLI (Jesuit)—Saggio teoretico di diritto naturale apoggiato sul fatto, 5 vols., 1844; Corso elementare di diritto naturale, 1845. Translated also into German.

Intorno alla filosofia del diritto e singolarmente intorno alle origine del diritto di punire; Letters from the Count Mamiani della Rover and from Prof. Mancini; Naples, 1841.

POLI—Della riforma della giurisprudenza come scienza del diritto. Milan, 1841.

TOLOMEI—Corso elementare di diritto naturale; 2nd ed. Padua, 1855.

ALBINI—Enciclopedia del diritto, 1846.

AMBROSOLI—Introduzione alla giurisprudenza filosofica. Milan, 1846.

BONCOMPAGNI—Introduzione alla scienza del diritto, 1847.

DE GIORGI—Saggio sul diritto filosofico, 1852.

GIUSEPPE CARLE—La vita del diritto nei suoi rapporti colla vita sociale. Turin, 1880.

WAUTRAIN CAVAGNARI—L'ideale del diritto, studio di filosofia giuridica. Genoa, 1883.

XVIII. TREATISES ON THE FUNDAMENTAL PRINCIPLES OF LAW (AHRENS).

FRANCIS BACON—Exemplum Tractatus de Justitia Universali sive de Fontibus Juris, extractum ex ejusdem Opere, De Dignitate et Augmentis Scientiarum, Parisiis, 1752. Spedding's edition of works, vol. i., London, 1879. Essai d'un traité de la justice universelle par Bacon, traduit par Devauxelles, avec le texte en regard. Paris, 1824.

VICO—De uno universo Juris Principio. Naples, 1720-4.

GOTT. HUFELAND—Ueber den Grundsatz des Naturrechts. Leipsic, 1785.

GENZ—Ueber den Ursprung und die ältesten Principien des Rechts; in the "Berliner Monatsschrift," April, 1791.

R. HEIDENREICH—Entwurf der Grundsätze des absoluten Naturrechts, in his Originalideen über die kritische Philosophie. Leipsic, 1793.

P. J. A. FEUERBACH—Versuch über den Begriff des Rechts, in Fichte and Niethammer's Philosophical Journal, 1793, part C. Kritik des natürlichen Rechts. Altona, 1796.

G. HENRICHI—Ideen zu einer wissenschaftlichen Begründung der Rechtslehre oder über den Begriff und die letzten Gründe des Rechts. Hanover, 1810; 2 parts, new edition, 1822.

C. Th. Weicker—Die letzten Gründe von Recht, Staat und Strafe. Giessen, 1813.

L. A. Warnkœnig—Versuch einer Begründung des Rechts durch eine Vernunftidee. Bonn, 1819—See head xi.

A. Baumbach—Einleitung in das Naturrecht als eine volksthümliche Rechtsphilosophie, 1823.

Lerminier—See head xii.

J. A. Bruckner—Essai sur la nature et l'origine des droits, ou déduction des principes de la science philosophique du droit; 2nd edition, Leipsic, 1818. "This is the first French work in which attention has been paid to the progress which the philosophical knowledge of law has made in modern times. The author follows Kant" (Ahrens).

Ueber das oberste Rechtsprincip als Grundlage der Rechtswissenshaft im Allgemeinen. Leipsic, 1825 (anonymous).

G. Hepp—Essai sur la théorie de la vie sociale et du gouvernement représentatif, pour servir d'introduction à l'étude de la science sociale ou du droit et des sciences politiques, 1833. "This volume contains in its first part a philosophical and methodical deduction of the fundamental principle of law" (Ahrens).

J. Oudot—Premiers essais de philosophie du droit, 1846; Conscience et science du devoir, 1856, 2 vols.

P. Pradier-Fodéré—Principes généraux de droit, 1869.

H. Thiercelin—Principes du droit; 2nd edition, 1865.

XIX. MODERN WORKS, PRINCIPALLY ON CONSTITUTIONAL OR STATE LAW (AHRENS).

J. W. Behr—Verfassung und Verwaltung des Staates; 2 vols., 1812.

L. v. Haller—Restauration der Staatswissenschaft; 3 vols., 1820-1823, and in French, Paris and Lyons, 1824-1830.

George Spence—An Inquiry into the Laws and Political Institutions of Modern Europe, and particularly those of England. London, 1826.

L. Jordan—Versuche über das allgemeine Staatsrecht, 1828.

L. ZACHARIAE—Vierzig Bücher vom Staate; 2nd edition, 1839–1847.
F. C. DAHLMANN—Die Politik, 1847.
BLUNTSCHLI—Allgemeines Staatsrecht; 2 vols., 4th edition, 1868.
J. HELD—Staat und Gesellschaft; 3 vols., 1861–1865.
J. SCHOEN—Die Staatswissenschaft geschichtlich und philosophisch begründet. 1831.
BENJAMIN CONSTANT—Principes de politique constitutionnelle, 1836.
SCHUTZENBERGER—Lois de l'ordre social; 2 vols., 1850.
v. EÖTVÖS—Der Einfluss der herrschenden Ideen des 19 Jahrhunderts auf den Staat; 2 vols., 1861–1864.
AUG. COMTE—Système de politique positive, 4 vols., 1854; 2nd edition, 6 vols., 1864. (English translation, London, 1851, &c.)
WILHELM VON HUMBOLDT—Ideen zu einem Versuch, die Gränzen der Wirksamkeit des Staats zu bestimmen, Berlin, 1852; translated, under the title of "The Sphere and Duties of Government," by Joseph Coulthard, jun. London: Trübner & Co.
W. DE GRAY—Essays on Political Science, 2 vols. London, 1853.
P. E. DOVE—The Elements of Political Science. Edinburgh, 1854.
J. v. HELD—Grundzüge des allgemeinen Staatsrechts oder Institutionen des öffentlichen Rechts, 1868.
F. PILGRAM—Nene Grundlagen der Wissenschaft vom Staate, 1870.
ALFRED FOUILLÉE—L'idée moderne du droit en Allemagne, en Angleterre, et en France. Paris, 1878.

XX. TREATISES ON THE HISTORY OF NATURAL LAW.

D. F. LUDOVICI—Dilineatio Historiae Juris Divini, Naturalis et Positivi Universalis. Halae, 1714.
HUBNER—Essai sur l'histoire du droit naturel, 2 vols. London, 1757.
G. HENRICI—The work cited under head xviii.
THEODORE SIMON JOUFFROY—Cours de droit naturel, 3 vols. Paris, 1834–1842.
F. L. G. VON BAUMER—Ueber die geschichtliche Entwickelung der Begriffe von Recht, Staat und Politik, 1827; 3rd ed., 1861.

LERMINIER—See head xii.
ROSBACH—Die Perioden der Rechtsphilosophie, 1842.
HINRICHS—Geschichte der Rechts-und Staatsprincipien seit der Reformation; 3 vols., 1848–1852. (The third volume stops short at the doctrine of Wolff.)
J. H. FICHTE—Die philosophischen Lehren von Recht, Staat und Sitte; part I., 1850.
STAHL—See head xiii.
JOHANN CASPAR BLUNTSCHLI—Geschichte des allgemeinen Staatsrecht und der Politik, vol. i. Munich, 1864—See head xix.
KARL HILDENBRAND—Geschichte und System der Rechts- und Staatsphilosophie, vol. i. Leipsic, 1860.
R. CAULFIELD HERON—An introduction to the History of Jurisprudence. London, 1860.

INDEX.

Abdy, Dr., 77, 79, 108.
Actio, sacramenti, 52; *Per pignoris capionem*, 53; *Publiciana*, 139, 140.
Action, early forms of, 52.
Acts of Parliament—see Statutes.
Acts of Sederunt, 66, 69.
Adoption, 47, 67.
Advocates, 57, 220.
Æsthetics, 10, 26, 362-368.
Æthelbirht, Laws of, 49.
Aged persons, 291.
Ahrens, 201, 253, 349, 382, 408.
Alabama Arbitration, 115, 242, 395.
Aleatory Contracts, 223—see Gaming debt.
Aliment, duty of, between members of family, 167.
Allies, 247.
Amendment of Law, 60, 346.
American Civil War, 232, 399.
Amos, Prof., 15, 108, 417.
Amphiktyonic Council, 243.
Ancestors, worship of, 176, 185, 275; respect for, 317, 361.
Ancient Law, 46—see Maine.
Anglo-Saxon Law, 47-49.
Animals, rights of, 293, 316, 320.
Antinomics of pure reason, 236, 315, 338, 357, 360.
Aquinas, St. Thomas, 353, 382.
Arbitration, 56, 70; international, 243.
Aristotle, 248.
Arrestment on dependence, 53.
Art and part, 384.
Art, progress of, 355; and religion, 368-370; and science of law, 5; comparison of fine arts with law, morality, and religion, 362; law as an, 1, 2, 5, 23, 38, 368, 377.
Arts of life, 369.
Augustus, laws against celibates, 154.
Austin, 13, 15, 24, 41, 43, 59, 70, 280, 359, 417.

Balance of power, 405, 406.
Bankruptcy, 227.
Bar, influence of, on law, 70, 390.

Bentham, 17, 293, 321, 378. 417.
Berkeley, 30.
Bet, nature of a, 214.
Blockade, 242, 406.
Body, rights over living, 121, 288; dead, 258.
Breach of promise to marry, 160.
Brett, Mr. Justice, 58.
Buller, Mr. Justice, 65.

Canon Law, 295.
Capital punishment, 98-101.
Capitis diminutio, 296.
Cartesian theory of Universe, 11.
Cases quoted or commented on :—
    H.M. Advocate *v*. Kerr, 82.
    Aitchison *v*. Aitchison, 260.
    Baird *v*. Hamilton, 388.
    Barr *v*. Neilsons, 387.
    Bartonshill cases, 390.
    Bradlaugh *v*. De Rin, 240.
    Caroline, Queen, 67.
    Cookney *v*. Anderson, 240.
    Findlater *v*. Duncan, 391.
    Fletcher *v*. Rylands, 106.
    Fraser *v*. Dunlop & Montgomerie, 388.
    Gordon, 393.
    Hawthorne, *in re*, 240.
    Honck *v*. Muller, 58.
    Hunter or Niven *v*. E. & G. Canal Co., 389.
    Léotade, The Monk, 96.
    Lickbarrow *v*. Mason, 64.
    Macgregor *v*. Ross and Marshall, 106, 112.
    M'Naughten, 109.
    Mersey Docks Trustees *v*. Gibbs, 391.
    Moffat *v*. Park, 386.
    Orr-Ewing, 265.
    Phosphate Co. *v*. Molleson. 59, 379.
    Priestley *v*. Fowler, 387.
    Sibbald *v*. Lady Rosyth, 387.
    Smith, Madeleine, 96.
    Sword *v*. Cameron, 390.

Cases quoted or commented on :
  Thurburn *v.* Stewart, 174.
  Virtue *v.* Alloa Police Commissioners, 391.
  Waldie *v.* Duke of Roxburghe, 388.
  Wardrope *v.* Duke of Hamilton, 387.
  Watt Brothers *v.* Foyn, 79.
  Woodhead *v.* Gartness Mineral Co., 384.
Caste, 187, 251, 403.
Casuistry, 351-353.
Categories, The Legal, 303-338 ; The Logical, 304; Kant's, 304-313.
Caucus, the, 188.
Cause, Law as idea of. 374.
Causes célèbres, 83, 395.
Celibacy, laws as to, 154.
Censors, 347.
Ceremonies, 343.
Charles I., 80.
Children, 112, 168, 281, 291 ; punishment of, 101 ; property of, 129—see Education, Property, Succession.
Christianity, 195, 362 : and the individual, 302, 352, 360 ; and the Roman law, 12.
Church and State, 190, 198, 202, 273, 318, 365.
Cicero, 14, 15, 17, 321.
Citizen, 189.
Civil injury, 48, 92, 95, 304, 306—see Crime.
Civilisation, 370.
Classes, upper, 187, 318, 320.
Classification of men, 402.
Clotûre, 192.
Code, method of arrangement, 1, 2.
Coexistence of men, impossible to conceive mere, 15, 151, 329.
Collaborateur, doctrine of, 384.
Comity, 317.
Commandment, the fourth, 340.
Commerce, effect of, 204, 237.
Committees of parliament, judicial, 67; grand, 69.
Communism, 146, 244, 245, 266.
Community of states, 229-249.
Compulsory sale of land, 128.
Comtist development, 4, 232.
Conditions in contracts, 216.
Condominium, 132.
Conduct, as a source of law, 31-40.
Confarreatio, 158.
Confederation, 247.
Confessional, 353.

Consciousness, 5, 36-39, 108, 119, 130, 292, 299, 319, 332, 369.
Conservatism, 40, 148, 244, 370; of savages, 343—see Liberal.
Consolat del mar, 59.
Constitutional, Law,'63, 75, 186, 400 ; idea, 175, 189, 197, 302; despotism, 185.
Contract, 84, 104, 118, 135, 171, 204, 229, 304, 307, 309, 330; social, 39, 178, 207, 243; in ethical relations, 156, 222; Roman, 208-211.
Conveyancing, 2, 310.
Copyright, 127, 149.
Corporations, their personality, 287, 367; their responsibility, 47, 112.
Court of Session, a legislative body, 66, 69.
Cousins, marriages of, 165 ; succession of, 264.
Credit system, modern, 149.
Crime, 92, and foll., 304, 305, 309, 347; late definition of, 50 — see Civil Injury.
Criminal law, 48.
Crown, as *ultimus heres*, 264.
Culpa tenet suos auctores, 317.
Cumberland, 376, 410.
Custom, 14, 68, 342, 346, 369; and morality, 344.

Darwin, 166.
Dead's part, 169, 260, 267.
Death, effect of rights, 317—see Succession.
Debtor, meaning of, 210.
Decalogue, 90, 340, 376.
De facto principle—see Lorimer.
Degrees, prohibited in marriage, 162.
Demangeat, 381.
Democracy, 195, 244, 300.
Dens, Peter, 353, 380.
Design, argument from, 12.
Development—see Evolution.
Dickens, 157, 290.
Digby, 132, 268.
Diocletian, 57.
Disestablishment, 72, 190, 341.
Distress, law of, 51.
Distributions, statute of, 259.
Divorce, 67, 170.
Doge of Venice, 62.
Donation *mortis causa*, 254.
Drunkard, rights of, 364.
Duelling, 117; in war, 114, 117.
Dutch law of marriage settlements, 174.
Duties on succession, 263.

INDEX.

ECCLESIASTICAL COURTS, 347—see Church.
Economics—see Political Economy.
Edict—see Praetor.
Edictum perpetuum, 66.
Education by mother, 162; by schoolmaster, 171; by state, 183, 284.
Embassies, 232, 236.
Employers' Liability Act, 61, 391.
Englishman's house is his castle, an, 236, 318.
Entail, law of, 134, 269.
Equality, 299.
Equity, 41, 48, 60, 62, 349.
Erskine, 67, 379, 380, 384.
Ethics, 10; an art of conduct, 5, 23, 32; derivation of, 342; in Greece, 4.
Etiquette, 345.
Evolution, 31-40, 303, 305, 308, 336, 360; from lower to higher categories, 329.
Examples, learning by, 79, 301.
Execution, summary, 50, 54; in public, 100.
Executioner, 62.
Experiments in politics, 7, 301.

FACTORY ACTS, 340.
Factors as guardians, 172, 183.
Facts—see Law.
Faliero, Marino, 80.
Family, 47, 48, 50, 150 et foll., 176, 187, 204, 286—see Marriage, Succession, State, Person.
Farmers, 218.
Fashions, 345.
Father—see Family.
Females, exclusion of, in succession, 271, 275.
Feudalism, 245, 405.
Fiat justitia ruat cœlum, 18.
Fictions, 28, 44, 60, 61, 72, 186, 213, 240, 355.
"Fire and sword," letters of, 113.
Force and fear, 215.
Foreign enlistment, 115—see Statutes.
Foreigners, rights of, 145, 230, 238, 241, 265, 317.
Form and matter, 177, 212, 219, 278.
Formalism in law, 49, 79, 88, 111, 130, 212, 219; in religion, 352.
Fountainhall, Lord, 387.
France, 244, 273.
Franchise, a trust, 189, 191, 369; extension of, 195; female, 193; manhood, 188.

Fraud, 98, 154, 161, 166, 211, 215, 218, 228.
Free trade, 238.
Freedom, 71-73, 179, 182, 216, 278; of contract, 174, 217, 220—see Contract.
French code, 264.
Froude, J. A., 397.

GAMING DEBT, 214.
Gardens, &c., property in, 144.
George, Henry, 130, 146.
Germanic Empire, 86, 177, 199, 280.
God, as legislator, 10, 334, 335, 381; idea of, solution of antinomies, 337; law of, 379; rights against, 316, 320.
Gratuitous contracts, disappearing, 220.
Greek, art, 356; ethics 4, 359; lawgivers, 11; state, 297, 300.
Grotius, 253, 405.
Ground-annuals, 61, 133, 310.
Guardianship, 168, 172, 201, 361.
Gundling, 258.

HABITUAL DRUNKARDS' ACT, 364.
Hadrian, 66.
Hallam, 80, 373.
Hamilton, 30.
Hanseatic league, 231.
Happiness, greatest, principle of, 17.
Heaven, kingdom of, 338.
Hegel, 6, 30, 41, 91, 96, 99, 201, 257, 298, 355.
Heredity, 317.
High church parties, 341.
Hindus, retiral into religious life of aged, 261.
Historical and comparative methods, 46, 414, 415.
Historicus, 77, 81.
History, of law, 3, 400; taught through law, 397—see Roman law, Constitutional law, International law.
Hobbes, 4, 13, 15, 23, 417; definition of civil law, 14.
Holland, Professor, 4, 322, 396.
Holmes, jr., O. W., 191, 223, 400.
Homeric division of mankind, 403.
Hosack, 396.
Hospitality, 247.
House of Lords, 65, 193, 251.
Howard, the philanthropist, 49.
Humanity, unity of, 249, 276.
Hume, 15, 30.
Hunter's *Roman Law*, 210.

Husband, responsibility of, for wife, 387—see Family, Marriage, Succession, Property.
Hutcheson, 5.
Huxley, 375.

Idea of Right, 44; made explicit in judicial decisions, 59; the essence of the relations between parties, 57; underlies all the forms of law, 46.
Ideals in law, &c., 354.
Ignorantia juris neminem excusat, 213.
Illegitimate children, 167.
Illiterate voters, 197.
Imbeciles, personality of, 286.
Immoral contracts, 214; laws and exhibitions, 363.
Imprisonment, for debt, 60, 94, 101, 358; for life, 99.
Independence of states, 236, 319.
India, 62, 91, 96, 99, 185, 190, 346, 353, 358.
Individual, and society, 19, 128, 151, 172, 241, 277, 306, 312; and the world, 249, 301, 314, 347, 371—see Christianity.
Individualism, 116, 241, 245, 300.
Infanticide, 26, 171, 182, 283.
Ingratitude, in *code civil*, 136; Roman law as to, 363.
Innes, Cosmo, 398.
Insanity, 109, 111, 170, 365.
Instinct, 30, 34, 39.
Insurance, 106, 116, 222, 225, 386, 391.
Interdicts, 140.
International law, 26, 46, 75, 81, 229–249, 359; and inter-family law, 50; and constitutional law, 85, 86; historical, 400—see Private.
Interpretation of law, 68; of contracts, 212.
Intervention, 81, 234, 236, 246.
Ipso jure investiture, 265, 393.
Ireland, 15, 55, 73, 218, 353.
Irish Land Act, 1881—see Statutes.
Irish Land Court, 58.

Jevons, Stanley, 294.
Judex, the Roman, 56.
Judge, 62.
Judge-made law, 55, 59, 64, 66, 87.
Judgments, synthetic, 40, 44.
Judicial decisions, law, 59, 379.
Jural relation, 40, 43; moments of, 91, 126, 211, 234, 241, 274, 282, 311.
Jury, trials by, 58; question for a, 60.

Jus naturale, 376—see Law.
Jus gentium, 85, 204, 237, 349.
Jus relictæ, 169, 260.
Justice, 345.
Justinian, 1, 49, 154, 230.

Kames, Lord, 51, 55.
Kant, 153, 156, 159, 160, 179, 182, 244, 304, 333, 357, 378, 412.
Kent, Chancellor, 78.
King, prerogatives of, 63, 200, 331; can do no wrong, 64, 319.

Labour, hours of, 341; and property, 126.
Laissez-faire, 219, 298, 307.
Land, property in, 122, 145.
Laurent, 241, 245, 403.
Law, a science, 30, 382; and fact, 56, 58; and history, 395–407—see History; and language, 16; and natural punishment, 18; as mechanical contrivance, 16, 21, 38, 377; civil, defined by Hobbes, 14; confusion in English, 395; common and statute, 354, 373; declaratory, 41, 67, 72, 330; divisions of, 84; early, nature of, 46; eternity of, 320; foreign words for, 373; innate, denied by Locke, 25; involved in all human relations, 22, 40, 59, 376; laws of, 27, 378; mathematical, 374; mode of learning, 2; natural, 11, 29, 30, 314, 379, 381; objective and subjective, 41; of contract, &c., 379; of nature, 27, 377; a, of nature, 29, 376, 379, 380; of single case, 25, 59, 379; physical, 27, 321, 367, 375, 376; positive, defined, 9, 11, 29, 314, 357, 375, 382 — see Art; positive and natural, 24–29, 308, 381; substantive and adjective, 89—see also Anglo-Saxon, Roman, Nature and Nations, Morality, War.
Lawyers, as advocates and judges, 57, 240; as legislators, 59, 70.
Laymen prone to quibble, 61.
Lecky, 286.
Leges Angliæ nolumus mutare, 355.
Legislation, 16, 38, 186, 205, 304, 308 — see Judge-made Law; development of, 69, 81; in contracts, 71, 226; in wills, 268, 273; by treaty, 84; in theology, 355; by Corporations, 199 —see Statute.
Legislative bodies, 67; the world one such body, 249.

Legislator, qualifications of, 377.
Legitim, 169, 260.
Leibnitz, 257, 411.
Leviathan, 13.
Liability, restricted, 385; for servants, 387, 392.
Liberal, and conservative, 8, 333, 337; party and intervention, 235.
Life, differentiation in, 46, 339; conceptions of, 369.
Limitations, Statute of, 227.
Litiscontestation, a judicial contract, 56.
Locke, 25.
Logical question in law, 9, 27, 28.
Lord Advocate, 96.
Lords, House of, 251, 273; as a judicial body, 65; reform of, 194.
Lorimer, Prof., 9, 12, 24, 26, 28, 30, 41, 253, 376, 406.
Louis XVI., 80.
Lubbock, Sir John, 164.
Lunatics, property of, 129, 185, 286.
Lyall, Sir A., 190, 340.
Lynch law, 50, 304.

MAGISTRATE, function of, 52, 56, 57.
Maills and duties, action of, 53.
Maine, Sir H., 47, 48, 52, 60, 67, 152, 208, 210, 260, 266, 272, 307, 400.
Majorities, 192, 318.
Man, rights of, 298, 315.
Mancipatio, 310.
Mancipi, Res, 124, 153, 207, 385.
Manners, 342.
Manu, laws of, 286.
Maritime codes, 59.
Marriage, dissolution of, 169; legal results of, 167; physical and ethical ends of, 157, 167; the relation one of status not contract, 156, 330; rudimentary idea of, 153; with deceased wife's sister, 164.
Martyrdom, 346.
Master and servant, 104, 216.
Material rights, 120-149.
Mathematics, 37.
Maudsley, Dr., 110.
May, Sir T. E., 244.
Medicine, analogies of law and, 23, 37, 356.
Melior est conditio defendentis, 54.
Mercantile law and merchants, 58.
Mercenaries, 222, 242.
Metaphysical question in law, 9, 10, 44.
Might and Right, 74, 307, 316.
Millennium, 361.

Milton, 317, 336, 380.
Minorities—see Majorities.
Miracle, 377.
Mobilia sequuntur personam, 265.
Modality, categories of, 307, 313.
Mohammedanism, 362, 365.
Monsters, 287.
Montesquieu, 23, 32, 41, 331, 415.
Morality, 158, 166, 339-371; not at first distinguished from religion, 355.
Mortis causâ and *inter vivos* deeds contrasted, 253.
Mortmain, law of, 255, 271.
Mortuus sasit vivum, 265.
Moses, 10, 11.
Motives, 15, 347, 356.
Müller, Max, 153.
Murder, 47, 99; child, 283.

NATION, idea of, 326.
Nationalisation of land, 146.
Natural Law—see Law.
Naturalisation, 88, 179, 241.
Nature, law of—see Law.
Nature and nations, law of, 314—see *Jus Gentium*.
Nautæ, Caupones, &c., 386.
Negative movement in thought, 72, 119, 346.
Negative servitudes, 135.
Negligence, 103-106 — see Police Offence; Responsibility.
Netherlands, the, 86, 131, 199, 231.
Neutrality, 115.
Newspapers, 187, 243, 249.
Nexus, 209.
Non-belligerents' property at sea, 116, 242.
Non-intervention—see Intervention.
North Sea fishermen, legislation as to, 85.
Notary's functions judicial, 70.

OATH, in contracts, 209; parliamentary, 342.
Obligation, from delict and contract, 89; implied obligations, 90; in property, 133, 205; inheritance of, 208, 257, 263.
Opposition, Her Majesty's, 192.
Outlawry, 296.

PAIN, affecting evolution, 31.
Paine, 80, 273, 318, 331.
Paley, 244, 340, 379.

Parents and children, 161, 168, 184; responsibility, 113, 385; in succession, 262.
Paris, declaration of, 87, 116.
Parliament, powers of, 63; its nature, 188.
Party, 197, 246, 337.
Paterfamilias—see Husband.
Pathology of society, 23, 37.
Paul (Jurist), 349, 384.
Paul, St., 344, 345, 351, 352, 356.
Paupers, 181, 289, 310, 331, 332—see Poor.
Peculium in Roman law, 172, 208, 229.
Peers—see Lords.
Perception, compared with legal judgment, 42.
Permissive Bill, 363.
Persecution, 352, 366.
Person, 277-302; idea of, 45, 120, 275, 297, 304, 310, 322, 360; extension into property, 121, 146, 252; in case of infant, 283; of women, 155, 160, 169, 175, 286; in contract, 211, 214, 216, 219; of corporations, 287, 367; in animals, 293, 316, 320.
Personality—see Person.
Pessimism, 370.
Philanthropy, 369.
Philip II., 131.
Philosophy of law, 3-10; utility of, 6-8, 377.
Physiology, 23, 37.
Pindar, 256.
Piracy, 242.
Plato, 155, 297.
Pleasure, 17-21; measurement of, 18; cause of evolution, 31.
Poinding of the ground, 53.
Police, 179, 237.
Police-man-made law, 55.
Police offence, 90, 106, 119, 385; statute, 108.
Political economy, 122, 146, 181, 377.
Pollock, Prof., 383, 417.
Polygyny, 159—see Marriage.
Poor law, 180; statutes, 289.
Pope, The, 231, 341, 404.
Positive law; morality; religion—see Law, Morality, Religion.
Possession, 124, 137; and property, 125; Roman law of, 139.
Postal union, 237.
Posterity, pleasure of, 20; rights of, 19, 317, 361.

Poverty, 325.
Præcepta juris, 306, 381.
Prætor, the Roman, 57.
Prætorian legislation, 66.
Pre-established harmony, 45.
Prescription, 139, 227.
Primogeniture, 263, 271 and foll.
Private international law, 85, 88, 239, 407.
Prodigal son, parable of, 261.
Professions and trades, 221.
Property, 120-150, 304, 305, 310, 322, 323, 330, 332, 360; in wife and children, 153, 169; and contract, 208; of monarch in state, 191, 231; as inferring liability, 386; of wife, 172—see Person, Children.
Proportioning of votes, 191.
Prosecutor, in England, &c., 96.
Protestantism, 352, 405.
Proudhon, 300, 306.
Prussia, 341.
Psychological, question in law, 9; and analytical methods, 281.
Punch, quoted, 349.
Punishment, 49, 55, 91; theories of, 96, 105; nature of, 110, 343.

QUALITY, categories of, 305 — see Categories.
Quantity, categories of, 305, 309—see Categories; rights as a, 138, 292, 305, 322, 324, 326; of pleasure, 18.
Queen's Bench, court of, 61.

REBELLION, 77-79.
Reciprocity, 307, 338—see Categories.
Recognition of rights by state, 126, 137, 311.
Recognition of states, 234, 331.
Reformation, The, 200, 231, 353, 405.
Regiam Majestatem, 309.
Reid, 30.
Relation, categories of, 306, 310—see Modality, Jural; physical, involves law, 40, 150, 229, 247, 376.
Relationship, constructive, in marriage, 165, 178.
Religion, conceptions of, 343, 344; classification of, 362; in marriage, 158—see Morality; as a bond of states, 403, 405.
Religious and other establishments, 182, 366—see Disestablishment.
Representation, 317—see Succession.
Res mancipi—see *Mancipi*.

INDEX. 431

Responsibility, secondary, 384-392.
Revelation of law, 10, 11.
Revenge, instinct, 18, 102.
Revolutions, lesson of, 232.
Right and Might — see Might and Right.
Right, idea of, 9, 44; acts absolutely, 31.
Rights, origin of, 120, 306; natural, 383.
Riot Act, reading of, 113.
Roman Catholics, legislation against, 202.
Roman law, 12, 43, 47, 57, 137, 207, 209, 279, 385, 404; in Scotland, 399.
Rousseau, 39, 207, 244.
Ruskin, 26, 356, 419.
Rustici, &c., legislation for, 218.

SACRIFICE, 369.
Sailors, 218.
Sale, 310, 393.
Sanction, not necessary to make law, 18, 358; different kinds of, 348, 356.
Sasine registers, 126.
Savages, 116, 230, 316, 343.
Savigny, 85, 137, 265.
Science, object of, 5; progress of, 43, 56; and philosophy, 3, 4; and religion, 368; abstract science of law, 37, 314.
Scott, Sir Walter, 113, 236.
Scottish school of philosophy, 30; of jurisprudence, 419.
Sea can be appropriated by use, 122, 124.
Seeley's *Expansion of England*, 402.
Serfs in Germany, 279.
Servant—see Master.
Servitudes, 135, 205, 252.
Session—see Court.
Shakespere, 18, 82, 316.
Shand, Lord, on liability for servants, 391.
Sheriff in Scotland and England, 62, 63; as legislator, 66.
Sic utere tuo ut alienum non lædas, 319.
Sidgwick, and utilitarianism, 23.
Sin, 347.
Sittlichkeit, 342.
Slave, status of, in Roman law, 385.
Slavery, 121, 149, 212, 217, 238, 389.
Space and time, 360.
Spencer, Herbert, 31-40, 152, 159, 163, 377, 416.
Spiritual independence, 201 — see Church.

Sport, 145, 294.
Stahl, 11, 355, 357, 416.
Stair, 373.
State, 41, 91, 95, 102, 112, 152, 162, 176-204, 321, 322, 323—see Community of states, Church, Family.
Status to Contract, progress from, 153, 201, 207, 216, 306; modification of formula, 307.
Statute, nature of, 29, 68.
Statutes, quoted or referred to :—
  1425, cap. 48, 88.
  1621, cap. 18, 66.
  1690, cap. 26, 393.
  1695, cap. 24, 263, 393.
  52 Henry III., cap. 1, 51.
  4 Geo. IV., cap. 98, 393.
  12 and 13 Vict., cap. 51, 172.
  13 Vict., cap. 13, 394.
  18 Vict., cap. 23, 172, 258.
  19 and 20 Vict., cap. 25, 65.
  24 and 25 Vict., cap. 86, 172.
  25 and 26 Vict., cap. 101, 107.
  32 and 33 Vict., cap. 62, 94.
  35 and 36 Vict., cap. 38, 183.
  37 and 38 Vict., cap. 31, 172.
  39 and 40 Vict., cap. 70, 66, 79.
  40 and 41 Vict., cap. 29, 172.
  41 and 42 Vict., cap. 43, 159.
  42 and 43 Vict., cap. 19, 364.
  43 and 44 Vict., cap. 26, 173.
  43 and 44 Vict., cap. 35, 296.
  44 and 45 Vict., cap. 21, 168, 172, 261.
  44 and 45 Vict., cap. 44, 66.
  45 and 46 Vict., cap. 66, 365.
  46 and 47 Vict., cap. 22, 85, 237.
  46 and 47 Vict., cap. 47 (Provident Nominations' Act), 268.
  Agricultural Holdings' Act, 1883. 217.
  Ballot Act, 197.
  Catholic Emancipation Act, 81. 280.
  Companies' Act, 1862, 71.
  Contagious Diseases' Acts, 297.
  Conveyancing (Scotland) Act, 1874, 71, 134, 142, 287, 394.
  Court of Session Act, 1868, 79.
  Debtors' (Scotland) Act, 1880, 94, 228.
  Ecclesiastical Titles' Act, 328.
  Employers' Liability Act, 61, 391.
  Entail Amendment Act, 1868, 270.
  Factory Acts, 340.
  Foreign Enlistment Acts, 242.
  Ground Game Act, 1880, 217.

Statutes quoted or referred to:—
　Jewish Disabilities' Act, 81, 280.
　Land-Law (Ireland) Act, 1881, 58, 64, 218.
　Law-Agents' Act, 1873, 203.
　Naturalisation Act, 1870, 81, 280.
　Peace-Preservation (Ireland) Act, 1881, 55, 87, 218.
　Presumption of Life (Scotland) Act, 1881, 264.
　Reform Acts, 81, 280.
　Sheriff-Court Act, 1876, 79, 274.
　Summary Procedure Act, 309.
　Thellusson Act, 143.
　Titles to Land Consolidation (Scotland) Act, 1868, 254, 394.
Stephen, Sir J. F., 49, 100, 108, 396, 416.
Stoicism, 362.
Strafford, Earl of, 80.
Suarez, 379, 380.
Succession, 169, 250-276, 311, 317, 360, 361.
Suffrage—see Franchise.
Suicide, 155, 288.
Summons, 54.
Summum jus est summa injuria, 131, 136, 143, 155, 212, 338, 357.
Suttee, 350.
Swiss Cantons, legislation in, 185, 187.

TAXATION, a voluntary contribution by state, 143, 144, 180.
Ten thousand a-year, 61.
Testing, right of, 136, 253, 266, 311.
Theft and robbery, 137.
Theology, 7, 8, 377, 382; rational, 315; and law, 335; an art, 340, 369.
Theological school, 10-13, 416.
Thing, 121-123, 289.
Thought and its embodiment, 33; and facts, 26; necessary, 27.
Titles of nobility, succession to, 251, 272.
Tort—see Civil Injury.
Toys, property of children, 129.
Trade, guilds, 202, 238; unions, 217; hereditary, 251.
Transcendental law, 382.
Treaties, 70, 81, 84, 85, 247, 248; a source of history, 407.
Treatises on law, use of, 2.
Trebonian, 400.

Trendelenburg, 9, 30, 96, 101, 283, 357, 382, 414.
Tribunals of commerce, 58.
Trinity, doctrine of, 282.
Twelve tables, 49, 53, 75, 90.
Type, conformity to, 363.

ULPIAN, 382, 386.
Ultramontanes, 341.
United States of America, 64, 85, 86, 233, 241, 399.
Universal dominion, 202, 325, 327.
Universities, powers of, 203.
University Commissioners, the Scottish, 397.
Usage—see Custom.
Utilitarianism, 13, 23, 348, 417.
Utility as an explanation of law, 16, 17, 23.

VEGETABLES, rights of—see Animals.
Venice, 86, 187.
Vice, legislative suppression of, 363.
Vienna, Congress of, 83, 406.
Violation of law in physical and jural sense, 378.
Violence in self-defence, 51.
Vivisection, 293.
Volenti non fit injuria, 288.
Vote—see Franchise.
Vox populi vox Dei, 318.

WAGER OF BATTLE, 52.
Wallace, A. R., 131, 147.
Wallace, Prof., 5.
War, 48, 81, 86, 113-118, 243.
Westbury, Lord, 240.
Westlake, 375.
Widow's third, 109, 260.
Wife—see Husband, Polygyny, &c.
Wild birds, 296.
Will, 71, 267—see Testing.
Witenagemot, 67.
Women, personality of, 286.
Work, State, for poor, 180.
World, religious, scientific, &c., 328; literary in legislation, 186—see Individual.
Worship, 362, 368, 370.
Wreck commissioner, 58.
Wrong, 32, 91, 103, 347—see Negligence, Spencer, Right.

A

CATALOGUE

OF

STANDARD WORKS

PUBLISHED BY

CHARLES GRIFFIN & COMPANY.

	PAGE
I.—Religious Works, ...	1
II.—Scientific „	6
III.—Educational „	22
IV.—Works in General Literature, . .	27

LONDON:
12 EXETER STREET, STRAND.

NOTICE.

New Issue of this Important Work—Enlarged, in part Re-written, and thoroughly Revised to date.

TWENTIETH EDITION, *Royal 8vo.*   *Handsome Cloth,* 10s. 6d.

A DICTIONARY OF
DOMESTIC MEDICINE AND HOUSEHOLD SURGERY,

BY

SPENCER THOMSON, M.D., EDIN., L.R.C.S.,

REVISED, AND IN PART RE-WRITTEN, BY THE AUTHOR,

AND BY

JOHN CHARLES STEELE, M.D.,

OF GUY'S HOSPITAL.

With Appendix on the Management of the Sick-room, and many Hints for the Diet and Comfort of Invalids.

In its New Form, DR. SPENCER THOMSON'S "DICTIONARY OF DOMESTIC MEDICINE" fully sustains its reputation as the "Representative Book of the Medical Knowledge and Practice of the Day" applied to Domestic Requirements.

The most recent IMPROVEMENTS in the TREATMENT OF THE SICK—in APPLIANCES for the RELIEF OF PAIN—and in all matters connected with SANITATION, HYGIENE, and the MAINTENANCE of the GENERAL HEALTH—will be found in the New Issue in clear and full detail; the experience of the Editors in the Spheres of Private Practice and of Hospital Treatment respectively, combining to render the Dictionary perhaps the most thoroughly practical work of the kind in the English Language. Many new Engravings have been introduced—improved Diagrams of different parts of the Human Body, and Illustrations of the newest Medical, Surgical, and Sanitary Apparatus.

*** *All Directions given in such a form as to be readily and safely followed.*

FROM THE AUTHOR'S PREFATORY ADDRESS.

"Without entering upon that difficult ground which correct professional knowledge and educated judgment can alone permit to be safely trodden, there is a wide and extensive field for exertion, and for usefulness, open to the unprofessional, in the kindly offices of a *true* DOMESTIC MEDICINE, the timely help and solace of a simple HOUSEHOLD SURGERY, or, better still, in the watchful care more generally known as 'SANITARY PRECAUTION,' which tends rather to preserve health than to cure disease. 'The touch of a gentle hand' will not be less gentle because guided by knowledge, nor will the *safe* domestic remedies be less anxiously or carefully administered. Life may be saved, suffering may always be alleviated. Even to the resident in the midst of civilization, the 'KNOWLEDGE IS POWER,' to do good; to the settler and emigrant it is INVALUABLE."

"Dr. Thomson has fully succeeded in conveying to the public a vast amount of useful professional knowledge."—*Dublin Journal of Medical Science.*

"The amount of useful knowledge conveyed in this Work is surprising."—*Medical Times and Gazette.*

"WORTH ITS WEIGHT IN GOLD TO FAMILIES AND THE CLERGY."—*Oxford Herald.*

LONDON : CHARLES GRIFFIN & CO., EXETER STREET, STRAND.

CHARLES GRIFFIN & COMPANY'S
LIST OF PUBLICATIONS.

RELIGIOUS WORKS.

ALTAR OF THE HOUSEHOLD (The); a Series of Prayers and Selections from the Scriptures, for Domestic Worship, for every Morning and Evening in the Year. By the Rev. Dr. HARRIS, assisted by eminent Contributors, with an Introduction by the Rev. W. LINDSAY ALEXANDER, D.D. *New Edition, entirely Revised.* Royal 4to, with Steel Frontispiece. Cloth, gilt edges, 22/.

Illustrated with a Series of First-class Engravings on Steel, 28/.

May also be had bound in the following styles: half-bound calf, marbled edges; and levant morocco, antique, gilt edges.

ANECDOTES (CYCLOPÆDIA OF RELIGIOUS AND MORAL). With an Introductory Essay by the Rev. GEORGE CHEEVER, D.D. *Thirty-fourth Thousand.* Crown 8vo. Cloth, 3/6.

*** These Anecdotes relate to no trifling subjects; and they have been selected, not for amusement, but for instruction. By those engaged in the tuition of the young, they will be found highly useful.

BIBLE HISTORY (A Manual of). By the Rev. J. WYCLIFFE GEDGE, Diocesan Inspector of Schools for Winchester. Small 8vo. Cloth, neat, 7d.

"This small but very comprehensive Manual is much more than a mere summary of Bible History."—*Church Sunday School Magazine.*

BUNYAN'S PILGRIM'S PROGRESS. With Expository Lectures by the Rev. ROBERT MAGUIRE, Incumbent of St. Olave's, Southwark. With Steel Engravings. *Second Edition.* Imperial 8vo. Cloth, gilt, 10/6.

THE LARGE-TYPE BUNYAN.

BUNYAN'S PILGRIM'S PROGRESS. With Life and Notes, Experimental and Practical, by WILLIAM MASON. Printed in large type, and Illustrated with full-page Woodcuts. *Twelfth Thousand.* Crown 8vo. Bevelled boards, gilt, and gilt edges, 3/6.

BUNYAN'S SELECT WORKS. With an Original Sketch of the Author's Life and Times. Numerous Engravings. *New Edition.* Two vols., super-royal 8vo. Cloth, 36/.

CHRISTIAN YEAR (The): Thoughts in Verse
for the Sundays and Holy Days throughout the Year. With an original Memoir of the Rev. JOHN KEBLE, by W. TEMPLE, Portrait, and sixteen beautiful Engravings on Steel, after eminent Masters. In 4to. Handsome cloth, 12/6.

    Unique walnut boards, . . . 21/.
    Morocco antique, . . . 25/.

ILLUSTRATIONS.

Morning .. .. after H. HOWARD, R.A.	The Old Mansion .. after C. W. RADCLYFFE.
Sunset .. .. ,, G. BARRETT.	The Cathedral Choir ,, LEVAINT.
A Mountain Stream ,, C. BENTLEY.	Sunset (after CLAUDE),, G. BARRETT.
A River Scene ,, C. W. RADCLYFFE.	Moonlight ,, HOPLAND.
A Mountain Lake ,, J. M. W. TURNER.	Pastoral Landscape ,, C. W. RADCLYFFE.
A Greek Temple ,, D. ROBERTS, R.A.	Halt in the Desert ,, D. ROBERTS, R.A.
A Village Church ,, C. W. RADCLYFFE.	Guardian Angels ,, H. HOWARD, R.A.
The Wayside Cross ,, TONY JOHANNOT.	The Church Gate ,, C. W. RADCLYFFE.

"An Edition *de luxe*, beautifully got up . . . admirably adapted for a gift-book."—*John Bull*.

CHRISTIAN YEAR (The): With Memoir of the
Author by W. TEMPLE, Portrait, and Eight Engravings on Steel, after eminent Masters. *New Edition*. Small 8vo, toned paper. Cloth gilt, 5/.
    10/6.
    Morocco elegant, ... 10/6.
    Malachite, ... 12/6.

*** The above are the only issues of the "Christian Year" with Memoir and Portrait of the Author. In ordering, Griffin's Editions should be specified.

COMMENTARIES ON THE HOLY SCRIPTURES.

HENRY (Matthew): The HOLY BIBLE. With a Commentary and Explanatory Notes. *New Edition*. In 3 vols., super-royal 8vo. Strongly bound in cloth, 50/.

SCOTT (Rev. Thomas): A COMMENTARY
ON THE BIBLE; containing the Old and New Testaments according to the Authorised Version, with Practical Observations, copious Marginal References, Indices, &c. *New Edition*. In 3 vols., royal 4to. Cloth, 63/.

CRUDEN'S COMPLETE CONCORDANCE
TO THE OLD AND NEW TESTAMENTS AND THE BOOKS CALLED APOCRYPHAL. Edited and Corrected by WILLIAM YOUNGMAN. With fine Portrait of CRUDEN. *New Edition*. Imperial 8vo. Cloth, handsome gilt top, 7/6.

DICK (Thos., LL.D.): CELESTIAL
SCENERY; or, The Wonders of the Planetary System Displayed. This Work is intended for general readers, presenting to their view, in an attractive manner, sublime objects of contemplation. Illustrated. *New Edition*. Crown 8vo, toned paper. Handsomely bound, gilt edges, 5/.

DICK (Dr.): CHRISTIAN PHILOSOPHER
(The); or, The Connection of Science and Philosophy with Religion. Revised and enlarged. Illustrated with 150 Engravings on Wood. *Twenty-eighth Edition*. Crown 8vo, toned paper. Handsomely bound, with gilt edges, 5/.

STANDARD BIBLICAL WORKS
BY
THE REV. JOHN EADIE, D.D., LL.D.,
Late a Member of the New Testament Revision Company.

This SERIES has been prepared to afford sound and necessary aid to the Reader of Holy Scripture. The VOLUMES comprised in it form in themselves a COMPLETE LIBRARY OF REFERENCE. The number of Copies already issued greatly exceeds A QUARTER OF A MILLION.

I. **EADIE (Rev. Prof.): BIBLICAL CYCLO-**
PÆDIA (A); or, Dictionary of Eastern Antiquities, Geography, and Natural History, illustrative of the Old and New Testaments. With Maps, many Engravings, and Lithographed Facsimile of the Moabite Stone. Large post 8vo, 700 pages. *Twenty-third Edition.* Handsome cloth, 7/6.
    Half-bound, calf, . . . 10/6.
    Morocco antique, gilt edges, . . 16/.
"By far the best Bible Dictionary for general use."—*Clerical Journal.*

II. **EADIE (Rev. Prof.): CRUDEN'S CON-**
CORDANCE TO THE HOLY SCRIPTURES. With Portrait on Steel, and Introduction by the Rev. Dr. KING. Post 8vo. *Fiftieth Edition.* Handsome cloth, ... 3/6.
    Half-bound, calf, ... 6/6.
    Full calf, gilt edges, ... 8/6.
    Full morocco, gilt edges. . . 10/6.
*** Dr. EADIE's has long and deservedly borne the reputation of being the COMPLETEST and BEST CONCORDANCE extant.

III. **EADIE (Rev. Prof.): CLASSIFIED BIBLE**
(The). An Analytical Concordance. Illustrated by Maps. Large Post 8vo. *Sixth Edition.* Handsome cloth, . . 8/6.
    Full morocco, antique, . . 17/.
"We have only to add our unqualified commendation of a work of real excellence to every Biblical student."—*Christian Times.*

IV. **EADIE (Rev. Prof.): ECCLESIASTICAL**
CYCLOPÆDIA (The). A Dictionary of Christian Antiquities, and of the History of the Christian Church. By the Rev. Professor EADIE, assisted by numerous Contributors. Large Post 8vo. *Sixth Edition.* Handsome cloth, ... 8/6.
    Full morocco, antique, . . 17/.
"The ECCLESIASTICAL CYCLOPÆDIA will prove acceptable both to the clergy and laity of Great Britain. A great body of useful information will be found in it."—*Athenæum.*

V. **EADIE (Rev. Prof.): A DICTIONARY OF**
THE HOLY BIBLE; for the use of Young People. With Map and Illustrations. Small 8vo. *Thirty-sixth Thousand.* Cloth, elegant, 2/6.
    Full morocco, gilt edges, . . 7/6.

**FOSTER (Charles): THE STORY OF THE
BIBLE**, from Genesis to Revelation—including the Historical Connection between the Old and New Testaments. Told in Simple Language.

Large Post 8vo, with Maps and over 250 Engravings (many of them Full-page, after the Drawings of Professor CARL SCHÖNHERR and others), illustrative of the Bible Narrative, and of Eastern Manners and Customs.

Now Ready. Third Edition.

Home and School Edition, cloth elegant, . . 6/.
Prize and Presentation Edition, beautifully gilt, . 7/6.

OPINIONS OF THE PRESS.

"A book which, once taken up, is not easily laid down. When the volume is opened, we are fairly caught. Not to speak of the well-executed wood engravings, which will each tell its story, we find a simple version of the main portions of the Bible, all that may most profitably be included in a work intended at once to instruct and charm the young —a version couched in the simplest, purest, most idiomatic English, and executed throughout with good taste, and in the most reverential spirit. *The work needs only to be known to make its way into families*, and it will (at any rate, it *ought* to) become a favourite Manual in Sunday Schools."—*Scotsman.*

"A HOUSEHOLD TREASURE."—*Western Morning News.*

"This attractive and handsome volume . . . written in a simple and transparent style. . . . Mr. Foster's explanations and comments are MODELS OF TEACHING."—*Freeman.*

"This large and handsome volume, abounding in Illustrations, is just what is wanted. . . . The STORY is very beautifully and reverently told."—*Glasgow News.*

"There could be few better Presentation Books than this handsome volume."—*Daily Review.*

"This elegant volume will prove a valuable adjunct in the Home Circle and Sunday Class."—*Western Daily Mercury.*

"WILL ACCOMPLISH A GOOD WORK."—*Sunday School Chronicle.*

"In this beautiful volume no more of comment is indulged in than is necessary to the elucidation of the text. Everything approaching Sectarian narrowness is carefully eschewed."—*Methodist Magazine.*

"This simple and impressive Narrative . . . succeeds thoroughly in rivetting the attention of children; . . . admirably adapted for reading in the Home Circle."—*Daily Chronicle.*

"The HISTORICAL SKETCH connecting the Old and New Testaments is a very good idea; it is a common fault to look on these as distinct histories, instead of as parts of *one grand whole.*"—*Christian.*

"Sunday School Teachers and Heads of Families will best know how to value this handsome volume."—*Northern Whig.*

**KITTO (John, D.D., F.S.A.): THE HOLY
LAND**: The Mountains, Valleys, and Rivers of the Holy Land; being the Physical Geography of Palestine. With eight full-page Illustrations. *Eleventh Thousand. New Edition.* Fcap 8vo. Cloth, 2/6.

** Contains within a small compass a body of most interesting and valuable information.

THE PICTORIAL SUNDAY BOOK:
Containing nearly two thousand Illustrations on Steel and Wood, and a Series of Maps. *Seventy-third Thousand.* Folio. Cloth, gilt, 30/.

PALEY (Archdeacon): NATURAL THEOLOGY.
The Evidences of the Existence and the Attributes of the Deity. With Illustrative Notes and Dissertations, by HENRY, Lord BROUGHAM, and Sir CHARLES BELL. Many Engravings. One vol., 16mo. Cloth, 4/.

PALEY (Archdeacon): NATURAL THEOLOGY.
With Lord BROUGHAM'S NOTES AND DIALOGUES ON INSTINCT. Many Illustrations. Three vols., 16mo. Cloth, 7/6.

"When Lord Brougham's eloquence in the Senate shall have passed away, and his services as a statesman shall exist only in the free institutions which they have helped to secure, his discourse on Natural Theology will continue to inculcate imperishable truths, and fit the mind for the higher revelations which these truths are destined to foreshadow and confirm."—*Edinburgh Review.*

RAGG (Rev. Thomas): CREATION'S TESTIMONY TO ITS GOD: the Accordance of Science, Philosophy, and Revelation. *Thirteenth Edition.* Large crown 8vo. Handsome cloth, bevelled boards, 5/.

"We are not a little pleased again to meet with the author of this volume in the new edition of his far-famed work. Mr. Ragg is one of the few original writers of our time to whom justice is being done."—*British Standard.*

*** This work has been pronounced "The Book of the Age," "The best popular Text-Book of the Sciences," and "The only complete Manual of Religious Evidence, Natural and Revealed."

RELIGIONS OF THE WORLD (The): Being Confessions of Faith contributed by Eminent Members of every Denomination of Christians, also of Mahometanism, Parseeism, Brahminism, Mormonism, &c., &c., with a Harmony of the Christian Confessions of Faith by a Member of the Evangelical Alliance. Crown 8vo. Cloth bevelled, 3/6.

*** In this volume, each denomination, through some leading member, has expressed its own opinions. There is no book in the language on the same plan. All other works on the subject, being written by one individual, are necessarily one-sided, incomplete, and unauthentic.

SOUTHGATE (Henry): SUGGESTIVE THOUGHTS ON RELIGIOUS SUBJECTS. (See page 35.)

SOUTHGATE (Mrs. H.): THE CHRISTIAN LIFE: Thoughts in Prose and Verse from Five hundred of the Best Writers of all Ages. Selected and Arranged for Every Day in the Year. Small 8vo. With Red Lines and unique Initial Letters on each page. Cloth Elegant, 5/. Morocco, 10/6. *Second Edition.*

"A volume as handsome as it is intrinsically valuable."—*Scotsman.*
"The readings are excellent."—*Record.*
"A library in itself."—*Northern Whig.*

TAIT (Rev. James): MIND IN MATTER: A Short Argument on Theism. Demy 8vo. Handsome Cloth, 8/6.

GENERAL CONTENTS.—Evolution in Nature and Mind—Mr. Darwin and Mr. Herbert Spencer—Inspiration, Natural and Supernatural—Deductions.

"An able and original contribution to Theistic literature. . . . The style is pointed, concise, and telling to a degree.'—*Glasgow Herald.*
"Mr. TAIT advances many new and striking arguments . . . highly suggestive and fresh."—*Brit. Quarterly Review.*

WORDS AND WORKS OF OUR BLESSED LORD: and their Lessons for Daily Life. Two Vols. in One Foolscap, 8vo. Cloth, gilt edges, 6/.

SCIENTIFIC WORKS.

MEDICAL WORKS
By WILLIAM AITKEN, M.D., Edin., F.R.S.,

PROFESSOR OF PATHOLOGY IN THE ARMY MEDICAL SCHOOL; EXAMINER IN MEDICINE FOR THE MILITARY MEDICAL SERVICES OF THE QUEEN; FELLOW OF THE SANITARY INSTITUTE OF GREAT BRITAIN; CORRESPONDING MEMBER OF THE ROYAL IMPERIAL SOCIETY OF PHYSICIANS OF VIENNA; AND OF THE SOCIETY OF MEDICINE AND NATURAL HISTORY OF DRESDEN.

SEVENTH EDITION.

The SCIENCE and PRACTICE of MEDICINE.

In Two Volumes, Royal 8vo., cloth. Illustrated by numerous Engravings on Wood, and a Map of the Geographical Distribution of Diseases. To a great extent Rewritten; Enlarged, Remodelled, and Carefully Revised throughout, 42/.

In reference to the Seventh Edition *of this important Work, the Publishers would only remark, that no labour or expense has been spared to sustain its well-known reputation as* "*The Representative Book of the Medical Science and Practice of the Day.*" *Among the More Important Features of the New Edition, the subject of* DISEASES OF THE BRAIN AND NERVOUS SYSTEM *may be specially mentioned.*

Opinions of the Press.

"The work is an admirable one, and adapted to the requirements of the Student, Professor, and Practitioner of Medicine. . . . The reader will find a large amount of information not to be met with in other books, epitomised for him in this. We know of no work that contains so much, or such full and varied information on all subjects connected with the Science and Practice of Medicine."—*Lancet.*

"Excellent from the beginning, and improved in each successive issue, Dr. Aitken's GREAT and STANDARD WORK has now, with vast and judicious labour, been brought abreast of every recent advance in scientific medicine and the healing art, and affords to the Student and Practitioner a store of knowledge and guidance of altogether inestimable value. . . . The first 530 Pages of the Second Volume would, if printed separately, form perhaps the best text-book in our language for the student of Neurology and Insanity. A masterly and philosophical review, characterised by the precision of the specialist, and the breadth of the catholic physician, is presented in these pages of the varied phenomena connected with morbid conditions of the nervous system in their relation to anatomical structure, chemical composition, physiological uses, and pathological changes. . . . A classical work which does honour to British Medicine, and is a compendium of sound knowledge.". *Extract from Review in "Brain," by J. Crichton-Browne, M.D., F.R.S., Lord Chancellor's Visitor in Lunacy.*

"The SEVENTH EDITION of this important Text-Book fully maintains its reputation. . . . Dr. Aitken is indefatigable in his efforts. . . . The section on DISEASES of the BRAIN and NERVOUS SYSTEM is completely remodelled, so as to include all the most recent researches, which in this department have been not less important than they are numerous."—*British Medical Journal.*

"The STANDARD TEXT-BOOK in the English Language. . . . There is, perhaps, no work more indispensable for the Practitioner and Student."—*Edin. Medical Journal.*

"In its system, in its scope, and in its method of dealing with the subjects treated of, this work differs from all other Text-Books on the Science of Medicine in the English language."—*Medical Times and Gazette.*

"The extraordinary merit of Dr. Aitken's work. . . . The author has unquestionably performed a service to the profession of the most valuable kind."—*Practitioner.*

"Altogether this voluminous treatise is a credit to its Author, its Publisher, and to English Physic. . . . Affords an admirable and honest digest of the opinions and practice of the day. . . . Commends itself to us for sterling value, width of retrospect, and fairness of representation."—*Medico-Chirurgical Review.*

"Diseases are here described which have hitherto found no place in any English systematic work."—*Westminster Review.*

"We can say with perfect confidence, that no medical man in India should be without Dr. Aitken's 'Science and Practice of Medicine.' The article on Cholera is by far the most complete, judicious, and learned summary of our knowledge respecting this disease which has yet appeared."—*Indian Medical Gazette.*

PROF. AITKEN'S WORKS—*(Continued).*

—— OUTLINES OF THE SCIENCE AND
PRACTICE OF MEDICINE. A Text-Book for Students. *Second Edition.* Crown 8vo, 12/6.

"Students preparing for examinations will hail it as a perfect godsend for its conciseness."—*Athenæum.*

"Well-digested, clear, and well-written, the work of a man conversant with every detail of his subject, and a thorough master of the art of teaching."—*British Medical Journal.*

"In respect of both the matter contained, and the manner in which it is conveyed, our examination has convinced us that nothing could be better. . . . We know of no summary of the use of Electricity as a means of diagnosis, equal to that contained in the Section on Diseases of the Nervous System." *Medico-Chirurgical Review.*

—— THE GROWTH OF THE RECRUIT,
and the Young Soldier, with a view to the Selection of "Growing Lads" and their Training, 2/6.

ANSTED (Prof., M.A., F.R.S.): NATURAL
HISTORY OF THE INANIMATE CREATION, recorded in the Structure of the Earth, the Plants of the Field, and the Atmospheric Phenomena. With numerous Illustrations. Large post 8vo. Cloth, 8/6.

BAIRD (W., M.D., F.L.S., late of the Brit. Mus.):
THE STUDENT'S NATURAL HISTORY; a Dictionary of the Natural Sciences: Botany, Conchology, Entomology, Geology, Mineralogy, Palæontology, and Zoology. With a Zoological Chart, and over 250 Illustrations. Demy 8vo. Cloth gilt, 10/6.

"The work is a very useful one, and will contribute, by its cheapness and comprehensiveness, to foster the extending taste for Natural Science."—*Westminster Review.*

BROWNE (Walter R., M.A., M. Inst. C.E.,
F.G.S., late Fellow of Trinity College, Cambridge):

THE STUDENT'S MECHANICS: An Introduction to the Study of Force and motion. With Diagrams. Crown 8vo. Cloth, 4/6.

Contents.
I. FIRST PRINCIPLES.
II. STATICS.
III. KINEMATICS.
IV. DYNAMICS.
V. AXIOMS, DEFINITIONS, AND LAWS.
VI. EXAMPLES WORKED & UNWORKED.

"Clear in style and practical in method, 'THE STUDENT'S MECHANICS,' is cordially to be recommended from all points of view. . . . Will be of great value to Studen desirous to gain full knowledge." *Athenæum.*

"The merits of the work are especially conspicuous in its clearness and brevity . . . deserves the attention of all who have to teach or learn the elements of Mechanics. . . . An excellent conception." *Westminster Review.*

—— FOUNDATIONS OF MECHANICS.
Papers reprinted from the *Engineer.* In crown 8vo, 1/.

—— FUEL AND WATER: A Manual for
Users of Steam and Water. By Prof. SCHWACKHÖFER and W. R. BROWNE, M.A. (See p. 19.)

WORKS by A. WYNTER BLYTH, M.R.C.S., F.C.S.,
Public Analyst for the County of Devon, and Medical Officer of Health for St. Marylebone.

HYGIÈNE AND PUBLIC HEALTH (a Dictionary of): embracing the following subjects:—

I.—SANITARY CHEMISTRY: the Composition and Dietetic Value of Foods, with the Detection of Adulterations.
II.—SANITARY ENGINEERING: Sewage, Drainage, Storage of Water, Ventilation, Warming, &c.
III.—SANITARY LEGISLATION: the whole of the PUBLIC HEALTH ACT, together with portions of other Sanitary Statutes (without alteration or abridgment, save in a few unimportant instances), in a form admitting of easy and rapid Reference.
IV.—EPIDEMIC AND EPIZOOTIC DISEASES: their History and Propagation, with the Measures for Disinfection.
V.—HYGIÈNE—MILITARY, NAVAL, PRIVATE, PUBLIC, SCHOOL.

Royal 8vo, 672 pp., cloth, with Map and 140 Illustrations, 28/.

Opinions of the Press.

"Excellently done . . . the articles are brief, but comprehensive. We have tested the book, and can therefore recommend Mr. Blyth's Dictionary with confidence."—*Westminster Review.*

"A very important Treatise . . . an examination of its contents satisfies us that it is a work which should be highly appreciated."—*Medico-Chirurgical Review.*

"A work that must have entailed a vast amount of labour and research. . . . Will become a STANDARD WORK IN HYGIENE AND PUBLIC HEALTH."—*Medical Times and Gazette.*

"Contains a great mass of information of easy reference."—*Sanitary Record.*

FOODS: THEIR COMPOSITION AND ANALYSIS. Price 16/. In Crown 8vo, cloth, with Elaborate Tables, Folding Litho-Plate, and Photographic Frontispiece.

General Contents.

History of Adulteration—Legislation, Past and Present—Apparatus useful to the Food Analyst—"Ash"—Sugar—Confectionery—Honey—Treacle—Jams and Preserved Fruits—Starches—Wheaten-Flour—Bread—Oats—Barley—Rye—Rice—Maize—Millet—Potato—Peas—Chinese Peas—Lentils—Beans—MILK—Cream—Butter—Cheese—Tea—Coffee—Cocoa and Chocolate—Alcohol—Brandy—Rum—Whisky—Gin—Arrack—Liqueurs—Beer—Wine—Vinegar—Lemon and Lime Juice—Mustard—Pepper—Sweet and Bitter Almond—Annatto—Olive Oil—Water. *Appendix:* Text of English and American Adulteration Acts.

"Will be used by every Analyst."—*Lancet.*

"Full of great interest. . . . The method of treatment excellent. . . . Gives just that amount of information which those able to appreciate it will desire."—*Westminster Review.*

"STANDS UNRIVALLED for completeness of information. . . . A really 'practical' work for the guidance of practical men."—*Sanitary Record.*

"An admirable digest of the most recent state of knowledge. . . . Interesting even to lay-readers."—*Chemical News.*

POISONS: THEIR EFFECTS AND DETECTION. Price 16/.

General Contents.

Historical Introduction—Statistics—General Methods of Procedure—Life Tests—Special Apparatus—Classification: I. ORGANIC POISONS: (*a.*) Sulphuric, Hydrochloric, and Nitric Acids, Potash, Soda, Ammonia, &c.; (*b.*) Petroleum, Benzene, Camphor, Alcohols, Chloroform, Carbolic Acid, Prussic Acid, Phosphorus, &c.; (*c.*) Hemlock, Nicotine, Opium, Strychnine, Aconite, Atropine, Digitalis, &c.; (*d.*) Poisons derived from Animal Substances; (*e.*) The Oxalic Acid Group. II.—INORGANIC POISONS: Arsenic, Antimony, Lead, Copper, Bismuth, Silver, Mercury, Zinc, Nickel Iron, Chromium, Alkaline Earths, &c. *Appendix:* A. Examination of Blood and Blood-Spots. B. *Hints for Emergencies:* Treatment—Antidotes.

"Should be in the hands of every medical practitioner."—*Lancet.*

"A sound and practical Manual of Toxicology, which cannot be too warmly recommended. One of its chief merits is that it discusses substances which have been overlooked."—*Chemical News.*

"One of the best, most thorough, and comprehensive works on the subject."—*Saturday Review.*

THE CIRCLE OF THE SCIENCES: A
SERIES OF POPULAR TREATISES ON THE NATURAL AND PHYSICAL SCIENCES, AND THEIR APPLICATIONS, by Professors OWEN, ANSTED, YOUNG, and TENNANT; Drs. LATHAM, EDWARD SMITH, SCOFFERN, BUSHNAN, and BRONNER; Messrs. MITCHELL, TWISDEN, DALLAS, GORE, IMRAY, MARTIN, SPARLING, and others. Complete in nine volumes, illustrated with many thousand Engravings on Wood. Crown 8vo. Cloth lettered. Each vol., 5/.

VOL. 1.—ORGANIC NATURE.—Part I. Animal and Vegetable Physiology: the Skeleton and the Teeth; Varieties of the Human Race.
VOL. 2.—ORGANIC NATURE.—Part II. Structural and Systematic Botany—Invertebrated Animals.
VOL. 3.—ORGANIC NATURE.—Part III. Vertebrated Animals.
VOL. 4.—INORGANIC NATURE.—Geology and Physical Geography; Crystallography; Mineralogy; Meteorology, and Atmospheric Phenomena.
VOL. 5.—NAVIGATION; PRACTICAL AND NAUTICAL ASTRONOMY.
VOL. 6.—ELEMENTARY CHEMISTRY.
VOL. 7.—PRACTICAL CHEMISTRY.—Electro-Metallurgy; Photography; Chemistry of Food; and Artificial Light.
VOL. 8.—MATHEMATICAL SCIENCE.—Arithmetic; Algebra; Plane Geometry; Logarithms; Plane and Spherical Trigonometry; Mensuration and Practical Geometry, with use of Instruments.
VOL. 9.—MECHANICAL PHILOSOPHY.—Statics; Dynamics; Hydrostatics; Pneumatics; Practical Mechanics; and the Steam Engine.

IN SEPARATE TREATISES. Cloth.

1. ANSTED'S Geology and Physical Geography, . . . 2/6.
2. BREEM'S Practical Astronomy, ... 2/6.
3. BRONNER and SCOFFERN'S Chemistry of Food and Diet, . 1/6.
4. BUSHNAN'S Physiology of Animal and Vegetable Life, . 1/6.
5. GORE'S Theory and Practice of Electro-Deposition, . . 1/6.
6. IMRAY'S Practical Mechanics, ... 1/6.
7. JARDINE'S Practical Geometry, ... 1/.
8. LATHAM'S Varieties of the Human Species, . . . 1/6.
9. MITCHELL and TENNANT'S Crystallography and Mineralogy, 3/.
10. MITCHELL'S Properties of Matter and Elementary Statics, 1/6.
11. OWEN'S Principal Forms of the Skeleton and the Teeth, . 1/6.
12. SCOFFERN'S Chemistry of Heat, Light, and Electricity, . 3/.
13. SCOFFERN'S Chemistry of the Inorganic Bodies, . . 3/.
14. SCOFFERN'S Chemistry of Artificial Light, . . . 1/6.
15. SCOFFERN and LOWE'S Practical Meteorology, . . . 1/6.
16. SMITH'S Introduction to Botany: Structural and Systematic, 2/.
17. TWISDEN'S Plane and Spherical Trigonometry, . . 1/6.
18. TWISDEN on Logarithms, ... 1/.
19. YOUNG'S Elements of Algebra, ... 1/.
20. YOUNG'S Solutions of Questions in Algebra, . . . 1/.
21. YOUNG'S Navigation and Nautical Astronomy, . . . 2/6.
22. YOUNG'S Plane Geometry, ... 1/6.
23. YOUNG'S Simple Arithmetic, ... 1/.
24. YOUNG'S Elementary Dynamics, ... 1/6.

DALLAS (W. S., F.L.S.):

A POPULAR HISTORY OF THE ANIMAL CREATION: The Habits, Structure, and Classification of Animals. With coloured Frontispiece and many hundred Illustrations. *New Edition.* Crown 8vo. Cloth, 8/6.

DOUGLAS (John Christie, Mem. Soc. Tel. Eng., East India Govt. Telegraph Department, &c.):

A MANUAL OF TELEGRAPH CONSTRUCTION. For the use of Telegraph Engineers and others. With numerous Diagrams. Crown 8vo. Cloth, bevelled, 15/.

** *Second Edition. Published with the approval of the Director-General of Telegraphs in India.*

GENERAL CONTENTS.

PART I.—GENERAL PRINCIPLES OF STRENGTH AND STABILITY: with the Strength of Materials.

PART II.—PROPERTIES AND APPLICATIONS OF MATERIALS, WITH SPECIFICATIONS.

PART III.—TELEGRAPH CONSTRUCTION, MAINTENANCE, AND ORGANISATION, treating of the Application of the Information conveyed in Parts I. and II. to the case of Combined Structures: including the Construction of Overground, Subterranean, and Subaqueous Lines; Office Fittings; Estimating; Organisation, &c.

"Mr. Douglas deserves the thanks of Telegraphic Engineers for the excellent 'Manual' now before us . . . he has ably supplied an existing want . . . the subject is treated with great clearness and judgment . . . good practical information, given in a clear, terse style."—*Engineering.*

"The amount of information given is such as to render this volume a most useful guide to any one who may be engaged in any branch of Electric Telegraph Engineering.".—*Athenæum.*

"Calculated to be of great service to Telegraphic Engineers." —*Iron.*

DUPRÉ (Auguste, Ph. D., F.R.S., Prof. of Chemistry at the Westminster Hospital) and HAKE (H. W., Ph. D., F.C.S., of Queenwood College):

A MANUAL OF CHEMISTRY, Organic and Inorganic, for the use of Students. In crown 8vo.

GRIFFIN (John Joseph, F.C.S.):

CHEMICAL RECREATIONS: A Popular Manual of Experimental Chemistry. With 540 Engravings of Apparatus. *Tenth Edition.* Crown 4to. Cloth.

Part I.—Elementary Chemistry, 2/.

Part II.—The Chemistry of the Non-Metallic Elements, including a Comprehensive Course of Class Experiments, 10/6.

Or, complete in one volume, cloth, gilt top, . . 12/6.

GURDEN (Richard Lloyd, Authorised Surveyor for the Governments of New South Wales and Victoria):

TRAVERSE TABLES: computed to Four Places Decimals for every Minute of Angle up to 100 of Distance. For the use of Surveyors and Engineers. In folio, strongly half-bound, 30/.

** Published with Concurrence of the Surveyors-General for New South Wales and Victoria.

"Mr. GURDEN is to be thanked for the extraordinary labour which he has bestowed on facilitating the work of the Surveyor. . . . An almost unexampled instance of professional and literary industry."—*Athenæum.*

"Those who have experience in exact SURVEY-WORK will best know how to appreciate the enormous amount of labour represented by this valuable book. The computations enable the user to ascertain the sines and cosines for a distance of twelve miles to within half an inch, and this BY REFERENCE TO BUT ONE TABLE, in place of the usual Fifteen minute computations required. This alone is evidence of the assistance which the Tables ensure to every user, and as every Surveyor in active practice has felt the want of such assistance, few knowing of their publication will remain without them."—*Engineer.*

"We cannot sufficiently admire the heroic patience of the author, who, in order to prevent error, calculated each result by two different modes, and, before the work was finally placed in the Printers' hands, repeated the operation for a third time, on revising the proofs."—*Engineering.*

"Up to the present time, no Tables for the use of Surveyors have been prepared, which, in minuteness of detail, can be compared with those compiled by Mr Gurden. . . . With the aid of this book, *the toil of calculation is reduced to a minimum;* and not only is time saved, but the risk of error is avoided. Mr. Gurden's book has but to be known, and no Engineer's or Architect's office will be without a copy."—*Architect.*

"A valuable acquisition to those employed in extensive surveys."—*Building News.*

"These Tables are Characterised by ABSOLUTE SIMPLICITY; the saving of time effected by their use is most material. . . . Every one connected with Engineering or Survey should be made aware of the existence of this elaborate and useful set of Tables." *Builder.*

JAMES (W. Powell, M.A.):

FROM SOURCE TO SEA: or, Gleanings about Rivers from many Fields. A Chapter in Physical Geography. Cloth elegant, 3/6.

"Excellent reading . . . a book of popular science which deserves an extensive popularity."—*Saturday Review.*

"A spiritedly-written little book . . . very pleasant matter."—*Northern Whig.*

"A very charming little volume."—*Birmingham Post.*

JAMIESON (Andrew, C.E., F.R.S.E.):

STEAM AND THE STEAM ENGINE (A Manual of) for the use of Students preparing for Government and other Competitive Examinations. With Numerous Diagrams. Crown 8vo.

JAMIESON (Andrew, C.E.), and MUNRO (John C.E.):

A POCKET-BOOK OF ELECTRICAL RULES AND TABLES. —(*See* Munro, John.)

Professors **LANDOIS** and **STIRLING**.

HUMAN PHYSIOLOGY
(A TEXT-BOOK OF):
Including Histology and Microscopical Anatomy.
WITH SPECIAL REFERENCE TO PRACTICAL MEDICINE,
By Dr. L. LANDOIS,
PROF. OF PHYSIOLOGY, UNIVERSITY OF GREIFSWALD.

Translated from the Fourth German Edition, with Annotations and Additions,

By WM. STIRLING, M.D., Sc.D.,
REG. PROF. INST. OF MED., UNIVERSITY OF ABERDEEN.

With very Numerous Illustrations.

In Two Parts, Royal 8vo, Handsome Cloth.

GENERAL CONTENTS.

PART I.—Physiology of the Blood, Circulation, Respiration, Digestion, Absorption, Animal Heat, Metabolic Phenomena of the Body. Price 18s.

PART II.—Secretion of Urine: Structure of the Skin: Physiology of the Motor Apparatus; the Voice and Speech: General Physiology of the Nerves; Electro-Physiology; the Brain; Organs of Vision, Hearing, Smell, Taste, Touch; Physiology of Development.
[*In February*, 1885.

*** Since its first appearance in 1880, Prof. LANDOIS' TEXT-BOOK OF PHYSIOLOGY has been translated into three Foreign languages, and passed through four large editions. In the English version will be found many Annotations by the Editor, calculated to render the work still more valuable to English Practitioners and Students, while, with the same object in view, the number of Illustrations has been increased from 106 in the Fourth German Edition to 176 in the English Version.

" The characteristic which has thus commended the work will be found mainly to lie in its eminent *practicality*; and it is this consideration which has induced the Editor to undertake the task of putting it into an English dress for English readers.

" Landois' work, in fact, forms a *Bridge* between Physiology and the Practice of Medicine. It never loses sight of the fact that the Student of to-day is the practising Physician of to-morrow. Thus, to every Section is appended—after a full description of the normal processes—a short *résumé* of the pathological variations, the object of this being to direct the attention of the Student, from the outset, to the field of his future practice, and to show him to what extent pathological processes are a disturbance of the normal activities.

" In the same way, the work offers to the busy Physician in practice a ready means of refreshing his memory on the theoretical aspects of Medicine. He can pass *backwards* from the examination of pathological phenomena to the normal processes, and, in the study of these, find new indications and new lights for the appreciation and treatment of the cases under consideration.

" With this object in view, all the methods of investigation which may with advantage be used by the Practitioner, are carefully and fully described; and Histology, also, occupies a larger place than is usually assigned to it in Text-Books of Physiology."—*Extract from Editor's Preface.*

" So great are the advantages offered by Prof. LANDOIS' TEXT-BOOK from the EXHAUSTIVE and EMINENTLY PRACTICAL manner in which the subject is treated, that, notwithstanding it is one of the largest works on Physiology, it has yet passed through four large editions in the same number of years. It has been translated by one who is well-known for the scientific work he has accomplished, and who is in all respects competent for the very serious task he has undertaken. . . . Dr. STIRLING'S annotations have materially added to the value of the work. . . . Admirably adapted for the practitioner. . . . with this Text-Book at his command, no Student could fail in his examination".—*Lancet.*

LEARED (Arthur, M.D., F.R.C.P., late Senior Physician to the Great Northern Hospital):

IMPERFECT DIGESTION: Its Causes and Treatment. Post 8vo. *Seventh Edition.* Cloth, 4/6.

"It now constitutes about the best work on the subject."—*Lancet.*

"Dr. Leared has treated a most important subject in a practical spirit and popular manner."—*Medical Times and Gazette.*

LINN (S.H., M.D., D.D.S., Dentist to the Imperial Medico-Chirurgical Academy of St. Petersburg):

THE TEETH: How to preserve them and prevent their Decay. A Popular Treatise on the Diseases and the Care of the Teeth. With Plates and Diagrams. Crown 8vo. Cloth, 2/6.

"Everyone who values his teeth—(and who does not?)—should study this practical little book."

"Many important truths on the preservation of the teeth and the irregularity of children's teeth are here set forth; and on the subject of artificial teeth there is sound advice, which most of us may sooner or later be glad of."—*Medical Times and Gazette.*

"Contains much useful information and excellent advice." *Leeds Mercury.*

"Deserves to be widely read."—*Northern Whig.*

"We heartily recommend the treatise."—*John Bull.*

LONGMORE (Surgeon-General, C.B., Q.H.S., F.R.C.S., &c., Professor of Military Surgery in the Army Medical School):

THE SANITARY CONTRASTS OF THE CRIMEAN WAR. Demy 8vo. Cloth limp, 1/6.

"A most valuable contribution to Military Medicine."—*British Medical Journal.*

"A most concise and interesting Review."—*Lancet.*

McNAB (W. Ramsay, M.D., F.L.S., Professor of Botany at the Royal College of Science, Dublin):

A MANUAL OF BOTANY, Structural and Systematic, for the use of Students.

MOFFITT (Staff-Assistant-Surgeon A., late of the Royal Victoria Hospital, Netley):

A MANUAL OF INSTRUCTION FOR ATTENDANTS ON THE SICK AND WOUNDED IN WAR. With numerous Illustrations. Post 8vo. Cloth, 5/.

*** *Published under the sanction of the National Society for Aid to the Sick and Wounded in War.*

"A work by a practical and experienced author. After an explicit chapter on the Anatomy of the Human Body, directions are given concerning bandaging, dressing of sores, wounds, &c., assistance to wounded on field of action, stretchers, mule litters, ambulance, transport, &c. All Dr. Moffitt's instructions are assisted by well-executed illustrations."—*Public Opinion.*

MUNRO (John, C. E.) and JAMIESON (Andrew, C.E., F.R.S.E.):

A POCKET-BOOK OF ELECTRICAL RULES AND TABLES, for the use of Electricians and Engineers. Pocket Size. Leather, 7/6. *Second Edition.*

GENERAL CONTENTS.—Units of Measurement; Measures; Testing; Conductors; Dielectrics; Submarine Cables; Telegraphy; Electro-Chemistry and Metallurgy; Batteries; Dynamos and Motors; Electric Lighting; Miscellaneous; Logarithms.

"WONDERFULLY PERFECT. . . . Worthy of the highest commendation we can give it."—*Electrician.*

"The STERLING VALUE of Messrs. MUNRO and JAMIESON's POCKET-BOOK."—*Electrical Review.*

"A Veritable Pocket-Companion."—*Telegraphist.*

"Furnished with a capital Index; can be consulted at any moment."—*Scottish Engineer.*

NAPIER (James, F.R.S.E., F.C.S.):

A MANUAL OF THE ART OF DYEING AND DYEING RECEIPTS. Illustrated by Diagrams and Numerous Specimens of Dyed Cotton, Silk, and Woollen Fabrics. Demy 8vo. *Third Edition, thoroughly revised and greatly enlarged.* Cloth, 21/.

"A Manual of necessary reference to all those who wish to master their trade, and keep pace with the scientific discoveries of the time."—*Journal of Applied Science.*

"In this work Mr. Napier has done good service . . . being a Practical Dyer himself, he knows the wants of his *Confrères* . . . the Article on Water is a very valuable one to the Practical Dyer. The Dyeing Receipts are very numerous, and well illustrated."—*Textile Manufacturer.*

——— A MANUAL OF ELECTRO-METAL-

LURGY. With numerous Illustrations. Crown 8vo. Cloth. *Fifth Edition, revised and enlarged,* 7/6.

"An established authority on Electro-Metallurgy, . . . of immense use to the Manufacturer in *economising the quantity of the precious metals absorbed.*"—*Journal of Applied Science.*

"The fact of Mr. Napier's Treatise having reached a FIFTH EDITION is good evidence of an appreciation of the Author's mode of treating his subject."—*Iron.*

"The Fifth Edition has all the advantages of a new work, and of a proved and tried friend. Mr. Napier is well known for the carefulness and accuracy with which he writes."—*Jeweller and Watchmaker.*

PARKER (Prof. W. Kitchen, F.R.S., Hunterian Professor, Royal College of Surgeons):

MAMMALIAN DESCENT: being the Hunterian Lectures for 1884. Adapted for General Readers. With Illustrations. In 8vo. Handsome cloth, 10s. 6d.

"This is a remarkable book. . . . Accuracy of statement, skill in marshalling facts, lucidity, impartiality, all these we might have expected to find, as we do find them. But Prof. PARKER goes beyond these things; he has varied learning, keen philosophic insight, and a poetic range of intellectual vision. Our advice is: *Get this book, and read it.* You will be first interested; then absorbed."—*Scotsman.*

"A very striking book . . . as readable as a book of travels. Prof. PARKER is no Materialist."—*Leicester Post.*

By MM. ETHERIDGE and SEELEY.

A MANUAL OF GEOLOGY,

BY

JOHN PHILLIPS, M.A., L.L.D., F.R.S.,

LATE PROF. OF GEOLOGY IN THE UNIVERSITY OF OXFORD.

Re-written and Edited by

ROBERT ETHERIDGE, F.R.S.,

OF THE NATURAL HISTORY DEPARTMENT, BRITISH MUSEUM, LATE PALÆONTOLOGIST TO THE GEOLOGICAL SURVEY OF GREAT BRITAIN, PAST-PRESIDENT OF THE GEOLOGICAL SOCIETY; AND

HARRY GOVIER SEELEY, F.R.S.,

PROFESSOR OF GEOGRAPHY IN KING'S COLLEGE, LONDON.

In Two Parts, 8vo, Handsome Cloth.

PART I.—Physical Geology and Palæontology. By Prof. SEELEY. 18s.
PART II.—Stratigraphical Geology and Palæontology. By R. ETHERIDGE, F.R.S.

With Numerous Tables, Sections, and Figures of Characteristic Fossils.

Extract from Review in the "Geological Magazine" for Dec., 1884.

"The Publishers have evidently acted upon the conviction that the name of JOHN PHILLIPS is a tower of strength. . . . It is most satisfactory to be able to say that Professor H. G. SEELEY has maintained in his 'PHYSICAL GEOLOGY AND PALÆONTOLOGY' the high reputation he already deservedly bears as a teacher, and that the work reflects credit on the name of PHILLIPS, with which it is associated.

"It is difficult, in the space at our command, to do fitting justice to so large a work. Commencing with the definition and origin of the Science, Professor SEELEY points out the various lines of inquiry which the geologist may follow. . . . We have next to consider the mineral constituents of the Aqueous and Igneous Rocks, and their characteristic structure, then the mode of formation of each, and all the subsequent changes they have undergone from agents of denudation and by upheaval, faulting, dislocation, &c. This naturally leads us to the consideration of Earth-Sculpture into Islands and Continents, diversified by Mountains, Valleys, Table-lands, and Plains, producing local variations in climate, and all the modifications in the scenery of this and other lands.

"Then follow chapters on Volcanic Energy and its manifestation in active Volcanoes, on the Nature and Origin of Igneous Rocks, their History, and the concomitants and results of volcanic energy. To this succeed chapters on Metamorphism, Mineral Veins, and on the chief Mineral Deposits in Britain.

"The final chapters, which are replete with interest, deal with the Biological aspect of Palæontology. Here we find discussed the origin, the extinction, succession; migration, persistence, distribution, relation, and variation of species—with other considerations, such as the Identification of Strata by Fossils, Homotaxis, Local Faunas, Natural History Provinces, and the relation of Living to Extinct forms.

"There is a noble and kindly sentiment suggested in the retention of PHILLIPS' name on the title page: and it is satisfactory to know that, notwithstanding the large additions and revisions, the *spirit* of the old work has been maintained.

"In its completed form, the work will probably be more than twice as large as the original by PHILLIPS."—Dr. HENRY WOODWARD, F.R.S., in the *Geological Magazine*.

"Professor SEELEY'S edition of PHILLIPS' GEOLOGY is substantially a new and modern work, forming a deeply interesting volume, well arranged, valuable as a work of reference— dealing with Physical Geology as a whole, and also presenting us with an animated summary of the leading doctrines and facts of Palæontology, as looked at from a modern standpoint." —*Scotsman.*

"Professor SEELEY'S work includes one of the most satisfactory Treatises on Lithology in the English language. . . . So much that is not accessible in other works, is presented in this volume, that no Student of Geology can afford to be without it."—*American Journal of Engineering.*

PHILLIPS (J. Arthur, F.R.S., M. Inst. C.E., F.C.S., F.G.S., Ancien Élève de l'Ecole des Mines, Paris):

ELEMENTS OF METALLURGY: a Practical Treatise on the Art of Extracting Metals from their Ores. With over 200 Illustrations, many of which have been reduced from Working Drawings. Royal 8vo, 764 pages, cloth, 34/-

General Contents.

I.—A TREATISE on FUELS and REFRACTORY MATERIALS.
II. A Description of the principal METALLIFEROUS MINERALS, with their DISTRIBUTION.
III. STATISTICS of the amount of each METAL annually produced throughout the World, obtained from official sources, or, where this has not been practicable, from authentic private information.
IV.—The METHODS of ASSAYING the different ORES, together with the PROCESSES of METALLURGICAL TREATMENT, comprising:

Refractory Materials.	Antimony.	Iron.
Fire-Clays.	Arsenic.	Cobalt.
Fuels, &c.	Zinc.	Nickel.
Aluminium.	Mercury.	Silver.
Copper.	Bismuth.	Gold.
Tin.	Lead.	Platinum.

"'Elements of Metallurgy' possesses intrinsic merits of the highest degree. Such a work is precisely wanted by the great majority of students and practical workers, and its very compactness is in itself a first-rate recommendation. . . . In our opinion, the BEST WORK EVER WRITTEN ON THE SUBJECT with a view to its practical treatment."—*Westminster Review.*

"In this most useful and handsome volume, Mr. Phillips has condensed a large amount of valuable practical knowledge. . . . We have not only the results of scientific inquiry most cautiously set forth, but the experiences of a thoroughly practical man very clearly given."—*Athenæum.*

"For twenty years the learned author, who might well have retired with honour on account of his acknowledged success and high character as an authority in Metallurgy, has been making notes, both as a Mining Engineer and a practical Metallurgist, and devoting the most valuable portion of his time to the accumulation of materials for this his Masterpiece."—*Colliery Guardian.*

"The VALUE OF THIS WORK IS ALMOST INESTIMABLE. There can be no question that the amount of time and labour bestowed upon it is enormous. . . . There is certainly no Metallurgical Treatise in the language calculated to prove of such general utility to the Student really seeking sound practical information upon the subject, and none which gives greater evidence of the extensive metallurgical knowledge of its Author."—*Mining Journal.*

PORTER (Surgeon-Major J. H., Late Assistant Professor of Military Surgery in the Army Medical School, and Hon. Assoc. of the Order of St. John of Jerusalem):

THE SURGEON'S POCKET-BOOK: an Essay on the Best Treatment of the Wounded in War; for which a Prize was awarded by Her Majesty the Empress of Germany. Specially adapted to the PUBLIC MEDICAL SERVICES. With 152 Illustrations, 16mo, roan. *Second Edition, Revised and Enlarged*, 7/6.

"Every Medical Officer is recommended to have the 'Surgeon's Pocket-Book' by Surgeon-Major Porter, accessible to refresh his memory and fortify his judgment."—*Précis of Field-Service Medical Arrangements for Afghan War.*

"A complete *vade mecum* to guide the military surgeon in the field."—*British Medical Journal.*

"A capital little book . . . of the greatest practical value. . . . A surgeon with this Manual in his pocket becomes a man of resource at once."—*Westminster Review.*

"So fully illustrated that for LAY-READERS and AMBULANCE WORK it will prove eminently useful."—*Medical Times and Gazette.*

SCIENTIFIC MANUALS
BY
W. J. MACQUORN RANKINE, C.E., LL.D., F.R.S.,
Late Regius Professor of Civil Engineering in the University of Glasgow.

In Crown 8vo. Cloth.

I. RANKINE (Prof.): APPLIED MECHANICS:
comprising the Principles of Statics and Cinematics, and Theory of Structures, Mechanism, and Machines. With numerous Diagrams. *Eleventh Edition*, 12/6.

"Cannot fail to be adopted as a text-book. . . . The whole of the information is so admirably arranged that there is every facility for reference."—*Mining Journal*.

II. RANKINE (Prof.): CIVIL ENGINEERING:
comprising Engineering Surveys, Earthwork, Foundations, Masonry, Carpentry, Metal-work, Roads, Railways, Canals, Rivers, Water-works, Harbours, &c. With numerous Tables and Illustrations. *Fifteenth Edition*, 16/.

"Far surpasses in merit every existing work of the kind. As a manual for the hands of the professional Civil Engineer it is sufficient and unrivalled, and even when we say this, we fall short of that high appreciation of Dr. Rankine's labours which we should like to express." *The Engineer*.

III. RANKINE (Prof.): MACHINERY AND MILLWORK: comprising the Geometry, Motions, Work, Strength, Construction, and Objects of Machines, &c. Illustrated with nearly 300 Woodcuts. *Fifth Edition*, 12/6.

"Professor Rankine's 'Manual of Machinery and Millwork' fully maintains the high reputation which he enjoys as a scientific author; higher praise it is difficult to award to any book. It cannot fail to be a lantern to the feet of every engineer."- *The Engineer*.

IV. RANKINE (Prof.): THE STEAM ENGINE and OTHER PRIME MOVERS. With Diagram of the Mechanical Properties of Steam, Folding-Plates, numerous Tables and Illustrations. *Eleventh Edition*, 12/6.

V. RANKINE (Prof.): USEFUL RULES and TABLES for Engineers and others. With Appendix: TABLES, TESTS, and FORMULÆ for the use of ELECTRICAL ENGINEERS; comprising Submarine Electrical Engineering, Electric Lighting, and Transmission of Power. By ANDREW JAMIESON, C.E., F.R.S.E. *Sixth Edition*, 10/6.

"Undoubtedly the most useful collection of engineering data hitherto produced."—*Mining Journal*.
"Every Electrician will consult it with profit."--*Engineering*.

VI. RANKINE (Prof.): A MECHANICAL TEXT-BOOK. by Prof. MACQUORN RANKINE and E. F. BAMBER, C.E. With numerous Illustrations. *Third Edition*, 9/.

"The work, as a whole, is very complete, and likely to prove invaluable for furnishing a useful and reliable outline of the subjects treated of."--*Mining Journal*.

*** THE MECHANICAL TEXT-BOOK forms a simple introduction to PROFESSOR RANKINE'S SERIES of MANUALS on ENGINEERING and MECHANICS.

PROF. RANKINE'S WORKS—(*Continued*).

VII. RANKINE (Prof.): MISCELLANEOUS SCIENTIFIC PAPERS. Royal 8vo. Cloth, 31/6.

Part I. Papers relating to Temperature, Elasticity, and Expansion of Vapours, Liquids, and Solids. Part II. Papers on Energy and its Transformations. Part III. Papers on Wave-Forms, Propulsion of Vessels, &c. With Memoir by Professor TAIT, M.A. Edited by W. J. MILLAR, C.E. With fine Portrait on Steel, Plates, and Diagrams.

"No more enduring Memorial of Professor Rankine could be devised than the publication of these papers in an accessible form. . . . The Collection is most valuable on account of the nature of his discoveries, and the beauty and completeness of his analysis . . . The Volume exceeds in importance any work in the same department published in our time."—*Architect*.

SIR EDWARD REED'S NEW WORK.

Royal 8vo, Handsome Cloth, 25s.

THE STABILITY OF SHIPS.

BY

SIR EDWARD J. REED, K.C.B., F.R.S., M.P.,

KNIGHT OF THE IMPERIAL ORDERS OF ST. STANILAUS OF RUSSIA; FRANCIS JOSEPH OF AUSTRIA; MEDJIDIE OF TURKEY; AND RISING SUN OF JAPAN; VICE-PRESIDENT OF THE INSTITUTION OF NAVAL ARCHITECTS.

With numerous Illustrations and Tables.

THIS work has been written for the purpose of placing in the hands of Naval Constructors, Shipbuilders, Officers of the Royal and Mercantile Marines, and all Students of Naval Science, a complete Treatise upon the Stability of Ships, and is the only work in the English Language dealing exhaustively with the subject.

The plan upon which it has been designed is that of deriving the fundamental principles and definitions from the most elementary forms of floating bodies, so that they may be clearly understood without the aid of mathematics; advancing thence to all the higher and more mathematical developments of the subject.

The work also embodies a very full account of the historical rise and progress of the Stability question, setting forth the results of the labours of BOUGUER, BERNOULLI, DON JUAN D'ULLOA, EULER, CHAPMAN, and ROMME, together with those of our own Countrymen, ATWOOD, MOSELEY, and a number of others.

The modern developments of the subject, both home and foreign, are likewise treated with much fulness, and brought down to the very latest date, so as to include the labours not only of DARGNIES, REECH (whose famous *Mémoire*, hitherto a sealed book to the majority of English naval architects, has been reproduced in the present work), RISBEC, FERRANTY, DUPIN, GUYOU, and DAYMARD, in France, but also those of RANKINE, WOOLLEY, ELGAR, JOHN, WHITE, GRAY, DENNY, INGLIS, and BENJAMIN, in Great Britain.

In order to render the work complete for the purposes of the Shipbuilder, whether at home or abroad, the Methods of Calculation introduced by Mr. F. K. BARNES, Mr. GRAY, M. REECH, M. DAYMARD, and Mr. BENJAMIN, are all given separately, illustrated by Tables and worked-out examples. The book contains more than 200 Diagrams, and is illustrated by a large number of actual cases, derived from ships of all descriptions, but especially from ships of the Mercantile Marine.

The work will thus be found to constitute the most comprehensive and exhaustive Treatise hitherto presented to the Profession on the Science of the STABILITY OF SHIPS.

"Sir EDWARD REED'S 'STABILITY OF SHIPS' is INVALUABLE. In it the STUDENT, new to the subject, will find the path prepared for him, and all difficulties explained with the utmost care and accuracy; the SHIP-DRAUGHTSMAN will find all the methods of calculation at present in use fully explained and illustrated, and accompanied by the Tables and Forms employed; the SHIPOWNER will find the variations in the Stability of Ships due to differences in forms and dimensions fully discussed, and the devices by which the state of his ships under all conditions may be graphically represented and easily understood; the NAVAL ARCHITECT will find brought together and ready to his hand, a mass of information which he would otherwise have to seek in an almost endless variety of publications, and some of which he would possibly not be able to obtain at all elsewhere."—*Steamship*.

"This important and valuable work supplies a long-felt want. . . . Cannot be too highly recommended, not only to Naval Architects and Students, but to all connected with Shipping interests. Nothing can be more simple than Sir Edward Reed's method."—*Iron*.

SCHWACKHÖFER and BROWNE:

FUEL AND WATER: A Manual for Users of Steam and Water. By Prof. FRANZ SCHWACKHÖFER of Vienna, and WALTER R. BROWNE, M.A., C.E., late Fellow of Trinity College, Cambridge. Demy 8vo, with Numerous Illustrations, 9/.

GENERAL CONTENTS.—Heat and Combustion; Fuel, Varieties of; Firing Arrangements, Furnace, Flues, Chimney; The Boiler, Choice of; Varieties; Feed-Water Heaters; Steam Pipes; Explosions; Water; Composition, Purification, Prevention of Scale, &c., &c.

"The Section on Heat is one of the best and most lucid ever written."—*Engineer.*
"Contains a vast amount of useful knowledge. . . . Cannot fail to be valuable to thousands compelled to use steam power."—*Railway Engineer.*
"Goes into minute details as to how economies may be effected in use of fuel and management of boilers."—*Sheffield Daily Telegraph.*
"The result of wide experience."—*Scotsman.*
"Its practical utility is beyond question."—*Mining Journal.*

SEATON (A. E., Lecturer on Marine Engineering

at the Royal Naval College, Greenwich, and Member of the Institute of Naval Architects):

A MANUAL OF MARINE ENGINEERING; Comprising the Designing, Construction, and Working of Marine Machinery. With numerous Illustrations. *Fourth Edition.* Demy 8vo. Cloth, 18/.

GENERAL CONTENTS.

I. PRINCIPLES OF MARINE PROPULSION.
II. PRINCIPLES OF STEAM ENGINEERING.
III. DETAILS OF MARINE ENGINES.
IV. PROPELLERS.
V. BOILERS.
VI. MISCELLANEOUS.

Opinions of the Press.

"The important subject of Marine Engineering is here treated with the thoroughness that it requires. No department has escaped attention. . . . Gives the results of much close study and practical work."—*Engineering.*
"By far the best MANUAL in existence. . . . Gives a complete account of the methods of solving, with the utmost possible economy, the problems before the Marine Engineer."—*Athenæum.*
"In the three-fold capacity of enabling a Student to learn how to design, construct, and work a modern Marine Steam-Engine, Mr. Seaton's Manual has no rival."—*Times.*
"The Student, Draughtsman, and Engineer will find this work the most valuable Handbook of Reference on the Marine Engine now in existence."—*Marine Engineer.*

SHELTON (W. Vincent, Foreman to the Imperial

Ottoman Gun Factories, Constantinople):

THE MECHANIC'S GUIDE: A Hand-Book for Engineers and Artizans. With Copious Tables and Valuable Recipes for Practical Use. Illustrated. *Second Edition.* Crown 8vo. Cloth, 7/6.

GENERAL CONTENTS.

PART I.—Arithmetic.
PART II.—Geometry.
PART III.—Mensuration.
PART IV.—Velocities in Boring and Wheel-Gearing.
PART V.—Wheel and Screw Cutting.
PART VI.—Miscellaneous Subjects.
PART VII.—The Steam Engine.
PART VIII.—The Locomotive.

"The MECHANIC'S GUIDE will answer its purpose as completely as a whole series of elaborate text-books."—*Mining Journal.*
"Ought to have a place on the bookshelf of every Mechanic."—*Iron.*
"Much instruction is here given without pedantry or pretension."—*Builder.*
"A *sine quâ non* to every practical Mechanic."—*Railway Service Gazette.*

*** This Work is specially intended for Self-Teachers, and places before the Reader a concise and simple explanation of General Principles, together with Illustrations of their adaptation to Practical Purposes.

STIRLING (William, M.D., D.Sc., Reg. Prof.
Inst. of Med., University of Aberdeen):
A TEXT-BOOK OF HUMAN PHYSIOLOGY: Including Histology and Microscopical Anatomy. From the German of Prof. LANDOIS, Director of the Physiological Institute, University of Greifswald. *From the Fourth German Edition.* With Numerous Illustrations. Royal 8vo.
(*See under Landois and Stirling.*)

THOMSON (Spencer, M.D., L.R.C.S., Edinburgh,
and J. C. STEELE, M.D., of Guy's Hospital):
DOMESTIC MEDICINE AND HOUSEHOLD SURGERY (A Dictionary of). Thoroughly Revised and in part Re-Written by the Editors. With a Chapter on the Management of the Sick-room, and many Hints for the Diet and Comfort of Invalids. With many new Engravings. *Twentieth Edition.* Royal 8vo. Cloth, 10/6.

THORBURN (John), M.D., Prof. of Obstetric
Medicine, Victoria University, Manchester.
GYNÆCOLOGY: A Manual of. Prepared with Special Reference to the Requirements of the General Practitioner.
[*In Preparation.*

WYLDE (James, formerly Lecturer on Natural
Philosophy at the Polytechnic):
THE MAGIC OF SCIENCE: A Manual of Easy and Amusing Scientific Experiments. With Steel Portrait of Faraday and many hundred Engravings. *Third Edition.* Crown 8vo. Cloth gilt and gilt edges, 5/.

" To those who need to be allured into the paths of Natural Science by witnessing the wonderful results that can be produced by well-contrived experiments, we do not know that we could recommend a more useful volume."—*Athenæum.*

OFFICIAL YEAR-BOOK

OF THE

SCIENTIFIC AND LEARNED SOCIETIES OF GREAT BRITAIN AND IRELAND. PRICE 7/6.

Compiled from Official Sources. FIRST ISSUE. Giving an Account of over 400 Societies engaged in the following Departments of Research:—

§ 1. Science Generally: *i.e.*, Societies occupying themselves with several Branches of Science, or with Science and Literature jointly.
§ 2. Mathematics and Physics.
§ 3. Chemistry and Photography.
§ 4. Geology, Geography, and Mineralogy.
§ 5. Biology, including Microscopy and Anthropology.
§ 6. Economic Science and Statistics.
§ 7. Mechanical Science and Architecture.
§ 8. Naval and Military Science.
§ 9. Agriculture and Horticulture.
§ 10. Law.
§ 11. Medicine.
§ 12. Literature.
§ 13. Psychology.
§ 14. Archæology.

With Appendix on the Leading Scientific Societies throughout the world.

A few of the Opinions of the Press.

"The YEAR-BOOK OF SOCIETIES meets an obvious want, and promises to be a valuable work of reference." *Athenæum.*

"The YEAR-BOOK OF SCIENTIFIC AND LEARNED SOCIETIES meets a want, and is therefore sure of a welcome." *Westminster Review.*

"In the YEAR-BOOK OF SOCIETIES we have the FIRST ISSUE of what is, without doubt, a very useful work."- *Spectator.*

"A most praiseworthy and useful compilation. . . . We can testify to its accuracy; the whole work, attended as it must have been with great trouble and patience, is creditable." —*Notes and Queries.*

"The YEAR-BOOK OF SOCIETIES fills a very real want. The volume will become a Scientific Directory, chronicling the work and discoveries of the year, and enabling the worker in one branch to try his hand in all that interests him in kindred lines of research. We trust that it will meet with an encouraging reception."—*Engineering.*

"We have no hesitation in saying that the YEAR-BOOK OF SOCIETIES supplies a real want to scientific workers. . . . A most valuable feature will be the Index to the Papers read before the various Societies throughout the kingdom during each year."—*Science Monthly.*

"The OFFICIAL YEAR-BOOK OF SOCIETIES, which has been prepared to meet a want long felt by scientific workers of a Representative Book, will form a yearly record of Scientific Progress, and a Handbook of Reference. . . . It is carefully printed, and altogether well got up."—*Public Opinion.*

The ISSUE of the YEAR-BOOK OF SOCIETIES for 1885 will be compiled from official sources, and will comprise (in addition to the necessary information as to official changes) the TITLES of the PAPERS read before the various SOCIETIES during 1884, with the NAMES of their AUTHORS.

The YEAR-BOOK OF SOCIETIES will thus form a complete INDEX TO THE SCIENTIFIC WORK of the year in the various Departments. It will be used as a ready HANDBOOK in all our great SCIENTIFIC CENTRES, MUSEUMS, and LIBRARIES throughout the Kingdom, and will become an INDISPENSABLE BOOK OF REFERENCE to every one engaged in Scientific Work.

"We predict that the YEAR-BOOK OF SOCIETIES will speedily become one of those Year-Books WHICH IT WOULD BE IMPOSSIBLE TO DO WITHOUT."—*Bristol Mercury.*

EDUCATIONAL WORKS.

*** *Specimen Copies of all the Educational Works published by Messrs. Charles Griffin and Company may be seen at the Libraries of the College of Preceptors, South Kensington Museum, and Crystal Palace; also at the depôts of the Chief Educational Societies.*

BRYCE (Archibald Hamilton, D.C.L., LL.D.,
Senior Classical Moderator in the University of Dublin):

THE WORKS OF VIRGIL. Text from HEYNE and WAGNER. English Notes, original, and selected from the leading German, American, and English Commentators. Illustrations from the antique. Complete in One Volume. *Fourteenth Edition.* Fcap 8vo. Cloth, 6/.

Or, in Three Parts:

    Part I. BUCOLICS and GEORGICS, . . 2/6.
    Part II. THE ÆNEID, Books I.-VI., . 2/6.
    Part III. THE ÆNEID, Books VII.-XII., . 2/6.

"Contains the pith of what has been written by the best scholars on the subject. . . . The notes comprise everything that the student can want."—*Athenæum.*

"The most complete, as well as elegant and correct edition of Virgil ever published in this country."—*Educational Times.*

"The best commentary on Virgil which a student can obtain."—*Scotsman.*

COBBETT (William): ENGLISH GRAMMAR,
in a Series of Letters, intended for the use of Schools and Young Persons in general. With an additional chapter on Pronunciation, by the Author's Son, JAMES PAUL COBBETT. *The only correct and authorised Edition.* Fcap 8vo. Cloth, 1/6.

"A new and cheapened edition of that most excellent of all English Grammars, William Cobbett's. It contains new copyright matter, as well as includes the equally amusing and instructive 'Six Lessons intended to prevent Statesmen from writing in an awkward manner.'"—*Atlas.*

COBBETT (William): A FRENCH GRAMMAR.
Fifteenth Edition. Fcap 8vo. Cloth, 3/6.

"Cobbett's 'French Grammar' comes out with perennial freshness. There are few grammars equal to it for those who are learning, or desirous of learning, French without a teacher. The work is excellently arranged, and in the present edition we note certain careful and wise revisions of the text."—*School Board Chronicle.*

"Business men commencing the study of French will find this treatise one of the best aids. . . . It is largely used on the Continent."—*Midland Counties Herald.*

COBBIN'S MANGNALL: MANGNALL'S
HISTORICAL AND MISCELLANEOUS QUESTIONS, for the use of Young People. By RICHMAL MANGNALL. Greatly enlarged and corrected, and continued to the present time, by INGRAM COBBIN, M.A. *Fifty-fourth Thousand. New Illustrated Edition.* 12mo. Cloth, 4/.

COLERIDGE (Samuel Taylor): A DISSERTATION ON THE SCIENCE OF METHOD. (*Encyclopædia Metropolitana.*) With a Synopsis. *Ninth Edition.* Cr. 8vo. Cloth, 2/.

CRAIK'S ENGLISH LITERATURE.
A COMPENDIOUS HISTORY OF ENGLISH LITERATURE AND OF THE ENGLISH LANGUAGE FROM THE NORMAN CONQUEST. With numerous Specimens. By GEORGE LILLIE CRAIK, LL.D., late Professor of History and English Literature, Queen's College, Belfast. *New Edition.* In two vols. Royal 8vo. Handsomely bound in cloth, 25/.

GENERAL CONTENTS.
INTRODUCTORY.
I.—THE NORMAN PERIOD—The Conquest.
II.—SECOND ENGLISH—Commonly called Semi-Saxon.
III.—THIRD ENGLISH—Mixed, or Compound English.
IV.—MIDDLE AND LATTER PART OF THE SEVENTEENTH CENTURY.
V.—THE CENTURY BETWEEN THE ENGLISH REVOLUTION AND THE FRENCH REVOLUTION.
VI.—THE LATTER PART OF THE EIGHTEENTH CENTURY.
VII.—THE NINETEENTH CENTURY (*a*) THE LAST AGE OF THE GEORGES.
(*b*) THE VICTORIAN AGE.

With numerous Excerpts and Specimens of Style.

"Anyone who will take the trouble to ascertain the fact, will find how completely even our great poets and other writers of the last generation have already faded from the view of the present, with the most numerous class of the educated and reading public. Scarcely anything is generally read except the publications of the day. YET NOTHING IS MORE CERTAIN THAN THAT NO TRUE CULTIVATION CAN BE SO ACQUIRED. This is the extreme case of that entire ignorance of history which has been affirmed, not with more point than truth, to leave a person always a child. . . . The present work combines the HISTORY OF THE LITERATURE with the HISTORY OF THE LANGUAGE. The scheme of the course and revolutions of the language which is followed here is extremely simple, and resting not upon arbitrary, but upon natural or real distinctions, gives us the only view of the subject that can claim to be regarded as of a scientific character."—*Extract from the Author's Preface.*

"Professor Craik's book going, as it does, through the whole history of the language, probably takes a place quite by itself. The great value of the book is its thorough comprehensiveness. It is always clear and straightforward, and deals not in theories but in facts."—*Saturday Review.*

"Professor Craik has succeeded in making a book more than usually agreeable."—*The Times.*

CRAIK (Prof.): A MANUAL OF ENGLISH LITERATURE, for the use of Colleges, Schools, and Civil Service Examinations. Selected from the larger work, by Dr. CRAIK. *Ninth Edition.* With an Additional Section on Recent Literature, by HENRY CRAIK, M.A., Author of "A Life of Swift." Crown 8vo. Cloth, 7/6.

"A Manual of English Literature from so experienced and well-read a scholar as Professor Craik needs no other recommendation than the mention of its existence."—*Spectator.*

"This augmented effort will, we doubt not, be received with decided approbation by those who are entitled to judge, and studied with much profit by those who want to learn. . . . If our young readers will give healthy perusal to Dr. Craik's work, they will greatly benefit by the wide and sound views he has placed before them."—*Athenæum.*

"The preparation of the NEW ISSUE has been entrusted to Mr. HENRY CRAIK, Senior Examiner in the Scotch Education Department, and well known in literary circles as the author of the latest and best Life of Swift. . . . A Series of TEST QUESTIONS is added, which must prove of great service to Students studying alone."—*Glasgow Herald.*

WORKS BY CHARLES T. CRUTTWELL, M.A.,
Fellow of Merton College, Oxford, and Head Master of Malvern College.

I.—A HISTORY OF ROMAN LITERA-
TURE: From the Earliest Period to the Times of the Antonines. *Third Edition.* Crown 8vo. Cloth, 8/6.

"Mr. CRUTTWELL has done a real service to all Students of the Latin Language and Literature. . . . Full of good scholarship and good criticism."—*Athenæum*.

"A most serviceable—indeed, indispensable—guide for the Student. . . . The a general reader' will be both charmed and instructed."—*Saturday Review*.

"The Author undertakes to make Latin Literature interesting, and he has succeeded. There is not a dull page in the volume."—*Academy*.

"The great merit of the work is its fulness and accuracy."—*Guardian*.

"This elaborate and careful work, in every respect of high merit. Nothing at all equal to it has hitherto been published in England."—*British Quarterly Review*.

Companion Volume. Second Edition.

II.—SPECIMENS OF ROMAN LITERA-
TURE: From the Earliest Period to the Times of the Antonines. Passages from the Works of Latin Authors, Prose Writers, and Poets:

Part I.—ROMAN THOUGHT: Religion, Philosophy and Science, Art and Letters, 6/.

Part II.—ROMAN STYLE: Descriptive, Rhetorical, and Humorous Passages, 5/.

Or in One Volume complete, 10/6.

Edited by C. T. CRUTTWELL, M.A., Merton College, Oxford; and PEAKE BANTON, M.A., some time Scholar of Jesus College, Oxford.

"'Specimens of Roman Literature' marks a new era in the study of Latin."—*English Churchman*.

"Schoolmasters and tutors will be grateful for a volume which supplies them at once with passages of every shade of difficulty for testing the most different capacity, or which may be read with advantage in the higher forms of schools. There is no other book of the kind in this country which can be more safely recommended, either for its breadth, cheapness, or interest."—*Prof. Ellis in the "Academy."*

"A work which is not only useful but necessary. . . . The plan gives it a standing-ground of its own. . . . The sound judgment exercised in plan and selection calls for hearty commendation."—*Saturday Review*.

"It is hard to conceive a completer or handier repertory of specimens of Latin thought and style."—*Contemporary Review*.

*** KEY to PART II., PERIOD II. (being a complete TRANSLATION of the 85 Passages composing the Section), by THOS. JOHNSTON, M.A., may now be had (by Tutors and Schoolmasters only) on application to the Publishers. Price 2/6.

CURRIE (Joseph, formerly Head Classical Master of Glasgow Academy):

THE WORKS OF HORACE: Text from ORELLIUS. English Notes, original and selected, from the best Commentators. Illustrations from the antique. Complete in One Volume. Fcap 8vo. Cloth, 5/.

Or in Two Parts:
    Part I.—CARMINA, ... 3/.
    Part II.—SATIRES AND EPISTLES, . . 3/.

"The notes are excellent and exhaustive."—*Quarterly Journal of Education*.

EXTRACTS FROM CÆSAR'S COM-
MENTARIES; containing his description of Gaul, Britain, and Germany. With Notes, Vocabulary, &c. Adapted for Young Scholars. *Fourth Edition.* 18mo. Cloth, 1/6.

D'ORSEY (Rev. Alex. J. D., B.D., Corpus Christi Coll., Cambridge, Lecturer at King's College, London):

SPELLING BY DICTATION: Progressive Exercises in English Orthography, for Schools and Civil Service Examinations. *Sixteenth Thousand.* 18mo. Cloth, 1/.

EDUCATIONAL PUBLICATIONS. 25

FLEMING (William, D.D., late Professor of Moral Philosophy in the University of Glasgow):
THE VOCABULARY OF PHILOSOPHY: MENTAL, MORAL, AND METAPHYSICAL. With Quotations and References for the Use of Students. Revised and Edited by HENRY CALDERWOOD, LL.D., Professor of Moral Philosophy in the University of Edinburgh. *Third Edition, enlarged.* Crown 8vo. Cloth bevelled, 10/6.

"The additions by the Editor bear in their clear, concise, vigorous expression, the stamp of his powerful intellect, and thorough command of our language. More than ever, the work is now likely to have a prolonged and useful existence, and to facilitate the researches of those entering upon philosophic studies."—*Weekly Review.*

McBURNEY (Isaiah, LL.D.,): EXTRACTS FROM OVID'S METAMORPHOSES. With Notes, Vocabulary, &c. Adapted for Young Scholars. *Third Edition.* 18mo. Cloth, 1/6.

MENTAL SCIENCE: S. T. COLERIDGE'S celebrated Essay on METHOD; Archbishop WHATELY's Treatises on LOGIC and RHETORIC. *Tenth Edition.* Crown 8vo. Cloth, 5/.

MILLER (W. Galbraith, M.A., LL.B., Lecturer on Public Law, including Jurisprudence and International Law, in the University of Glasgow):
THE PHILOSOPHY OF LAW, LECTURES ON. Designed mainly as an Introduction to the Study of International Law. In 8vo. Handsome Cloth, 12/. *Now Ready.*

"Mr. MILLER's 'PHILOSOPHY OF LAW' bears upon it the stamp of a wide culture and of an easy acquaintanceship with what is best in modern continental speculation. . . . Interesting and valuable, because suggestive."- *Journal of Jurisprudence.*

WORKS BY WILLIAM RAMSAY, M.A.,
Trinity College, Cambridge, late Professor of Humanity in the University of Glasgow.

A MANUAL OF ROMAN ANTIQUITIES. For the use of Advanced Students. With Map, 130 Engravings, and very copious Index. *Twelfth Edition.* Crown 8vo. Cloth, 8/6.

"Comprises all the results of modern improved scholarship within a moderate compass."—*Athenæum.*

RAMSAY (Professor): AN ELEMENTARY MANUAL OF ROMAN ANTIQUITIES. Adapted for Junior Classes. With numerous Illustrations. *Seventh Edition.* Crown 8vo. Cloth, 4/.

———— **A MANUAL OF LATIN PROSODY,** Illustrated by Copious Examples and Critical Remarks. For the use of Advanced Students. *Sixth Edition.* Crown 8vo. Cloth, 5/.

"There is no other work on the subject worthy to compete with it."—*Athenæum.*

———— **AN ELEMENTARY MANUAL OF LATIN PROSODY.** Adapted for Junior Classes. Crown 8vo. Cloth, 2/.

THE SCHOOL BOARD READERS:
A NEW SERIES OF STANDARD READING-BOOKS.
EDITED BY A FORMER H.M. INSPECTOR OF SCHOOLS.

Adopted by many School Boards throughout the Country.

Elementary Reader, Part I., 1d.	Standard III.,	9d.
" " " II., 2d.	" IV.,	1s. 0d.
Standard I., . . 4d.	" V.,	1s. 6d.
" II., . . . 6d.	" VI.,	2s. 0d.

Key to the Questions in Arithmetic in 2 Parts, each 6d.

*** Each Book of this Series contains within itself all that is necessary to fulfil the requirements of the Revised Code—viz., Reading, Spelling, and Dictation Lessons, together with Exercises in Arithmetic for the whole year. The paper, type, and binding are all that can be desired.

"THE BOOKS GENERALLY ARE VERY MUCH WHAT WE SHOULD DESIRE."—*Times.*
"The Series is DECIDEDLY ONE OF THE BEST that have yet appeared."—*Athenæum.*

THE SCHOOL BOARD MANUALS
ON THE SPECIFIC SUBJECTS OF THE REVISED CODE,
BY A FORMER H.M. INSPECTOR OF SCHOOLS,
Editor of the "School Board Readers."

64 pages, stiff wrapper. 6d. ; neat cloth, 7d. each.

I.—ALGEBRA.	V.—ANIMAL PHYSIOLOGY. (Well Illustrated with good Engravings.)
II.—ENGLISH HISTORY.	VI.—BIBLE HISTORY. (Entirely free from any Denominational bias.)
III.—GEOGRAPHY.	
IV.—PHYSICAL GEOGRAPHY.	

"These simple and well-graduated Manuals, adapted to the requirements of the New Code, are the most elementary of elementary works, and extremely cheap. They are more useful as practical guide-books than most of the more expensive works."—*Standard.*

SENIOR (Nassau William, M.A., late Professor of Political Economy in the University of Oxford).
A TREATISE ON POLITICAL ECONOMY: the Science which treats of the Nature, the Production, and the Distribution of Wealth. Sixth Edition. Crown 8vo. Cloth. (*Encyclopædia Metropolitana*), 4/.

THOMSON (James): THE SEASONS. With an Introduction and Notes by ROBERT BELL, Editor of the "Annotated Series of British Poets." *Third Edition.* Fcap 8vo. Cloth, 1/6.
"An admirable introduction to the study of our English classics."

WHATELY (Archbishop): LOGIC—A Treatise on. With Synopsis and Index. (*Encyclopædia Metropolitana*), 3/.

——— RHETORIC—A Treatise on. With Synopsis and Index. (*Encyclopædia Metropolitana*), 3/6.

WYLDE (James): A MANUAL OF MATHEMATICS, Pure and Applied, 10/6.

WORKS IN GENERAL LITERATURE.

BELL (Robert, Editor of the "Annotated Series of British Poets"):

GOLDEN LEAVES FROM THE WORKS OF THE POETS AND PAINTERS. Illustrated by Sixty-four superb Engravings on Steel, after Paintings by DAVID ROBERTS, STANFIELD, LESLIE, STOTHARD, HAYDON, CATTERMOLE, NASMYTH, Sir THOMAS LAWRENCE, and many others, and engraved in the first style of Art by FINDEN, GREATBACH, LIGHTFOOT, &c. *Second Edition*, 4to. Cloth gilt, 21/.

"'Golden Leaves' is by far the most important book of the season. The Illustrations are really works of art, and the volume does credit to the arts of England."—*Saturday Review*.

"The Poems are selected with taste and judgment."—*Times*.

"The engravings are from drawings by Stothard, Newton, Danby, Leslie, and Turner, and it is needless to say how charming are many of the above here given."—*Athenæum*.

CHRISTISON (John): A COMPLETE SYSTEM OF INTEREST TABLES at 3, 4, 4½, and 5 per Cent.; Tables of Exchange or Commission, Profit and Loss, Discount, Clothiers', Malt, Spirit, and various other useful Tables. To which is prefixed the Mercantile Ready-Reckoner, containing Reckoning Tables from one thirty-second part of a penny to one pound. *New Edition. Greatly enlarged.* 12mo. Bound in leather, 4/6.

THE WORKS OF WILLIAM COBBETT.

THE ONLY AUTHORISED EDITIONS.

COBBETT (William): ADVICE TO YOUNG Men and (incidentally) to Young Women, in the Middle and Higher Ranks of Life. In a Series of Letters addressed to a Youth, a Bachelor, a Lover, a Husband, a Father, a Citizen, and a Subject. *New Edition. With admirable Portrait on Steel.* Fcap 8vo. Cloth, 2/6.

"Cobbett's great qualities were immense vigour, resource, energy, and courage, joined to a force of understanding, a degree of logical power, and above all a force of expression, which have rarely been equalled. . . . He was the most English of Englishmen."—*Saturday Review*.

"With all his faults, Cobbett's style is a continual refreshment to the lover of 'English undefiled.'"—*Pall Mall Gazette*.

WILLIAM COBBETT'S WORKS—*(Continued).*

COBBETT (Wm.): COTTAGE ECONOMY:
Containing information relative to the Brewing of Beer, Making of Bread, Keeping of Cows, Pigs, Bees, Poultry, &c.; and relative to other matters deemed useful in conducting the affairs of a Poor Man's Family. *Eighteenth Edition*, revised by the Author's Son. Fcap 8vo. Cloth, 2/6.

────── EDUCATIONAL WORKS. (See page 22.)

────── A LEGACY TO LABOURERS: An Argument showing the Right of the Poor to Relief from the Land. With a Preface by the Author's Son, JOHN M. COBBETT, late M.P. for Oldham. *New Edition*. Fcap 8vo. Cloth, 1/6.

"The book cannot be too much studied just now."—*Nonconformist*.

"Cobbett was, perhaps, the ablest Political writer England ever produced, and his influence as a Liberal thinker is felt to this day. . . . It is a real treat to read his strong racy language."—*Public Opinion*.

────── A LEGACY TO PARSONS: Or, have the Clergy of the Established Church an Equitable Right to Tithes and Church Property? *New Edition*. Fcap 8vo. Cloth, 1/6.

"The most powerful work of the greatest master of political controversy this country has ever produced."—*Pall Mall Gazette*.

COBBETT (Miss Anne): THE ENGLISH
HOUSEKEEPER; or, Manual of Domestic Management. Containing Advice on the conduct of Household Affairs and Practical Instructions, intended for the Use of Young Ladies who undertake the superintendence of their own Housekeeping. Fcap 8vo. Cloth, 3/6.

COOK'S VOYAGES. VOYAGES ROUND
THE WORLD, by Captain COOK. Illustrated with Maps and numerous Engravings. Two vols. Super-Royal 8vo. Cloth, 30/.

DALGAIRNS (Mrs.): THE PRACTICE OF
COOKERY, adapted to the business of Every-day Life. By Mrs. DALGAIRNS. *The best book for Scotch dishes.* About Fifty new Recipes have been added to the present Edition, but only such as the Author has had adequate means of ascertaining to be valuable. *Seventeenth Edition*. Fcap 8vo. Cloth. (*In preparation.*)

"This is by far the most complete and truly practical work which has yet appeared on the subject. It will be found an infallible 'Cooks' Companion,' and a treasure of great price to the mistress of a family."—*Edinburgh Literary Journal*.

"We consider we have reason strongly to recommend Mrs. Dalgairns' as an economical, useful, and practical system of cookery, adapted to the wants of all families, from the tradesman's to the country gentleman's."—*Spectator*.

D'AUBIGNÉ (Dr. Merle): HISTORY OF THE
REFORMATION. With the Author's latest additions and a new Preface. Many Woodcuts, and Twelve Engravings on Steel, illustrative of the life of MARTIN LUTHER, after LABOUCHÈRE. In one large volume. Demy 4to. Elegantly bound in cloth, 21/.

"In this edition the principal actors and scenes in the great drama of the Sixteenth Century are brought vividly before the eye of the reader, by the skill of the artist and Engraver."

DONALDSON (Joseph, Sergeant in the 94th
Scots Regiment):

RECOLLECTIONS OF THE EVENTFUL LIFE OF A SOLDIER IN THE PENINSULA. *New Edition.* Fcap 8vo. Gilt sides and edges, 4/.

EARTH DELINEATED WITH PEN AND
PENCIL (The): An Illustrated Record of Voyages, Travels, and Adventures all round the World. Illustrated with more than Two Hundred Engravings in the first style of Art, by the most eminent Artists, including several from the master-pencil of GUSTAVE DORÉ. Demy 4to, 750 pages. Very handsomely bound, 21/.

MRS. ELLIS'S CELEBRATED WORKS
On the INFLUENCE and CHARACTER of WOMEN.

THE ENGLISHWOMAN'S LIBRARY:

A Series of Moral and Descriptive Works. By Mrs. ELLIS. Small 8vo. Cloth, each volume, 2/6.

1.—THE WOMEN OF ENGLAND: Their Social Duties and Domestic Habits. *Thirty-ninth Thousand.*
2.—THE DAUGHTERS OF ENGLAND: Their Position in Society, Character, and Responsibilities. *Twentieth Thousand.*
3.—THE WIVES OF ENGLAND: Their Relative Duties, Domestic Influence, and Social Obligations. *Eighteenth Thousand.*
4.—THE MOTHERS OF ENGLAND: Their Influence and Responsibilities. *Twentieth Thousand.*
5.—FAMILY SECRETS; Or, Hints to make Home Happy. Three vols. *Twenty-third Thousand.*
6.—SUMMER AND WINTER IN THE PYRENEES. *Tenth Thousand.*
7.—TEMPER AND TEMPERAMENT; Or, Varieties of Character. Two vols. *Tenth Thousand.*
8.—PREVENTION BETTER THAN CURE; Or, the Moral Wants of the World we live in. *Twelfth Thousand.*
9.—HEARTS AND HOMES; Or, Social Distinctions. Three vols. *Tenth Thousand.*

THE EMERALD SERIES OF STANDARD AUTHORS.

Illustrated by Engravings on Steel, after STOTHARD, LESLIE, DAVID ROBERTS, STANFIELD, Sir THOMAS LAWRENCE, CATTERMOLE, &c., Fcap 8vo. Cloth, gilt.

Particular attention is requested to this very beautiful series. The delicacy of the engravings, the excellence of the typography, and the quaint antique head and tail pieces, render them the most beautiful volumes ever issued from the press of this country, and now, unquestionably, the cheapest of their class.

BURNS' (Robert) SONGS AND BALLADS.
With an Introduction on the Character and Genius of Burns. By THOMAS CARLYLE. Carefully printed in antique type, and illustrated with Portrait and beautiful Engravings on Steel. *Second Thousand.* Cloth, gilt edges, 3/.

BYRON (Lord): CHILDE HAROLD'S PILGRIMAGE.
With Memoir by Professor SPALDING. Illustrated with Portrait and Engravings on Steel, by GREATBACH, MILLER, LIGHTFOOT, &c., from Paintings by CATTERMOLE, Sir T. LAWRENCE, H. HOWARD, and STOTHARD. Beautifully printed on toned paper. *Third Thousand.* Cloth, gilt edges, 3/.

CAMPBELL (Thomas): THE PLEASURES OF HOPE.
With Introductory Memoir by the Rev. CHARLES ROGERS, LL.D., and several Poems never before published. Illustrated with Portrait and Steel Engravings. *Second Thousand.* Cloth, gilt edges, 3/.

CHATTERTON'S (Thomas) POETICAL WORKS.
With an Original Memoir by FREDERICK MARTIN, and Portrait. Beautifully illustrated on Steel, and elegantly printed. *Fourth Thousand.* Cloth, gilt edges, 3/.

GOLDSMITH'S (Oliver) POETICAL WORKS.
With Memoir by Professor SPALDING. Exquisitely illustrated with Steel Engravings. *New Edition.* Printed on superior toned paper. *Seventh Thousand.* Cloth, gilt edges, 3/.

GRAY'S (Thomas) POETICAL WORKS.
With Life by the Rev. JOHN MITFORD, and Essay by the EARL of CARLISLE. With Portrait and numerous Engravings on Steel and Wood. Elegantly printed on toned paper. *Eton Edition, with the Latin Poems. Sixth Thousand.* Cloth, gilt edges, 5/.

HERBERT'S (George) POETICAL WORKS.
With Memoir by J. NICHOL, B.A., Oxon, Prof. of English Literature in the University of Glasgow. Edited by CHARLES COWDEN CLARKE. Antique headings to each page. *Second Thousand.* Cloth, gilt edges, 3/.

KEBLE (Rev. John): THE CHRISTIAN YEAR.
With Memoir by W. TEMPLE, Portrait, and Eight beautiful Engravings on Steel. *Second Thousand.*

Cloth, gilt edges,	5/.
Morocco, elegant,	10/6.
Malachite,	12/6.

THE EMERALD SERIES—(*Continued*).

POE'S (Edgar Allan) COMPLETE POETICAL
WORKS. Edited, with Memoir, by JAMES HANNAY. Full-page Illustrations after WEHNERT, WIER, &c. Toned paper. *Thirteenth Thousand.*
Cloth, gilt edges, ... 3/.
Malachite, ... 10 6.
Other volumes in preparation.

FINDEN'S FINE ART WORKS.

BEAUTIES OF MOORE: being a Series of
Portraits of his Principal Female Characters, from Paintings by eminent Artists, engraved in the highest style of Art by EDWARD FINDEN, with a Memoir of the Poet, and Descriptive Letterpress. Folio. Cloth gilt, 42/.

DRAWING-ROOM TABLE BOOK (The): a
Series of 31 highly-finished Steel Engravings, with descriptive Tales by Mrs. S. C. HALL, MARY HOWITT, and others. Folio. Cloth gilt, 21/.

GALLERY OF MODERN ART (The): a Series
of 31 highly-finished Steel Engravings, with descriptive Tales by Mrs. S. C. HALL, MARY HOWITT, and others. Folio. Cloth gilt, 21/.

FISHER'S READY-RECKONER. The best
in the World. *New Edition.* 18mo. Cloth, 1/6.

GILMER'S INTEREST TABLES; Tables for
Calculation of Interest, on any sum, for any number of days, at ½, 1, 1½, 2, 2½, 3, 3½, 4, 4½, 5 and 6 per Cent. By ROBERT GILMER. Corrected and enlarged. *Eleventh Edition.* 12mo. Cloth, 5/.

GRÆME (Elliott): BEETHOVEN: a Memoir.
With Portrait, Essay, and Remarks on the Pianoforte Sonatas, with Hints to Students, by DR. FERDINAND HILLER, of Cologne. *Second Edition slightly enlarged.* Crown 8vo. Cloth gilt, elegant, 5/.
"This elegant and interesting Memoir. . . . The newest, prettiest, and most readable sketch of the immortal Master of Music.—*Musical Standard.*
"A gracious and pleasant Memorial of the Centenary."—*Spectator.*
"This delightful little book — concise, sympathetic, judicious." - *Manchester Examiner.*
"We can, without reservation, recommend it as the most trustworthy and the pleasantest Memoir of Beethoven published in England."—*Observer.*
"A most readable volume, which ought to find a place in the library of every admirer of the great Tone-Poet."—*Edinburgh Daily Review.*

—— A NOVEL WITH TWO HEROES.
Second Edition. In 2 vols. Post 8vo. Cloth, 21/.
"A decided literary success."—*Athenæum.*
"Clever and amusing . . . above the average even of good novels . . . free from sensationalism, but full of interest . . . touches the deeper chords of life . . . delineation of character remarkably good."—*Spectator.*
"Superior in all respects to the common run of novels."—*Daily News.*
"A story of deep interest. . . . The dramatic scenes are powerful almost to painfulness in their intensity."—*Scotsman.*

HOGARTH: The Works of William Hogarth, in
a Series of 150 Steel Engravings by the First Artists, with descriptive
Letterpress by the Rev. JOHN TRUSLER, and Introductory Essay by JAMES
HANNAY. Folio. Cloth, gilt edges, 52/6.

"The Philosopher who ever preached the sturdy English virtues which have made us what we are."

KNIGHT (Charles): PICTORIAL GALLERY
OF THE USEFUL AND FINE ARTS. With Steel Engravings, and
nearly 4,000 Woodcuts. Two vols. Folio. Cloth gilt, 42/.

—— PICTORIAL MUSEUM OF ANIMA-
TED NATURE. Illustrated with 4,000 Woodcuts. Two vols. Folio.
Cloth gilt, 35/.

MACKEY'S FREEMASONRY:
A LEXICON OF FREEMASONRY. Containing a definition of its
Communicable Terms, Notices of its History, Traditions, and Antiquities,
and an Account of all the Rites and Mysteries of the Ancient World. By
ALBERT G. MACKEY, M.D., Secretary-General of the Supreme Council
of the U.S., &c. *Seventh Edition*, thoroughly revised with APPENDIX by
Michael C. Peck, Prov. Grand Secretary for N. and E. Yorkshire. Hand-
somely bound in cloth, 6/.

"Of MACKEY'S LEXICON it would be impossible to speak in too high terms; suffice it to say, that, in our opinion, it ought to be in the hands of every Mason who would thoroughly understand and master our noble Science. . . . No Masonic Lodge or Library should be without a copy of this most useful work."—*Masonic News.*

HENRY MAYHEW'S CELEBRATED WORK ON THE STREET-FOLK OF LONDON.

LONDON LABOUR AND THE LONDON
POOR: A Cyclopædia of the Condition and Earnings of *those that will
work and those that cannot work.* By HENRY MAYHEW. With many
full-page Illustrations from Photographs. In three vols. Demy 8vo.
Cloth. Each vol. 4/6.

"Every page of the work is full of valuable information, laid down in so interesting a manner that the reader can never tire."—*Illustrated London News.*
"Mr. Henry Mayhew's famous record of the habits, earnings, and sufferings of the London poor."—*Lloyd's Weekly London Newspaper.*
"This remarkable book, in which Mr. Mayhew gave the better classes their first real insight into the habits, modes of livelihood, and current of thought of the London poor."—*The Patriot.*

The Extra Volume.

LONDON LABOUR AND THE LONDON
POOR: *Those that will not work.* Comprising the Non-workers, by
HENRY MAYHEW; Prostitutes, by BRACEBRIDGE HEMYNG; Thieves,
by JOHN BINNY; Beggars, by ANDREW HALLIDAY. With an Introductory Essay on the Agencies at Present in Operation in the Metropolis
for the Suppression of Crime and Vice, by the Rev. WILLIAM TUCKNISS,
B.A., Chaplain to the Society for the Rescue of Young Women and
Children. With Illustrations of Scenes and Localities. In one large
vol. Royal 8vo. Cloth, 10/6.

"The work is full of interesting matter for the casual reader, while the philanthropist and the philosopher will find details of the greatest import."—*City Press.*

Mr. MAYHEW's LONDON LABOUR—(*Continued*).

Companion volume to the preceding.

THE CRIMINAL PRISONS OF LONDON,

and Scenes of Prison Life. By HENRY MAYHEW and JOHN BINNY. Illustrated by nearly two hundred Engravings on Wood, principally from Photographs. In one large vol. Imperial 8vo. Cloth, 10/6.

"This volume concludes Mr. Henry Mayhew's account of his researches into the crime and poverty of London. The amount of labour of one kind or other, which the whole series of his publications represents, is something almost incalculable."—*Literary Budget.*

*** This celebrated Record of Investigations into the condition of the Poor of the Metropolis, undertaken from philanthropic motives by Mr. HENRY MAYHEW, first gave the wealthier classes of England some idea of the state of Heathenism, Degradation, and Misery in which multitudes of their poorer brethren languished. His revelations created, at the time of their appearance, universal horror and excitement—that a nation, professedly *Christian*, should have in its midst a vast population, so sunk in ignorance, vice, and very hatred of Religion, was deemed incredible, until further examination established the truth of the statements advanced. The result is well known. The London of Mr. MAYHEW will, happily, soon exist only in his pages. To those who would appreciate the efforts already made among the ranks which recruit our "dangerous" classes, and who would learn what yet remains to be done, the work will afford enlightenment, not unmingled with surprise.

MILLER (Thomas, Author of "Pleasures of a Country Life," &c.):

THE LANGUAGE OF FLOWERS. With Eight beautifully-coloured Floral Plates. Fcap 8vo. Cloth, gilt edges. *Fourteenth Thousand*, ... 3/6.
        Morocco, ... 7/6.

"A book
In which thou wilt find many a lovely saying
About the leaves and flowers."—KEATS.

——— THE LANGUAGE OF FLOWERS

Abridged from the larger work by THOMAS MILLER. With coloured Frontispiece. *Cheap Edition.* Limp cloth, 6d.

POE'S (Edgar Allan) COMPLETE POETICAL

WORKS. Edited, with Memoir, by JAMES HANNAY. Full-page Illustrations after WEHNERT, WEIR, and others. In paper wrapper. Illustrated, 1/6.

POETRY OF THE YEAR: Or, Pastorals from

our Poets, illustrative of the Seasons. With Chromo-Lithographs from Drawings after BIRKET FOSTER, R.A., S. CRESWICK, R.A., DAVID COX, HARRISON WEIR, E.V.B., and others. *New Edition.* Toned paper. Cloth gilt, elegant, 16/.

RAPHAEL: THE CARTOONS OF

RAPHAEL. Engraved on Steel in the first style of Art by G. GREATBACH, after the Originals at South Kensington. With Memoir, Portrait of RAPHAEL, as painted by himself, and Fac-simile of his Autograph. Folio. Elegantly bound in cloth, 10/6.

"Forms a handsome volume."—*Art and Letters.*

SCHILLER'S MAID OF ORLEANS: (*Die Jungfrau von Orleans*).
Rendered into English by LEWIS FILMORE, translator of GOETHE'S FAUST. With admirable Portrait of SCHILLER, engraved on Steel by ADLARD, and Introductory Notes. In Crown 8vo. Toned paper. Cloth, elegant, gilt edges, 2/6.

"Mr. Filmore's excellent translation deserves to be read by all."—*Northern Whig.*
"The drama has found in Mr Filmore a faithful and sympathetic translator."—*Public Opinion.*

SHAKSPEARE: THE FAMILY.
The Dramatic Works of WILLIAM SHAKSPEARE, edited and expressly adapted for Home and School Use. By THOMAS BOWDLER, F.R.S. With Twelve beautiful Illustrations on Steel. *New Edition.* Crown 8vo.

Cloth, gilt, ... 10/6.
Morocco antique, . . . 17/6.

*** *This unique Edition of the great dramatist is admirably suited for home use; while objectionable phrases have been expurgated, no rash liberties have been taken with the text.*

"It is quite undeniable that there are many passages in Shakspeare which a father could not read aloud to his children—a brother to his sister—or a gentleman to a lady; and every one almost must have felt or witnessed the extreme awkwardness, and even distress, that arises from suddenly stumbling upon such expressions. . . . Those who recollect such scenes must all rejoice that Mr. BOWDLER has provided a security against their recurrence. . . . This purification has been accomplished with surprisingly little loss, either of weight or value; the base alloy in the pure metal of Shakspeare has been found to amount to an inconceivably small proportion. . . . It has in general been found easy to extirpate the offensive expressions of our great poet without any injury to the context, or any visible scar or blank in the composition. They turn out to be not so much cankers in the flowers, as weeds that have sprung up by their side—not flaws in the metal, but impurities that have gathered on its surface—and, so far from being missed, on their removal the work generally appears more natural and harmonious without them."—*Lord Jeffrey in the Edinburgh Review.*

SHAKSPEARE'S DRAMATIC & POETICAL WORKS.
Revised from the Original Editions, with a Memoir and Essay on his Genius by BARRY CORNWALL; and Annotations and Introductory Remarks on his Plays, by R. H. HORNE, and other eminent writers. With numerous Woodcut Illustrations and full-page Steel Engravings by KENNY MEADOWS. *Tenth Edition.* Three vols. Super-royal 8vo. Cloth, gilt, 42/.

SHAKSPEARE'S WORKS. Edited by T. O.
HALLIWELL, F.R.S., F.S.A. With Historical Introductions, Notes, Explanatory and Critical, and a Series of Portraits on Steel. Three vols. Royal 8vo. Cloth gilt, 50 .

SOUTHGATE (Mrs. Henry): THE CHRISTIAN LIFE:
Thoughts in Prose and Verse from the Best Writers of all Ages. Selected and Arranged for Every Day in the Year. *Second Edition.* Cloth Elegant, ... 5/.
Morocco Antique, . . . 10/6.

GENERAL PUBLICATIONS. 35

MR. SOUTHGATE'S WORKS.

"No one who is in the habit of writing and speaking much on a variety of subjects can afford to dispense with Mr. SOUTHGATE'S WORKS."—*Glasgow News.*

FIRST SERIES—THIRTY-THIRD EDITION. SECOND SERIES—EIGHTH EDITION.

MANY THOUGHTS OF MANY MINDS:

Selections and Quotations from the best Authors. Compiled and Analytically Arranged by

HENRY SOUTHGATE.

In Square 8vo, elegantly printed on Toned Paper.

Presentation Edition, Cloth and Gold, ... Each Vol.	12/6.
Library Edition, Roxburghe, ... ,,	14/.
Ditto, Morocco Antique, ... ,,	21/.

Each Series complete in itself, and sold separately.

"The produce of years of research."—*Examiner.*
"A MAGNIFICENT GIFT-BOOK, appropriate to all times and seasons."—*Freemasons' Magazine.*
"Not so much a book as a library."—*Patriot.*
"Preachers and Public Speakers will find that the work has special uses for them."—*Edinburgh Daily Review.*

BY THE SAME AUTHOR.

Now Ready, THIRD EDITION.

SUGGESTIVE THOUGHTS ON RELIGIOUS SUBJECTS:

A Dictionary of Quotations and Selected Passages from nearly 1,000 of the best Writers, Ancient and Modern.

Compiled and Analytically Arranged by HENRY SOUTHGATE. In Square 8vo, elegantly printed on toned paper.

Presentation Edition, Cloth Elegant, ...	10/6.
Library Edition, Roxburghe, ...	12/.
Ditto, Morocco Antique, ...	20/.

"The topics treated of are as wide as our Christianity itself: the writers quoted from, of every Section of the one Catholic Church of JESUS CHRIST."—*Author's Preface.*
"This is another of Mr. Southgate's most valuable volumes. . . . The mission which the Author is so successfully prosecuting in literature is not only highly beneficial, but necessary in this age. . . . If men are to make any acquaintance at all with the great minds of the world, they can only do so with the means which our Author supplies."—*Homilist.*
"A casket of gems."—*English Churchman.*
"Mr. Southgate's work has been compiled with a great deal of judgment, and it will, I trust, be extensively useful."—*Rev. Canon Liddon, D.D., D.C.L.*
"Many a busy Christian teacher will be thankful to Mr. Southgate for having unearthed so many rich gems of thought; while many outside the ministerial circle will obtain stimulus, encouragement, consolation, and counsel, within the pages of this handsome volume."—*Nonconformist.*
"The special value of this most admirable compilation is discovered, when attention is concentrated on a particular subject, or series of subjects, as illustrated by the various and often brilliant lights shed by passages selected from the best authors in all ages. . . . A most valuable book of reference."—*Edinburgh Daily Review.*
"Mr. SOUTHGATE is an indefatigable labourer in a field which he has made peculiarly his own. . . . The labour expended on 'Suggestive Thoughts' must have been immense, and the result is as nearly perfect as human fallibility can make it. . . . Apart from the selections it contains, the book is of value as an index to theological writings. As a model of judicious, logical, and suggestive treatment of a subject, we may refer our readers to the manner in which the subject 'JESUS CHRIST' is arranged and illustrated in 'Suggestive Thoughts.'"—*Glasgow News.*

THE SHILLING MANUALS.
By JOHN TIMBS, F.S.A.,
Author of "The Curiosities of London," &c.

A Series of Hand-Books, containing Facts and Anecdotes interesting to all Readers. *Second Edition.* Fcap 8vo. Bound in neat cloth.

Price One Shilling each.

I.—TIMBS' CHARACTERISTICS OF EMINENT MEN.

II.—TIMBS' CURIOSITIES OF ANIMAL AND VEGETABLE LIFE.

III.—TIMBS' ODDITIES OF HISTORY AND STRANGE STORIES FOR ALL CLASSES.

IV.—TIMBS' ONE THOUSAND DOMESTIC HINTS on the Choice of Provisions, Cookery, and Housekeeping; new Inventions and Improvements; and various branches of Household Management.

V.—TIMBS' POPULAR SCIENCE: Recent Researches on the Sun, Moon, Stars, and Meteors; the Earth; Phenomena of Life, Sight, and Sound; Inventions and Discoveries.

VI.—TIMBS' THOUGHTS FOR TIMES AND SEASONS.

Opinions of the Press on the Series.

"It is difficult to determine which of these volumes is the most attractive. Will be found equally enjoyable on a railway journey or by the fireside."—*Mining Journal.*

"These additions to the Library, produced by Mr. Timbs' industry and ability, are useful, and in his pages many a hint and suggestion, and many a fact of importance is stored up that would otherwise have been lost to the public."—*Builder.*

"Capital little books of about a hundred pages each, wherein the indefatigable Author is seen at his best."—*Mechanic's Magazine*

"Extremely interesting volumes."—*Evening Standard.*

"Amusing, instructive, and interesting. . . . As food for thought and pleasant reading, we can heartily recommend the 'Shilling Manuals.'"—*Birmingham Daily Gazette.*

TIMBS (John, F.S.A.): PLEASANT HALF-
HOURS FOR THE FAMILY CIRCLE. Containing Popular Science, One Thousand Domestic Hints, Thoughts for Times and Seasons, Oddities of History, and Characteristics of Great Men. *Second Edition.* Fcap 8vo. Cloth gilt, and gilt edges, 5/.

"Contains a wealth of useful reading of the greatest possible variety."—*Plymouth Mercury.*

WANDERINGS IN EVERY CLIME; Or,
Voyages, Travels, and Adventures All Round the World. Edited by W. F. AINSWORTH, F.R.G.S., F.S.A., &c., and embellished with upwards of Two Hundred Illustrations by the first Artists, including several from the master-pencil of GUSTAVE DORÉ. Demy 4to. 800 pages. Cloth and gold, bevelled boards, 21/.

INDEX.

	PAGE
AINSWORTH (W. F.), Earth Delineated,	29
—— Wanderings in Every Clime,	36
AITKEN (W., M.D.), Science and Practice of Medicine,	6
—— Outlines,	7
—— Growth of the Recruit,	7
ANSTED (Prof.), Geology,	9
—— Inanimate Creation,	7
BAIRD (Prof.), Student's Natural History,	7
BELL (R.), Golden Leaves,	27
BLYTH (A. W.), Hygiène and Public Health,	8
—— Foods and Poisons,	8
BROUGHAM (Lord), Paley's Natural Theology,	5
BROWNE (W. R.), Student's Mechanics,	7
—— Foundations of Mechanics,	7
—— Fuel and Water,	19
BRYCE (Dr. H.), Works of Virgil,	22
BUNYAN'S Pilgrim's Progress (Mason),	1
—— Select Works,	1
CHEEVER'S (Dr.), Religious Anecdotes,	1
CHRISTISON (J.), Interest Tables,	27
CIRCLE OF THE SCIENCES, 9 vols.,	9
—— Treatises,	9
COBBETT (Wm.), Advice to Young Men,	27
—— Cottage Economy,	28
—— English Grammar,	22
—— French do.,	22
—— Legacy to Labourers,	28
—— Do. Parsons,	28
COBBIN'S Mangnall's Questions,	22
COLERIDGE on Method,	23
COOK (Captain), Voyages of,	28
CRAIK (G.), History of English Literature,	23
—— Manual of do.	23
CRUDEN'S CONCORDANCE, by Eadie,	3
—— by Youngman,	3
CRUTTWELL'S History of Roman Literature,	24
—— Specimens of do.,	24
—— Do. do. (in Parts),	24
CURRIE (J.), Works of Horace,	24
—— Cæsar's Commentaries,	24
DALGAIRN'S COOKERY,	28
DALLAS (Prof.), Animal Creation,	10
D'AUBIGNÉ'S History of the Reformation,	29
DICK (Dr.), Celestial Scenery,	2
—— Christian Philosopher,	2
DONALDSON (Jas.), Life of a Soldier,	29
D'ORSEY (A. J.), Spelling by Dictation,	24
DOUGLAS (J. C.), Manual of Telegraph Construction,	10
DUPRE AND HAKE, Practical Chemistry,	10
EADIE Rev. Dr.), Biblical Cyclopædia,	3
—— Cruden's Concordance,	3
—— Classified Bible,	3
—— Ecclesiastical Cyclopædia,	3
—— Dictionary of Bible,	3
ELLIS (Mrs.), Englishwoman's Library,	29
EMERALD SERIES OF STANDARD AUTHORS,	30
FINDEN'S FINE-ART WORKS,	31
FISHER'S READY-RECKONER,	31
FLEMING (Prof.), Vocabulary of Philosophy,	25
FOSTER (Chas.), Story of the Bible,	4
GEDGE (Rev. J. W.), Bible History,	1
GILMER (R.), Interest Tables,	31
GORE (G.), Electro-deposition,	9
GRAEME (Elliott), Beethoven,	31
—— Novel with Two Heroes,	31
GRIFFIN (J. J.), Chemical Recreations,	10
—— Do. (in Parts),	10

	PAGE
GURDEN (R.), Traverse Tables,	11
HARRIS (Rev. Dr.), Altar of Household,	1
HENRY (M.), Commentary on the Bible,	2
HOGARTH, Works of,	32
JAMES (W. P.), From Source to Sea,	11
JAMIESON (A.), Manual of the Steam Engine	11
KEBLE'S CHRISTIAN YEAR, 4to,	2
—— Do. Fcap,	2
KITTO (Rev. Dr.), The Holy Land,	4
—— Pictorial Sunday Book,	4
KNIGHT (Charles), Pictorial Gallery,	32
—— Do. Museum,	32
LANDOIS AND STIRLING'S Physiology,	12
LEARED (Dr.), Imperfect Digestion,	13
LINN (Dr.), On the Teeth,	13
LONGMORE (Prof.), Sanitary Contrasts,	13
M'BURNEY (Dr.), Ovid's Metamorphoses,	25
MACKEY (A. G.), Lexicon of Freemasonry,	32
M'NAB (Dr.), Manual of Botany,	13
MAYHEW (H.), London Labour,	32
MENTAL SCIENCE (Coleridge and Whately),	25
MILLER (T.), Language of Flowers,	33
MILLER (W. G.), Philosophy of Law,	25
MOFFITT (Dr.), Instruction for Attendants on Wounded,	13
MUNRO AND JAMIESON'S Electrical Pocket-Book,	14
NAPIER (Jas.), Dyeing and Dyeing Receipts,	14
—— Electro-Metallurgy,	14
PARKER (Prof.), Mammalian Descent,	14
PHILLIPS (John), Manual of Geology,	15
PHILLIPS (J. A.), Elements of Metallurgy,	16
POE (Edgar), Poetical Works of,	33
POETRY OF THE YEAR,	33
PORTER (Surg.-Maj.), Surgeon's Pocket-Book,	16
RAGG (Rev. T.), Creation's Testimony,	5
RAMSAY (Prof.), Roman Antiquities,	25
—— Do. Elem^{ry}.,	25
—— Latin Prosody,	25
—— Do. Elem^{ry}.	25
RANKINE'S ENGINEERING WORKS,	17, 18
RAPHAEL'S CARTOONS,	33
REED (Sir E. J.), Stability of Ships,	18
RELIGIONS OF THE WORLD,	5
SCHILLER'S MAID OF ORLEANS,	34
SCHOOL BOARD MANUALS,	26
READERS,	26
SCOTT (Rev. Thos.), Commentary on the Bible,	2
SEATON (A. E.), Marine Engineering,	19
SENIOR (Prof.), Political Economy,	26
SHAKSPEARE, Bowdler's Family,	34
—— Barry Cornwall's,	34
—— Halliwell's,	34
SHELTON (W. V.), Mechanic's Guide,	19
SOUTHGATE (H.), Many Thoughts of Many Minds,	35
—— Suggestive Thoughts,	35
—— (Mrs.), Christian Life,	5
STIRLING & LANDOIS, Manual of Physiology,	12
TAIT (Rev. J.), Mind in Matter,	5
THOMSON (Dr. Spencer), Domestic Medicine,	20
THOMSON'S SEASONS,	26
THORBURN (Dr.), Manual of Gynæcology,	20
TIMBS' (John), Shilling Manuals,	36
—— Pleasant Half Hours,	36
WHATELY (Archbishop), Logic, and Rhetoric,	26
WORDS AND WORKS OF OUR LORD,	5
WYLDE (Jas.), Magic of Science,	20
—— Manual of Mathematics,	22
YEAR-BOOK OF SCIENTIFIC SOCIETIES,	21

FIRST SERIES—THIRTY-THIRD EDITION.
SECOND SERIES.—EIGHTH EDITION.

MANY THOUGHTS OF MANY MINDS:
A TREASURY OF REFERENCE,
Consisting of Selections from the Writings of the most Celebrated Authors.
FIRST AND SECOND SERIES. COMPILED AND ANALYTICALLY ARRANGED
By HENRY SOUTHGATE.

In Square 8vo, elegantly printed on Toned Paper.

Presentation Edition, Cloth and Gold,	. . .	12s. 6d. each Volume.
Library Edition, Half-Bound, Roxburghe,	. .	14s. ,,
Do., Morocco Antique,	. . .	21s. ,,

Each Series is Complete in itself, and sold separately.

"'MANY THOUGHTS,' &c., are evidently the produce of years of research. We look up any subject under the sun, and are pretty sure to find something that has been said—generally *well* said—upon it."—*Examiner*.

"Many beautiful examples of thought and style are to be found among the selections."—*Leader*.

"There can be little doubt that it is destined to take a high place among books of this class."—*Notes and Queries*.

"A treasure to every reader who may be fortunate enough to possess it. Its perusal is like inhaling essences; we have the cream only of the great authors quoted. Here all are seeds or gems."—*English Journal of Education*.

"Mr. Southgate's reading will be found to extend over nearly the whole known field of literature, ancient and modern."—*Gentleman's Magazine*.

"Here is matter suited to all tastes, and illustrative of all opinions—morals, politics, philosophy, and solid information. We have no hesitation in pronouncing it one of the most important books of the season. Credit is due to the publishers for the elegance with which the work is got up, and for the extreme beauty and correctness of the typography."—*Morning Chronicle*.

"Of the numerous volumes of the kind, we do not remember having met with one in which the selection was more judicious, or the accumulation of treasures so truly wonderful."—*Morning Herald*.

"Mr. Southgate appears to have ransacked every nook and corner for gems of thought."—*Allen's Indian Mail*.

"The selection of the extracts has been made with taste, judgment, and official nicety."—*Morning Post*.

"This is a wondrous book, and contains a great many gems of thought."—*Daily News*.

"As a work of reference, it will be an acquisition to any man's library."—*Publishers' Circular*.

"This volume contains more gems of thought, refined sentiments, noble axioms, and extractable sentences, than have ever before been brought together in our language."—*The Field*.

"Will be found to be worth its weight in gold by literary men."—*The Builder*.

"All that the poet has described of the beautiful in nature and art; all the wit that has flashed from pregnant minds; all the axioms of experience, the collected wisdom of philosopher and sage, are garnered into one heap of useful and well-arranged instruction and amusement."—*The Era*.

"The mind of almost all nations and ages of the world is recorded here."—*John Bull*.

"This is not a law-book; but, departing from our usual practice, we notice it because it is likely to be very useful to lawyers."—*Law Times*.

"The collection will prove a mine, rich and inexhaustible, to those in search of a quotation."—*Art Journal*.

"There is not, as we have reason to know, a single trashy sentence in this volume. Open where we may, every page is laden with the wealth of profoundest thought, and all aglow with the loftiest inspirations of genius. To take this book into our hands is like sitting down to a grand conversazione with the greatest thinkers of all ages."—*Star*.

"The work of Mr. Southgate far outstrips all others of its kind. To the clergyman, the author, the artist,

and the essayist, 'Many Thoughts of Many Minds' cannot fail to render almost incalculable service."—*Edinburgh Mercury*.

"We have no hesitation whatever in describing Mr. Southgate's as the very best book of the class. There is positively nothing of the kind in the language that will bear a moment's comparison with it."—*Manchester Weekly Advertiser*.

"There is no mood in which we can take it up without deriving from it instruction, consolation, and amusement. We heartily thank Mr. Southgate for a book which we shall regard as one of our best friends and companions."—*Cambridge Chronicle*.

"This work possesses the merit of being a magnificent gift-book, appropriate to all times and seasons—a book calculated to be of use to the scholar, the divine, or the public man."—*Freemasons' Magazine*.

"It is not so much a book as a library of quotations."—*Patriot*.

"The quotations abound in that *thought* which is the mainspring of mental exercise."—*Liverpool Courier*.

"For purposes of apposite quotation it cannot be surpassed."—*Bristol Times*.

"It is impossible to pick out a single passage in the work which does not, upon the face of it, justify its selection by its intrinsic merit."—*Dorset Chronicle*.

"We are not surprised that a Second Series of this work should have been called for. Mr. Southgate has the catholic tastes desirable in a good editor. Preachers and public speakers will find that it has special uses for them."—*Edinburgh Daily Review*.

"The SECOND SERIES fully sustains the deserved reputation of the First."—*John Bull*.

LONDON: CHARLES GRIFFIN & COMPANY.

www.ingramcontent.com/pod-product-compliance
Lightning Source LLC
Chambersburg PA
CBHW051235300426
44114CB00011B/741